THE
PARADOXICAL
PRIME MINISTER

ALSO BY SHASHI THAROOR

NON-FICTION
Why I Am a Hindu
An Era of Darkness: The British Empire in India
India Shastra: Reflections on the Nation in Our Time
India: the Future is Now (ed.)
Pax Indica: India and the World of the 21st Century
Shadows Across the Playing Field: 60 Years of India-Pakistan Cricket (with Shahryar Khan)
India (with Ferrante Ferranti)
The Elephant, the Tiger, and the Cell Phone: Reflections on India in the 21st Century
Bookless in Baghdad
Nehru: The Invention of India
Kerala: God's Own Country (with M. F. Husain)
India: From Midnight to the Millennium and Beyond
Reasons of State

FICTION
Riot
The Five Dollar Smile and Other Stories
Show Business
The Great Indian Novel

THE PARADOXICAL
PRIME MINISTER

NARENDRA MODI AND HIS INDIA

SHASHI THAROOR

ALEPH

ALEPH BOOK COMPANY
An independent publishing firm
promoted by *Rupa Publications India*

First published in India in 2018
by Aleph Book Company
7/16 Ansari Road, Daryaganj
New Delhi 110 002

ISBN: 978-93-88292-17-7

3 5 7 9 10 8 6 4 2

For sale in the Indian subcontinent only

Printed by Parksons Press Pvt. Ltd., Mumbai

To
The People of India
Who deserve better

CONTENTS

INTRODUCTION

I told you so.

In 2014, I published *India Shastra*, a volume of essays about contemporary India. In it I examined the then new prime minister of India, Narendra Modi, six months into his assumption of office. This is what I wrote then:

> There is a paradox at the heart of Mr Modi's ascent to the prime ministership. His speeches and rhetoric appear to recognize, and harness, a vital shift in our national politics from a politics of identity to a politics of performance. Yet he has ridden to power at the helm of a party, the BJP, which is ill-suited to the challenge of delinking India's polity from the incendiary issue of religious identity that it had built its base on. And his rise to office has empowered the khaki-shorts wearing 'cultural organization', the Rashtriya Swayamsevak Sangh (RSS), whose views on every subject—economics, politics, history, culture, morality, gender relations, even matters of appropriate dress or conduct—are totally illiberal. Mr Modi has built his appeal by putting the focus on what the Indian people manifestly need—more development, better governance, wider socio-economic opportunities. But having won an election by attracting voters to these themes, he has given free rein to the most retrograde elements in Indian society, who are busy rewriting textbooks, extolling the virtues of ancient science over modern technology, advocating protectionism and self-reliance against free trade and foreign investment, and asserting that India's identity must be purely Hindu. Mr Modi cannot be oblivious to this fundamental contradiction, but he can only resolve it by jettisoning the very forces that have helped ensure his electoral victory. I am not sure whether such a fundamental contradiction can even

1

be resolved, and in that may lie the seeds of Mr Modi's future failure.[1]

Four years later, that failure is clearly apparent. The story of these last years is a story of missed opportunities and dashed hopes, of waiting for 'achhe din' that never came, of seeing expectations raised to the heights by lofty rhetoric, only to come crashing down in the face of depressing reality. These years have been an era of disappointment for believers, of vindication for the sceptics, and of frustration for all who want India to thrive.

In writing such a book, of course, I cannot pretend to be a neutral observer. I am a Member of Parliament from the Opposition Congress party, and there will be some who will inevitably make the 'well, he would say that, wouldn't he?' argument about the analysis in this book. In extenuation I can only point out that I have tried over Mr Modi's years in office to be as fair to him as possible, incurring the wrath of many of my own party colleagues by accepting his invitation to join the first group of prominent Indians asked to endorse his Swachh Bharat (Clean India) campaign, and being at the receiving end of much political opprobrium for my initial willingness to give him the benefit of the doubt. Part of this willingness was the hope I shared with most Indians to see a changed man between the campaigner and the victor—now that he was actually PM, perhaps he was prepared to govern for all Indians? And part of it was respect for the electorate—they had elected him and, as a democrat, I felt an obligation to respect their collective judgement enough to see if Modi would live up to the voters' faith in his words and promises.

As I show in this book, he did not. But I do not regret that initial suspension of criticism, though in some ways it was the worst of both worlds, since I got the backs up of the government for my subsequent criticisms anyway, while provoking the suspicions of some on my side who alleged I was planning to switch my allegiance to Mr Modi (something that anybody with the slightest

[1]Shashi Tharoor, *India Shastra*, New Delhi: Aleph Book Company, 2015, p. xv.

familiarity with my more than three-decade-long paper trail of trenchantly liberal opinions should have known was impossible). The middle of the road, after all, is the place where you get hit by traffic from both directions.

One of the things the twenty-first century is supposed to have taught us is that few things in life are black and white, that much of human reality involves complex, alternating shades of grey. The one field, however, that is exempt from this simple principle is Indian politics. Our political life and discourse are the last refuge of Manichaeism, the doctrine that divided the world into mutually incompatible ideas of good and evil.

Consider the evidence from just one episode: in mid-2015, I found myself launching and discussing a book by the scholar and columnist Raja Mohan, *Modi's World*, on the NDA government's foreign policy. Since what was expected was an overall assessment, I began by crediting the prime minister for the personal energy he brought to the conduct of policy, with his wide-ranging travels which had made a positive impression on the countries receiving him, and for having leveraged India's soft power as an instrument of our diplomacy through such initiatives as International Yoga Day—though I qualified this by observing that the pursuit of the Guinness World Records was unnecessarily tacky and unworthy of a government. I then went on to point out that the Modi government had not only continued the foreign policy of the UPA but done so by reversing most of the BJP's positions in Opposition, on issues ranging from the Indo-US nuclear deal to the Bangladesh Land Boundary Agreement. Even the emphasis on economic diplomacy with which the prime minister was being credited, I said, was nothing more than the implementation of what I have dubbed the Manmohan Doctrine, which posits that the overriding objective of Indian foreign policy is the economic transformation and development of India. I added, for good measure, that where the Modi government had departed from its predecessor it had embarrassed itself and the nation—pointing, in detail, to the yo-yo like pendulum swings of our policy pronouncements and actions on Pakistan and Israel.

It was, in other words, a nuanced analysis, mixed but far more critical than laudatory, as anyone present in the audience (or a glance at the video—https://www.youtube.com/watch?v=_xaOpGxnVvk where I start at 5:30 and go on for nine minutes) will confirm. What I wasn't prepared for was the slew of 'Tharoor praises Modi again' headlines that promptly followed my remarks. 'Tharoor sings Modi's tune again, says he's leaving "positive impression"', declared ANI. 'PM leaves "positive impression" during foreign visits: Tharoor', echoed PTI. 'Modi's "Personal Energy" Brought New Dimension to Diplomatic Relations: Tharoor', announced *Outlook*.[2] There were several more in similar vein, all omitting the 80 per cent of my speech that fell short of praise. It was as if all I had done that evening was applaud Mr Modi. There were a couple of exceptions. *The Wire*'s description of the event was 'Book Launch Sees Sharp Debate on Modi's Foreign Policy'; IANS, referring to the foreign secretary's remarks as well, wrote 'Jaishankar lauds Modi's proactive foreign policy, Tharoor slams "yo-yo" on Pakistan'. But these more accurate stories got far less traction; accuracy isn't saleable in the world of political news.

The reason is clear: our politics is not supposed to be nuanced. Our media sees every debate in the binary terms made famous by George W. Bush: 'Are you with us or against us?' (It is said, apocryphally, that when asked this question by former US Secretary of State John Foster Dulles, Nehru-ji replied: 'Yes'.) Our media analysis admits of no other possibilities: one must be either for Modi, or against Modi; seeing 20 per cent worth praising, 60 per cent worth criticizing and 20 per cent neither-good-nor-bad in his statements and policies is too complicated for our scribes and analysts to digest. Even *The Wire* and IANS stories mentioned above fell into the same trap; where other journalists had reported only my praise, these outlets had room only for my criticism.

---

[2]Vinayak Hegde, 'When Tharoor speaks on Modi, headline-writers struggle', sify. com, 21 July 2015; 'Seminal Shift or Continuity, Book Launch Sees Sharp Debate on Modi's Foreign Policy', *The Wire*, 19 July 2015.

Whereas I had admitted some positives before weighing in strongly on the shortcomings of Mr Modi's foreign policy, readers of the news would only think that I had 'again' praised him or attacked him—nothing in between.

The problem became more acute a few days later when Prime Minister Modi was kind enough to speak positively at a public forum about a speech of mine in Oxford that had 'gone viral'. Immediately, speculation began that I must be about to switch sides; indeed, television anchors asked me if I was about to do so. I pointed out (again) that I had thirty years of published work at odds with what Mr Modi and his party stood for, but this was irrelevant to the commentators: the prime minister had praised me, so that must mean I was on his side.

There's something terribly wrong with this picture. Why shouldn't our politics allow for mutual expressions of respect across the political divide? Why should we not, by praising politicians on the other side when they say or do the right thing, raise the bar for the standards by which we can judge their subsequent conduct? Why shouldn't we be able to see or hear the good things said or done by those we fundamentally disagree with and oppose? Nehru-ji was remarkably cordial to, and respectful of, the Opposition parliamentarians who routinely savaged him and his policies, notably winning the approbation of future BJP prime minister Atal Bihari Vajpayee in the process, and even took criticism on the chin from some of his own party MPs. One could disagree with a party's ideology, worldview or policies as a whole, but find common ground with it on some things. But we have reduced our politics to black and white today: either for or against, nothing in between. *Fifty Shades of Grey* could never be the title of a book about Indian politics.

This view of our politics, reinforced daily by the reports in our media, vitiates our political discourse. It reduces democracy to a zero-sum game where everything done by one side is automatically bad and unacceptable to the other. It explains the destructive Opposition politics of the recent past, when the BJP ferociously opposed even policies it had itself worked for, merely because they were being implemented by the UPA. It precludes the possibility of fair-minded debate and prevents the public from seeing our politicians as well-rounded human beings with minds of their own. Instead, everyone is reduced to a stock caricature, defined in absolute terms by their party affiliation alone.

This is a disservice to our democracy—which, as the Nobel Prize-winning economist Amartya Sen has pointed out, is supposed to be a process of deliberative reasoning, resulting in the best outcomes for the nation as a whole. Democracy is supposed to be an on-going process, one in which there must be give and take, dialogue and compromise among differing interests. Let us not reduce it to a game of kabaddi. Though unlike kabaddi, don't hold your breath expecting the score to change.

How then, as a fair-minded Opposition MP, does one look back at the Modi years? What can one make of a man who speaks of tolerance and accommodation while condoning hate speech by party members he has appointed as ministers?[3] How does one interpret a PM who speaks of 'minimal government, maximum governance' but is in the process of running the most centralized, top-down, bureaucracy-driven, personality-cult dominated central government since Indira Gandhi's Emergency rule? What conclusion can one reasonably derive about a leader who says, 'the government has no business to be in business'[4] but has never said a word to question the anomaly of his government owning and running airlines and hotels?[5] How can one interpret the intentions of a prime minister elected on a promise of delivering results, whose very fine speeches

---

[3]'A sinister campaign has been unleashed to create social and communal tension with the objective of polarizing our society. The PM's silence and inaction has only conveyed the impression that he condones all that has been happening', from 'Sonia Gandhi leads protest march, questions PM Modi's silence', *Indian Express*, 4 November 2015.
[4]'Government Has No Business Being in Business, PM Modi Tells US Investors', *NDTV*, 1 October 2014.
[5]As repeatedly pointed out even by a Modi supporter, Tavleen Singh, in her columns in the *Indian Express*.

and liberal pronouncements appear completely disconnected from any tangible action plan, adequate funding or execution capacity? Economics is clearly a vital prism to understand the answer: after all, numbers cannot be partisan. Mr Modi came to power boasting about his prowess at economic development, telling the nation he had been a successful CEO of Gujarat Inc. and was ready to do for India what he had done for his state. Against that yardstick, we have a checklist of spectacular failures, headed by a GDP growth rate that fell by 2.2 per cent as also the twin, self-inflicted blows of demonetization (a bad idea implemented badly)[6] and the botched rollout of GST (a good idea implemented badly). Manufacturing has contracted, exports have declined, growth in industrial production has slowed, and agriculture is stagnating (or worse, given the annual rise in the number of farmer suicides). Credit growth stood at 5.3 per cent in 2016-17, the lowest in over sixty years.[7] After declaring 'no more tax terrorism', the Modi government inflicted tax demands on entire new categories of victims, shaking investor confidence.[8]

A government that promised 2 crore new jobs a year—8 crore in four years—has generated precisely 18 lakh jobs in that time, most of them classified by the International Labour Organization (ILO) as vulnerable employment, and the thrasonical prime minister has been reduced to claiming that pakoda-sellers on sidewalks should also be counted in the employment figures. The unemployment rate has gone up from 4.91 per cent in 2014 to 6.23 per cent in 2018. India has more unemployed people than any country in the world.[9]

---

[6]Mihir Sharma, 'Truth is that on growth, Modi govt's performance has been astoundingly poor', *Business Standard*, 27 August 2018; 'It Turns Out, Manmohan Singh Was Prophetic In His Growth Prediction After Demonetisation', *Huffington Post*, 1 September 2017.
[7]'Credit growth plunges to over 60-year low at 5 per cent in 2017', *Times of India*, 16 April 2017.
[8]Minhaz Merchant, 'Biggest let-down of Modi government is its failure to end tax terrorism', *DailyO*, 28 March 2018.
[9]Shreya Shah, 'Three years of Modi govt: Job-creation promise falls short as unemployment rate up', *Hindustan Times*, 23 May 2017; Pragya Srivastava, 'Where

During the campaign a popular slogan was 'Bahut hui mehengai ki maar/Ab ki baar, Modi sarkaar!'[10] The BJP government earned a windfall of US $40 billion or ₹233,000 crore in its first three years, thanks to a collapse in benchmark crude oil prices from $108.05 to $48.82 (May 2014 to May 2017) whose benefits it refused to pass on to the aam aadmi.[11] Instead it levied in extra taxes what might have been saved at the pump, failing to produce a stimulus to the economy; it is estimated that the government earned ₹4.5 lakh crore every year since 2014 through excise on petrol and diesel alone.[12] Given the subsequent rise in global prices, the Indian driver was left stuck with record high prices at the pump, even as the rupee tumbled to record lows (crossing ₹71 to the dollar in August 2018).[13]

Then there was the disastrous experiment of demonetization, to which this book devotes an entire chapter. According to the Centre for Monitoring Indian Economy, demonetization cost India 15 lakh jobs between January and April 2017 alone.[14] As I point out, it achieved not a single one of its objectives as announced by the prime minister; indeed, 99 per cent of the money that was demonetized has now come back into circulation.[15] Worse is the intangible damage done to investor confidence in India's economy; the fear of similar surprises has intimidated investors

---

are the jobs? Not in India; unemployment rate doubles, jobs decline', *Financial Express*, 24 April 2018; 'India is the nation of the most unemployed in the world: Labour Bureau Statistics', *Outlook*, 5 April 2018.

[10](We have had enough of being battered by high prices; it's time for a Modi government!)

[11]Rajesh Pandathil and Kishor Kadam, '#Explained: If crude prices are at 2004 levels, why are we paying double the price for petrol, diesel?', *FirstPost*, 22 May 2016.

[12]'Excise duty on petrol, diesel to give big boost to Centre's revenue kitty', *Hindu BusinessLine*, 11 February 2018.

[13]'Rupee continues steep fall, hits 71 per dollar', Reuters, 31 August 2018.

[14]Aanchal Magazine and Sunny Verma, 'Demonetisation anniversary: New numbers are in, 1.5 million jobs lost in January-April this year', *Indian Express*, 8 November 2017.

[15]Dinesh Unnikrishnan, 'Demonetisation: RBI says 99 per cent banned notes are back; where is the black money?', *FirstPost*, 3 November 2017; 'Mitron, your score: 99.3% My score: 0.7%', *The Telegraph*, 30 August 2018.

and depressed demand. Demonetization was such a spectacular failure that Prime Minister Modi chose not to mention it at all in his final pre-election Independence Day address in 2018.

Instead of being a game-changing government, the BJP has turned out to be a name-changing one. The only successes it can point to are of schemes that were initiated by the UPA and often criticized at the time by the Opposition BJP: MGNREGA (which the PM sneered at, but now seeks credit for increasing its funding, even though states complain the promised subventions from the centre have not come); Aadhaar (which Mr Modi vowed to dismantle but has instead made compulsory, in many cases linking it to such things as credit cards and mobile phones that often have no links to government benefits); Direct Benefits Transfer, attractively renamed Jan Dhan as if the BJP had not criticized its adoption; Nirmal Bharat Abhiyan, now packaged as 'Swachh Bharat' with lower outgoes but five times the publicity budget; FDI in retail, the Financial Inclusion Scheme, liberalization of insurance and GST (Goods and Services Tax) itself, all of which the BJP had ferociously opposed and now wants to be congratulated for adopting. The UPA's skill development mission has been renamed the Pradhan Mantri Kaushal Vikas Yojana; the National e-Governance Plan is now 'Digital India'; the Rajiv Gandhi Grameen Vidyutikaran Yojana has been rebaptized the Deen Dayal Upadhyaya Gram Jyoti Yojana; the UPA's Accelerated Irrigation Benefits Programme has become the Pradhan Mantri Krishi Sinchayee Yojana; and the Jawaharlal Nehru National Urban Renewal Mission has been shrunk to Atal Mission for Rejuvenation and Urban Transformation—while the Modi government pretends these are all new schemes launched from the imagination of its visionary leader. One must concede that the Modi government creates better acronyms than its predecessors did—AMRUT is markedly more euphonious than JNNURM, for instance—but it cannot demonstrate better results on the ground.

Other promises have been dashed with impunity. The PM grandiloquently pledged to bring back the nation's 'black money' stashed abroad and put ₹15 lakh into every Indian's bank account; neither has happened.[16] During the sarkar of the man who promised to be the country's chowkidar, or watchman, there have been over 23,000 bank frauds amounting to ₹1 lakh crore since 2014.[17] On the watch of the leader who said 'na khaunga aur na khane dunga' (won't take bribes, nor let others take them) there have been a bewildering variety of world-class scams—from the Vyapam scandal in Madhya Pradesh to a PDS scam in Chhattisgarh, a GSPC scam in Gujarat and a mining scam in Rajasthan, as well as the suspected defence scam on the purchase of the Rafale fighter aircraft[18]—even as his own foreign minister bypassed official channels to seek protection for an Indian fugitive in London and the Panama Papers were given a quiet burial. Before 2014, Narendra Modi had supported the demand for an anti-corruption ombudsman, or Lokpal—but four years later, he had still not appointed a Lokpal.

The prime minister's priorities—as reflected in his Budgets—do not match his rhetoric. Agriculture has stagnated, with the agricultural growth rate dropping to 2.4 per cent per annum between 2014–18 compared to an average growth rate of 5.2 per cent per annum the preceding four years.[19] A staggering 36,420 farmers committed suicide between 2014 and 2016; figures for 2017 and 2018 were still awaited from the government at the time of writing, but judging by media reporting, the suicide rate will certainly be worse. The central government's Budget spending on education has declined dramatically during the Modi regime, from 4.57 per cent of the government budget in 2013–14 to 3.71 per cent in 2017–18, and from 0.63 per cent of GDP in 2013–14

[16]'What about 15 lakh in accounts promised by PM Modi, asked RTI. The reply', *NDTV*, 23 April 2018.

[17]'Over 23,000 bank frauds worth ₹1 lakh crore reported in 5 years: RBI', *Times of India*, 2 May 2018.

[18]Bhasha Singh, 'Rafale Jet Deal: Mother of all defence scams', *National Herald*, 18 February 2018.

[19]'Four years of Modi govt: "Problem of plenty", agriculture slowdown challenges for NDA', *Hindustan Times*, 26 May 2018.

to 0.47 per cent in 2017-18.[20] The private sector makes up for some of it, but not nearly enough.

The plight of India's women graphically illustrates the emptiness of many of the prime minister's slogans and speeches. He announced a scheme to support the girl child through enhanced education—Beti Bachao, Beti Padhao—but 90 per cent of the funds allocated last year remain unutilized.[21] In 2018, horrific rape incidents in Kathua and Unnao (and their politicized aftermath, with BJP leaders rushing to protect the accused[22]) are a stark reminder of how unsafe India has become for women. The National Crime Records Bureau (NCRB) found that, overall, rape cases had seen an increase of 12.4 per cent from 34,651 cases in 2015 to 38,947 in 2016.[23] In just one year, India slipped twenty-one places on the World Economic Forum's (WEF) Global Gender Gap index, from 87th to 108th—behind even our supposedly notorious neighbours China (where aborted female foetuses have contributed to a gender imbalance) and Bangladesh, where Islam has allegedly made the society unfriendly to women.[24] Sadly, not only does India remain unsafe for women, but in the Modi era there have even been ministers who have supported or tried to protect perpetrators of such violence towards women.[25] Today, India ranks 148th in the world for the number of women in Parliament; Pakistan ranked 89th and Bangladesh 91st.[26] The UPA's Women's Reservation Bill, which would guarantee women 33 per

---

[20]Subodh Varma, 'Budget analysis: Share of spend in government expenditure, GDP on education falling for 3 years', *Times of India*, 6 February 2017.

[21]'90% of Beti Bachao Beti Padhao funds unutilised: Parliamentary panel', *Times of India*, 21 March 2017.

[22]Sameer Yasir, 'Kathua rape case: BJP ministers backing accused quit but not before they mocked law, government and humanity', *FirstPost*, 14 April 2018.

[23]Azaan Javaid, 'Crimes across India spike by 2.6%, rape cases up by 12.4% in 2016: NCRB data', *Hindustan Times*, 30 November 2017.

[24]'India falls 21 places in global gender equality report, ranks 108 in 144-nation list', *Scroll.in*, 2 November 2017.

[25]Shuja-ul-Haq, 'Kathua rape case: 2 BJP ministers attend rally in support of accused', *India Today*, 4 March 2018.

[26]'India ranks 148th in the world for number of women MPs, says a new UN report', *Scroll.in*, 16 March 2017.

cent of the seats in Parliament, still languishes in the Lok Sabha
where Mr Modi has a brute majority.

Among Mr Modi's most emotionally-expressed commitments
was to the Ganga River, which he often describes as his 'mother',
saying she has 'called him' to serve her. But his Namami Ganga
scheme to clean up the grossly polluted river is a spectacular
failure, and India ranks 177th in the Environmental Performance
Index out of 180 countries.[27] Modi's own constituency of Varanasi
is a byword for dirt, grime and unmanageable waste.

National security was an area that brought out the most
bombastic pronouncements in the election campaign four years
ago. It has witnessed the most palpable failures. Our borders have
been rendered completely unsafe in these years of BJP rule: repeated
terrorist attacks, border ceasefire violations, massive infiltration of
terrorists from across the border, incursion into Indian territory
by Chinese and Pakistani soldiers and the frequency of terrorist
attacks on Indian army bases and military installations in Kashmir
do not speak well of the competence of our government in keeping
us safe. The domestic record is no better, with the continuing
incidence of Naxalism proving that the BJP's claim of sorting out
internal security issues is hollow.

Every proud Indian wishes to say a good word about foreign
policy: I have long argued that there is no such thing as a Congress
foreign policy or a BJP foreign policy, only Indian national interests
which any government of any party must uphold. Unfortunately,
though the PM has undoubtedly brought a great deal of personal
energy to his extensive travels around the globe, which have
enhanced his image and marked India's presence on the world stage,
few tangible gains can be seen for the country from his frequent
flyer miles. The government's foreign policy record over the years of
Modi's sarkar has been marked by the absence of a coherent policy
on Pakistan, where India's approaches have featured more ups and

---

[27]'India ranks 177 out of 180 in Environmental Performance Index', *The Hindu*,
24 January 2018.

downs than a child's yo-yo; the incapacity to define and achieve a stable relationship with China, which continues to oppose India's vital interests at every opportunity; deteriorating relationships with indispensable neighbours like Bangladesh, Nepal and Sri Lanka; the alienating of a time-tested ally like Russia; the excessive deference to a right-wing administration in America; and indiscreet and vainglorious rhetoric on subjects like the 'surgical strike' against Pakistan and the raid on Myanmar, with the unwarranted TV bravado of ministers causing consternation in the neighbourhood.

The Modi government has meanwhile wasted its limited time and resources on grandiose statuary, announcing one large monument after another: the Sardar Patel 'Statue of Unity' in Gujarat, which will cost ₹3,000 crore, the Shivaji statue off the coast of Mumbai, which will cost ₹2,500 crore, and the statue to Lord Rama in Ayodhya, which will cost ₹330 crore.[28] It is hard to see what benefit these statues will bring to the country. (The statues won't even help fulfil Modi's 'Make in India' slogan, since reports tell us that even the Statue of Unity of Sardar Patel in Gujarat has been outsourced to a foundry in China!)[29] This is not to mention, of course, the ₹4,343 crore the government has spent on advertising and publicity the last four years.[30]

It says something about the prime minister that his taste is for the extravagant and the flamboyant—for instance, agreeing to a wholly unnecessary Japanese 'bullet train' project between Mumbai and Ahmedabad that will cost ₹1.1 lakh crore[31] and is doomed to unviability, considering the modest price of air tickets and the

---

[28]'₹3,000-Crore "Statue Of Unity" of Sardar Patel in Gujarat to be ready for inauguration on October 31', *Indiatimes*, 14 February 2018; 'L&T bags Shivaji statue contract for ₹2,500 cr', *Times of India*, 1 March 2018; Alok Pandey, 'Yogi Adityanath wants corporates to fund ₹330 crore Ram statue in Ayodhya', *NDTV*, 30 March 2018.

[29]'Statue of Unity to be "made in China", Gujarat govt says it's contractor's call', *Indian Express*, 20 October 2015.

[30]'Modi govt spent ₹4,343 crore on publicity, reveals RTI query', *The Hindu*, 14 March 2018.

[31]'Narendra Modi, Shinzo Abe inaugurate India's first bullet train project in Ahmedabad', *Scroll.in*, 14 September 2017.

number of passengers who can afford a ticket on the bullet train, in a country where frequent railway accidents have occurred (even prompting the resignation of Modi's railway minister) because of a lack of resources for track maintenance and basic safety of the railway infrastructure. 'The bullet train is not moving', observed Congress president Rahul Gandhi during his interaction with the Indian Journalists' Association in London in August 2018. 'You can have a fancy poster of a bullet train, but the cost of a ticket in a bullet train is more than an airline ticket. If we were offered the bullet train money by the Japanese, our response would be, give us the money and help us strengthen Indian railway infrastructure,' Gandhi added.[32]

The saddest people in India must be those outside the core BJP fold who took him at his word and believed his commitment to 'good governance' and the transformation of the country. As I have written elsewhere, whether we grow at 9 per cent or at 5 per cent, we have to ensure the benefits reach the bottom 25 per cent of our population. Some of us deluded ourselves into thinking that Narendra Modi intended to do this, and to connect millions of our citizens in a functioning democracy to their own government: not just to announce entitlements that they are expected to grasp for themselves, but to create delivery mechanisms that ensure that these entitlements are not just theoretical, but real and accessible. Prime Minister Modi seemed to understand this in his speeches; but it has become painfully clear that in Narendra Modi's India, the right diagnosis does not always result in the right prescription, and even when it does, there is no guarantee that it will cure the condition—implementation has remained a crippling national weakness.

Rather than make this introductory threnody twice as long and thrice as painful, I will look at everything else that has been disastrous about the Modi sarkar in various chapters in the book—

[32]'Bullet train ticket will be costlier than airplane's: Rahul Gandhi', *Economic Times*, 25 August 2018.

among other things, the overt, triumphalist majoritarianism that has set alarm bells off among the minorities, the excesses of the 'cow vigilantes' and 'mob lynchers' and the subversion of institutions. The Modi slogan 'sabka saath, sabka vikas' (together with all, development for all) has found its reality: India's minorities are daily being made to feel unwelcome by the majoritarian discourse flourishing under the BJP, with ruling party MPs, including ministers, uttering Hindu-chauvinist sentiments never heard before from people in authority. Ghar wapsi, saffronization, statues of Godse, Ramzade and Haramzade, have all entered into and seared our political discourse, while the prime minister has largely remained silent, refusing to discipline or dismiss his errant ministers.[33]

In the essay which I cited at the beginning of this Introduction, I wrote that 'Prime Minister Modi's speeches and sound bites since his election could certainly have been scripted by a liberal, though the gap between articulation and implementation, in his case, remains currently wide enough to drive a rath through.' The liberal mask has long since fallen off. The gap has widened. The result is another paradox: a prime minister of lofty ambition, laid low by underachievement.

◆

In writing this book about Narendra Modi and his effect on India, I have elected not to write a straightforward political biography or a history of Modi's sarkar. Rather, in order to give myself the widest possible canvas on which to depict the contradictions within his personality, style of functioning and methods of governance, I have adopted an editorial structure that owes a lot to movie-making techniques such as cross-cutting, slow-cutting and jump-cutting, which I hope has allowed me to probe my subject much more effectively than a standard linear structure would have allowed.

This book is divided into five sections, each of which looks at a discrete aspect of the prime minister's personality or the

---

[33]M. V. Rajeev Gowda, 'A counter narrative', *Seminar*, November 2017.

way in which his government has functioned. Each section is further sub-divided into various chapters that provide an even more distilled examination of Mr Modi and his followers. The five sections are i) 'The Paradoxical Prime Minister', a long, probing profile of the PM; ii) 'The Modi-fication of India', which shines a light on the myriad ways in which Mr Modi's government and followers are damaging India's plural and secular nature, rendering the country unsafe for minorities, liberals, Dalits and women, stifling freedom of expression, enabling the faking of history and so on; iii) 'Moditva and Misgovernance', which takes apart the fraudulent claims that Moditva has led to the overall betterment of our lives and the strengthening of our institutions of governance; iv) 'The Failure of Modinomics' which takes a searching look at the damage Mr Modi has done to the economy; and v) 'Flights of Fancy' which gives the lie to his much-vaunted foreign policy initiatives. The book concludes with the chapters, 'A Man of Destiny? Not Quite', which sums up Narendra Modi and his contradictions and a final version of 'The New India We Seek', and deserve—a country that is far removed from the one that Mr Modi has given us. Together, the fifty chapters in the book are intended give the reader a view that is both panoramic and in-depth of Narendra Modi, the paradoxical prime minister.

'You gave Congress sixty years,' Mr Modi used to say, 'just give me sixty months and I will transform India'. His comprehensive failure to do so has his followers now going around the country saying that he needs at least ten years for the task.

Everyone is entitled to their own opinions, but not to their own facts. This book relies on incontrovertible facts; the glowing polls being cited by Mr Modi's supporters are opinions. At this rate, the facts will continue to speak for themselves in the only poll that matters—the one that's coming in 2019. Our only hope is that by the fifth anniversary of the BJP's ascent, we won't need to worry about any of these, because this disastrous government will be gone.

I

THE PARADOXICAL PRIME MINISTER

Each of the five sections in the book examines a particular aspect of Narendra Modi's personality or the manner in which his government functions. Taken together, they are intended to give the reader a clear sense of his style of functioning as prime minister and of India under his leadership. In this section, I take a close look at his life and times, beginning with his humble beginnings in Vadnagar, Gujarat, and ending with his ascent to the prime ministership of India. I have also explained in the introduction and here why I think of him as a paradoxical prime minister. This is because of the fundamental contradiction within him as prime minister—he advocates liberal principles and objectives, but if these are to be fulfilled he would need to jettison the very illiberal forces that have helped ensure his electoral victories. The tension between his indulgence of the Hindutva brigades and his responsibilities as prime minister of India has become increasingly apparent. He may say all the right things himself, but he will not condemn the bigots in his own ranks, and by his refusal to condemn them, he empowers and emboldens them. That will prove to be his undoing, and if allowed to prevail, will destroy everything that is good, noble and decent about our country.

chapter one

THE PARADOXICAL PRIME MINISTER

I

The very first time I met Narendra Modi, it was entirely by accident.

Not yet in politics, I was invited to address, and chair a session at, the Pravasi Bharatiya Divas in Chennai in January 2009. A ministerial friend invited me to join him for lunch at a private room in the conference hall. I arrived a little late—my session had run over time—and joined my host and four other guests already seated at a small round table. Somewhat to my surprise (since the minister in question was a Congress party stalwart), I discovered that one of my fellow guests, in smart short-sleeved shirt, rimless glasses and neatly trimmed white beard, was the chief minister of Gujarat, Narendra Modi.

I knew of Mr Modi only from the media, and what I knew was not flattering. He was seen by many as the chief villain of the Gujarat riots of 2002, which had killed over a thousand people, mainly Muslims, on his watch.[34] Some of my friends routinely demonized him; just over a year earlier, Congress president Sonia Gandhi had called him a 'maut ka saudagar', a merchant of death.[35] And here he was, smiling amiably at me.

Unexpectedly, he greeted me by name; he knew who I was. Taken aback, I reciprocated. But I am not one to leave well enough alone. I might not have sought a meeting with him, given his reputation, but now that I was with the man himself, I decided to question him.

The lunch soon became a dialogue between Mr Modi and myself, with the others too polite to chip in. Regrettably, I did

---

[34]'Timeline of the Riots in Modi's Gujarat', *New York Times*, 19 August 2015.
[35]Javed M. Ansari, 'Who coined "maut ka saudagar"?', *DNA*, 18 December 2007.

not write any notes that day of our conversation, and many of the details are now lost in the mists of memory. But one part of the exchange stays vividly in my mind.

I had asked him about the 2002 riots and his role in them, and he had replied predictably that he had done all he could, and called in the army when the police proved inadequate. I then switched to the present: what about the lingering effects on the Muslims of his state? I had heard dismaying reports of their being marginalized and ghettoized. How were they faring?

'Let me tell you a story,' Mr Modi replied, looking me straight in the eye. 'The same question you are asking me, I was asked by some very important people from Delhi. Some committee appointed by the central government had come to see me. [I surmised this was the Sachar Commission, which had been tasked by the UPA government to prepare a detailed report on the condition of Indian Muslims.] So I received them in my office, and they said to me, "We hear you have done nothing for Muslims in Gujarat."'

'*You have done nothing for Muslims in Gujarat,*' he repeated for emphasis. 'I replied, "Sit down, and please write this,"' Narendra Modi's eyes glinted behind his glasses. 'They all took out their notebooks and pens. And I told them, "You are right. I have done nothing for Muslims in Gujarat." They all started writing this in their notebooks. Then I added, "Write this also: I have done nothing for Hindus in Gujarat either."' He paused for dramatic effect. '"I have done nothing for Muslims or Hindus. I have only worked for Gujaratis."'

It was highly effective, as was much else that he said that day. He was in Chennai to address non-resident Indian delegates about the investment opportunities available in his state. It was clear he knew how to impress an audience, even if, at our lunch, it was just an audience of five.

But there was another side to Mr Modi's charm that I would not take long to discover.

Less than a year later, by now minister of state for external affairs, I found myself on an official visit to the United Arab

Emirates. One of my tasks was to urge my interlocutors to invest in India. But the UAE government had a problem. Their company, Dubai Ports World, had acquired the British P&O, and taken over all of P&O's existing contracts relating to the management of ports around the world. In three Indian states they had had no problem converting the existing contracts with P&O to new ones with Dubai Ports World. But in Gujarat, they were stuck; the state government was simply not heeding their request. Could I help?

With the confidence borne of my lunchtime exchange, I telephoned the chief minister of Gujarat. 'We're trying to get the UAE to increase their investments in India,' I explained, 'but they say they have this issue in Gujarat. What seems to be the problem?'

There was no beating about the bush on the telephone. Mr Modi's answer was chillingly blunt: a company controlled by an Arab country could not run a Gujarati port.

He went on: 'You want these UAE people to invest in India? Tell them to come to Gujarat. I will give them land, 24/7 electricity, good roads, all the cooperation they want. But I won't let them run a port.'

I mentioned that the same arrangement was working elsewhere in India, but the Gujarat chief minister refused to see my point of view. He was adamant that this would be detrimental to India's national interest.[36]

I felt this was irrational and tried to plead with him, but he was implacable. I had to admit failure to my interlocutors.

II

Narendra Damodardas Modi was born in the Gujarati town of Vadnagar on 17 September 1950, the third of six children, to Damodardas Mulchand Modi and his wife, Heeraben, a couple of modest means who belonged to the Ghanchi caste, which had traditionally made their living as oil-pressers. (His caste ought not to matter in a twenty-first-century profile, but Mr Modi

---

[36]Shashi Tharoor, 'Beyond Beijing and Delhi', *India Today*, 30 November 1999.

subsequently ensured that it would, by describing himself as India's first backward-caste prime minister, a claim that could more properly have been made by H. D. Deve Gowda, prime minister 1996-97.[37]) Like other Ghanchis, the Modis seem to have practised this profession too, but Damodardas Modi also operated a tea stall at the Vadnagar railway station. Here, he had the help of his son, Narendra, from a young age. 'The boy was an average student,' reported one of his biographers, Nilanjan Mukhopadhyay, quoting one of his teachers, Prahladbhai G. Patel.[38] Prahladbhai Patel, who taught Narendra at the BN High School, remembered him as 'an argumentative child who would often defy teachers'. He said he had once 'asked Narendra to show his homework to one of the class monitors and he refused—he said that if he has to show it to anyone for evaluation, it must be the teacher himself or no one'. Patel was also unequivocal about Modi's performance as a student. He said Narendra was not 'a very bright student' and 'ranked medium and at best could have been called a mediocre student'. He is said to have shown less interest in his studies than in debates and theatre.

His prowess as a student may have been less than stellar but Narendra was someone who never shied away from hard work. He would assist his father during the busy hours before school started, while his mother and siblings operated the oil mill. The experience taught him the value of hard work and a respect for labour that are still cited among Narendra Modi's basic characteristics. Mr Mukhopadhyay says that Narendra Modi told him in the course of an interview: 'I sleep very less—just three-and-a-half or four hours...[and I am up] about 4:30 to 4:45 a.m. If it gets late then 5 a.m. at the latest.'

Narendra Modi took these attitudes with him to the organization

---

[37]"Modi is a Teli-Ghanchi OBC": BJP', *Times of India*, 23 April 2014; Sowmya Aji, 'I was India's first OBC PM, not Narendra Modi: H D Deve Gowda', *Economic Times*, 13 July 2015.
[38]Nilanjan Mukhopadhyay, *Narendra Modi: The Man, The Times*, New Delhi: Tranquebar, 2013.

that formed him and shaped his beliefs, the Rashtriya Swayamsevak Sangh (RSS), founded in 1925 as the vanguard of an aggressive Hindu political revival after centuries of British and Muslim rule. The RSS emerged from the prevalent ideological currents of the 1920s, believing in many of the ideas Mussolini's Fascists or Hitler's National Socialists were propagating at the same time, notably race pride, military discipline, effective organization and fiercely chauvinist nationalism that targeted minorities and dissenters. Its leaders were contemptuous of the secularism and pluralism of the freedom movement led by the Indian National Congress, advocating instead an uncompromising Hindu Rashtra. In the first few decades of its existence, the RSS's ideas did not acquire a wide following, but its adherents were fanatically devoted to it.

The RSS regarded the partition of the country that accompanied Independence as a betrayal, and blamed the Congress and Mahatma Gandhi for it. It was a former member of the organization, Nathuram Godse, who assassinated the Mahatma in 1948, leading to the RSS being banned for two years. When it re-emerged, it focused on spreading its organizational wings, seeking young recruits who could be moulded in the ideas and ethos of the RSS. One of them, joining the organization as a bal swayamsevak (child volunteer) on Diwali day in 1958 at the tender age of eight, was Narendra Modi.

Narendra Modi immersed himself early in the teachings of the RSS. Leaving home soon after high school—having left a child bride to whom his marriage had been arranged when he was thirteen—he is reported to have spent time in Rajkot, near Kolkata, Guwahati and Almora, living in ashrams dedicated to the Ramakrishna Mission and Swami Vivekananda in an attempt at self-discovery. (His authorized biographer, Andy Marino, claims that Mr Modi was told by the missionaries at Belur Math that the life of a monk was not suited to him.[39]) This demonstration

---

[39]Andy Marino, *Narendra Modi: A Political Biography*, New Delhi: HarperCollins, 2014, pp. 25–27.

of independence and self-reliance would mark him for all time. After returning to Gujarat and brief stints working in his uncle's canteen in Ahmedabad and operating a tea cart, Narendra Modi became a full-time RSS worker.

It is a measure of his devotion to the cause that he spent at least a year performing menial chores like cooking and cleaning for his superiors in the RSS hierarchy in Gujarat. But he soon graduated to the role of a pracharak, a full-time disseminator of the RSS message. His efficiency and appetite for work soon impressed his seniors, and he was sent to RSS headquarters in Nagpur for successive levels of training that equipped him for higher responsibilities in the RSS setup. Mr Modi has stated that his experience as a pracharak taught him that 'your life should be disciplined', and that 'what work you get, do it well'.[40]

He did. He rose rapidly up the ranks, first of the RSS organization and then of its political arm, the Bharatiya Janata Party (BJP). During the Emergency, when the RSS was banned, he disguised himself as a Sikh and conducted a variety of subversive activities, including ferrying wanted Opposition leaders to safe houses. In 1987, Mr Modi was deputed to the BJP by the RSS as general secretary of the party's Gujarat unit. Initially he was entrusted with organizational responsibilities—managing events, marches and rallies, including for two BJP presidents (a section of L. K. Advani's rath yatra in 1990 and Murli Manohar Joshi's Kanyakumari-to-Kashmir Ekta or Unity Yatra in 1991–92). He was also credited for his organizational role in ensuring the BJP's victory in the Gujarat state elections of 1995. He soon rose to the national level as the BJP's organization secretary, and became a stalwart spokesman for the BJP on national television. But the day soon came when he was entrusted with substantive political responsibilities in his own right. In October 2001, after a crisis in the BJP-run state government in Gujarat, the fifty-one-year-old

---

[40]Ross Colvin and Satarupa Bhattacharjya, 'Special Report: The remaking of Narendra Modi', *Reuters*, 12 July 2013.

Narendra Modi was despatched to Ahmedabad by the party to serve as chief minister.[41] One story claims he was initially asked to be deputy to the ailing chief minister, Keshubhai Patel; Mr Modi is said to have replied that he would either be fully in charge of Gujarat or decline to move there at all.

When Narendra Modi was made CM, the assembly elections were just a year away. His principal challenge was to hit the ground running in order to ensure his party's re-election. 'I have come here to play a one-day match,' CM Modi told the press in the state capital, Gandhinagar, using a cricketing metaphor. 'I need fast and performing batsmen to score runs in the limited overs game.'[42] He made it clear that he himself would lead from the front—the captain, opening batsman and fastest bowler, all rolled into one.

But just four months later, on 27 February, 58 men, women and children, kar sevaks returning from a trip to Ayodhya—where they had travelled in support of constructing a Ram Janmabhoomi temple on the site of the destroyed Babri Masjid, on the tenth anniversary of its demolition—were killed when a fire broke out on their train as it passed through the Muslim-dominated town of Godhra, 160 kilometres east of Ahmedabad. Given the widespread assumption that they had deliberately been targeted by Muslims in Godhra for their political affiliation,[43] the authorities feared retaliation, but the Modi government did little to prepare for it. A state-wide bandh was declared and the bodies of the kar sevaks were reportedly paraded in public (other accounts deny this, though it was widely reported at the time). Enraged Hindu leaders began fanning the flames, taking out processions to condemn what they denounced as a Muslim assault on Hindutva activists. They were neither dissuaded nor stopped in their tracks by the government.

---

[41]Vinod K. Jose, 'The Emperor Uncrowned: The Rise of Narendra Modi', *Caravan*, 1 March 2012.

[42]Ranjit Bhushan, 'Cadre Raj, Phase Two', *Outlook*, 19 November 2001.

[43]Some suggest the train fire could well have been accidental. However, the police did not agree, and trials were held of 94 accused; 31 were convicted, 11 sentenced to death, 20 received life imprisonment, and the rest were acquitted.

Soon tempers boiled over, and attacks began on Muslims, as well as on Muslim homes and Muslim-owned shops.[44] In the frenzy of mob violence that followed, over 1,000 people, mainly Muslims, were massacred in a pogrom against that community that blighted the state's normally tranquil capital, Ahmedabad, and other places in Gandhi's homeland.

The scale of the tragedy was horrific. According to an affidavit filed by the then Director-General of Police (Intelligence) in Gujarat, R. B. Sreekumar, before the Justice Nanavati inquiry commission, 1,044 were killed, 2,500 injured, and 223 were reported missing; more than 4,500 houses were destroyed and 18,500 damaged; Muslim Gujaratis suffered property damage worth approximately ₹600 crore, and Hindus approximately ₹40 crore.[45] It was estimated a few months after the riots that 132,532 persons had been displaced or forced to leave their homes.[46]

The Modi government was accused of condoning—or at the very least not taking prompt action—to stop the killings and destruction, which ceased only after the army was called in three days after they began. Narendra Modi has long had to battle the perception that he did not do enough to stop the bloodshed, though it must be noted that a Supreme Court investigation found there was no case for him to answer. He has consistently insisted, as he did with me, that he did all he could to control the rioters. Others disagree. Human Rights Watch, for instance, issued a report entitled 'We Have No Orders to Save You' arguing that at best the police had been 'passive observers, and at worst they acted in concert with murderous mobs.'[47] In her book, *The Clash Within: Democracy, Religious Violence, and India's Future*, the American

---

[44]Shreeya Sinha and Mark Suppes, 'Timeline of the Riots in Modi's Gujarat', *New York Times*, 19 August 2015.
[45]'Gujarat riot death toll revealed', *BBC*, 11 May 2005; 'NHRC Reports and Timeline', *CJP.org.in*, 7 June 2017.
[46]Report of the Parliamentary Committee on the Empowerment of Women, August 2002.
[47]'"We Have No Orders To Save You": State participation and complicity in communal violence in Gujarat', Human Rights Watch, April 2002.

scholar Martha Nussbaum concludes, "There is by now a broad consensus that the Gujarat violence was a form of ethnic cleansing, that in many ways it was premeditated, and that it was carried out with the complicity of the state government and officers of the law.'[48]

Narendra Modi's authorized biography by Andy Marino describes these events very differently and advances a compelling case that Mr Modi was indeed blameless on the 2002 riots: 'the facts show that Modi did not want them to happen, did not help them to happen, and did everything within his power as quickly as he could to stop them happening'.[49] This is far from a widely accepted conclusion, but it must be recorded, in an environment where too many are convinced of their own versions of the truth.

Narendra Modi's actions may not amount to direct complicity in the killings, but his attempts to downplay the tragedy—or at least his role in it—have not helped either. His infamous declaration at the time that the riots 'result[ed] from the natural and justified anger of people' did not go over well with world public opinion, and considerably damaged his reputation, not least internationally.[50] (Instead of condemning those—mainly Hindu—who were responsible for the violence and terror, let alone acting against them, he accused the people of Godhra of possessing 'criminal tendencies' which had instigated retaliatory violence.[51] Days after the riots, in an interview with Zee TV on 1 March 2002, he said, 'This is a chain of action and reaction. We want both the action and the reaction to stop.'[52])

Modi later told Reuters (in what may be a poor translation

---

[48]Martha C. Nussbaum, *The Clash Within: Democracy, Religious Violence, and India's Future*, Cambridge, MA: Harvard University Press, 2007, p. 51.

[49]Andy Marino, *Narendra Modi: A Political Biography*, New Delhi: HarperCollins, 2014.

[50]'Overview of the attacks against Muslims', *Outlook*, 1 May 2002.

[51]Vidya Subramanian, 'SIT says Ehsan Jafri "provoked" murderous mobs', *The Hindu*, 11 May 2012.

[52]'Modi "action-reaction" statement not sufficient to make a case: SIT', *Indian Express*, 11 May 2002.

of his Hindi): 'We feel that we used our full strength to set out to do the right thing.' Asked if he regretted the violence, Modi compared his feelings to the occupant of a car involved in an accident. If 'someone else is driving a car and we're sitting behind, even then if a puppy comes under the wheel, will it be painful or not? Of course it is. If I'm a chief minister or not, I'm a human being. If something bad happens anywhere, it is natural to be sad,' he said.[53]

To compare the brutal massacre, rape and destruction of human lives and property in 2002 to the accidental running over of a puppy betrayed a heartlessness and a lack of proportion that many found unforgivable. His lack of compassion for the victims is disappointing in a state chief executive: there is only one known instance of Mr Modi visiting a relief camp. Instead, he described the camps as Muslim 'baby-making factories'.[54]

Lawyer and Congress MP Kapil Sibal has further pointed out that 'not all the accused [in the riots] were brought to book and many were released on bail during the course of the trial.'[55] Some who were convicted of rioting have been released on appeal; Maya Kodnani, a former BJP minister, sentenced to twenty-eight years in prison for leading the rioters in the biggest single massacre, was acquitted by the Gujarat High Court in April 2018, after having enjoyed several furloughs earlier during which she was spotted at yoga retreats.[56] Some witnesses turned 'hostile', recanting their earlier damning testimony, allegedly under duress. Some cases are still dragging on. Given that the Godhra accused were denied bail, kept in jail throughout the trial and justice was swiftly dispensed, the double standards are glaring.

---

[53]Ross Colvin and Sruthi Gottipati, 'Interview with BJP leader Narendra Modi', *Reuters*, 12 July 2013.
[54]"Should We Run Relief Camps? Open Child Producing Centres?', *Outlook*, 30 September 2002.
[55]Kapil Sibal, *Shades of Truth*, New Delhi: Rupa Publications, 2018, p. 39.
[56]"BJP's Maya Kodnani Cleared Of Charges In Worst Massacre Of 2002 Riots', *NDTV*, 20 April 2018; 'Gujarat riots convict Maya Kodnani takes selfie at yoga retreat; Twitter gets angry', *Catch News*, 25 November 2015.

It was reported that the late Prime Minister Vajpayee wanted to dismiss Narendra Modi as chief minister for his failure to prevent the massacre, but was dissuaded by the Hindutva hardliners in his administration. Senior BJP leader, and current vice president of India, Venkaiah Naidu confirmed this story on the record as an example of his party's democratic decision-making: according to Mr Naidu, Prime Minister Vajpayee wanted Narendra Modi to resign as Gujarat chief minister after the riots, but had to give in to the party's 'collective decision' against the idea.[57] Mr Modi prepared well to resist his ouster, persuading senior leaders to back him: at the national executive meeting of the BJP in Goa in April 2002, he theatrically offered to resign as Gujarat CM, only to be drowned in a chorus of 'No's', showing Vajpayee-ji clearly how much influence he held within the party.[58] Vajpayee-ji gave in.

Be that as it may, the Gujarati public rallied behind him. Mr Modi was re-elected as chief minister of Gujarat in elections later that year in a landslide—the BJP winning 69.8 per cent of seats to the Congress's 28 per cent, a lopsided victory that bolstered Mr Modi's image at a time when the BJP was facing major defeats in other parts of the country—and returned to office again with ever-larger majorities in 2007 and 2012.[59] (He is by far the longest-serving chief minister Gujarat has ever had.) While his campaign rhetoric vehemently expressed Hindutva ideas, he increasingly claimed to be governing Gujarat effectively and promoting robust economic development, a message that resonated well beyond his state and gave him a credible national reputation for decisive and impactful leadership.

Indeed, Modi's credibility as a prime ministerial contender rested largely on his reputation for the excellent economic management of his own state. He was portrayed as a hands-on

---

[57]'Vajpayee wanted Modi to quit over Gujarat riots, but party said no: Venkaiah Naidu', *Indian Express*, 9 March 2014.
[58]Ibid.
[59]Darshan Desai, 'The Gujarat vote share trend conundrum', *Economic and Political Weekly*, Vol. 51, Issue No. 28, 9 July 2016.

chief executive, whose vaulting success—showcased in a series of 'Vibrant Gujarat' summits that attracted India's top businessmen and foreign investors—had created a 'Gujarat Model' that the rest of India could learn from. (Narendra Modi himself declared that Gujarat under him was the 'engine of India's economic growth'.[60]) Mr Modi's 'Gujarat Model' was anchored in generous encouragement for free enterprise, more efficient and profitable public sector undertakings, state expenditure targeted at identified deliverables, and an impressive growth rate—among the highest in India (an average of 10 per cent a year during his dozen years as chief minister[61]). Mr Modi made it easier for corporate houses to use agricultural land for industrial purposes in Gujarat and also eased land acquisition and labour laws. It helped, of course, that CM Modi ran a tightly controlled state government, which justifiably boasted that it had prevented a recurrence of communal riots after 2002.

One episode sealed Narendra Modi's image as a can-do 'vikas purush' (development man). When, in 2008, political violence and farmers' opposition to the acquisition of their land to build a factory for Tata Motors in Singur, West Bengal, erupted and prompted the Tatas to pull out of that state, Mr Modi immediately stepped into the breach, offering the company land, facilities and generous tax concessions to relocate to Gujarat. 'I will never forget the way he found solutions for a company that was looking for a home,' said then Tata chief Ratan Tata. 'That just does not happen in India.'[62]

All this was deftly portrayed through skilled marketing: the product was the chief minister himself, the sales pitch was slick and tirelessly repeated, and the 'consumer' was the Indian voter, first in Gujarat but thereafter across the nation. Mr Modi did

---

[60]Ross Colvin and Satarupa Bhattacharjya, 'Special Report: The remaking of Narendra Modi', *Reuters*, 12 July 2013.
[61]'Bursting the bubble', *Business Standard*, 24 January 2013.
[62]'Ratan Tata votes for Narendra Modi; says, Prime Minister capable of delivering New India', *Financial Express*, 20 September 2017.

not hesitate to spend top dollar to rehabilitate his image, which he knew had been tarnished by the events of 2002. Narendra Modi's Gujarat government engaged the services of an assortment of domestic and foreign public relations agencies—in particular, APCO Worldwide, one of the largest American firms in the field— to help his image makeover.[63] In India he employed top-notch consultants to enhance his brand, including some of the stars of the advertising business, such as Piyush Pandey of Ogilvy and Mather, Prasoon Joshi of McCann, and Sam Balsara of Madison World.[64] The objective was dual: to sell Modi to Indian voters using the most advanced modern techniques, but also to make sure that foreign governments thought better of him.

After Narendra Modi was again re-elected chief minister in 2007, his nationwide projection gathered pace, and it intensified with his third election victory in 2012, which clinched his reputation as the BJP's most successful national figure. A key part of his public appeal was his decision to bypass the mainstream media, which he felt had been unfair to him in (and since) 2002, in favour of reaching out directly to the public on social media. His Twitter account became a key vehicle of his messaging—in the interests of full disclosure, I should say, with due immodesty, that I had anticipated him in this regard, but he eclipsed me on 4 July 2013 as the country's most 'followed' politician on Twitter, and multiplied his lead several times soon thereafter; he is now the third most followed current world leader on Twitter, after US President Donald Trump and Pope Francis, with over 43 million followers.[65] In addition to his Twitter page, Narendra Modi—or perhaps more accurately, his personal social media cell—ran a Facebook page, a YouTube channel, a LinkedIn account, and also posted widely on other social media including, when they became

---

[63]Binoy Prabhakar, 'How an American lobbying company Apco Worldwide markets Narendra Modi to the world', *Economic Times*, 9 December 2012.

[64]Shamni Pande, 'Just the Right Image', *Business Today*, 8 June 2014.

[65]'PM Modi third most followed world leader…', *Indian Express*, 11 July 2018. (Former President Obama, though no longer a current 'world leader', remains number one.)

popular, Pinterest, Instagram and Tumblr.

Both through his choice of medium and the nature of his posts on these social media services, Mr Modi projected a compelling picture of himself to the world. His photographs showed a modern, hands-on man of action, laptop at the ready, financial newspaper in hand, or wielding a DSLR camera. Other images portrayed a cosmopolitan sophisticate—there was Mr Modi reading an Obama biography, Mr Modi in a tracksuit, Mr Modi sporting a cowboy hat. These social media images were a vital part of a larger branding exercise designed to achieve the visual reimagining of Narendra Modi.

The photographs sought to portray a man who was both *not* what people assumed he was, and *was* something people thought he might not be. The first message was that he was not the typical 'socialist' politician, clad hypocritically in khadi, whom the Indian public had seen too many of over the years; and equally that he was not the khaki-shorts-wearing, lathi-wielding RSS pracharak with antediluvian ideas about modern society and economics. Instead, the new brand image showed Narendra Modi as a man who comfortably occupied two spaces—that of Hindu values and traditions embodied in his ideology and politics, but also that of globalized modernity reflected in his activities as the progressive-minded CEO of Gujarat Inc. Narendra Modi had, from childhood, a taste for different ways of doing things, and saw himself as a man of innovation; this self-image was what the pictures sought to project to the wider world.

The pictures spoke of a figure not associated in the public mind with the RSS—a modern man adept at using the latest communications technology, at home with international economic thought, and with titans of global business. Mr Modi wished to convey that he had a globalized vision for the nation, unlike most of the members of his old organization, the RSS, who were associated with the nativist and protectionist ideas advocated by that body's Swadeshi Jagran Manch. As Mr Modi declared in an address to the Shri Ram College of Commerce in Delhi in

2007[66] (in a metaphor he was to use seven years later, as prime minister, in a memorable address in Madison Square Garden, New York), Indians in the past had been known as snake charmers, but Indian youth in the future were moving from the snake to charming the mouse—the latter, of course, attached to a computer. As prime minister, Modi told overseas Indians that his aim was to create a 'technology-driven society' through 'technology-driven development'.[67]

This reinvention of the right-wing project by Narendra Modi and its propagation by social media did a number of things at once. It challenged the conventional wisdom about his and the RSS's politics and economics. It associated him with a willingness to learn and profit from the West, whereas the RSS had traditionally been seen as resistant to the West and globalization. It identified him with young India's aspirations for modernity. In the process, it allowed Narendra Modi to change the public perception of the party he sought to lead. (It helped, of course, that much of his target audience were young people, first-time voters, Facebook and Twitter users, hailing from a generation that had grown up with little memory of the 2002 riots. It's a startling fact that half of India's population is under twenty-five, and so the oldest of the youths voting for the first time in the 2019 elections would have been barely six years old when that tragedy occurred.) Many had seen the BJP as a political vehicle for old men speaking in Hindi about the glories of Hindu culture, preferably while wearing saffron and sandalwood paste on their foreheads. Instead, here was a new standard-bearer, a smartly attired modern man who could click a mouse with one hand while brandishing a trishul in the other.

But the Vibrant Gujarat summits, with their extravagant pledges of investment and the associated hoopla, masked some unimpressive facts and figures. In the eight editions of the summit,

---

[66]'We are a nation of mouse-charmers now: Narendra Modi at SRCC', *NDTV*, 7 February 2013.
[67]Speech to Indian community in Washington DC, 25 June 2017, www. narendramodi.in.

the state signed 51,738 MoUs worth more than ₹84 lakh crore, most of which never materialized; investment came in at about 10 per cent of the pledges, and the implementation percentage of the projects promised and announced, as of 2017, was only 25 per cent.[68] Vibrant Gujarat—in a problem that now afflicts Modi at the national level—was much more show than substance. It was true that CM Modi's state ranked fifth out of India's big states in terms of per capita income. But Gujarat was not exactly an economic backwater before Narendra Modi's ascent; it was already one of India's most prosperous states, long industrialized and with a hoary tradition of entrepreneurship—despite this it attracted less foreign investment than five other Indian states did during CM Modi's rule. However impressive the state's GDP growth was, it was not significantly higher than in the previous two decades under Congress governments. But Gujarat under Narendra Modi performed badly on a number of key social indicators, notably malnutrition, child welfare, education for girls, maternal mortality, access to health, the education of minorities, availability of clean drinking water for the poor and the percentage of its budget devoted to health-related expenditure. These were not the chief minister's priorities.

The figures are damning. Between 2008 and 2015, Gujarat slipped from the 6th to 11th rank on the national Human Development Index (HDI) among all states. When Mr Modi left office, the state was ranked 19th in the availability of household TVs, Internet connections and mobile networks; 18th in terms of literacy; 22nd in primary school enrolment; 23rd in its infant mortality rate; and 11th in its maternal mortality rate. The number of people living below the poverty line has increased in Gujarat since the 1990s. The daily income of farmers, ₹264 in 2016, was ₹77 less than the national average. The number of educated

---

[68]Rutam Vora, 'Vibrant Gujarat—Brushing up the numbers', *Hindu BusinessLine*, 16 January 2017; Virendra Pandit, 'Vibrant Gujarat summit. Wait, where's the "investor"?', *Hindu BusinessLine*, 6 January 2017.

unemployed in the state stood at 6.12 lakh in 2016.[69] The state's high rate of growth evidently masked several inequities.

Yet the absence of progress in social development did little to dent Chief Minister Modi's popularity. His personal 'stage presence' had a great deal to do with that. He was a compelling orator in Gujarati and Hindi, arguably the best modern India has ever seen. The journalist Vinod K. Jose listened to one of his speeches in his home state in 2012 and came away mesmerized: 'On stage before an adoring audience, Modi has a sure command of the theatrical. He was loud, firm and confident: the kind of leader who makes his followers sure that everything will be taken care of... He spoke extemporaneously and flawlessly, his eyes constantly fixed on the audience before him. The tent fell completely silent while he was speaking: no one played with their mobile phones; there was no rustling of plastic bags. Many people had their mouths wide open.'[70]

The powerful oratory was accompanied by a strong message: the country was in a mess and he was the man to change it. The second term of the UPA government had, for various reasons, run aground: the economy took a hit from the global recession; the skyrocketing price of fuel (which reached as high as $140 a barrel during the last year of the government) affected the price of everything else and the cost-sensitive Indian voter blamed his rulers; an effective anti-corruption campaign led by an octogenarian Gandhian, Anna Hazare, captured the popular imagination and created an image of the ruling party as entrenched in sleaze; and the soft-spoken but reticent prime minister, Manmohan Singh, a highly respected economist, was widely portrayed as weak, indecisive, silent and in thrall to the Gandhi family, whose matriarch, the

---

[69]Maitreesh Ghatak, 'Gujarat model: The gleam of state's high growth numbers hides dark reality of poverty, inequality', *Scroll.in*, 25 October 2017; Christophe Jaffrelot , 'Gujarat model?', *Indian Express*, 20 November 2017; 'Gujarat model is Modi model supportive of crony capitalism: Prithviraj Chavan', *Economic Times*, 3 December 2017.
[70]Vinod K. Jose, 'The Emperor Uncrowned: The Rise of Narendra Modi', *Caravan*, 1 March 2012.

Italian-born Sonia Gandhi, was depicted as pulling the strings behind the scenes. Mr Modi, by contrast, claimed to be strong in every area where the UPA was weak: he projected himself as an able, effective and decisive chief executive, a true Indian nationalist, unbeholden to anyone else, who had risen from the grassroots, and one without the baggage of a poor governance record in national politics (glossing over the 2002 riots themselves, which by now were more than a decade in the past).

Narendra Modi used his compelling oratory in Hindi to demonize the UPA government, which he effectively blamed for every single failure or misfortune in the country, while promising the voters everything they sought if he came to power. He painted an arresting picture of the 'achhe din' that would come if he was brought to power: he pledged to farmers that he would end their suicides, give them more money for their produce and revive agriculture; he told the millions of unemployed youth who thronged his rallies that he would provide them with jobs; he assured urban women, traumatized by the rising incidence of rapes and assaults even in the nation's capital, that he would create conditions of security for women; he convinced the middle class, struggling to make do on limited means and eyeing the mega-rich with resentment, that he would bring back billions of dollars of 'black money' stashed abroad, putting 15 lakh rupees into the bank accounts of every Indian citizen; he assured the citizenry at large, shaken by the terror attacks by Pakistan-sponsored jihadi groups, that he was not weak and soft like the government and would stand up to Pakistani terror; and he assured the business community that he would transform the investment climate and send India soaring up the World Bank's 'ease of doing business' rankings. The public lapped it up. The improbability of many of these promises, the inaccuracy of the figures he was citing (notably for black money) were overlooked and not seriously challenged; this was what people wanted to hear. He established an emotional connection with his audiences: he told various groups that he 'would not be able to sleep at night' until he had resolved their problems. Narendra Modi might not have been the 'maut ka saudagar' (merchant of death) that Sonia Gandhi described him as being in 2007, but he was undoubtedly a 'sapnon ka saudagar' (merchant of dreams) by 2014.

III

In December 2012, soon after his resounding third election win in the state assembly elections in Gujarat, Narendra Modi had clearly emerged as an irresistible force, a man who could not be ignored. The changing perception became apparent, for example, in New Delhi's diplomatic corps, which had, for the most part, ostentatiously avoided him. That month, at a social lunch, I was approached by an old friend, German ambassador Michael Steiner, seeking a private word. 'How would you feel,' he asked, 'about the European ambassadors meeting the chief minister of Gujarat, whom we have so far ostracized?'

I was no longer in the External Affairs Ministry and this was a totally unofficial conversation. I replied carefully that I was venturing a personal opinion as a friend, not as a member of the government. I said that I felt there was nothing inappropriate, in a democracy, in diplomats meeting a member of the Opposition. 'Why don't you do it in an informal social setting,' I suggested, 'rather than a formal meeting, which might seem to be giving him a degree of official recognition?' He thought that made sense, but was less enthusiastic when I added that he might want to balance Modi by inviting another politician or two of differing political views on the same occasion. 'We need to know him,' Mr Steiner said, somewhat helplessly; '...without seeming to endorse him,' I added. He nodded. In the event, Mr Steiner hosted Narendra Modi, in January 2013, at a lunch at the German embassy with all the EU ambassadors in New Delhi. The ice of Narendra Modi's diplomatic isolation was broken.

Domestically, the clamour for him became unstoppable. Mr Modi eclipsed the former president (and defeated 2009 prime ministerial candidate) of the BJP, the veteran Sangh leader, Lal

Krishna Advani—who had been assumed to be the party's likely
standard-bearer in 2014—by supplanting him in that capacity
at a meeting of the BJP national executive; the street-smart Mr
Modi comprehensively outmanoeuvred the veteran Mr Advani to
be officially anointed as the BJP's candidate for prime minister in
the 2014 general elections. He spent the next year in a nationwide
campaign of unparalleled reach, intensity and impact, which
propelled him to an unchallengeable position of dominance by
the time ballots were cast.

Narendra Modi's message resonated with those who had
little and with those who had much, and the latter helped sell it
to the former. Business houses, excited at the prospect of being
able to flourish in the new Modi-directed order, lent themselves
willingly to the cause, with generous campaign contributions. The
print and electronic media, which was largely owned by them,
devoted themselves to an almost fawning dissemination of the
Modi message. There was no escaping his image, his sonorous
speeches, his ubiquitous slogans: 'achhe din', 'sabka saath, sabka
vikas', 'ab ki baar, Modi Sarkar'.[71] Mr Modi eloquently projected
a decisiveness and can-do attitude that people were yearning for;
his omnipresence both reflected and reinforced their dreams.

But Mr Modi still polarized opinions: passionate critics
denounced him as an extremist and even a fascistic would-be
dictator; supporters, often even more passionate in their views,
believed he alone could transform India's economy into a larger
version of Gujarat's and, with his Hindu pride and global instincts,
make India the superpower his followers felt it deserved to be.
Opinions were divided, but so was the Opposition. Narendra
Modi's BJP won just 31 per cent of the national vote—up from
19 per cent in 2009—but it was enough to ensure a resounding
victory in the parliamentary elections, as the Westminster-style,
first-past-the post system gave the BJP an absolute majority with

---

[71]'good days', 'together with everyone, development for all', and 'this time, a
Modi government', respectively.

52 per cent of the seats.[72] One of the most memorable moments in Twitter history—and certainly the most 'retweeted' and 'favourited' message in India's social media—came on 15 May 2014, when the newly-victorious Narendra Modi issued the pungent tweet: 'India has won'.[73]

It had been a spectacular victory; the BJP under his leadership had risen from 116 to 282 seats of the 543 elected members of the Lok Sabha, the first time in history that the BJP had enjoyed an absolute majority in the all-important Lower House of Parliament.[74] Together with the BJP's pre-election allies, the National Democratic Alliance, or NDA, led by Modi, enjoyed 333 seats; plus they could nominate two more members from the Anglo-Indian community. It was clear they would completely command, and could get anything done by, the Lower House.

The Congress party had been decimated, falling from 216 seats in the outgoing House to a mere 44 in the new one.[75] Though I had won my own seat, my majority had fallen from 100,000 to 15,700; for the first time, a BJP candidate had come second in my constituency, Thiruvananthapuram. It was only in the evening, as the results poured in and the size of his majority became apparent, that I issued a somewhat grudging tweet: 'Still touring my constituency to thank party workers, but before it's too late, congratulations @NarendraModi & BJP on an astonishing victory'. Within minutes this tweet came back from him: '@ShashiTharoor: Many thanks. Congratulations for your victory as well. Let's work together to create a better India!'

This was remarkable, not least because it came at his moment of triumph, when he could be forgiven for having other things on his mind than reaching out to opponents. Narendra Modi's extraordinary journey from chai-wallah to prime minister had

---

[72]Ian Bremmer, 'How far can Modi take India—and how fast?', *Reuters*, 21 May 2014.
[73]'Victory tweet "India has won!" creates record', *The Hindu*, 17 May 2014.
[74] G. S. Mudur, 'Quirky outcomes from the box', *The Telegraph*, 19 May 2014.
[75]Shubham Ghosh, 'May 16: Three years since Congress was reduced to 44 seats in a general election, its all-time low', *IBN Times*, 16 May 2017.

caught the imagination of the Indian people; he could have been excused for savouring his victory rather than replying to an Opposition MP. It even seemed to me an early sign that Mr Modi was seeking to convey a willingness to work with the other side.

It didn't last very long. As I have explained in the introduction, I was one of those prepared to see some prospect of a Narendra Modi 2.0, reinventing the old Hindutva warrior of the past as a development-oriented statesman who would move his party away from a politics of identity to a politics of performance. While critical of specific steps of the government, I was therefore willing to give him the benefit of the doubt on initiatives I considered non-political, and support such ideas as the International Day of Yoga, the World Buddhist and Sufi conferences in Delhi, and the Swachh Bharat campaign.

By inviting me to be among the nine prominent Indians associated with the launch of his Swachh Bharat initiative, Narendra Modi showed a capacity to reach out to the Opposition; as I have noted earlier, a few months later he again surprised me by echoing the Lok Sabha speaker's praise of my speech in Oxford on British colonialism, declaring publicly that I had 'said the right thing in the right place at the right time'. It was with all this in the background that, on his birthday in 2015, I tweeted: 'Happy Birthday @NarendraModi. May you continue to serve India with energy & commitment. Will continue to disagree with your politics, but with respect!' Again his response, barely a couple of hours later, impressed me: 'Thank you, Dr. Tharoor. And, what is our democracy without constructive criticism! Debate makes us stronger.'

It was this capacity to speak across the political divide to opponents that struck me at the time as the most unexpected personal characteristic of the prime minister. I had, after all, used the occasion of his birthday to remind him again of our political differences; yet he had not only taken that in his stride, but turned it around into a positive message of conciliation and collegiality. That was the spirit in which I wished Narendra Modi a happy birthday. As I declared in a public message to him: 'Let us, Government and Opposition, work together to create a better India. When your policies are manifestly in the national interest, let us support you; and when, in our view, they are not, let us take opposition constructively, respecting each other's sincere faith in different paths to India's betterment.'

In saying this, I was perhaps being naïve, and certainly there has been little sign of such a spirit on either side of the aisle since, not least in Prime Minister Narendra Modi's own attitudes. The @PMOIndia twitter handle tweeted on 18 April 2016, on behalf of the prime minister, words very similar to those he had addressed to me: 'I want this Government to be criticized. Criticism makes democracy strong.' And yet criticism has been unwelcome to the government. Many Indians—teachers, students, businessmen, auto-rickshaw drivers, and members of the police and paramilitary forces—have been booked or even arrested for 'insulting' Modi.[76] The prime minister himself has not been above sharp and often below-the-belt attacks on political opponents; in 2018 he suffered the indignity of becoming the first prime minister to have his words expunged from the parliamentary record, in the course of a speech where he also seemed to mock Mrs Gandhi's accent in a demonstration of schoolboy insecurity rather than statesmanlike leadership.[77] Each passing year has made him more combative and truculent, the political atmosphere in the country more polarized and intractable. Part of the reason is Narendra Modi himself, or more precisely the congeries of elements that collectively make up his ethos of governance—what some have dubbed, in a conflation of 'Modi' and 'Hindutva', 'Moditva'.

[76]Piyasree Dasgupta, 'What happens to the people arrested for insulting Modi?', *Huffington Post*, 13 February 2018.
[77]'PM remark expunged in rare decision', *The Telegraph*, 11 August 2018; Ashok Swain, 'Modi Mocking Sonia Gandhi's Italian Accent In Parliament Is Disgusting And Shameful', *NewsCentral*, 22 July 2018.

IV

Narendra Modi has emerged from the RSS and the Hindutva movement and is unquestionably of them—his 2008 book, *Jyotipunj*, recounts the biographies of sixteen people who inspired him, every single one of them a male RSS leader.[78] But for all his deep immersion in the RSS, he has also managed to be above the organization. It can be argued that he is no longer a pure and simple RSS pracharak, and that what he stands for is Hindutva with a personalized Modi ethos, immersed in muscular Hindu nationalism and yet devoted to a cult of personality that has little to do with Hindutva. These elements constitute what may be termed 'Moditva', at the centre of which, towering over his followers like a Colossus, is the man himself.

'Modi understands only one alphabet, and that is the capital I,' declared Gordhan Zadaphia, former minister of state for home affairs in Gujarat.[79] During his 2007 Gujarat election campaign, a national newspaper's front-page headline for its account of his speech was telling: 'In 30 minutes, Modi names himself 29 times, BJP 6, and in slip asks: me as PM?'[80] The personality cult he encouraged in Gujarat is in full bloom around the nation today, but it really reached its apogee during the 2014 elections, when a children's comic book extolling his childhood in near-mythic terms was released. The stories in *Bal Narendra* (Boy Narendra) range from the relatively mundane (Narendra helping his parents with their work) to the mildly heroic (Narendra freeing a pigeon entangled in a kite string) to the hagiographic (Narendra using his meagre pocket money to set up a tea stall for flood victims; Narendra swimming through a crocodile-infested lake to a marooned temple).[81] The unabashed lionizing of Narendra Modi

[78]'Narendra Modi On MS Golwalkar, Translated By Aakar Patel—Part 1', *Caravan*, 31 May 2014.
[79]Vinod K. Jose, 'The Emperor Uncrowned: The Rise of Narendra Modi', *Caravan*, 1 March 2012.
[80]*Indian Express*, 13 December 2007 (front page).
[81]'"Bal Narendra" in pics: comic book shows "fearless" young Narendra Modi

is a key element that distinguishes Moditva from Hindutva.

If Modi's authorized biographer, Andy Marino, is to be believed, Modi was not a supporter of the Ayodhya movement and had a strong antipathy to the Hindu extremism of the VHP and Bajrang Dal, whom he proceeded to marginalize in Gujarat.[82] This makes it all the more puzzling that he did not adopt the same approach in Delhi, instead empowering such forces by his refusal to condemn their excesses as soon as they occurred—one more example of the Modi paradox.

Of course, Modi remains strongly committed to Hindutva. As he told Reuters in 2013: 'I'm a nationalist. I'm patriotic. Nothing is wrong. I'm a born Hindu. So yes, you can say I'm a Hindu nationalist.'[83] This is clearly part of his core beliefs. Moditva borrows from Hindutva the idea of a pristine Hindu Rashtra, a nation emerging from the mists of time immemorial, the Bharatvarsha of the *Rig Veda*; it asserts a majoritarian nationalism in the name of the Hindu people, marginalizing or vilifying minorities—particularly Muslims and Christians—as interlopers;[84] it articulates a cultural nationalism anchored in the Hindu dharma, but extending beyond it. Moditva nationalism unabashedly declares that India is a 'natural home for persecuted Hindus' while offering no similar welcome mat for other Indians; at the same time it extends its appeal to Hindus living abroad, with whom Modi professes a tie of blood that transcends a passport.[85] On top of this foundation of Hindutva, it builds the idea of a strong leader, a man with a 56-inch chest, powerful and decisive, who embodies the nation and will lead it to triumph. This is the element that makes the ruling credo 'Moditva'.

---

saving drowning boy, taking on crocodiles, bullies', *News18.com*, 27 March 2014.
[82]Andy Marino, *Narendra Modi: A Political Biography*, New Delhi: HarperCollins, 2014.
[83]Ross Colvin and Satarupa Bhattacharjya, 'The Remaking of Narendra Modi', *Reuters*,12 July 2013.
[84]Ramachandra Guha, 'The guru of hate', *The Hindu*, 26 March 2012.
[85]Speech to Indian community at Wembley Stadium, London, 13 November 2015, www.narendramodi.in

The 56-inch chest is an instructive detail. During the build-up to the 2014 election, Modi replied to criticism by Samajwadi Party chief Mulayam Singh Yadav with the words: 'Netaji has said Modi does not have what it takes to make another Gujarat out of UP. Do you know what making another Gujarat requires?... It requires a chhappan-inch ki chhati (56-inch chest).' BJP sources indicated the figure was to be taken literally as representing what Narendra Modi had to offer, but when Babasaheb Bhimrao Ambedkar University officials were asked to design an achkan for PM Narendra Modi to wear, authorities said they were given a 50-inch chest size measurement to be shared with the tailor.[86]

Moditva is assertively masculinist, as the chest measurement (about which Mr Modi himself boasted) implies, and chauvinist, contemptuous of weakness and dissent, dismissive of rivals and resolute against enemies, whether domestic or foreign. Mr Modi and the BJP have effectively invoked the army and the 'suffering of our jawans' in any discussions where they are losing on pure logic and facts (such as the suffering of people when standing in ATM lines after demonetization, when an effective social media meme asked the grumbling public: 'If our jawans can stand at our borders 24/7 to keep our country safe, why can't we stand a few hours in a bank queue?') For Moditva, the sacrifice and suffering of the armed forces has increasingly become a reliable weapon a tool for political point-scoring by the ruling party to justify PM Modi's actions, as opposed to serious topics that need redressal in themselves. Military fervour and pride seem to have become mandatory for any 'self-respecting and patriotic Indian' under a Moditva regime. That the Indian military largely deserves the encomia that have been showered on it is beside the point; it is the instrumentalization of the military for political purposes (most brazenly after the so-called 'surgical strike' on terrorists along the Line of Control with Pakistan) that marks Moditva as a

---

[86]Isha Jain, 'PM Narendra Modi's chest now said to measure 50 inches', *Times of India*, 21 January 2016.

departure from India's previous ruling ethos. The military always enjoyed deep respect, if in a somewhat patronizing way, as the mid-1960s slogan 'jai jawan, jai kisan' testifies. But this is the first time they have been exalted to near-mythic proportions to serve the political objectives of the ruling party, such as when the Modi government broadcast news of the army's 'surgical strike' against Pakistan in what was clearly an attempt to impress the electorate (although, ironically, as I show in Chapter 24, the military haven't been treated especially well by the Modi sarkar).

This is also a legacy of Hindutva, since Sangh Parivar thinkers have consistently rejected Gandhian pacifism. The longtime RSS chief Golwalkar rejected the identification of Hinduism with non-violence, pointing out that in Hindu iconography, every Hindu god is armed. Hindutva leaders have often spoken of abandoning the soft Brahminism of the Congress party, with its emphasis on ahimsa and the devotional traditions of the Bhakti movement, in favour of the tough Kshatriya warrior tradition, with its emphasis on shakti or strength. It is no accident that in mid-2018 the Modi government floated a proposal to provide military training to a million boys and girls each year, to 'instil values of nationalism, discipline and self-esteem into the youth, which in turn will help make India a "Vishwaguru" and achieve Prime Minister Narendra Modi's vision of New India 2022.'[87] Moditva builds on such beliefs, and projects its leader as the embodiment of strength and power. Moditva also adores its leader; on top of a purely BJP government, we see a fiery and articulate ideologue, projected as all-knowing and infallible, the hero on a white stallion who will gallop at the head of the nation's massed forces with upraised sword, knowing all the answers, ready to cut through the Gordian knots of the nation's problems. Since the leader represents the nation, support for him is seen as patriotic and opposition anti-national.

This is not typical of the Sangh Parivar, but from his earliest

---

[87]Ritika Chopra, 'To instil discipline, nationalism: Govt discusses military training plan for disciplined 10-lakh "force of youth"', *Indian Express,* 20 July 2018.

days, Narendra Modi did not conform to the anonymity required
of RSS workers. For all his talk of the importance of discipline,
he seems to have stretched its boundaries even within the RSS,
acquiring a reputation as a headstrong figure of stubbornly
independent ways. As a former senior of his in the BJP, Shankersinh
Vaghela,[88] observed of his one-time associate: 'He always used to
do things differently from others in the group—if all of us wore
long-sleeved kurtas, he used to wear short sleeves, and when all of
us wore khaki shorts, he wore white shorts. And I remember one
day the visiting RSS leader Golwalkar questioning Modi in public
for keeping a trimmed beard.' Modi always had a penchant for
the limelight; innumerable social media memes have been spawned
about his efforts to keep himself in the centre of photographs and
his keen awareness of the camera at any public appearance, even
unsubtly positioning himself to catch the lens during encounters
with world leaders. (On one occasion the prime minister was
so annoyed when one of his Special Protection Group personnel
blocked him from the sight of the cameras, that he barked 'Yahan
khade rehkar kya karoge? (Why are you standing here?)', before
ordering the hapless guard to maintain his distance. Discipline is
most attractive to he who exacts it from others. Narendra Modi's
eldest brother, Somabhai, has been quoted as saying that Modi
wanted to join the RSS ever since he was a child because 'he was
always greatly impressed by the fact that only one person gave all
the orders in the shakha and everyone followed the command'.[89]

Yet Narendra Modi has managed a complex modus vivendi
with the RSS, even while abandoning the personal restraint they
might have expected of him: as prime minister he has, for instance,
initiated a practice whereby his ministers dutifully report to the
organization's leadership about their performance and are graded,
admonished, advised or exhorted by senior swayamsewaks before

---

[88]Vinod K. Jose, 'The Emperor Uncrowned: The Rise of Narendra Modi', *Caravan*,
1 March 2012.
[89]G. Sampath, 'The Man in the Modi Mask,' *LiveMint*, 25 July 2013.

returning to their ministerial offices.[90] This combination of outsize personal ego and institutional supplication to the RSS is also a marker of Moditva.

Unlike Hindutva, Moditva has little patience for the economic autarchy traditionally espoused by RSS frontal organizations like the Swadeshi Jagran Manch; it seeks a globalized nation, deriving investment and profit from association with the wider world, and allied with corporate interests within the country who share the same worldview. It derives legitimacy from evoking the glories of the past, but it seeks to update them with an eye on the future, reconciling Hindu temples with high-tech, marrying the ancient to the modern, and capturing futuristic technologies to serve its national mission. This is the one significant way in which Moditva differs from the core assumptions of the Sangh Parivar.

The vocabulary of Moditva is therefore very different from Hindutva pure and simple: it speaks of good governance, economic growth, infrastructure investment, service delivery, and ease of doing business. These are not terms likely to have been employed by RSS leaders in the past, but they are applied to the same ends; economic development is portrayed as part of a nationalist awakening, prosperity is a means to establishing the glorious Ram Rajya long promised by the votaries of Hindutva. 'Vikas', the Hindi word for development often cited by Modi in his speeches, is simultaneously slogan and trope; it redefines Hindu nationalism in terms of the well-being of the people, and associates it with the personality of the leader, the vikas purush. 'The rising [level of] aspiration is the biggest strength of Indian development,' Modi declared. 'When aspirations get proper leadership...aspiration in itself is achievement.'[91]

To Leftists, Moditva economics and Moditva cultural nationalism have come together in a new form of assertive conservatism. By seeking its success through foreign investment

---

[90]'BJP chief, ministers meet RSS top brass; deliberate over policies', 28 May 2018.
[91]Modi speech to Indian community in Washington DC, 25 June 2017, www.narendramodi.in.

and 'Make in India', Leftists say, it is obliged to sell India as a land of cheap labour and affordable skills ready to serve the global financial system; but for India to remain attractive, labour must be kept cheap and skilled workers affordable, which requires clamping down on social unrest in the underclass. Thus, keeping the Dalits in their place and the minorities on the margins serves both a cultural and an economic purpose. Crony capitalism at home and quiescent collaboration abroad require no less. Moditva does not shrink from the violent imposition of social conformism by upper castes or by employers; it is silent in the face of communal violence or anti-Dalit atrocities, because both serve to assert the social order that facilitates Moditva. This analysis explains why opposition to Narendra Modi extends beyond the widespread concern about his politics; his economics raises multiple concerns too.

V

Some, particularly on the Left, have gone further than this, evoking the dreaded term 'fascism' for Moditva. In a now-famous essay published in the magazine *Seminar* soon after the 2002 riots, sociologist (and trained clinical psychologist) Professor Ashis Nandy, who had interviewed Narendra Modi in the late 1980s, well before he began his spectacular political rise, laid out this chilling diagnosis. The future prime minister, Prof Nandy wrote, at the time 'a nobody, a small-time RSS pracharak trying to make it as a small-time BJP functionary', gave him a 'long, rambling interview' that 'left me in no doubt that here was a classic, clinical case of a fascist.' Prof Nandy added, 'I never use the term "fascist" as a term of abuse; to me it is a diagnostic category comprising not only one's ideological posture but also the personality traits and motivational patterns contextualizing the ideology. Modi, it gives me no pleasure to tell the readers, met virtually all the criteria that psychiatrists, psycho-analysts and psychologists had set up after years of empirical work on the authoritarian personality. He had the same mix of puritanical rigidity, narrowing of emotional life, massive use of the ego defence of projection, denial and fear of his own passions combined with fantasies of violence—all set within the matrix of clear paranoid and obsessive personality traits. I still remember the cool, measured tone in which he elaborated a theory of cosmic conspiracy against India that painted every Muslim as a suspected traitor and a potential terrorist.'[92]

Prof Nandy is a respected scholar and there is no reason to doubt the objectivity of his analysis. Some elements he identifies are in fact avowed by Modi followers themselves, though as virtues, not failings: the 'puritanical rigidity', for instance, is a Modi attribute—he told me himself that, as prime minister, he sees no movies, for instance; he is known neither to drink nor smoke, eats non-spicy fare, enjoys a simple khichdi (usually alone) and frequently observes fasts on specific Hindu occasions, in particular during the Navratri festival, when he only drinks nimbu paani and a cup of tea during the day.

Another is the 'narrowing of emotional life' Prof Nandy mentions. Narendra Modi lives alone, and maintains little contact with his mother, four brothers or sister, though he has not been above demonstrating his filial devotion by seeking his mother's blessings on his victory or being photographed wheeling her chair around the prime ministerial garden (before returning her to a life of anonymity away from him). Mr Modi has no relationship to speak of with his blood relatives, and advertises this as part of his incorruptibility. At an election rally in Hamidpur in Himachal Pradesh in February 2014, PM Modi said, 'I have no family ties. I am single. Who will I be corrupt for?' adding, 'this mind and body is totally devoted to the nation.'[93] His siblings are less enthusiastic about his rectitude. 'I wish he would help the next generation of our family. But I am sure he won't,' his younger brother, Prahlad Modi, said after Narendra Modi became PM. 'He won't even offer tea to someone without a reason—especially his family.'[94]

---

[92]Ashis Nandy, 'Obituary of a culture', *Seminar*, May 2002.
[93]"I am single, who will I be corrupt for?" says Narendra Modi', *NDTV*, 17 February 2014.
[94]Andrew North, 'Narendra Modi keeps family and hometown at arm's length', *BBC*, 16 May 2014.

Prahlad Modi is also the source of one of the few negative anecdotes about PM Modi as a youngster. When he was younger, Narendra Modi liked to fly kites. Being the younger brother, Prahlad would hold the spool of string, or manja, while Narendra Modi did all the flying. 'If I refused, he would get angry and he would hit me,' says Prahlad, 'I am still scared of him, even today.'[95]

As has been noted, Narendra Modi has said he sleeps about four hours a night; he rises at about 5 a.m. every day to do yoga and meditate, spends fifteen minutes reading the news on his iPad (this seems suspiciously little) and has not taken a holiday in nearly two decades. An official response to an RTI (Right to Information Act) petition filed in 2016 asking about the number of days of leave Modi had taken since becoming PM informed the applicant—in terms unusually obsequious for an RTI response—that he had not taken a single day of leave since coming to power: 'the Prime Minister can be said to be on duty all the time'.[96]

Much of this display of austerity and devotion to work is real—even Mr Modi's critics acknowledge he is a workaholic whose tireless energy amid a punishing schedule is remarkable—but it is also at odds with his expensive, rimless Bvlgari designer glasses, his Mont Blanc pens and luxury Movado watch, and his trademark half-sleeve kurtas and 'bundy' jackets tailored for him since 1989 by a bespoke Ahmedabad designer, Bipin Chauhan of Jade Blue, who now markets Modi's signature look as 'Modi kurtas' and 'Modi jackets'. (There was also the embarrassing episode of the ten-lakh rupee suit, with his name embossed on every pinstripe, which he wore to a meeting with President Obama in January 2015: he was mocked so mercilessly for this that he declared it to be a gift, reportedly from a manufacturer of diamond jewellery, Rameshkumar Bhikabhai Virani, and promptly auctioned it off for four crore rupees to benefit the Prime Minister's Relief Fund.[97])

[95]Ibid.
[96]'Narendra Modi has not taken a single leave till date; PM always on duty', Economic Times, 12 October 2016.
[97]'Rahul slams Modi for wearing "₹10 lakh suit"', The Tribune, 30 January 2015;

But there are two things that must be said about this. First, personal grooming and meticulousness about appearance are no sin. They also seem to be a lifelong characteristic: Modi's uncle, Jayantibhai, remembers that when Modi was young, he 'liked to dress properly and took care of his clothes—did not allow them to get frayed and ruffled like other children. He spent a lot of time in grooming.'[98] He is said to always carry a comb in his pocket, and has never been photographed with a hair out of place. Some have described him as obsessive about personal hygiene; he is said to change his clothes at least four or five times a day. He is conscious of the impression he makes on people, and this is not just about appearance: he reportedly never drinks cold water and takes great care of his voice. 'Modi had once told me, he cannot compromise on three things—his eyes, voice and clothes,' Bipin Chauhan has declared.[99] Second, if anyone has earned the right to such small signs of luxury as a handful of expensive accessories, it is surely Narendra Modi, who has devoted himself completely to his cause—or, as his followers see it, the cause of the nation. Mr Modi once told me that he has given away most of his salary to charity ever since becoming chief minister, a practice he continues, and there is no reason not to believe him.

It would be churlish to suggest that Mr Modi should not be given credit for his lack of acquisitiveness since he has, after all, disavowed the family obligations that inspire cupidity on the part of other Indian politicians. Still, many Indians are troubled that, after abandoning his wife in her childhood, he has been so neglectful of her. Narendra Modi's first mention of his wife, Jashodaben, whose existence he had failed to acknowledge for years, was in the poll affidavit he was obliged to submit when he filed his nomination for the Lok Sabha elections in 2014.[100]

'PM Narendra Modi's auctioned suit enters Guinness Book of World Records', *Times of India*, 20 August 2018.
[98]G. Sampath, 'The Man in the Modi Mask', *LiveMint*, 25 July 2013.
[99]'Bipin Chauhan: Meet Narendra Modi's personal tailor', *Economic Times*, 17 June 2013.
[100]Haima Deshpande, '"I am Narendra Modi's wife"', *Open*, 11 April 2009.

Divorce being unthinkable in their community, Mrs Modi has been condemned to a life of spinsterhood since her teens, eking out a living as a schoolteacher on a meagre government salary, with no financial support coming her way from her husband. She has had to travel by bus or on foot, for instance, even after he became prime minister; when she was provided a security detail by the government in keeping with standard protocols, she found herself in the absurd position of being tailed in a police vehicle by her guards while she herself used public transport.[101] No voter would have begrudged PM Modi providing his wife the basic comforts and dignity to which a prime minister's wife is entitled; his denial of it seems an inverse form of ostentation, as if it is more important to demonstrate rectitude than decency.

It is said that Narendra Modi acquiesced in his marriage to Jashoda because of his reverence for tradition and abandoned it because he was rejecting a choice that he had not made and a way of life that had been imposed upon him. This contradiction is not surprising. Mr Modi's attitude to women generally seems an odd compound of old-fashioned patriarchy and enlightened sloganeering. Just before being elected prime minister he dismayed an audience of businesswomen and female entrepreneurs assembled by the Federation of Indian Chambers of Commerce and Industry (FICCI) by talking about every clichéd stereotype inflicted on Indian women—'subservient wives, sacrificing mothers and cooking wizards', in the words of one observer.[102] While most of his audience consisted of women entrepreneurs, well-paid professionals and high-ranking corporate executives, Mr Modi hailed 'stree-shakti' (the strength of women) with examples of the housewife who burns her fingers making chapattis for her husband and another who hastily abandons a sari sale to run home and save her child

---

[101]'Jashodaben speaks out: Three reasons Modi's wife is upset with her security', *FirstPost*, 25 November 2014.
[102]'What the woman audience thought of Modi's Ficci speech', *FirstPost*, 20 December 2014.

from a fire.[103] As PM, he once praised his Bangladeshi counterpart, Sheikh Hasina, for her courage in fighting terrorism 'despite being a woman'.[104] The hashtag #DespiteBeingAWoman started trending on social media, but the prime minister was unfazed.[105] He has announced a number of women-friendly slogans and schemes, notably in favour of girls' education, while slashing the budget for the rape-crisis centres that had been intended for every district to such a level that revised plans would provide only a handful in the whole of India.[106] Women's empowerment appears to be a credo without conviction in Moditva.

Moditva certainly relies on radiating an impression of strength: it follows a policy of 'never apologize, never explain'. Unlike the Congress-led UPA government that preceded the NDA government he heads, Mr Modi has never allowed the Opposition, the media or even widespread public disapproval to force a member of his government out of office. When his external affairs minister, Sushma Swaraj, was revealed to have gone behind the back of her own foreign secretary and the Indian high commissioner in the UK to privately advise the British high commissioner in Delhi that her ministry would not object if a travel document were provided to an Indian fugitive economic offender in London, Lalit Modi—a resigning offence in any democracy, especially since the fugitive was her lawyer husband's client—Modi refused the Opposition clamour for her resignation, and prevailed.[107] He similarly stuck with two ministers who had made offensive public statements (one of which divided the people of India into Ramzade and Haramzade, or followers of Ram and bastards), despite an Opposition outcry

---

[103]Ibid.

[104]'PM Narendra Modi draws flak for "despite being a woman" remark on Sheikh Hasina', *Economic Times*, 5 June 2015.

[105]Rama Lakshmi, 'India's Modi just delivered the world's worst compliment', *Washington Post*, 8 June 2015.

[106]'Modi government says no to rape crisis centres in every district', *DNA*, 25 February 2015.

[107]Suparna Singh, 'New Lalit Modi Emails Renew Conflict of Interest Charges for Sushma Swaraj', *NDTV*, 2 July 2015.

in Parliament. Mr Modi's stubbornness in all these cases signalled that he would not give in to pressure; this attitude of invulnerability itself shored up the perception of strength around his government, by contrast with earlier governments which had caved in to public pressure.

The prime minister was similarly unmoved by calls to 'unfollow' social media supporters of his who had issued vile messages celebrating the murder of journalist Gauri Lankesh in September 2017. Mr Modi's silence amounted to tacit support for abusive Hindu right-wing trolls, but he stood by them even in the face of a social media uproar, with the hashtag #BlockNarendraModi trending on Twitter. The PM was unmoved, and again the campaign against him ran out of steam. His imperturbability and resoluteness reinforced his strongman image, while on all these issues, his critics subsided into a sullen silence.

None of this, however, necessarily adds up to a fascist personality, though Prof Nandy is the expert, not me. It must be said, too, that Mr Modi has not conducted himself in office in the manner Prof Nandy's impressions and analysis would have suggested. He has repeatedly spoken of being a prime minister for all Indians; arguably his most effective slogan has been 'sabka saath, sabka vikas'. But as I have pointed out throughout this book, he has allowed free rein to retrograde and often violent forces who conform collectively to Prof Nandy's archetype. These elements in the Sangh Parivar have been emboldened by Mr Modi's continued silence in the face of their repeated atrocities and empowered by his stirring rhetoric that implicitly, and sometimes explicitly, attacks Muslims.[108]

At this point, it might be instructive to cast a little light on what is best described as the superstructure of Moditva. This aspect of Moditva is borrowed wholesale from Hindutva; one of its central tenets is the denigration and mistreatment of the

---

[108]M. K. Venu, 'If Left can condemn Maoists, why is Narendra Modi silent on Sanghis?', *FirstPost*, 19 August 2014; 'Modi needs to do more to condemn hate mongers within Sangh Parivar', *Times of India*, 24 April 2014.

Muslim community.[109] There are numerous examples I could quote in support of the way in which Indian Muslims have been excluded, vilified, or worse. There is, of course, the 2002 massacre, that took place on the watch of a BJP government, with CM Modi at its head. There is also the fact that the BJP became the first governing party in the history of independent India to come to power without a single elected Muslim member of the Lok Sabha; the three Muslims who have served in its council of ministers are all appointees to the Rajya Sabha, elected by pliable BJP majorities in state assemblies, all representing states to which they do not belong.[110] The very fact that the BJP finds itself unable to put up electable Muslim candidates in any constituency speaks volumes about the party's attitude to Muslims and of the attitudes of Indian Muslims to it—as well as of the views of its core voters, whose bigotry would not predispose them to vote for a Muslim, not even one contesting on their own party's symbol. Strengthening this anti-Muslim bias is the fact that under Prime Minister Modi, the BJP has a sizeable parliamentary majority on its own that it had never enjoyed before and is, therefore, not obliged to dilute its agenda to accommodate less Hindutva-minded coalition partners, since it does not need any of them to make up its majority. (This has led one ally, the Telugu Desam Party, to leave the NDA, and another, the Shiv Sena, to publicly express its dissatisfaction, even abstaining in a vote of no-confidence in the Modi government of which it is a part.[111]) Also for the first time, Indian democracy finds itself facing the reality of its top three constitutional positions—president, vice president and prime minister—all being held by RSS members of the same ideological disposition.

---

[109]James Traub, 'Is Modi's India Safe for Muslims?', *Foreign Policy*, 26 June, 2015; Zoya Hasan, '4 years of Modi: Ostracisation of Muslims a hallmark of "new India"', *National Herald*, 27 May 2018.
[110]Anubhuti Vishnoi and Seema Chishti, 'BJP's Muslim score: 7 of 482 fielded, no winners', *Indian Express*, 19 May 2014.
[111]'Andhra Pradesh's Telugu Desam Party quits the NDA', *Times of India*, 16 March 2018; 'Shiv Sena, to publicly express its dissatisfaction, even abstaining in a vote of no-confidence in the Modi government', *The Telegraph*, 20 July 2018.

Below this Hindutva superstructure, worrying in itself, is the
ethos of Moditva that suffuses it. Mr Modi embodies the prejudices
about Muslims that are the marked characteristic of these forces.
During his election campaign Mr Modi alleged that the Congress
party-led UPA government was pro-Muslim and therefore 'anti-
Hindu'; he deplored what he portrayed as the Congress's policy of
'Muslim appeasement'; and he condemned it for dealing too softly
with Pakistan and feeding chicken biryani to visiting Pakistani
grandees.[112] After becoming prime minister, Modi initially seemed
to seek to outgrow his own prejudices, for instance inviting the
former prime minister of Pakistan, Nawaz Sharif, to his swearing-
in, exchanging saris and shawls with Nawaz Sharif (if not serving
him chicken biryani!) and adopting a more statesmanlike posture
towards the UAE than he had betrayed in his 2009 conversation
with me. And yet in domestic politics he did not hesitate to
exploit the same majoritarian bigotry he sought to conceal, or
disavow, abroad.

There is no doubt that Mr Modi has a blind spot about Muslims.
While he has made the occasional statement to demonstrate his
impartiality, while donning various types of colourful and exotic
headgear on his travels in India and abroad, he has never agreed
to put on a Muslim skullcap (which he has called a 'symbol of
appeasement of the minority').[113] In his campaign speeches he has
relished using overtly Muslim honorifics for those he was attacking,
speaking derisively of 'Mian' Musharraf or 'Mian' Ahmed Patel.[114]
When he sought to deride the Congress's Rahul Gandhi as a
princeling, he never used the Hindi term 'rajkumar', preferring the
Persian and Urdu 'shehzada', as if to further damn Rahul Gandhi by

[112]"Narendra Modi slams UPA's "biryani' foreign policy", *FirstPost*, 13 May 2013.
[113]Zahir Janmohamed, 'The rise of Narendra Modi: the man who doesn't wear
dark green', *Boston Review*, 28 June 201; Sunanda K. Datta-Ray, 'A turban and
a cap—India's national image is being reduced to that of the ruling party', *The
Telegraph*, 17 June 2017.
[114]Manoj Joshi, 'In his attempt to win elections, Narendra Modi does not seem
bound by propriety—or even dignity', *Scroll.in*. 12 December 2017.

association with Islamic terminology.[115] He remains unapologetic about the ghettoization of the Muslim community in Gujarat, as in the township of Juhapura in which almost every Muslim in Ahmedabad is now confined: he told me (in the lunchtime conversation that began this chapter) that 'they prefer it that way'. The mere fact that his fellow Gujaratis were now living proof that a minority community could seek trust and assurance only among people of their own religion, and that this was shameful, a blow against the development of a civic society and a recipe for psychological separation with incalculable negative consequences for the country, does not seem to have struck him at all.

Moditva grows out of Narendra Modi. And Narendra Modi in turn is rooted in the RSS. However, as I have pointed out earlier, in some ways Mr Modi seems to have outgrown his RSS prejudices. One of the most striking of these departures from the RSS way of thinking is in his views of Mahatma Gandhi.[116] He had to have been schooled, like other RSS pracharaks, in an intense dislike of Mahatma Gandhi, whose message of tolerance and pluralism was emphatically rejected as minority appeasement by the Sangh Parivar, and whose credo of non-violence, or ahimsa, was seen as an admission of weakness unworthy of manly Hindus.[117] Savarkar, whom Mr Modi has described as one of his heroes, had expressed contempt for Gandhi's 'perverse doctrine of non-violence and truth' and claimed it 'was bound to destroy the power of the country'.[118] But Prime Minister Modi, for all his Hindutva mindset, his admiration of Savarkar and his lifetime affiliation to the Sangh Parivar, has embraced Gandhi, hailing the Mahatma and even using his glasses as a symbol of the Swachh Bharat campaign.

---

[115]'Narendra Modi mimics "Shehzada" Rahul Gandhi at Chhattisgarh rally', *NDTV*, 15 November 2013.
[116]A. G. Noorani, 'The RSS and Gandhi: A Necessary Backstory', *The Wire*, 24 July 2016.
[117]Ibid.
[118]Rachel Fell McDermott et al (ed.), *Sources of Indian Tradition*, Vol. II, New York: Columbia University Press, 2014, p. 439.

This may or may not represent a sincere conversion to Gandhism. PM Modi is hardly unaware of the tremendous worldwide reputation that Mahatma Gandhi enjoys, and is too savvy a marketing genius not to recognize the soft-power opportunity evoking Gandhi-ji provides, not to mention the global public relations disaster that would ensue if he were to denounce an Indian so universally admired. There may, therefore, be an element of insincerity to his newfound love for the Mahatma, as well as a shrewd domestic political calculation—wrapping himself in the mantle of other distinguished Gujaratis, notably Gandhi-ji and (Sardar Vallabhbhai) Patel, would enable some of their lustre to rub off on him at home.

A digression here: in the Czech novelist Milan Kundera's brilliant novel of his native country under communist rule, *The Book of Laughter and Forgetting,* he tells the story of a Party stalwart, Politburo member and hero of the Soviet-backed revolution that ended democracy in Czechoslovakia for half a century.[119] The gentleman, Clementis, was among the select band of leaders who stood on a balcony waving to assembled party supporters as the annual military parade filed past in 1948. A famous photo shows him, sturdy and stone-faced as befitted the communist apparatchiks of that era, on the balcony, acknowledging the dutiful cheers of the throng, along with his party boss, Gottwald. Since it is snowy and cold, and Gottwald is bareheaded, Clementis has taken off his fur hat and solicitously placed it on his comrade's head.

But soon after the photo was published, Clementis fell out of favour. Some ideological heresy, no doubt, led to him being denounced as a class enemy, a traitor to the party and an enemy of the people. His fall was swift: he was dismissed and executed. Once a hero of the revolution, he became a non-person. His role in the revolution was not just forgotten; it was erased from the official histories authorized by the party. His portraits were taken

---

[119]Milan Kundera, *The Book of Laughter and Forgetting*, New York: HarperPerennial, 1994.

down, his photos deleted from all communist documents. Then worse followed: records of his participation in historic events were expunged. His life's work as a committed communist revolutionary ceased to be. It was as if he had never done any of the things he had been hailed for doing before his disgrace.

There remained one problem, however. He had been a participant, along with those who were still in power, in a number of occasions that could not simply be struck from the record, including the annual National Day events at which he had joined the country's communist leaders in waving to the crowds. His presence in photographs of those events was a reminder that the communist leaders had once nurtured an apostate in their midst. This was intolerable.

Technology permitted a decisive solution to the problem. The original negatives were retrieved, and Clementis was carefully airbrushed out of the pictures in which he had appeared. The historical record no longer showed him at all. Where Clementis stood, there was now only a gap, a void, an absence. It was the ultimate communist repudiation: they not only destroyed his future, they abolished his past.

The famous picture on the balcony was no exception. Where he had once stood upright and unsmiling next to Gottwald, there was now a bare patch of wall, as if he had never been there that day in 1948. The photo was republished in various newspapers, documents and publicity materials, but the only version of it allowed to appear was the doctored one. The communists knew that human memory fades; only photographs remain. They wanted to ensure that the photographic record told only the story they wanted people to know.

But the diligent photographic artist who had applied his airbrush techniques to the original photograph had omitted one detail in expunging Clementis from the photograph. All traces of the man, his face, his upraised hand, were gone. But the fur hat he had taken off remained resting on Gottwald's head. The man had been erased, but his hat was still there—a silent reminder of his original presence.

Something similar has happened in our country. No, we are not yet a dictatorship where only authorized versions of the past can be circulated. But our rulers are busy airbrushing our history too: Maharashtra's history schoolbooks have now eliminated the Mughals altogether, and Rajasthan's tells us that Rana Pratap won the Battle of Haldighati.[120] Inconvenient facts—even emperors and military defeats—can be erased from our memory if we just don't acknowledge they happened.

And we now have our equivalent of Kundera's hat as well. Everything that Mahatma Gandhi stood for is being trashed by our current rulers. The apostle of ahimsa is betrayed daily by those who inflict violence on the defenceless. The man who said noble ends cannot be served by ignoble means is cited by rulers who will stop at nothing to get their way. The great soul who worked tirelessly for peace and communal harmony is invoked by a governing party some of whose MPs have said they want his assassin's statues installed in different places in India.[121]

But despite all this, Gandhi the brand is too valuable to be junked by the marketing gurus who now rule us. And so they have reduced his message to that of sanitation: the symbol of the government's Swachh Bharat campaign is a pair of the Mahatma's glasses. They adorn every advertisement, every poster, every letterhead, proclaiming Clean India. The Mahatma said one should start by cleansing one's own mind and heart first. This, our government is incapable of.

So the Mahatma's message, spirit and soul have vanished from today's India. His ideals are gone. Only his glasses remain.

And yet it is precisely Mr Modi's willingness to leap beyond his ideological past that makes one feel that a term like 'fascist' is too

[120]'Mughals disappearing from textbooks across the country as history seems subject to change', *FirstPost*, 7 August 2017; Manoj Ahuja, 'In Rajasthan's revised history, Maharana Pratap defeated Akbar in Haldighati', *Hindustan Times*, 23 September 2017.
[121]'Install Nathuram Godse's statues at different places in India: Hindu Mahasabha to govt', *FirstPost*, 19 December 2014.

much too soon. Fascism surely requires two elements—an outright rejection of democracy and a ruthless definition and application of repressive law and order—that are absent in Moditva. Living in democratic India, I am reluctant to follow Prof Nandy in applying the label to Narendra Modi. But then I read Fintan O'Toole in the *Irish Times* on 21 July 2018 about the Western world: 'Fascism doesn't arise suddenly in an existing democracy. It is not easy to get people to give up their ideas of freedom and civility. You have to do trial runs that, if they are done well, serve two purposes. They get people used to something they may initially recoil from; and they allow you to refine and calibrate. This is what is happening now and we would be fools not to see it. And then I wonder, applying these words to India, and to the "new normal" that has dawned since 2014, are we also fools not to see it?'[122]

Historically there are certain aspects of fascism that do seem to have appeared in recent years in India—the demonization of minorities within society to the extent that they are made to feel insecure;[123] the condemnation and reviling of critics to the point where the use of violence against them seems permissible; the whipping up of nationalist feelings, coupled with an identification of the ruling party with the nation and a disparagement of dissent as anti-national and disloyal to the country; an assertive foreign policy, especially towards neighbours, that is belligerent to the point of being willing to risk war; and contempt for rules-based liberal democracy and its independent institutions. O'Toole warns of 'the generation of tribal identities, the division of society into mutually exclusive polarities' that have indeed been a feature of Moditva. He warns, too, of the rigging of elections, noting that, historically, fascism has come to power on a minority vote and then consolidated itself through fear and intimidation. Seen through this prism, the BJP's 31 per cent certainly looks more ominous. 'And fascism,' he continues, 'needs a propaganda machine so effective

---

[122]Fintan O' Toole, 'Trial runs for fascism are in full flow', *Irish Times*, 26 June 2018.
[123]Nazia Erum, 'BJP is done marginalising Indian Muslims. It has now started demonising them', *Scroll.in*, 21 July 2018.

that it creates for its followers a universe of 'alternative facts' impervious to unwanted realities.' Again, echoes of India resonate.[124]

And the final ingredient O'Toole identifies is the intangible one: the undermining of moral boundaries, which inure people to be accepting of acts of extreme cruelty, particularly towards a despised 'out-group' that is portrayed a threat. At a time when it seems it might be safer in some parts of India to be a cow than a Muslim, is O'Toole right that the test-marketing for something more ominous is already happening? With mob lynchings creating an atmosphere of fear among many in the country, the BJP has given rise to a culture of impunity.

The thoughtful Indian columnist Santosh Desai, without mentioning the word fascism, writes of the 'atmosphere of fear' being 'achieved not only through harsh punitive measures, but through a complex and elaborate network of actions, real and symbolic...The sense of threat is more palpable. This government is deemed capable of much more than what it has actually done; the fear is evoked by latent violence in the body language of the government rather than in its actions alone. "Violence in the air" is a more effective way of fostering self-censorship than any direct method...Fear reproduces itself thanks to the elegant design of the ecosystem of intimidation that is in place today... Showing signs of fear itself becomes proof—unless you are an anti-national, why should you be afraid?'[125]

It is difficult to argue that Desai is being alarmist. His tone is measured as he goes on: 'The calibrated use of reward and punishment, the taking of action against victims rather than perpetrators, the penetration of virtually every institution that matters, the creation of voluntary and vocal cheerleaders for the actions of the state, the regular encouragement given from the highest level of the government to those that carry out intimidation, the periodic acts of brutal violence that indicate that the threats

---

[124]Ibid.
[125]Santosh Desai, 'An Ecosystem of Fear?', *Times of India*, 3 September 2018.

are not only symbolic in nature, the breeding of several kinds of private armies that publicly display their muscle, the succession of violently intemperate statements made by minor party leaders, and actions like the arrest of activists on charges that align with the larger narrative that is being built—these are all part of this ecosystem of fear.'

If one were to look for an Indian echo to O'Toole's anxiety about the West, Desai's 'ecosystem of fear' is troubling enough. Fear is as worrying an 'f' word as fascism.

It is a measure of my own concern about the substance of Prof Nandy's charge—rather than my ambivalence over the word for it—that I was struck by a paragraph in Madeleine Albright's recent *Fascism: A Warning*, in which she warns the readers about the lasting damage that has been caused to her nation by President Trump. He has 'degraded political discourse...shown an astonishing disregard for facts, libelled his predecessors...touted mindlessly nationalistic economic and trade policies, vilified immigrants and the countries from which they come and nurtured a paranoid bigotry toward the followers of one of the world's foremost religions'.[126] Much of this description finds resonance in present-day India: the degrading of political discourse from the very top, the disregard for facts (of which more below), the constant denigration of his predecessors (Mr Modi speaks as if Indian political history before him was a black hole of failure, and claims that Indians became proud of India only after his victory), the mindless economic policy of demonetization (which, as I describe in Chapter 35, all but destroyed the Indian economy), and the vilification of immigrants and minorities—it helps that the two can be conflated, since the Bangladeshi migrants are overwhelmingly Muslim).[127] If, as Albright suggests, all this amounts to warning signs of looming fascism, then Indians must consider themselves warned.

---

[126]Madeleine Albright, *Fascism: A Warning*, New York: HarperCollins Publishers, 2018.
[127]'India will not take Rohingya refugees, they are a security threat, says BJP', *Deccan Chronicle*, 17 September 2017.

One phrase of Albright's especially struck me in particular: the 'astonishing disregard for facts'. This has been a particular characteristic of Moditva, starting from the man himself and extending (as I explain in a later chapter) to many of his well-placed followers. Narendra Modi is an undoubtedly intelligent man: he is a quick study, masters a vast array of information and retails it with impressive recall. But he does not have the educational credentials of many of his predecessors and contemporaries: the prime minister claims to have obtained a formal degree by correspondence from Delhi University, but the university was unable to trace any record of it. Doubts were also raised over his MA degree in 'Entire Political Science' from Gujarat University, a subject that apparently does not even exist at the university.[128] And as his reading has been narrow, ideologically biased and selective, he often seems unaware of the contextual basis for evaluating the 'facts', real and imagined, that come his way. As a result, the prime minister has often played fast and loose with fact-based ideas and theories.

The best-known example is of his claim, soon after his election, that the appearance of the elephant-headed Hindu god Ganesha or Ganapathi was proof that the ancient Indians had mastered plastic surgery.[129] I have written before that it does not seem to have occurred to him that the smallest imaginable elephant head could not possibly fit onto the largest available human neck; worse, in saying what he did, he discredited ancient India's genuine accomplishments in surgery, which included the world's first known rhinoplasty operation to reconstruct a human nose, by Susruta in the first century CE, whose records and instruments have survived. This is not the only instance of Mr Modi's factual errors; there have literally been dozens. He has been known to mix up the dates of the Maurya dynasty and to place Taxila, which is in today's Pakistan, in Bihar instead. He once claimed that the thirteenth-

[128]Ashok Swain, 'Controversy over PM Modi's degree damages reputation of India's education system', *DailyO*, 2 March 2018.
[129]Maseeh Rahman, 'Indian prime minister claims genetic science existed in ancient times', *The Guardian*, 28 October 2014.

century Sun Temple at Konark is 2,000 years old.[130] In a 2018 speech in Maghar, Uttar Pradesh, he mentioned that 'this was the place where Sant Kabir, Guru Nanak and Baba Gorakhnath sat together and discussed spirituality'. The three were undoubtedly spiritual giants of India's medieval era, but Gorakhnath was born in the eleventh century, Kabir at the end of the fourteenth century and Guru Nanak in the fifteenth century, and they could not possibly have met and discussed anything together.[131]

Mr Modi claimed in a 2015 town hall meeting at San Jose with Mark Zuckerberg that the Indian economy was $8 trillion, whereas India's GDP is, in fact, less than a third of that, at $2.5 trillion—an elementary error but one hardly becoming of a head of government.[132] Exaggeration seems to be a recurring weakness of Mr Modi's: he claimed in Davos in 2018 that '600 crore voters' had given him a mandate in 2014, a figure that amounts to 6 billion, which would include most of the human race; in fact, India had 81.5 crore (815 million) registered voters in 2014, of whom about 60 per cent voted, and of whom 31 per cent voted for his party—in other words, 17.98 crore, approximately, voted for him, not 600 crore.[133] And in Parliament, rebutting a motion of no-confidence against his government in 2018, Narendra Modi delivered a string of far-fetched numerical arguments for his employment-generation claims (claiming, for instance, that each car sold implied the employment of two new persons for it) that confirmed his cavalier attitude to figures as well as facts.

These may be harmless errors and should arguably be excused, even if they reveal a worrying penchant for making tall claims. Some other factual errors, however, seem to be maliciously

[130]Adrija Bose, 'Sun Temple is 2000 years old? 7 times Prime Minister Narendra Modi got his History wrong', *Huffington Post*, 8 June 2016.
[131]'Prime Minister Modi gets history wrong again, this time in Maghar', *India Today*, 28 June 2018.
[132]Puja Mehra and Mehboob Jeelani, 'Congress says PM got it wrong on GDP', *The Hindu*, 29 September 2015.
[133]'6 billion Indian voters: PM Modi commits faux pas at WEF', *Times of India*, 23 January 2018.

and politically motivated, and recall O'Toole's warning that
fascism 'creates for its followers a universe of "alternative facts"
impervious to unwanted realities'. Two recent examples of such
misrepresentation arose in 2018: during the course of the election
campaign to the Karnataka Assembly, Mr Modi claimed that
Jawaharlal Nehru and the Congress had mistreated two generals
who hailed from the state, Field Marshal K. M. Cariappa and
Gen. K. S. Thimayya, whereas both had in fact been honoured
and promoted.[134] He also alleged that Pandit Nehru had never
called on the incarcerated revolutionary Bhagat Singh in jail,
whereas pictorial and archival evidence of Nehru-ji's doing just
that exists.[135] These allegations, relying on 'false facts', are part of
the Hindutva playbook against the Congress party and the Nehru
family, as are the allegations (mercifully not yet voiced by the
prime minister himself, but widely circulated by his followers on
social media) that Feroze Gandhi, Indira's husband, was actually
a Muslim and that Jawaharlal Nehru, who died of a stroke at the
age of seventy-four, had in fact succumbed to syphilis. Fantasies,
conspiracy theories and invented facts are the staple of extremist
movements everywhere, and the worry, when a prime minister
utters a falsehood, is what else lurks where that came from.

VI

The media has tended not to make too much of such errors; in
an era where politicians are frequently and widely lampooned for
the slightest slip, Narendra Modi has largely preserved an aura
of infallibility. Yet PM Modi has had a fraught relationship with
the press. He sees them as instruments of his interests, but not
as an institution to which he is in any way accountable. They
can be useful in promoting his image and his message, which is
why they sometimes need to be cajoled; they can also be harmful

---

[134]'Karnataka polls: Modi accuses Congress of insulting Cariappa and Thimayya',
Business Standard, 4 May 2018.
[135]'Twitter gives Modi a history lesson after he claims that no Congress leader
met Bhagat Singh in jail', *Scroll.in*, 10 May 2018.

in undermining his image and his message, which is why they sometimes need to be cudgelled. PM Modi monitors the media almost obsessively, but he does not indulge it, rarely gives interviews (except to pliant journalists who ask him embarrassingly unctuous questions) and (in India) has never held a press conference. When it is necessary to humour the media, he will do so, addressing a media organization's 'summit', delivering a media foundation's lecture or giving away journalism prizes; when it is necessary to curb the media, he will not hesitate to use the powers of his government to do so, though rarely overtly. A word to the wise is all it takes; since most media houses are owned and run by corporate houses with other business interests than their publications, the media's paymasters are vulnerable to pressures that a mere editor might have been inclined to resist. Thus several senior journalists and editors—most recently (in August 2018) three leading journalists from the popular Hindi TV channel ABP—are said to have lost their jobs after the government conveyed its displeasure with their reporting.[136] Some subjects tend to arouse the government's hostility: the editor of a prominent national daily was allegedly asked to leave for publishing a regular 'Hate Tracker' listing incidents of communal violence, and though cause and effect are speculative, the Hate Tracker was discontinued immediately upon his defenestration.[137] On at least half a dozen occasions, articles critical of highly placed figures in the ruling party have disappeared overnight from the websites of major media organizations.[138] Indeed, some stories have not been reported at all, outside the web-only outlets that are so modestly funded that their donors cannot be pressured.

---

[136]Amrita Nayak Dutta, 'Top ABP editors quit, staff say Modi govt may have "arm-twisted channel for criticism"', *The Print*, 3 August 2018.

[137]Anuj Srivas, 'Hindustan Times Editor's Exit Preceded by Meeting Between Modi, Newspaper Owner', *The Wire*, 24 September 2017; 'After Editor's Exit, Hindustan Times Pulls Down Controversial "Hate Tracker"', *The Wire*, 25 October 2017.

[138]'Newspaper pulls down article critical of Amit Shah, Twitter outrages', *FirstPost*, 13 July 2014; Karnika Kohli, '*Times of India* Takes Down a Story the BJP Finds Embarrassing, Again', *The Wire*, 26 September 2017.

The journalist Karan Thapar has the distinction of conducting Narendra Modi's most famous, or most notorious, television interview. It took place in 2007, and lasted all of three minutes.

Thapar began by recalling that Mr Modi had been hailed by independent voices as 'the most efficient chief minister' of 'the best-administered state'. But he went on: 'And yet despite that, people still call you to your face a mass murderer and they accuse you of being prejudiced against Muslims. Do you have an image problem?'

Narendra Modi briefly seemed willing to engage with him on this, but when Thapar continued in his distinctive (some might say combative, some condescending) style—'Even five years after the Gujarat killings of 2002, the ghost of Godhra still haunts you... Why can't you say that you regret the killings that happened? Why can't you say maybe the government should have done more to protect Muslims?'—Mr Modi's forbearance snapped. He pulled off his microphone and walked off the set.[139] The resultant news story did far more damage to Modi than the interview itself (which would inevitably have moved on to other subjects) might have done, and continues to enjoy viral status on YouTube.

There is a footnote to the Karan Thapar interview story that reveals Mr Modi to be, as many of those who have fallen out with him allege, a man who holds deep grudges. In his recent book, Devil's Advocate, Karan Thapar reveals that Narendra Modi and he parted gracefully, but that despite several attempts, Thapar was never able to meet him again; Mr Modi refused to see him. When he became prime minister, Karan Thapar alleges, he ordered a boycott of Karan Thapar's show by all BJP officials and spokespersons, severely undermining the veteran journalist's broadcast career.[140]

The Karan Thapar episode is revelatory of a broader attitude.

---

[139]'Modi walks out of TV interview after being quizzed on riots', Rediff.com, 20 October 2007.
[140]Karan Thapar, 'Why Modi Walked Out in 2007 and the BJP Now Shuns Me', The Wire, 22 July 2018.

After becoming prime minister, Mr Modi refused to hold a single press conference. He let it be known that he did not feel the need to connect with people through the media 'when he is already in direct touch with the people'. To the time of writing (August 2018), he has only appeared before the press when on visits to presidents and prime ministers abroad, where the local customs involved a media appearance for the visitor with his host. (PM Modi is sensitive about the foreign media; he is said to veer between exaggerated pride at articles from foreign sources praising him and thin-skinned anger at negative stories abroad, though his supporters prefer to dismiss the latter as products of ignorance or bias.) In India, he holds neither formal press conferences nor informal engagements with the press. Instead, Mr Modi communicates with the public through social media, especially Twitter, his favoured medium, and on monthly broadcasts on radio and YouTube called *Mann ki Baat* ('Words from the Heart'[141]) which lay out his thoughts for the month. Whereas all of Narendra Modi's predecessors have taken a press pool with them on their aircraft, Mr Modi has refused to do so, and there are no media briefings, neither informal nor on the record, on board the prime minister's flights.

To compensate, as it were, for the neglect and 'management' of the mainstream media, PM Modi has focused his time and attention generously on social media, which has become a ferocious echo-chamber for the ruling Sangh Parivar's orthodoxy. It is astonishing to observe the extent of moral policing and right-wing trolling that Moditva and the BJP's supporters have unleashed on social media in India. This is so powerful and so overwhelming that it in effect acts as a community censure of any dissenting voices or liberal-leaning criticism of Mr Modi and his policies. Though the Sangh's political opponents, notably the Congress party, have

---

[141]This is an unsatisfactory translation, since 'heart' is actually 'dil' in Hindi, and 'mann' means 'mind'. But there is a connotation of 'feelings' and 'spirit' in 'mann' which would be absent in the English 'mind', hence 'Words from the Heart' is closer to the thought evoked by the phrase *Mann ki Baat*. A non-literal translation could be *What's On My Mind*.

finally begun to strike back in the same forum, the pattern was established early in PM Modi's tenure: organized and orchestrated social-media voices, many operating hundreds of 'bot' accounts to repeat their views, hail the new Caesar and drown out his critics, while the few people who seek to challenge PM Modi's actions on social media end up being angrily branded as 'anti-national' or 'anti-Hindu' and worse, being subjected to vile threats of assault, rape or murder if they persist in their views.[142] Some of the targets of their bile have been the handful of professional journalists who have bravely continued to wage their lonely individual battle for their own and, by extension, society's, freedom of expression.[143]

The concern about, and influence over, what is said in the media also appears to extend beyond the news media. Comedian Shyam Rangeela—whose video imitating Narendra Modi (with 'Rahul Gandhi' making a 'guest appearance') went viral on social media—complained that a leading Hindi-language television channel, Star Plus, refused to telecast his act on its show, *The Great Indian Laughter Challenge*.[144] Apparently, he was told that he could re-record his mimicry of Rahul Gandhi but not that of the prime minister. Stand-up comic Kunal Kamra found himself suddenly disinvited by a prominent university in Mr Modi's home state of Gujarat on the eve of his appearance there, because the content of his act was deemed too critical of the ruling party.[145] Actor Prakash Rai, better known as Prakash Raaj, whose trenchant denunciations of Modi have attracted a loyal following on YouTube, has found himself ostracized in Bollywood.[146]

---

[142]Swati Chaturvedi, 'General Narendra Modi and His Troll Army', *The Wire*, 8 September 2017.
[143]Annie Gowen, 'In Modi's India, journalists face bullying, criminal cases and worse', *Washington Post*, 15 February 2018.
[144]Karnika Kohli, 'Star Plus drops telecast of comedian mimicking Modi on "Great Indian Laughter Challenge"', *The Wire*, 26 October 2017.
[145]Suhit Kelkar, 'Kunal Kamra: Indian comedian riles ruling party with edgy humour', *Al Jazeera*, 21 June 2018; '"Anti-national content": MS University cancels comedian Kunal Kamra's show', *Indian Express*, 24 July 2018.
[146]'Not getting Hindi film offers after criticising Modi: Prakash Rai', *Times of India*, 5 May 2018.

It is hardly surprising, then, that during the four years of Narendra Modi's rule, India's ranking in the World Press Freedom Index has plummeted to 138th in the world, a poor reflection on the media environment in the world's largest democracy.

VII

Comparisons are, of course, always invidious, all the more so when they involve political leaders from different countries. But there's something about the trajectories of Turkey's Recep Tayyip Erdoğan and India's Narendra Modi that makes comparisons irresistible.

Erdoğan rose to power eleven years before Narendra Modi, but their parallels are eerie. Both came from humble backgrounds and were born in small towns (Rize on Turkey's Black Sea coast, Vadnagar in India's Gujarat state): Erdoğan as a child sold lemonade and pastry in the streets, Mr Modi helped his father and brother run a tea stall on a railway platform. Both were associated young with deeply held convictions that tied them to religiously oriented groups at odds with the secularism sanctified by their countries' dominant official narratives.

The modern nation states of Turkey and India had both emerged from the collapse of multi-ethnic, multi-religious empires, and had been led for decades by a secular elite whose ideology had been derived from Western sources of inspiration. Both Erdoğan and Modi led parties—the Justice and Development Party (AKP) and the Bharatiya Janata Party (BJP) respectively—that claimed to be anchored in a more authentic, religiously inspired nationalist tradition than the ruling ideologies they sought to supplant.

Both won their first elections by uncannily similar margins in their respective electoral systems: Erdoğan with 32.26 per cent of the popular vote and 363 of 550 seats in Parliament, Narendra Modi with 31 per cent and 333 of 543 seats (including those of allies who won on his coat-tails).

Both did so, too, by appealing beyond their religiously driven support base. Erdoğan and Narendra Modi expressed pride in their Islamic and Hindu rootedness, respectively, but campaigned on modernist platforms, arguing that they could bring about greater economic prosperity than the establishment they sought to overthrow. They both claimed to be more business-friendly, less mired in the corrupt ways of the past, and determined to shake their countries out of the sloth with which younger voters had become impatient.

Both were self-made men, energetic and physically fit (Erdoğan was a pro footballer, Narendra Modi thumped his 56-inch chest), and highly effective orators. Both, for all their parties' religious-cultural atavism, presented themselves as dynamic, forward-looking men of change—larger-than-life colossuses striding their political worlds while dwarfing both their rivals and their allies.

The two men's political messaging fell on receptive ground because popular discontent was high when they began their rise. The religious-chauvinist discourse of both the AKP and BJP, their emergence as the parties of the middle-classes of the hinterlands and second-tier cities and towns, their narratives of grievance and resentment against the established secular elites who had ruled too long, their dabbling in deep historical revisionism, built on a kind of chip-on-the-shoulder political appeal. Both Erdoğan and Narendra Modi portrayed themselves as outsiders who would transform their societies: they promised an identitarian validation for the 'real' Turk or Indian who had been marginalized by the cosmopolitan secularists.

Erdoğan, coming to power at a time of booming global growth, soon had economic success to bolster his popularity, which emboldened him to transform the country's polity. Narendra Modi, whether consciously or unconsciously, sought to emulate the Erdoğan formula. This consisted of seven key elements: assertion of religious identity, triumphalist majoritarianism, hyper-nationalism, authoritarian rule with increasing dominance of the country's institutions, challenging and curbing of the media, and strong economic growth, all embodied in the seventh key element—a personal image of 'the man who gets things done'. Erdoğan managed all seven elements and succeeded in being re-elected three times. PM Modi wished to reshape India the way Erdoğan has reshaped Turkey, but has been tripped up by only one of the list: the sixth. He has mismanaged the economy and denied himself the political benefits of strong economic growth (ironically, Erdoğan, too, is now facing the challenge of dealing with an economy that seems to be going into a tailspin).

Today, the parallels continue. Both men rule vast multicultural democracies while practising forms of illiberal nationalism. Erdoğan has demonized and suppressed Kurds just as Narendra Modi's BJP has sought to marginalize Muslims. In India, the minorities feel beleaguered, the excesses of the 'cow vigilantes' and 'mob lynchers' have alienated many on the fringes of Indian society, dissenters in the media and the universities are intimidated, political loyalties are all too often purchased by rampant financial corruption, and the subversion of institutions to serve a narrow sectarian political agenda gathers pace. The nationalism espoused by PM Modi excludes all who do not conform to the new orthodoxy. The majoritarian language and sentiment, the polarization, the dangerous belief that the BJP's opponents are traitors, all echo similar sentiments pronounced by the AKP in Turkey.

Both history and the future are pressed into service by the two leaders. Erdoğan extols the old Ottoman imperial legacy and campaigns telling voters they would 'not only be choosing a president and deputies' in parliament, but 'making a choice for our country's upcoming century'.[147] PM Modi constantly evokes the achievements of ancient India and claims to be reviving those past glories in a golden future under his rule. Both men conduct activist foreign policies built around boosting their image at home, and both have cultivated diaspora audiences: Erdoğan's speeches in the Balkans might antagonize the US and Europe, and even Serbs and Croats, but they raise his stock with Turks; PM Modi addresses stadiums full of Indian expatriates on his visits to other countries

---

[147]Ishaan Tharoor, 'Erdogan's push for power creates new chaos', *Washington Post*, 24 May 2018.

in speeches aimed entirely at audiences back home. Erdoğan evokes potent Islamic symbols abroad; PM Modi worships at temples in Nepal to influence Hindu voters in India.

Even the words of a Turkish author, Soner Captagay, to the *Washington Post* about Erdoğan could be applied to Narendra Modi without change: 'Half of the country hates him, and thinks he can do nothing right. But at the same time, the other half adores him, and thinks he can do nothing wrong.'[148]

To be sure, there are obvious differences. Turkey is 98 per cent Muslim, India only 80 per cent Hindu. Islamism, as Hindu chauvinists never tire of pointing out, is a global problem; Hindutva is not. Turkey has no equivalent of Mahatma Gandhi, with his message of non-violence and coexistence infused into every Indian schoolchild. India was colonized, Turkey was not. India was partitioned on religious grounds (to create Pakistan), Turkey was not (though the exchange of populations that accompanied the separation from Greece comes close). Turkey has undergone bouts of military rule; India has not. Turkey's population, at 81 million, is less than half that of a single Indian state, Uttar Pradesh (210 million). Turkey is more or less a developed country; India has a far longer way to go on the path of development.

True, parallels can be taken too far, and the two countries are far from identical. India is a far more diverse and complex society with an entrenched democracy, much less amenable to capture by one-man rule. It is still difficult for many Indians to imagine their country becoming what Turkey seems to have become, a majoritarian illiberal democracy with open traces of autocracy. But Narendra Modi and the BJP, in power for only four years, are at an earlier stage of 'state capture' than Erdoğan, in charge for fifteen. And the trajectory chosen by their current political leaders is similar enough to invite comparison—and provoke concern.

Erdoğan has had some success with the results of his policies, PM Modi considerably less. Every major Modi initiative has

---

[148]Ibid.

remained at the level of exhortation—Make in India, Skill India, Start-Up India, Digital India—but the slogans are yet to find their reality. Even the otherwise admirable Swachh Bharat campaign can only be credited for raising public awareness about sanitation and hygiene and increasing the number of toilets built, but India remains as dirty as ever, many of the toilets are unused because of a lack of water or maintenance, and open defecation is still rampant. Erdoğan won elections to a newly created executive presidency in July 2018, whereas PM Modi faces Indian voters (and a more united Opposition) in parliamentary elections in early 2019. It would be interesting to see if, thanks to the voters, the parallels finally diverge.

VIII

Narendra Modi runs a parliamentary system in a presidential style. This gives Indians the worst of both worlds: an unfettered executive with an automatic parliamentary majority which, unlike true presidential systems, is not held in check by an independent legislature.

The Modi government's two most dramatic decisions—the overnight demonetization of 86 per cent of India's currency in value, and the so-called 'surgical strikes' across the Line of Control between India and Pakistan—were taken and announced by the PM with a handful of unelected advisers, rather than, as would be expected in a parliamentary system, by the cabinet. Both were unilateral decisions made by the executive without any legislative input, not even by those legislators entrusted with formal executive authority in his own government. They were implemented by a small handful of bureaucrats, who enjoyed the PM's trust, in total secrecy, in a manner that involved what former UN Secretary General Boutros Boutros-Ghali once called 'stealth and sudden violence'. Such dramatic and stunning actions, conceived and conducted essentially in and by the PM's office, appear to be a hallmark of Mr Modi's leadership style. From his days in Gujarat, when he reputedly bypassed his cabinet to work entirely with a trusted group of unelected officials, he has demonstrated more faith in bureaucrats who are, after all, trained administrators, than in politicians, who only know how to win elections.[149] In his last major cabinet reshuffle, it was telling that four of his five new ministerial appointees were all former bureaucrats, two of whom had subsequently to be elected to the Upper House as required by the Constitution.

None of the usual constraints of the parliamentary system inhibit Narendra Modi. He has a majority in the Lok Sabha and does not need to waste time in legislative deal-making. His cabinet meetings are said to be exercises in one-way communication and top-down decision-making; ministers make presentations and proposals on demand, conduct themselves deferentially and never challenge the prime minister's position. He has a few token ministers from his allies in the cabinet, but they have very little authority and if they bridle at that, they are dispensable, since he does not need their parties to make up a majority—and they know that. He spends a large proportion of his time travelling—fifty-nine foreign countries visited so far at the time of writing, and countless destinations in India, the latter almost entirely in perpetual campaign mode. (On his international visits he has demonstrated a tendency to envelop his unsuspecting foreign interlocutors in a bear hug, while maintaining a stiff reserve on his domestic travels where he greets all and sundry with a formal namaskar.)

Though it was an American president, Theodore Roosevelt, who spoke of his office as a 'bully pulpit' to preach to the nation, it is an Indian prime minister who has now discovered his position gives him a 'bully pulpit' too. Whereas it should be in Parliament that the prime minister exercises his considerable skills of oratorical persuasion, Narendra Modi has spoken more often in foreign assemblies than in his own Lok Sabha. He disdains the

---

[149]D. P. Bhattacharya, 'Meet Narendra Modi's core team of four bureaucrats who drive the Modi-machine', *Economic Times*, 25 April 2014.

legislative fray, for which he reveals thinly veiled contempt. As he has already demonstrated in Gujarat, in his view a legislative majority exists only to enable and legitimize his executive power; once he has that, he does not need the legislature, except for the unavoidable task of passing his Budget and pushing through laws, both of which his majority enables him to do without serious legislative input. The number of sittings of Parliament have declined precipitously, and when it meets disruptions are frequent (and sometimes engineered by the government itself, which in 2018 passed its Budget without debate amid the din.[150]) It is Narendra Modi's wilful railroading of the Indian Parliament that makes the case for a genuine presidential system amply clear—never has the separation of powers between executive and legislative organs been revealed to be more necessary than today.

Parliament is not the only institution he has undermined, as I describe in Chapter 19. Though Narendra Modi promised 'minimum government, maximum governance', the opposite has occurred: government control that many would describe as authoritarian, decision-making centralized in the Prime Minister's Office to a point that has disempowered the ministries, and an administrative style that some of his own party men have criticized as a 'tendency to control everything'. The Modi government has been accused of subverting institutions like the Reserve Bank of India, Central Vigilance Commission, Central Bureau of Investigation and the judiciary, coupled with attempts to emasculate the Fourth Estate through various attacks on freedom of speech and expression.[151] Mr Modi and his handpicked BJP president, Amit Shah, have been described as running both the government and the party as it suits them, pushing anyone who opposes them to the sidelines.

It would be useful here to digress briefly to take a look at Amit Shah, who can, without exaggeration, be called PM Modi's

---

[150]'Lok Sabha passes Union Budget without debate', *Times of India*, 14 March 2018.
[151]'CBI is "Captive Bureau of Investigation" under Modi govt, says Congress on FIR against Lalu', *Indian Express*, 16 March 2018; Hartosh Singh Bal, 'India's Embattled Democracy', *New York Times*, 30 May 2018.

consigliore. Mr Modi is famous for being a man who keeps his own counsel and takes decisions independently. So the immense amount of trust he reposes in Amit Shah is remarkable, and unique. Mr Shah has stated that he was only 'sixteen or seventeen' when he first met Mr Modi[152]; that suggests a very long relationship, which both explains and reflects the bond. Their friendship became strong in the early 1980s, when Mr Modi was a pracharak and Amit Shah a junior worker within the RSS. Narendra Modi was impressed by Amit Shah's abilities, and in 1986, began assigning political tasks to him, starting with booth management during polls. Amit Shah's election campaign experience grew and with it, his responsibilities. His record for effectiveness and loyalty were such that when Mr Modi became chief minister in 2002, Mr Shah was made one of the youngest ministers of state in his cabinet at thirty-eight, and rapidly established himself as his mentor's alter ego.[153] In 2012, he was handling seventeen portfolios in the state cabinet. When Narendra Modi was anointed his party's prime ministerial candidate in 2013, he ensured that Amit Shah became the BJP general secretary in charge of his campaign; Mr Shah is generally credited with masterminding the BJP's thumping majority in the elections of 2014. Shortly after that election victory, he was appointed BJP president at Narendra Modi's instance, and reappointed for a second three-year term in 2017. The massive win in the UP state election in 2017, as well as the party's gains across the Hindi heartland and in the Northeast, and adroit coalition-making in those states where the BJP did not win a majority—all of which put it in control of twenty-one of India's twenty-nine states as of mid-2018—were credited to Mr Shah's political statecraft and ruthless cunning.[154]

Amit Shah enjoys almost absolute immunity as Mr Modi's

[152]Patrick French, 'The "Shah" of BJP's game plan who wants to alter India's political culture', *Hindustan Times*, 17 July 2016.
[153]Uday Mahurkar, 'Power duo: of Narendra Modi-Amit Shah's unbeatable electoral machine and wins', *India Today*, 20 December 2017.
[154]Gyan Verma, 'Historic verdict, BJP's footprint increasing with every election: Amit Shah', *LiveMint*, 4 March 2018.

closest aide. Though he was named as one of the accused in the 'fake encounter killings' of Sohrabuddin Sheikh, Kauser bi and Tulsiram Prajapati in the Ishrat Jahan case, and though he allegedly misused state machinery to monitor the movements and meetings of a woman, reportedly at 'sahib's' behest (the 'Snoopgate' controversy) and has been held responsible for fanning communal tensions during the Muzaffarnagar riots, and though at one point he was even banned by a court from setting foot in his own state, Gujarat—most of the problems that he has faced in relation to these charges appear to have magically disappeared.[155] In the Sohrabuddin case, for instance, a judge who criticized Mr Shah's non-appearance was summarily transferred, and another, Judge Loya, died suddenly.[156] Mr Shah has skipped many recent hearings on the case, saying he is too busy to attend.

When Mr Shah, who enjoys the admiration of many of his colleagues (sometimes unabashed, more often grudging) was appointed as BJP president, there was dissent in the party from within as well as outside—all to no avail. The critics understood that Amit Shah was there to ensure that Narendra Modi's writ ran in the party, and that he spoke with the top man's authority as no one else could claim to. He was Narendra Modi's permanent campaign manager, the man who breathed his boss's vision and who executed the strategy as well as determined the tactics to carry it out. When Amit Shah was appointed to the Rajya Sabha in 2018, there was idle speculation within the party that he would give up his party post for the higher-ranking position of defence minister. But insiders knew that idea was always fanciful: others could be cabinet ministers, but only Amit Shah could run the

[155]'Narendra Modi aide Amit Shah used police to spy on woman at "saheb's" behest, accuse Cobrapost, Gulail', *Indian Express*, 29 November 2013; 'Amit Shah is chargesheeted in election "hate speech" case', *Indian Express*, 11 September 2014.
[156]Aarefa Johari, 'Sohrabuddin Sheikh case: Fresh questions as judge who lifted media gag and slammed CBI is replaced', *Scroll.in*, 27 February, 2018; Nikita Saxena, 'Death of Judge Loya: Post-mortem Examination Was Manipulated Under Directions of Doctor Related to Maharashtra Cabinet Minister', *Caravan*, 2 April 2018.

party for Narendra Modi. As one senior BJP leader was reported to have commented wryly, 'Why would you give up the second-most powerful position [in the country] to take the job of a mere mantri (minister)?'[157] Shah is seen as the kingmaker—the man who engineered the surprise appointment of Yogi Adityanath as the chief minister of UP, India's largest state—as well as the one man whose advice the prime minister takes. It is a position in which he brooks no challenge.

At the same time, while combative and pugnacious on the stump and now in the Upper House of Parliament, Amit Shah has been careful to always defer to his boss, never to challenge his authority and never to steal any of his limelight. He is the ideal number 2, strong enough to command respect in his own right but self-effacing enough to pose no threat whatsoever to his boss.

At the time of writing, Amit Shah's lustre had dulled a bit on account of reverses in some states and Lok Sabha bypolls in 2018, but he will, without a doubt, be the architect of the BJP's poll campaign in the run-up to the 2019 general election.

Amit Shah aside, PM Modi is notorious for rebuking his party members if they oppose him or do not work to his rules, and sidelining his rivals if they seem to pose a serious challenge to him. This style of functioning had already been prefigured in Gujarat, where three BJP leaders who spoke out against CM Modi in 2002 saw a swift end to their political careers. Former minister Haren Pandya, who gave a deposition to a private inquiry commission led by Justice V. R. Krishna Iyer regarding the Gujarat riots, was ostracized, and later died, murdered in mysterious circumstances while on his regular morning walk in 2003. Sanjay Joshi was forced to resign when a CD containing compromising pictures of him (later revealed to be doctored) was circulated among BJP leaders. Gordhan Zadaphia was pushed out of the cabinet for disloyalty to Narendra Modi, and later removed from the party,

---

[157]'What Modi wants with Amit Shah's election to Rajya Sabha', *NDTV*, 28 July 2017.

though he has now returned.[158]

In Delhi now, Mr Modi reigns supreme, brooking no challenge. His party colleagues have been cut to size: those more senior and experienced than him, the pillars of Atal Bihari Vajpayee's cabinet the last time the BJP was in power, including former party presidents Advani, and Murli Manohar Joshi, have been relegated to a Margdarshak Mandal (Guidance Council), which has, by design, never met since neither the government (Narendra Modi) nor the party (Amit Shah) has convened a single meeting of it.[159] One prominent face of that era, former finance minister and foreign minister Yashwant Sinha, has even resigned from the Modi/Shah-led BJP; another former minister, Arun Shourie, has been vocal in expressing his disenchantment with the Modi government.[160] There is only one centre of power in the council of ministers, and that is PM Modi. His office calls Secretaries in the various ministries directly on pending issues, bypassing and thus undermining the ministers, who are sometimes reduced to mouthing decisions made behind their backs.

Not everyone in the BJP, or even in the RSS, is therefore entirely happy with Narendra Modi. In his 2012 profile of Mr Modi, the journalist Vinod K. Jose quoted an unnamed RSS leader describing his feelings about the Gujarat supremo with 'a bitter sigh': 'Shivling mein bichhu baitha hai. Na usko haath se utaar sakte ho, na usko joota maar sakte ho.' ('A scorpion is sitting on a Shiva lingam, the holy symbol of Lord Shiva. It can neither be removed by hand nor slapped with a shoe.'[161]) Try to remove the scorpion, and it will sting you; slap it with a shoe and you

[158]Vinod K. Jose, 'The Emperor Uncrowned: The Rise of Narendra Modi', *Caravan*, 1 March 2012.

[159]'Margdarshak mandal: Shabby treatment of seniors, or a brave new BJP?', *FirstPost*, 27 August 2014; Panini Anand, 'How Modi's rivals in the BJP have been cut to size', *Catch News*, 10 July 2015.

[160]'Arun Shourie says falsehood is hallmark of Narendra Modi government, alleges centralisation of power at PMO', *FirstPost*, 27 November 2017.

[161]Vinod K. Jose, 'The Emperor Uncrowned: The Rise of Narendra Modi', *Caravan*, 1 March 2012.

will be insulting your own faith. That remains a brilliant summary of the RSS's dilemma with Narendra Modi. A new book[162] by respected scholars of Sanghi politics asserts that the RSS leadership is currently struggling with a critical dilemma—whether or not the Sangh Parivar should continue to support the Bharatiya Janata Party in the 2019 Lok Sabha elections, despite its disapproval of the 'personality cult' around Narendra Modi. Even if this assertion proves to be true, those in the Hindutva movement who might prefer another leader find themselves helpless: they cannot remove or displace Narendra Modi because, at least for now, their own project would be destroyed with him.

And one must not forget that the electorate has continued to reward Narendra Modi so far. The BJP now rules, either by itself or with a partner, twenty-one out of twenty-nine Indian states—the highest such proportion since the Congress held power in eighteen states a quarter of a century ago. The psephologist Yogendra Yadav has remarked that 'the BJP today is perhaps the most formidable election machine that this country has witnessed in the last 70 years.'[163] When the failures of demonetization and the botched implementation of a new Goods and Services Tax (see chapters 35 and 36), along with anti-incumbency and an effective Congress party campaign, brought the BJP in Gujarat perilously close to defeat in the state assembly elections of December 2017, Modi made the vote a referendum on himself. He dramatically asked his fellow Gujaratis to demonstrate their pride in having him, their representative, as the nation's prime minister. 'Do you trust me?' he asked; 'Will you let me down? When everyone is against me, will you stand by me? Who else but me, sitting in Delhi, can work for you?'[164] It worked; the BJP scraped through by the skin of its teeth, albeit with a sharply reduced majority.

---

[162]Walter K. Andersen and Shridhar Damle, *RSS: A View to the Inside*, New Delhi: Penguin Books, 2018.

[163]'Modi's growing domination of Indian electoral politics', *National World*, 4 March 2018.

[164]'PM Modi comes to BJP's rescue, yet again', *Hindustan Times*, 18 December 2017.

Modi's honour was saved.

But then he also has 'the people'. As I have noted, Narendra Modi excels at direct communication with the masses, using his compelling oratory, monthly broadcasts and extensive social media presence to reach out directly to the masses. In the 2014 election, the lavishly funded Narendra Modi spent a small fortune on a hologram technology that projected a three-dimensional image of him addressing an audience to multiple locations simultaneously, enabling him to give several crowds the illusion of 'seeing' him at the same time. He single-handedly started the 'selfie' craze in India by tweeting his selfies and encouraging visitors to take them. The hashtag #SelfiewithModi encouraged Indians to tweet their selfies with their prime minister even when they couldn't meet him personally. Photo booths were set up across Delhi, for instance, in which people could have their picture taken with a cutout of him.[165] He has introduced a mobile telephone app, the Narendra Modi app, which the BBC called, in a reference to the international dating app, 'a Tinder for good governance'.[166] The app lets users share news of PM Modi, receive his updates and take part in polls. It includes a video game in which the user scores points for approving Mr Modi's policies.

So Moditva is a combination of Hindutva, nationalism, economic development and overweening personal leadership. It is carefully packaged and marketed, with considerable attention (and expense) being paid to disseminating its message to the public. It is always sold in terms of ideals—Narendra Modi is selfless and devoted, a man who has given up all personal interests for the nation, a man with no Swiss bank accounts or hideaway homes, a man with no sons or nephews to groom as successors, a man dedicated solely to the greater good of India. Even his mistakes are presented as well-meaning and motivated by his sincere convictions of the national interest. If some see him as power-hungry, many

---

[165]Isabelle Fraser, '"Selfie diplomacy": How India's prime minister Modi became such a hit on social media', *The Telegraph*, 12 November 2015.
[166]'Narendra Modi app is "like Tinder for good governance"', *BBC*, 7 July 2015.

Indians prefer a leader who is motivated by power rather than money. Even as a politician, the message goes, his mission is to serve the people, never himself.

His populism, direct appeal to the public and personal image of selflessness have proved huge political assets in a period of failing policies and economic setbacks. 'People are ready to trust what he says,' observed Jitendra Singh, minister of state in the PMO, with quiet satisfaction. This enabled him to get away with his calamitous demonetization decision (see Chapter 35)—'there may have been hardship involved in the transition phase,' Singh admits, 'but people were ready to cooperate because they thought if Modi is saying so, it is for the benefit of the country.'[167]

Moditva is careful not to appear to be in contradiction to Hindutva; rather, it builds upon it. But by identifying the message so completely with the personal life, values, and behaviour of the leader, Moditva has transformed Hindutva into something more than it ever was—a cult devoted to the greater glory of one man, in the name of exalting values that he epitomizes as no one before him has. In the process Hindutva itself is modified, or as some might have it, Modi-fied.

Of course, Narendra Modi is careful not to challenge the basic assumptions of Hindutva; rather he portrays his efforts as extending the conceptual reach of Hindutva and thus ensuring its ultimate triumph. He wants to be seen as strong and powerful, decisive and able, but he also wants to be considered honest, self-denying and above all, nationalistic.

As chief minister of Gujarat, Narendra Modi had already portrayed himself as embodying the identity and pride of the Gujarati people—'Gujarati asmita'. Now he seeks to do the same to, and for, the Indian people. He is the nation. And the nation's own self-identification must undergo a change to internalize his embodiment of it.

[167]Aman Sharma, 'On a roll, PM Narendra Modi made 775 speeches in 41 months', *Economic Times*, 24 October 2017.

It was once said of US President Woodrow Wilson that his biggest problem was that he believed his own press releases. Narendra Modi seems to buy into his own personality cult, at least judging by the evidence of his government websites, which depict him in larger-than-life terms, using language rarely seen in government publications before. His personal website, narendramodi.in, is full of articles describing his 'heart of gold', 'simplicity', his ability to never lose his cool, and stories of his exemplary childhood.[168] It is clear that Mr Modi wants his supporters to view him as a messianic figure, a superman who can save them from their problems. It would not surprise me to see the *Bal Narendra* comic book of 2014 being succeeded by a Superman Modi comic book in 2019.

IX

Today, Narendra Modi ranks 9th on the *Forbes* 2018 list of 'The World's Most Powerful People'.[169] And yet there is little doubt that for all his evident self-confidence, Narendra Modi bears a massive chip on his shoulder. Something he said to me was revelatory in this regard. When, in a rare one-on-one conversation in late 2017, I raised an aspect of Opposition criticism of something he had said or done, the prime minister replied: 'You know, in some parts of India, if a man of low caste sports a moustache or dares to ride a horse, he is beaten up by the higher castes for his presumption. That is what is happening to me. Some people will never accept that a man like me is the prime minister of India. That is why they keep attacking me.'

It is a curiously insecure comment for a man who radiates confidence, but it helps partly explain what drives him. A sense of resentment, a keen anger at economic and social deprivation, allied with a burning sense of mission to reverse the traditional narrative, displace the old elites and stamp his authority on the

---

[168]'Biography', www.narendramodi.in.
[169]'The World's Most Powerful People', *Forbes*, 31 May 2018.

country, all impel Narendra Modi and Moditva. The chapters to follow examine in greater detail how he has gone about it, and why, in my view, he has failed. But the final verdict on whether Narendra Modi's government proves just a blip in Indian democracy's long and complex history, or whether what we have witnessed is merely the first stage of a profound transformation that will create a nation unrecognizably different from that in which he assumed power in 2014, must await the electorate of 2019.

II

THE MODI-FICATION OF INDIA

Pierre Trudeau (1919–2000), one of the world's great statesmen, who served as the prime minister of Canada for over fifteen years, once tried to define 'a just society'. Among other things, he said, 'The Just Society will be one in which the rights of minorities will be safe from the whims of intolerant majorities.' If there is one thing that Narendra Modi will be remembered for when he is no longer prime minister, it is the intolerance his victory has let loose—and he has at least condoned—in Indian society. Diversity, acceptance of difference and cultural harmony are indispensable elements of the Indian ethos, but the current atmosphere of violence and persecution, for which the prime minister must take a large share of the blame, has jeopardized these integral values. The rise of gau-rakshaks, the assassinations of rationalists, mob lynchings, episodes of beef-related violence, virulent attacks on all and sundry by BJP trolls on social media and in various public forums, are some of the things he has enabled through his unwillingness to condemn fundamentalists and through his own criticism and broadsides against minorities and opponents. In this section I take a close look at the impact Prime Minister Modi and his followers have had on some of the most fundamental ideas and values of India.

chapter two

FAKE HISTORY AND
PSEUDO-NATIONALISM

I

For almost three quarters of a century now, the Hindu right wing has been trying to assail the very idea of India. Its ideologues, notably K. B. Hedgewar, M. S. Golwalkar, V. D. Savarkar and Deen Dayal Upadhyaya, have propagated various theories to prove that India was and should again be a Hindu Rashtra. In my last book, *Why I Am a Hindu*, I laid bare many of their falsehoods and exaggerations, but my fear is that in Narendra Modi's India they will leave a permanent mark on the country's psyche, and on its collective historical imagination, because of the support they receive from the prime minister and the BJP leadership. While assorted Hindutva thugs and goons are busily engaged in assaulting minorities, Dalits, liberals and women, another battle is being fought for the hearts and minds of all Indians. This accounts for the spread of false history and pseudo-nationalism. Not for nothing is 'feku' (congenital teller of tall tales) one of the epithets used for Mr Modi. It, therefore, seems appropriate to begin this section with a chapter on the dangerous falsehoods that are being propagated by Narendra Modi and his associates about our history, nationalism, pluralism and other core beliefs and constructs that objectively form our idea of India.

The essence of India is its diversity and concomitant secularism and pluralism—and this is why this characteristic is being attacked by the Hindutva right from the beginning. Since *India: From Midnight to the Millenium* (1996), and in many of my other books and articles, I have written at length about the reasons why the essence of India—the basic 'idea of India'—is wholly and unequivocally secular, or more accurately, plural, and it is worth

repeating some of these unalterable truths in order to give the lie
to what the right wing is trying hard to bring about.

The irony is that India's secular coexistence was paradoxically
made possible by the fact that the overwhelming majority of
Indians are Hindus. Their acceptance of difference characterized the
Hinduism propagated by Vivekananda and other visionary Hindu
seers. This meant that it came naturally to Hindus to coexist with
practitioners of other faiths. In a plural society, religious pluralism
was merely one more kind of difference everyone accepted, just
as we knew that around us were people who spoke different
languages, ate different foods, dressed differently and had different
shades of skin colour from ours.

Secularism in India, therefore, did not mean separation of
religion from state. Instead, secularism in India means a state
that was equally indulgent of all religious groups, and favoured
none. There was no 'established' state religion; the adherent of
every faith was a stakeholder in the Indian state.

Nor did it mean secularity in the French sense, or laïcité. The
French concept keeps religion out of governmental institutions
like schools and government out of religious institutions in turn,
whereas Indian secularism cheerfully refuses to forbid such religious
interpenetration. Whereas it is impermissible to sport any visible
sign of religious affiliation in a French government school or office
(a Catholic may not wear a crucifix, a Muslim sport a hijab, or a
Sikh don a turban) all these are permitted in the equivalent Indian
institutions. Conversely, the Government of India embraces the
practice of providing financial support to religious schools and the
persistence of 'personal law' for different religious communities.

Until fairly recently, an Indian's sense of nationhood lay in
the slogan, 'unity in diversity'. My generation was brought up to
take pluralism for granted, and to reject the communalism that
had partitioned the nation when the British left. In rejecting the
case for Pakistan, Indian nationalism also rejected the very idea
that religion should be a determinant of nationhood. We never
fell into the insidious trap of agreeing that, since Partition had

established a state for Muslims, what remained was a state for Hindus. To accept the idea of India you had to spurn the logic that had divided the country.

In some ways, this kind of Indian secularism has ancient roots in our history. Admired monarchs from Ashoka, in the third century BCE, to Harsha, in the sixth century CE, gave their recognition and patronage to different religions. Ashoka's Rock Edict XII forbade people from honouring their own sects at the expense of others, and condemning the beliefs of others. Citizenship and political status in his state were never linked to one's religion. The coexistence of religions is evident from the fact that the Ellora Cave temples, some Jain, some Hindu and some Buddhist, were carved next to each other between the fifth and tenth centuries. While this traditional approach to secular or pluralist practice was not that of the Islamic kingdoms that established themselves from the twelfth century onwards, even Muslim rulers bound to uphold the less welcoming tenets of their faith had to reconcile themselves to ruling an overwhelmingly non-Muslim populace and accommodating prominent Hindus in government and the military. One monarch, the Mughal Emperor Akbar, went so far as to create his own syncretic religion, Din-e-Ilahi, to meld the best features of Islam, Hinduism and the other faiths of which he knew into a new 'national faith'. It did not outlast his reign, but the attempt was extraordinary. And Akbar's contemporary, Ibrahim Adil Shah II of Bijapur, was a Sunni Muslim who saw no contradiction in also styling himself 'son of Guru Ganapati and the pure Saraswati' and wearing rudraksha beads.[170]

The concept of sarva dharma sambhava—accepting the equality of all religions—was propounded by great Hindu sages like Ramakrishna and Vivekananda and upheld by Mahatma Gandhi and the Indian nationalist movement. While it was an

---

[170]Manu S. Pillai, *Rebel Sultans: The Deccan from Khilji to Shivaji*, New Delhi: Juggernaut Books, 2018.

axiomatic tenet of the post-Independence India in which I grew up, sarva dharma sambhava has been increasingly rejected by some proponents of Hindutva who spurn the notion of religious universalism in favour of a more robust assertion of Hindu cultural identity and Hindus' political rights. They are unembarrassed about rejecting 'unity in diversity'; the farthest the Sangh Parivar is prepared to go is to accept 'diversity in unity', or variations of practice within an all-encompassing Hindu identity.[171]

Yet the lived reality of Indian syncretism is difficult to deny. Indians of all religious communities have long lived intertwined lives, and even religious practices were rarely exclusionary: thus Muslim musicians played and sang Hindu devotional songs, Hindus thronged Sufi shrines and worshipped Muslim saints there. Northern India celebrated what was called a 'Ganga-Jamuni tehzeeb', a syncretic culture that melded the cultural practices of both Hinduism and Islam. Indeed, the reality of syncretism runs deep into social practice. Muslim artisans create the masks for the major Hindu festival of Dussehra in the holy city of Varanasi; the Ram Leela could not be performed without their work. Muslim Patachitra painters sing and paint pats (scrolls) about Hindu divinities. And among the most famous exponents of Hindu devotional music are the Muslim Dagar brothers—not to mention the Baul singers, a legacy of the Bhakti tradition, who sing Sufi-inspired folk songs in praise of a universal God. Muslim sociologists and anthropologists have argued that Islam in rural India is more Indian than Islamic, in the sense that the faith as practised by the ordinary Muslim villagers reflects the considerable degree of cultural assimilation that has occurred between Hindus and Muslims in their daily lives. Everywhere in this remarkable land you will find quotidian examples of this sort of syncretism.

---

[171]Valson Thampu, 'The RSS, Pranab and Adi Shankara', *New Indian Express*, 15 June 2018; For a fuller discussion of the issues summarized over the next dozen pages, see Shashi Tharoor, *Why I Am a Hindu*, New Delhi: Aleph Book Company, 2018.

So the idea of India is of one land embracing many. As I have written before, it is the idea that a nation may endure differences of caste, creed, colour, culture, cuisine, conviction, costume and custom, and still rally around a consensus. That consensus is around the simple principle that in a diverse democracy you don't really need to agree—except on the ground rules of how you will disagree. The reason India has survived all the stresses and strains that have beset it for over seventy years, and that led so many to predict its imminent disintegration, is that it maintained consensus on how to manage without consensus.

But the twentieth-century politics of deprivation has eroded the culture's confidence. Hindu chauvinism has emerged from the competition for resources in a contentious democracy. Politicians of all faiths across India seek to mobilize voters by appealing to narrow identities; by seeking votes in the name of religion, caste and region, they have urged voters to define themselves on these lines. As religion, caste and region have come to dominate public discourse, to some it has become more important to be a Muslim, a Bodo or a Yadav than to be an Indian.

III

As I wrote at length in *Why I Am a Hindu*, Hindutva ideologues find the principles of tolerance and acceptance emasculating. The RSS sarsanghchalak and ideologue M. S. Golwalkar wrote that India's independence from colonial rule in 1947 did not constitute real freedom because the new leaders held on to the 'perverted concept of nationalism' that located all who lived on India's territory as equal constituents of the nation. 'The concept of territorial nationalism,' he wrote, 'has verily emasculated our nation and what more can we expect of a body deprived of its vital energy? ...And so it is that we see today the germs of corruption, disintegration and dissipation eating into the vitals of our nation for having given up the natural living nationalism in the pursuit of an unnatural, unscientific and lifeless hybrid concept of territorial nationalism.'[172] M. S. Golwalkar's *Bunch Of Thoughts* argues that territorial nationalism is a barbarism, since a nation is 'not a mere bundle of political and economic rights' but an embodiment of national culture—in India, 'ancient and sublime' Hinduism. It sneers at democracy, which Golwalkar sees as alien to Hindu culture, and lavishes praise on the Code of Manu, whom Golwalkar salutes as 'the first, the greatest, and the wisest lawgiver of mankind'.[173]

This is why the development of 'Hindu fundamentalism' and the resultant change in the public discourse about Indianness is so dangerous. The suggestion that only a Hindu, and only a certain kind of Hindu, can be an authentic Indian, is an affront to the very premise of Indian nationalism. An India that denies itself to some of us could end up being denied to all of us.

The reduction of non-Hindus to second-class status in their homeland is unthinkable. It would be a second Partition: and a partition in the Indian soul would be as bad as a partition in the Indian soil.

◆

Hindutva sees culture differently; as Golwalkar wrote, culture 'is but a product of our all-comprehensive religion, a part of its body and not distinguishable from it'.[174] For the Hindutvavadis, India's national culture is Hindu religious culture, and cultural nationalism cloaks plural India in a mantle of Hindu identity. Since Hindutva's conception of nationalism is rooted in the primacy of culture over politics, the historian K. N. Panikkar has pointed out, the Hindutva effort is to create an idea of the Indian nation in which the Hindu religious identity coincides with the cultural.

As the Hindutva ideologue David Frawley (Pandit Vamadeva

---

[172]M. S. Golwalkar, *We, or Our Nationhood Defined*, 3rd edition, Nagpur: Bharat Prakashan, 1945, pp. 52–53.
[173]M. S. Golwalkar, *Bunch of Thoughts*, 4th impression, Bangalore: Vikrama Prakashan, 1968, p. 156.
[174]M. S. Golwalkar, *We, or Our Nationhood Defined*, 3rd edition, Nagpur: Bharat Prakashan, 1945, p. 22.

Shastri) explains, after being ruled by Westernized Hindus for many decades after Independence, today, Hindus are rediscovering their roots. 'This movement is not simply a regressive return to medieval Hindu values, but a rediscovery of the validity and importance of Hindu culture and spirituality for both the future as well as the past. It includes discovering the importance of Hindu Yoga, Vedanta, Ayurveda, Vedic astrology, classical Indian art and culture, and the Hindu view of society and government'.[175] What he calls 'the Bharatiya spiritual urge', he says, after extolling Yoga and meditation, 'did not arise from the suppression of other human urges but from a full flowering of human nature in all aspects, including the arts and the sciences. This we see lavishly embodied in Indian music and dance, mathematics and medicine'. This sounds reasonable enough, except when he adds that 'Hindus must learn to project a united front and reclaim the greater field of Hindu Dharma that covers all aspects of life and culture'.[176] This call for unity replaces variety with uniformity and dissent with dogma—a notion of Hindu dharma that is all-encompassing and covers 'all aspects of life and culture' has no room for difference or for heterodoxy, let alone for deviance.

The inclusive, self-interrogating Hinduism propagated by the thinkers like Vivekananda, Dayanand Saraswati, Aurobindo and Mahatma Gandhi is not acceptable to the Sangh Parivar. The Hindutva premise, in Panikkar's words, is 'that national regeneration and resurgence would require the recreation of an authentic culture by reclaiming the indigenous and purging the exogenous. Hindutva's cultural project, encoded in the slogan "nationalise and spiritualise", therefore, is twofold: First, to retrieve and disseminate the cultural traditions of the "golden" Hindu past; and second, to eliminate all accretions that had become part of the heritage.'[177]

---

[175]David Frawley, *Arise Arjuna: Hinduism and the Modern World*, New Delhi: Voice of India, 1995, p. 15.
[176]Ibid., p. xxv.
[177]K. N. Panikkar, 'In the Name of Nationalism', *Frontline*, 13 March 2004.

IV

In 2016, the Ministry of Culture appointed a committee to examine ancient Indian history. Its members included the National Museum chief, B. R. Mani, Lal Bahadur Shastri Rashtriya Sanskrit Vidyapeetha vice chancellor, R. K. Pandey, retired Delhi University linguistics professor, R. C. Sharma, and Sanskrit scholars Santosh Kumar Shukla from Jawaharlal Nehru University and Balram Shukla from Delhi University. By all accounts, the committee is being coordinated by the Archaeological Survey of India, whose former director general, Rakesh Tewari, is a member as well.[178]

The committee's chairman, K. N. Dikshit, told Reuters, 'I have been asked to present a report that will help the government rewrite certain aspects of ancient history.' The committee's creator, Culture Minister Mahesh Sharma, confirmed in an interview that the group's work was part of larger plans to revise India's history.

Balmukund Pandey, the head of the historical research wing of the RSS, said he meets regularly with Culture Minister Sharma. 'The time is now,' Pandey said, to restore India's past glory by establishing that ancient Hindu texts are fact not myth.[179]

Mahesh Sharma told Reuters he expects the conclusions of the committee to find their way into school textbooks and academic research. The panel is referred to in government documents as the committee for the 'holistic study of origin and evolution of Indian culture since 12,000 years before the present and its interface with other cultures of the world'.[180]

The rewriting of history to better represent its worldview, and execute its objectives, is a major project of Narendra Modi and his government. When I published my book, *An Era of Darkness: The British Empire in India*, I spoke critically of 200 years of foreign rule. In their turn, the Hindutva brigade, led by Prime Minister Modi himself, condemned 1,200 years of foreign rule.

---

[178]Rupam Jain and Tom Lasseter, 'By rewriting history, Hindu nationalists aim to assert their dominance over India', *Reuters*, 6 March 2018.
[179]Ibid.
[180]Ibid.

To them, the Muslim rulers of India—whether the Delhi Sultans, the Deccani Sultans or the Mughals (or the hundreds of other Muslims who occupied thrones of greater or lesser importance for several hundred years across the country)—were all foreigners. I responded that while the founder of a Muslim dynasty may well have come to India from abroad, he and his descendants stayed and assimilated in this country, married Hindu women, and immersed themselves in the fortunes of this land; each Mughal emperor after Babar had less and less connection of blood or allegiance to a foreign country. If they looted or exploited India and Indians, they spent the proceeds of their loot in India, and did not send it off to enrich a foreign land as the British did. The Mughals received travellers from the Ferghana Valley politely, enquired about the well-being of the people there and perhaps even gave some money for the upkeep of the graves of their Chingizid ancestors, but they stopped seeing their original homeland as home. By the second generation, let alone the fifth or sixth, they were as 'Indian' as any Hindu.

This challenge of authenticity, however, emerges from those Hindus who share the late novelist V. S. Naipaul's view of theirs as a 'wounded civilization', a pristine Hindu land that was subjected to repeated defeats and conquests over the centuries at the hands of rapacious Muslim invaders and was enfeebled and subjugated in the process. That Modi subscribes to this notion is clear from the way he has unhesitatingly articulated it, especially when he is in campaign mode. In speech after speech he has talked about the iniquities of Muslim India. To Modi and his followers, Independence was not merely freedom from British rule but an opportunity to restore the glory of their culture and religion, wounded by Muslim conquerors. Historians like Audrey Truschke, author of a sympathetic biography of Aurangzeb, *Aurangzeb: The Man and the Myth*[181], have argued that this account of Muslims

---

[181]Audrey Truschke, *Aurangzeb: The Man and the Myth*, New Delhi: Juggernaut Books, 2017.

despoiling the Hindu homeland is 'neither a continuous historical memory nor based on accurate records of the past'. But there is no gainsaying the emotional content of the Hindutva view of the past: it is for them a matter of faith that India is a Hindu nation, which Muslim rulers attacked, looted and sought to destroy, and documented historical facts that refute this view as grossly incomplete and partial are at best an inconvenience, at worst an irrelevance.

In this Hindutva-centred view, history is made of religion-based binaries, in which all Muslim rulers are evil and all Hindus are valiant resisters, embodiments of incipient Hindu nationalism. The Hindutvavadis believe, in Prof Truschke's words, 'that India was subjected to repeated defeats over the centuries, including by generations of Muslim conquerors that enfeebled the people and their land...their sentiments [are] often undergirded by modern anti-Muslim sentiments.'[182] K. N. Panikkar has pointed out that liberal and tolerant rulers such as Ashoka, Akbar, Jai Singh, Shahu Maharaj and Wajid Ali Shah do not figure in Hindutva's list of national heroes. (Indeed, where many nationalist historians extolled Akbar as the liberal, tolerant counterpart to the Islamist Aurangzeb, Hindutvavadis have begun to attack him too, principally because he was Muslim, and like most medieval monarchs, killed princes who stood in his way, many of whom happened to be Hindu.)

The debates over history are not confined to the distant past alone. Narendra Modi chose the anniversary of the 1942 Quit India movement to launch a campaign called '70 Saal Azadi: Zara Yaad Karo Qurbani' ('Seventy years of freedom: remember the sacrifices'). The BJP which, led by the PM, has sought to drape itself in the mantle of nationalism, is now seeking to appropriate the freedom struggle for its cause. Ironically, the Quit India movement is an occasion the BJP could well have chosen to criticize rather than celebrate, since it resulted in the jailing by the British of all

[182]'Hated in the Present for Digging Into the Past: Audrey Truschke on Writing About Aurangzeb', *The Wire*, 26 May 2017.

the leaders and thousands of workers of the nationalist movement, a resultant free hand to the Muslim League to build up a support base it had lacked in the elections of 1937, and thus, strengthened the hands of those who wanted Partition.

But the Modi government has no intention of repudiating Quit India as a Congress folly. It wants to make heroes of freedom fighters, by implication placing them on its own side in a contemporary retelling of history. The complication is that the political cause to which the BJP is heir—embodied in the Jana Sangh, the RSS, and the Hindutva movement—had no prominent freedom fighter of its own during the nationalist struggle for azadi. The BJP traces its origin to leaders who were not particularly active during the nationalist movement. The lack of inspiration for the people in the parent body of the BJP means people like Mr Modi have to look for role models elsewhere. Thus they extol the Marxist Bhagat Singh, various young men who (unlike Gandhi) resorted to violence against the British and were martyred, and other nationalists who they claim have been marginalized by the Congress's glorification of the Nehru dynasty.

The process had already begun, lest we forget, when then Chief Minister Modi moved aggressively to lay claim to the legacy of one of India's most respected founding fathers, Sardar Vallabhbhai Patel, before the 2014 election. As I have mentioned earlier in this book, in his quest to garb himself in a more distinguished lineage than his party can ordinarily lay claim to, Mr Modi called on farmers across India to donate iron from their ploughs to construct a giant, nearly 600-foot statue of the Iron Man in his state, which would be by far the tallest statue in the world, dwarfing the Statue of Liberty. But it will be less of a monument to the modest Gandhian it ostensibly honours than an embodiment of the overweening ambitions of its builder—who, as I have mentioned, decided to get a Chinese foundry to cast it, for his ambitions exceeded India's capacities.

Modi's motives are easy to divine. As his own image was tarnished by the communal massacre in Gujarat when he was chief minister in 2002, identifying himself with Sardar Patel (who is portrayed as the leader who stood up for the nation's Hindus during the horrors of Partition and was firm on issues like Kashmir) is an attempt at character-building by association—portraying Narendra Modi himself as an embodiment of the tough, decisive man of action that Sardar Patel was, rather than the destructive bigot his enemies decry.

It helps that Patel is widely admired for his extraordinary role in forging India that gave him an unchallenged standing as the Iron Man. Sardar Patel represents both a national appeal and a Gujarati origin that suits Modi. The Modi-as-latter-day-Patel message has been resonating well with many Gujaratis, who are proud to be reminded of a native son the nation looks up to, and with many of India's urban middle-class, who see in Narendra Modi a strong leader to cut through the confusion and indecision of India's messy democracy.

But Sardar Patel's conduct during the violence that accompanied Partition stands in stark contrast to Narendra Modi's in 2002. Both Sardar Patel and Narendra Modi were faced with the serious breakdown of law and order in their respective domains, involving violence and rioting against the Muslims. In Delhi in 1947, Sardar Patel immediately and effectively moved to ensure the protection of Muslims, herding 10,000 in the most vulnerable areas to the security of Delhi's Red Fort. Because Sardar Patel was afraid that the local security forces might have been affected by the virus of communal passions, he moved army troops from Madras and Pune to Delhi to ensure law and order. Sardar Patel also made it a point to send a reassuring signal to the Muslim community by attending prayers at the famous Nizamuddin Dargah to convey a clear message that Muslims and their faith belonged unquestionably on the soil of India. Sardar Patel went to the border town of Amritsar, where there were attacks on Muslims fleeing to the new Islamic state of Pakistan, and pleaded with Hindu and Sikh mobs to stop victimizing Muslim refugees. In each of these cases, Sardar Patel succeeded and there are literally tens of thousands of people who are alive today because of his interventions.

The contrast with what happened in Gujarat in 2002 is painful. Whether or not one ascribes direct blame to Narendra Modi for the pogrom that year, he can certainly claim no credit for acting in the way Patel did in Delhi. In Gujarat, there was no direct and immediate action by CM Modi, as the state's chief executive, to protect the Muslims. Nor did Mr Modi express any public condemnation of the attacks, let alone undertake any symbolic action of going to a masjid or visiting a Muslim neighbourhood to convey reassurance.[183]

There is a particular irony to a self-proclaimed 'Hindu nationalist' like Narendra Modi laying claim to the legacy of a Gandhian leader who would never have qualified his Indian nationalism with a religious label. Sardar Patel believed in equal rights for all irrespective of their religion or caste. It is true that at the time of partition Sardar Patel was inclined to believe, unlike Jawaharlal Nehru, that an entire community had seceded. In my biography, *Nehru: The Invention of India*,[184] I have given some examples of Nehru-ji and Sardar Patel clashing on this issue. But there are an equal number of examples where Sardar Patel, if he had to choose between what was the right thing for the Hindus and what was the right thing morally, invariably plumped for the moral Gandhian approach.

An example, so often distorted by the Sangh Parivar apologists, was his opposition to Jawaharlal Nehru's pact with Liaquat Ali Khan, the prime minister of Pakistan, on the question of violence in East Pakistan against the Hindu minority. The Nehru–Liaquat pact was indeed criticized by Sardar Patel and he disagreed quite ferociously with Jawaharlal Nehru on the matter. But when Pandit Nehru insisted on his position, it was Sardar Patel who gave in, and his reasoning was entirely Gandhian: that violence in West

[183]'Modi modern-day Nero: SC', *Times of India*, 12 April 2004; 'Narendra Modi trying to protect Godhra riots perpetrators: Minority minister', *DNA*, 5 December 2013.
[184]New Delhi: Penguin Books, 2003.

Bengal against Muslims essentially took away Indians' moral right to condemn violence against Hindus in East Pakistan. That was not a Hindu nationalist position but a classically Gandhian approach as an *Indian* nationalist.

The only true nationalism that deserves to be inculcated in each and every one of us is Indian nationalism; anything else is fake or pseudo-nationalism. Indian nationalism grows out of an idea of India that celebrates diversity, but our ruling party prefers uniformity, built on a triad of Hindi-Hindu-Hindutva, all of which are essential to India but not sufficient to exhaust the idea of Indianness. In doing so they are undermining the basic ethos of India, which recognizes the nation's diversity and celebrates multiple ways of being Indian.

chapter three

A GROWING WAVE OF COMMUNALISM

The ways in which Narendra Modi and his cohorts are seeking to modify India and its essence is not limited to redefining nationalism, rewriting textbooks, reshaping history or making incendiary speeches. Not a week passes without news of some new outrage. This is why it was startling to hear the union minister for minority affairs, Mukhtar Abbas Naqvi and the home minister, Rajnath Singh, announce in 2018 that there have been 'no big communal riots' in India over the past four years.[185] Mr Singh even asserted during the no-confidence debate in the Lok Sabha in July that year that communal violence had decreased during his government's tenure. He was wrong, of course, but it is instructive to analyse *how* wrong he was.

Since the ascent of the BJP to power, the forces unleashed by the dominance of Hindutva have resulted in many incidents of violence. In one grim reckoning, more than 389 individuals have been killed in anti-minority acts of violence since mid-2014, and hundreds of others injured, stripped, beaten and humiliated.[186] Particularly haunting is the story of fifteen-year-old Junaid Khan, returning home on a crowded train after buying new clothes for Eid, who was stabbed repeatedly because he was Muslim and thrown off the train to bleed to death on the tracks.[187] Headlines have spoken continually of riots and killing, Hindu against Muslim, of men being slaughtered because of the mark on a forehead or the absence of a foreskin.

As I have remarked earlier in this book, and as has been widely

---

[185]'"No big communal riot" in past 4 years, claims BJP: Data shows 389 dead in over 2,000 incidents since 2014', *FirstPost*, 6 July 2018.
[186]Ibid.
[187]Saumya Lakhani, 'On Eid, fear grips Junaid village: Kuch mat bolo, chup chaap sab sun lo', *Indian Express*, 27 June 2017.

observed, following the BJP's victory in the 2014 elections, a wave
of Hindu-majoritarian triumphalism has swept the land. In its wake
have come new laws to protect cows and vociferous demands for
their strict enforcement. Gau-rakshak or cow protection societies,
which I will write about in greater detail in the next chapter,
have been revived, and many have taken it upon themselves to
compel compliance. In the process, not only have they taken the
law into their own hands, but they have perpetrated grave crimes,
including murder, in the name of protecting the cow. Seventy cases
of cow-related violence have been reported in the last eight years,
of which 97 per cent (68 out of 70) have occurred during the first
four years of BJP rule and a majority of these have occurred in
BJP-ruled states. 136 people have been injured in these attacks and
28 killed: 86 per cent of the victims were, of course, Muslim.[188]

Many of the incidents are well known: the case of a dairy
farmer, Pehlu Khan, transporting cattle legally with a licence, being
beaten to death on 1 April 2017 while his tormentors filmed his
pleas for mercy on their mobile phones, is particularly egregious.
A cattle-herder in Haryana, Mustain Abbas, was murdered and
mutilated a year earlier for doing his job, transporting cattle.
Truckers, cattle traders and alleged cow smugglers have also been
killed by 'cow protection' groups. A sixteen-year-old Kashmiri
Muslim boy was murdered for having hitched a ride on a truck
that was transporting cattle.

In 2015, when a Muslim, Mohammed Akhlaq, father of
a serving Indian Air Force havildar, was lynched by a mob in
Uttar Pradesh on suspicions of having killed a cow, the authorities
launched a forensic investigation into whether the meat in his
refrigerator was beef (it was not). The fact that a man had been
killed and his son nearly beaten to death was equated with an
unfounded allegation of beef consumption, as if the latter 'crime'

---

[188]'Cow vigilantism in India: 2017 sees 26 cases of cattle-related violence; most in
8 years', *FirstPost*, 29 July, 2017; Delna Abraham and Ojaswi Rao, '86% killed in
cow-related violence since 2010 are Muslim, 97% attacks after Modi govt came
to power', *Hindustan Times*, 16 July 2017.

could extenuate the former.[189] Worse, when a man who was part of the lynch mob died of natural causes a few weeks later, his coffin was draped with the Indian flag and a serving union minister who attended his funeral hailed him—an unspeakable act, and coming from a high office-holder of the secular Indian state, an unacceptable one.

Muslims have not been the only targets of the cow vigilantes, of course. There are also Dalits. But the communal colour that marked each of these incidents speaks to the inaccuracy of the ministers' statements. Perhaps they would take refuge behind the assertion that these were isolated incidents rather than mass communal violence. Yet they speak of a pervasive pattern that has deeply affected society across the country. And when another minister is accused of condoning such incidents by garlanding members of a lynch mob, society shivers.[190] (He says these individuals were framed and are out on bail, but regrets having garlanded them: the damage, though, is done.)

There is a tragic vocabulary to the analysis of communal violence in our country. A 'major' communal incident is one that results in more than five deaths or leaves over ten people injured. An incident that results in one death or ten injured is termed as 'important or significant'. Mr Naqvi spoke of 'big' communal riots, but 'big' is not a term of definition in our national lexicology. 'Major', however, is surely 'big', and there are three 'major communal incidents' that have been reported during BJP rule—Saharanpur, Uttar Pradesh, in 2014, Hazinagar, West Bengal, in 2016 and Baduria-Basirhat, also in West Bengal, in 2017.[191]

When we move from 'major', however, to merely 'important', the number of 'communal incidents' in the last four years rises

---

[189]'Lynchistan: Mob Lynching Cases Across India', *The Quint*.
[190]'Minister In Modi's Cabinet Garlands Cow Vigilantes Convicted For Lynching A Muslim Trader In Jharkhand', *Huffington Post*, 7 July 2018.
[191]'"No Big Communal Riot' In Last 4 Years: BJP Minister. Fact: 389 Dead in Over 2,000 Communal Incidents', *FactChecker.in*, 5 July 2018; Alok Mishra, '"Communal violence up after BJP came to power"', *Times of India*, 9 October 2015.

to 2,920, in which 389 people were killed and 8,890 injured. My source is Rajnath Singh's own government: these figures come from a reply by the Home Ministry to questions in the Lok Sabha. According to the government, Uttar Pradesh (UP), somewhat predictably, reported the most incidents over the last four years, a staggering 645. UP also reported the most deaths in these communal incidents (121) between 2014 and 2017, followed by Rajasthan (36) and Karnataka (35). The venues for communal rioting on the BJP's watch ranged from Ballabgarh, Haryana, in 2015, to Bhima-Koregaon, Maharashtra, in 2017.[192]

The Home Ministry's National Crime Records Bureau (NCRB) collects and maintains nationwide crime records, which naturally includes riots. NCRB data confirm that over 2,885 communal riots were reported between 2014 and 2016. Many others may not have been recorded as communal; as many as 61,974 riots were reported in 2016 under sections 147 to 151 and 153A of the IPC (the latter records cases relating to 'promoting enmity on ground of religion, race and place of birth'). In 2016, 869 communal riots were reported, the largest number in Haryana (250).[193] The figures for 2017 haven't been released yet, more than halfway into 2018; I dread what they are likely to reveal.

We have a government that seems to believe it can issue statements with utter disregard for the truth and people will believe them. This is the only explanation for the two ministers' breathtaking assertions. It matches the prime minister's claims on the economy and the government's blandly disingenuous PR pronouncements on everything from electrification to women's empowerment. But facts and figures matter. And the numbers simply do not add up to the picture the government seeks to portray. According to NCRB data concerning incidents of rioting, the years under Dr Manmohan Singh's rule were the most peaceful in independent India's history.[194] That record appears in no danger

---

[192]Ibid.
[193]Ibid.
[194]Shivam Vij, 'Riot after riot: The Manmohan years were the most peaceful, data

of being rapidly overturned: 'peaceful' is not an adjective that can be applied to India under Moditva.

The context against which such violence is occurring is a noticeable change in the communal climate across the country. A Shiv Sena worker shoves a chapatti down the throat of a fasting Muslim caterer.[195] A BJP leader casts doubt on the national credentials of India's leading woman tennis player, because she is Muslim and married to a Pakistani.[196] The Bharatiya Shiksha Niti Ayog has been constituted by the RSS-affiliated Shiksha Sanskriti Utthan Nyas, under the leadership of the notorious Dinanath Batra, with a mandate to 'suggest corrective steps' to 'Indianize' the education system.[197] All of these incidents invite no rebuke, let alone punishment.

Intangible factors have also contributed to the sense of communal polarization across our country. Election campaigns have showcased egregious instances of such rhetorical transgressions. Bihar BJP MP Giriraj Singh declared during the 2014 Lok Sabha election campaign that 'those who want to stop' BJP prime ministerial candidate Narendra Modi would soon have 'no place in India...because their place will be in Pakistan'.[198] BJP president Amit Shah reportedly claimed in a speech that the election was a chance to seek 'revenge' for the 'insult' inflicted on the Hindu community during the riots in Muzaffarnagar in September 2013, in which nearly 60 were killed, hundreds raped and thousands displaced. (Most of the victims were Muslim.)[199]

Electoral victory has emboldened Hindutvavadi voices across the country. Goa State Cooperation Minister Deepak Dhavalikar

shows', *Scroll.in*, 5 August 2014.
[195]'Indians MPs "force-fed" fasting Muslim worker', *BBC*, 23 July 2014.
[196]Ayesha Perrera, 'Dear Mr Laxman, sorry but Sania Mirza will always be India's daughter', *FirstPost*, 5 August 2014.
[197]Dhirendra K. Jha, 'RSS sets up panel to supervise saffronisation of education', *Scroll.in*, 2 August 2014.
[198]'Modi's critics will have to live in Pakistan, not India: BJP leader Giriraj Singh', *FirstPost*, 20 April 2014.
[199]'Amit Shah is chargesheeted in election "hate speech" case', *Indian Express*, 11 September 2014.

told his state assembly, 'If we all support it and we stand by Narendra Modi systematically, then I feel a Hindu Rashtra will be established.'[200] Goa Deputy Chief Minister Francis D'Souza, supporting his party colleague, said 'India is already a Hindu nation' and 'all Indians in Hindustan are Hindus.' He added that he considers himself a 'Christian-Hindu'.[201] In July 2014, BJP MLA and party national executive member C. T. Ravi had issued a tweet advocating the 'Gujarat Model' to stem the Saharanpur riots. He said 'Only the Gujarat model, that worked from 2002 in containing their [i.e. Muslims] rioting elements, can work. Apply across Bharat.'[202]

It is easy to discount such verbal violence—and there have been worse from the likes of Pravin Togadia and Ashok Singhal, whom the BJP prefer to dismiss as fringe figures—but the words in fact reflect a harsher reality. As I have mentioned earlier, the first time in the history of India, the ruling party has no Muslim representation in the Lok Sabha. Indeed, the state that has historically sent Muslims to Parliament after every single general election, Uttar Pradesh, with a 20 per cent Muslim population, failed to do so in 2014, when the BJP and its Apna Dal ally swept 73 seats out of 80 there.[203] There is no starker evidence of polarization imaginable.

Prime Minister Modi has been either ambivalent or utterly silent on all these incidents, including the Muzaffarnagar riots, and has not expressed disapproval of any communal actions taken by groups within the Sangh Parivar. He has missed several opportunities to reach out and reassure the Muslim community. He has not even made the simple gesture of attending an iftar during Ramadan, let alone hosting one as his predecessors did.

On the rare occasion that he has actually condemned

---

[200]'India is a Hindu nation, I'm a Christian-Hindu: Goa Dy CM Francis D'Souza', *FirstPost*, 25 July 2014.
[201]Ibid.
[202]'Karnataka BJP MLA wants Gujarat model in Uttar Pradesh', *Deccan Chronicle*, 29 July 2014.
[203]Mohd Faisel Fareed, 'No Mulsim MP from Up', *Indian Express*, 16 May 2014.

communal violence, his statements have been blandly reassuring, if belated. Early into his reign, during a video conference with NRIs in the US, PM Modi said: 'My definition of secularism is simple: "India First". Whatever you do, wherever you work, India should be the top priority for all its citizens. [The] country is above all religions and ideologies.'[204]

In February 2015, Narendra Modi spoke more clearly on the subject. Addressing a Christian congregation in New Delhi that was meeting to celebrate the elevation to sainthood of two Catholic figures, Kuriakose Elias Chavara and Mother Euphrasia, and doing so in the wake of mounting concern over the vandalization of six Catholic churches in and around the capital, Mr Modi said his government would not 'accept violence against any religion, on any pretext.' He declared unequivocally. 'I strongly condemn such violence. My government will act strongly in this regard.'[205]

This was undoubtedly because of the concern many of us had expressed about the damage the irresponsible statements and actions of the Hindutva brigades were doing to the country. The attacks on the churches were symptomatic of a far larger problem that was leaving all minorities feeling insecure. Foreign leaders were taking note too, with visiting US President Barack Obama telling a Delhi audience that 'India will succeed so long as it is not splintered along the lines of religious faith,' and commenting adversely on religious intolerance in India at a Prayer Breakfast on his return to the US. This was clearly not the way the prime minister wished his government to be perceived.

'We consider the freedom to have, to retain, and to adopt, a religion or belief is the personal choice of a citizen,' Mr Modi averred. 'My government will ensure that there is complete freedom of faith and that everyone has the undeniable right to retain or adopt the religion of his or her choice without coercion or undue

---

[204] '"India First" is my definition of secularism: Narendra Modi', *Economic Times*, 10 March 2013.
[205] '"My govt will ensure complete freedom of faith," PM says', *Business Standard*, 18 February 2015.

influence. My government will not allow any religious group, belonging to the majority or the minority, to incite hatred against others, overtly or covertly. Mine will be a government that gives equal respect to all religions.'[206]

While foreign reporters were quick to portray this as a gesture to Christians and other minorities, rebuking his own followers in the BJP and Sangh Parivar, who had gleefully led the ghar wapsi and love jihad campaigns and repeatedly affirmed that India was a Hindu country rather than the pluralist land of constitutional practice, some Indian commentators saw it also as PM Modi signalling to the minorities that they too should look beyond minority rights to India's ancient heritage of tolerance. After all, he said: 'My government will not allow any religious group, *belonging to the majority or the minority* [italics added], to incite hatred against others, overtly or covertly. Mine will be a government that gives equal respect to all religions.'

It was striking, in this context, that the PM used the words 'without coercion or undue influence', which some saw as a swipe at alleged inducements offered by Christian proselytizers to low-caste Hindus. On the whole, though, there was less here for the Hindutva elements than for others: this was the speech every Indian pluralist was waiting for the PM to make. 'Equal respect for all religions,' he went on, 'must be in the DNA of every Indian... I appeal to all religious groups to act with restraint, mutual respect, and tolerance in the true spirit of this ancient nation which is manifest in our Constitution.'[207]

Lest his speech be seen as responding to Obama's tutelage, the PM was firm in affirming the indigenous roots of Indian religious tolerance. 'Our Constitution did not evolve in a vacuum. It has roots in the ancient cultural traditions of India. The principle of equal respect has been a part of India's ethos for thousands of years and that is how it became integral to the Constitution of

---

[206]Ibid.
[207]Ibid.

India... As Swami Vivekananda said: "We believe not only in universal toleration, but we accept all religions as true."'

That was a welcome reminder to those Hindutva activists who have been advocating Hinduism as a badge of identity rather than a set of principles and traditions which are at odds with their narrow-minded bigotry. Narendra Modi reminded them that 'We believe that there is truth in every religion. Ekam sat vipra bahudha vadanti (There is one truth, but the sages call it by many different names).'

The speech was welcome, but the real challenge for Prime Minister Modi, as I tweeted soon after he made the speech, would be to get the Sangh Parivar to live up to it. Unfortunately for us all, there is no sign of this; and the prime minister's advocacy of tolerance and repudiation of sectarian violence has too often been too little too late. Instead his more frequent response has been silence—an obdurate refusal to speak, let alone to condemn the atrocities. Mr Modi's silence when violence has occurred has emboldened its perpetrators to believe the prime minister condones their actions, thus empowering the worst elements in our society.[208] It is a central element of the Modi paradox that whenever he is torn between being a Hindutvavadi leader and an Indian statesman, his sectarian instincts prevail more often than his prime ministerial duty.

---

[208]'Sonia Gandhi leads protest march, questions PM Modi's silence', *Indian Express*, 4 November 2015.

chapter four

SACRED COWS AND UNHOLY POLITICS

I

Typhon was the most terrible creature in Greek myth. In the words of Hesiod, the Greek poet (circa 700 BCE), 'from his shoulders grew a hundred heads of a snake, a fearful dragon, with dark, flickering tongues, and from under the brows of his eyes in his marvelous heads flashed fire, and fire burned from his heads as he glared. And there were voices in all his dreadful heads which uttered every kind of sound unspeakable, for at one time they made sounds such that the gods understood, but at another, the noise of a bull bellowing aloud in proud, ungovernable fury; and, at another, the sound of a lion, relentless at heart; and at another, sounds like whelps...and again, at another, he would hiss, so that the high mountains re-echoed.'[209] This fearsome creature was invoked by a three-judge bench of the Supreme Court in 2018, to decry the monstrous phenomenon that has gained ground in the country ever since the Modi government came into power. The judgment, written by Chief Justice Dipak Misra, deplored 'lynching and mob violence' and warned that there were 'creeping threats that may gradually take the shape of a Typhon-like monster as evidenced in the wake of the rising wave of incidents of recurring patterns by frenzied mobs across the country, instigated by intolerance and misinformed by circulation of false news and false stories.'[210]

The judges added, 'There has been an unfortunate litany of spiralling mob violence and agonized horror, presenting a grim

---

[209]From Hesiod's *Theogony* in *The Homeric Hymns and Homerica* with an English translation by Hugh G. Evelyn-White, Cambridge: MA: Harvard University Press; and London: William Heinemann Ltd., 1914.
[210]'SC's Lynching Order: A Gentle Reminder That Law Still Exists', *The Quint*, 19 July 2018.

gruesome picture that compels us to reflect whether the populace of a great republic like ours has lost the value of tolerance to sustain a diverse culture.' In its judgment the court directed the government to pass a special law to deter such crimes. It said the 'recurrent pattern of violence...cannot be allowed to become the new normal.'[211] (As a Member of Parliament, I have, together with a colleague from the Upper House, the senior advocate K. T. S. Tulsi, submitted the draft of such a law to the government.)

The court's stepping in to voice its concern over lynchings was just the latest indictment of the Modi government's appalling track record in the matter. What is ironic about most of the lynchings is that the central protagonist in most of these incidents is that most peaceable and innocent of animals, the cow.

Many orthodox Hindus, particularly in the northern Indian states that comprise the so-called Cow Belt, venerate the cow as gau mata, the 'mother of all', which provides nourishment and sustenance through its milk—not its meat. Refusing to eat beef is common in these states.

But it is not always a personal choice. Several Indian states have passed laws outlawing cow slaughter, and some have prohibited the possession and consumption of beef altogether. Cow slaughter and beef consumption are fully legal in just five of India's twenty-nine states, mainly in the south and northeast.[212]

In the previous chapter, I have detailed various instances of the murder of innocent people just because they happened to be Muslim and were rumoured to have eaten beef or were accused of supplying cows to slaughter. Ninety-seven per cent of all such incidents in the seventy years of independent India's history have occurred in four and a half years of BJP rule under the Modi government.[213]

---

[211]Ibid.

[212]Saptarishi Dutta, 'Where you can and can't eat beef in India', *Wall Street Journal*, 6 August 2015.

[213]Delna Abraham and Ojaswi Rao, '97% cow-related attacks after PM Modi came to power in 2014', *Business Standard*, 29 June 2017.

Indeed, a signal illiberal achievement of Prime Minister Narendra Modi's BJP regime has been the revival of the cow as an instrument of political warfare. And the spate of attacks in the past few years reveals a serious problem with the country's trajectory under Mr Modi.

Of course, the cow has long had a place in Indian politics: the country's Constitution includes a provision explicitly urging a gradual movement towards the full prohibition of cow slaughter—a ban that has already been implemented in most states.

For most of India's existence, however, the default approach has essentially been 'live and let live'—make your own choice about beef, and let others do the same. Where beef was legally available, it was consumed not just by Muslims and other minorities, but also by many poorer Hindus, who could not afford other kinds of meat.

But that response was possible only so long as relatively liberal or moderate officials (including an earlier BJP-led coalition government) were in power. The Modi government does not fit that description. Instead, it is full of leaders who seem more concerned with what goes into other people's mouths than what comes out of their own.

II

One of the worst aspects of this repellent phenomenon that is sweeping across parts of the country has been the rise of the gau-rakshaks. Gau Rakshak Samitis, or 'cow protection societies,' saw a revival in India after the BJP's 2014 electoral win. Gau-rakshaks took it upon themselves to ensure that cows are not slaughtered or eaten.

Making matters worse, the cause of cow protection has now been linked to another persistent and destructive custom in Indian society: violence against Muslims and Dalits. Indeed, the Cow Belt, where cow vigilantism is most rampant, is also a hub of atrocities against Dalits, 63 per cent of which occur in just four states: Uttar Pradesh, Bihar, Madhya Pradesh, and Rajasthan.[214] It is no coincidence that these are also the states where the BJP fared best in 2014.

The link between cows and Dalits is well known. Cows may be considered holy, but they are not immortal, and when they die (ideally of natural causes), someone must dispose of their carcasses. For centuries, that job has fallen to Dalits, who collect the carcasses, skin them and sell their hides to tanners and leather-makers, deliver the meat to Muslim butchers (where it is legal), and bury or cremate what remains. It is a livelihood for a group with few economic opportunities—one that benefits the many Hindus who would not want to perform such an unpleasant task.

But several recent incidents have shaken the foundations of this arrangement. In the state of Gujarat, four Dalit youths caught skinning a cow were stripped, tied, and beaten with iron rods by cow vigilantes who accused them of killing the animal (they had not).[215] In BJP-ruled Madhya Pradesh, two Dalit women were assaulted for supposedly carrying illegal cow meat (it was legal buffalo meat).[216] In Haryana, two Dalit men were beaten and forced to eat cow dung for the same 'crime'.[217]

Such incidents have heightened the sense of vulnerability felt by many who do not necessarily share the vigilantes' reverence for cows. They have also led to serious economic challenges for some groups.

Farmers who raise their cows with care and respect may not be able to afford to continue caring for those that are too old to produce milk. In the past, they would address this by quietly selling the aged cows either to local butchers or to those who would transport them to states where cow slaughter is legal. But,

---

[214]Vikas Pathak and G. Sampath, 'U.P., Bihar lead in crimes against Dalits', The Hindu, 18 October 2016.
[215]'4 Dalits stripped, beaten up for skinning dead cow', Times of India, 13 July 2016.
[216]'Gau rakshaks on the rise: MP mob targets Muslim women over beef rumour, 26th attack this year', Hindustan Times, 29 July 2017.
[217]Nitin Jain, 'Two "beef transporters" forced to eat cow dung by Haryana's Gau Rakshak Dal', India Today, 27 June 2016.

because that would be far too dangerous in the current political climate, many farmers are being driven into debt caring for old cows, or simply abandoning them, while the cow population in India becomes increasingly unsustainable.

Moreover, Dalits are increasingly refusing to dispose of cow carcasses. After the Gujarat incident, one group of Dalits in the state declared outright their intention to suspend their traditional duties. 'If the cow is your mother,' they challenged upper-caste Hindus, 'why don't you bury her?'[218]

Where was the central government when all of this has been happening? Initially, it did not condemn cow vigilantism. India's social justice minister, whose principal responsibility is to promote the welfare of India's Dalits, expressed regret not for the vigilantes' violent actions, but for the fact that they were spurred by ill-founded rumours.

In August 2016, Prime Minister Narendra Modi finally broke his silence on the issue, warning people to beware of the fake gau-rakshaks who are trying to create social conflict, declaring that 'all states should take stern action against these people'. There were fifteen cases of mob lynching in the first half of 2018 alone.[219] But BJP-ruled Rajasthan has instituted rules that make it legal for 'civil society groups' to enforce cow protection, and there is little appetite for curbing them.

In July 2018 came the Supreme Court's condemnation following which Home Minister Rajnath Singh also spoke about how his government would be taking steps to curb the menace. But all the government's barely visible actions to prevent lynchings and mob violence have taken too long to come about, and this is indisputably because the cow has become the current instrument of choice in the ruling dispensation's relentless drive to promote its ideology of Hindutva.

---

[218]Asees Bhasin, '"Your mother, you bury her": Gujarat Dalits abandon cow carcasses', *The Quint*, 29 July 2017.
[219]Sneha Alexander and Jency Jacob, 'At least 15 deaths due to mob lynching in 2018 so far, NCRB to address data gap', *Boomlive.in*, 13 June 2018.

III

For the longest time, all those who did not subscribe to this ideology strongly resisted attempts to impose it on the rest of the country. Calls during the constituent assembly deliberations to ban cow slaughter, opposed by a vocal minority, were finally reduced to a 'directive principle' anchored in economics and not religion: Article 48 of the Constitution says that 'the State shall endeavour to organize agriculture and animal husbandry on modern and scientific lines and shall, in particular, take steps for preserving and improving the breeds, and prohibiting the slaughter, of cows and calves and other milch and draught cattle.' So this 'endeavour' (stopping well short of a ban) was related specifically to the needs of agriculture and animal husbandry, not of worship.

Gandhi-ji himself said that though he did not eat meat and was personally opposed to cow slaughter, in a multi-religious country like India, he could not justify imposing his Hindu views on the many who did not share his faith. Many Hindus feel the same way; I am a vegetarian and abhor the idea of consuming the corpses of animals, but I do not judge those who, for cultural or other personal reasons, do so. I only ask that animals be treated decently and without cruelty, and that even their slaughter, for purposes of consumption, be conducted humanely and with minimal pain and suffering for the poor creatures.

The furore that accompanied the Prevention of Cruelty to Animals Act (Regulation of Livestock Markets) Rules, 2016, rolled out by the Ministry of Environmental Affairs, polarized opinion across the country, especially in beef-eating states like Kerala. In Kerala, the new rules produced a strong reaction from an indignant chief minister, invited condemnation across the local political spectrum, forced the state to drag the central government to court, united warring student union factions to organize beef festivals across the state and even gave Twitterati a field day with #PoMoneModi (Go Away Modi)—used last when the prime minister compared Kerala to the African nation of Somalia—resurfacing as a popular hashtag.

The debate over the cow has raised fundamental questions the government cannot escape, even as it tries to shift the focus to the misbehaviour of a few young men.

The first issue is constitutional—the decision to institute the full prohibition of cow slaughter is a prerogative of the states, not the government at the centre. Entry 15 of the State List of the Seventh Schedule of the Constitution provides for the 'Preservation, protection and improvement of stock and prevention of animal diseases, veterinary training and practice', empowering state legislatures to legislate prevention of slaughter and preservation of cattle.

Different states have different approaches to cow welfare. Some states like Uttar Pradesh, Madhya Pradesh and Delhi have strict laws while others such as Kerala, Tamil Nadu, West Bengal, Manipur, Mizoram and Nagaland have milder rules or no rules governing the welfare of cows. The blanket new rule is clearly an infringement on the rights of the states, undermining the federal rights guaranteed by our Constitution.

The second objection is practical. The Constitution rightly speaks of milch and draught cattle. Cows produce milk for about eight years, at which point they are too old for either milch or draught purposes. But they go on to live another eight years. Farmers have to spend at least ₹60 a day on the food and fodder requirements and other maintenance costs of a cow.[220] That is ₹22,000 a year, or ₹1,76,000 for eight years, as the minimum expenditure for a poor farmer on a non-productive investment, which is a fortune for farmers who often live barely above subsistence level. This is why they sell non-lactating cows, normally for slaughter.

Even our highest courts, despite their variety of views on the matter, have recognized that 'a total ban on cattle slaughter [is] unreasonable if, under economic conditions, keeping useless bulls

[220]Harish Damodaran, 'What it might cost to save gauvansh countrywide', *Indian Express*, 24 April 2017.

or bullocks be a burden on the society and therefore not in the public interest.'[221]

India is already home to nearly 512 million cows, according to the 19th National Livestock Census 2012.[222] Aside from maintaining them decently, India would also have to deal with deforestation and overgrazing, as well as the problems caused by cattle abandoned by farmers who cannot afford to maintain unproductive animals and are no longer able to sell them for slaughter; these cows stray onto the streets and in many cases die of malnutrition in their old age. The previous policy recognized that banning cow slaughter would impose an economic burden on farmers, who, given the paucity of resources at their disposal, would struggle to maintain these animals.

As a result, India is also the largest exporter of buffalo meat in the world—a multibillion-dollar business.[223] Since the sale and transfer of animals is integral to keep this going, the new rules are likely to severely cripple the meat export, dairy, leather and other allied businesses, which provide employment for over a million individuals within the country, mainly from minority communities.

Take for instance, the state of Maharashtra's 2015 beef ban, which has already destroyed the livelihoods of around 3 lakh Muslim butchers and truckers in that state; a nationwide ban would push more people into poverty who are currently leading economically productive lives.

As I've noted, where beef was legally available to people, it was eaten not just by Muslims and other minorities, but also by sections of poorer Hindus, who could not afford to buy other kinds of meat. Statistics suggest that just 2 per cent of the Hindu population consume beef, but this 2 per cent translates to 12.5 million individuals, making them the second largest consumers

[221]Abusaleh Shariff, 'Why India must not disrupt its balanced bovine economy with a ban on beef', The Wire, 22 June 2015.
[222]Department of Animal Husbandry, Dairying and Fisheries' report, 'Salient features of 19th livestock census'.
[223]'Where Indian buffalo meat exports go', Indian Express, 12 April 2017.

of beef in the country.[224] And, in reality, many others who do so do not admit to the practice. Scheduled castes and tribes (SC/ST) comprise the overwhelming majority (more than 70 per cent) of the beef-eating Hindu population, while 21 per cent hail from the OBC community.[225] The government decision is therefore socially discriminatory, since it specifically and disproportionately harms the poorer and less privileged sections of Indian society.

But the real concern about the government's rules is not just about beef or the welfare of the cow, but about freedom.

Indians have generally felt free to be themselves, within our dynamic and diverse society. It is that freedom that the BJP's followers are challenging today.

In fact, Hindus who eat beef can, like those who abjure it, find support for their beliefs in the religion's ancient texts and scripture. (There are chapters and verses from the ancient texts supporting cow slaughter and beef consumption, as well as others which decry it as the worst of all sins.)

Narendra Modi's government has fostered what is a form of subjective intolerance, with supporters, emboldened by the BJP's absolute majority, imposing their particular view of what India should be, regardless of whom it hurts. This is why the reaction has been so visceral, even from non-beef eaters like myself. Our resistance is to the way India is being changed into something it never was—an intolerant majoritarian society with no place for minority tastes. There is no better symbol of the Modi paradox of extolling democracy while undermining its basic tenets than what he has allowed to be done to India in the name of the cow.

---

[224]Roshan Kishore, 'Who are the beef eaters in India?', *LiveMint*, 20 October 2015.
[225]Ibid.

chapter five

MINORITY REPORT

The magic of Indianness is that you can be a proud Bihari, a believing Muslim, a convinced leftist and a good Indian all at once. Indeed, all these identities are rendered secure by the overarching Indian identity that subsumes them all. Our nationalist heroes created a nation built on an ideal of pluralism and freedom; we have given passports to their dreams. The BJP would sadly reduce the soaring generosity of their founding vision to the petty bigotry of majoritarian chauvinism.

Since Narendra Modi came to power, there has been the overt declaration by RSS leader Mohan Bhagwat that all Indians are Hindus, and by implication that those who do not consider themselves Hindus aren't actually Indian, and don't belong here.[226] There was the statement by Giriraj Singh that those who don't vote for PM Modi should move to Pakistan, and the one by Sadhvi Niranjan Jyoti that people are either followers of Ram or bastards ('Ramzade ya Haraamzade')—both these offenders were rewarded with a place on Prime Minister Modi's council of ministers and neither was asked to resign.[227] The inflammatory statements hailing Gandhi's assassin Nathuram Godse, made by the BJP MP Sakshi Maharaj,[228] did not affect the BJP's allocating him the chair of a parliamentary committee or his selection to lead his party in prestigious debates on the floor of the Lok Sabha.

In the face of such implicit political approval, there have been the numerous incidents of communal violence I described

---

[226]'Everyone living in India is a Hindu: Mohan Bhagwat', *The Hindu*, 25 February 2018.
[227]'Niranjan Jyoti: A VHP "katha vachak" with an unpopular reputation', *FirstPost*, 3 December 2014.
[228]'BJP Lawmaker Sakshi Maharaj Calls Gandhi Assassin Nathuram Godse A "Patriot"', Then Retracts', *NDTV*, 11 September 2014.

earlier, which have instilled fear in the targeted minorities. And in December 2014, there was the episode of the mass conversion of fifty-seven bewildered Bengali Muslims in Agra by the Bajrang Dal, through a mix of intimidation and inducement, under the Sang Parivar's newly revived 'ghar wapsi' scheme.[229]

Prime Minister Modi must know that there is a great deal of concern throughout the country, and particularly among our Muslim fellow-citizens, about whether the Bharatiya Janata Party and its fellow travellers have the desire or the willingness to work for all of India's communities, or whether they seek to profit from dividing the nation on sectarian lines. A few words of reassurance to the Muslim community, in particular, from the master orator could go a long way towards calming their disquiet. Instead, as I have said earlier, the prime minister has mostly chosen to stay silent whenever insults are flung at Indian Muslims or they are invited to go to Pakistan (along with intellectuals, scholars, writers, and anyone else who happens to disagree with Mr Modi and his government).

His lack of empathy has emboldened those who follow him to demonize the minorities, especially the Muslim community. In 2016, I was at a hugely attended conclave in Delhi where a prominent television anchor began a discussion with Amit Shah by telling his audience to repeat after him, 'Bharat Mata ki jai!' Then he asked those in the audience who had done so to raise their hands. Almost everyone did.

I hadn't, and didn't. Not that I have any problem shouting this particular slogan: I had done so on numerous occasions, most notably with a busload of transiting Indian pilgrims on a European airport tarmac a few months earlier. It's just that I don't like the idea of doing so because a chauvinistic politician demands it of me in a public place.

When the anchor went on to ask those who would refuse to

---

[229]Pheroze L. Vincent, '350 Bengali Muslims "purified", says Bajrang Dal leader', *The Hindu*, 11 December 2014.

say the words to raise their hands, I did not do so either, because I wouldn't refuse to do so every time. I just believed in my right to choose whether and when I would say those words, or any other.

That seems to me to have been the principle at stake in the controversy that erupted over the refusal of MP Asaduddin Owaisi and a Maharashtra MLA belonging to his party, Waris Pathan, to chant this particular slogan. Both took their oaths as legislators in the name of God and swear by the Indian Constitution. They aver that they have no problem in hailing the nation with a robust 'Jai Hind' or 'Hindustan Zindabad!'[230] But to them, 'Bharat Mata ki Jai' sounds overtly Hindu, the deification of the nation as a mother goddess, and as Muslims they don't feel comfortable with it. They pointed out, not unreasonably, that the Constitution does not require them to raise this slogan, and they should not be compelled to do so.

The other side of the argument—the side passionately advocated by Amit Shah and the BJP—says that every Indian nationalist should say these words upon demand, and the 'one per cent' who don't should be made to understand that their opposition to the slogan is unjustified. The BJP and its fellow travellers have made something of a fetish of nationalism (as they define it) as the major issue at stake in the country today. 'Bharat Mata ki Jai' appears to have become the latest acid test of Indian nationalism.

As I said, I have nothing against the slogan. I believe, as Javed Akhtar memorably pointed out in his farewell speech on exiting the Rajya Sabha, that many Muslims don't have a problem with it either. But some do, and the issue is their right to dissent from this test of loyalty.

Let's accept that Mr Owaisi and his AIMIM party deliberately exploited this issue for political purposes—as part of their efforts to differentiate themselves as the only authentic and courageous voices of the Muslim community who are willing to stand up against the majoritarian chauvinism of the ruling party. So what?

Indian politics affords plenty of examples of principles being advanced to mask simple political opportunism, and I am prepared to concede that this might have been yet another example of this. Still, however, the principle remains valid, and should not be vitiated. No Indian should be compelled to mouth a form of nationalism he does not feel.

India must protect its largest minority population, empower them politically, and enable them to partake fully of the opportunities the state offers. This would require education, training and the resources to take advantage of such opportunities—from recruitment to the police forces to seed capital for entrepreneurship. If the BJP disdains quotas for Muslims, it could offer them a helping hand through special training schemes that equip Indian Muslims to, for example, take the entrance examinations to the police services. The government consciously needs to send regular signals of reassurance to minorities—and to Muslims in particular, since their vulnerability is accentuated by the circumstances of India's Partition, and because so many terrorist groups derive support and funding from Islamist groups across the border.

The Modi regime does not appear to fully appreciate the importance of this. In professing to be religion-neutral, but giving free rein to Hindu chauvinists to spew bigotry and division for petty political purposes, including electorally useful 'polarization', the government is missing an opportunity to embrace the Muslim minority in its narrative of aspiration. Promoting development and integration of minorities into the national mainstream is essential for India if it wishes to minimize the numbers of those who might be seduced by the siren call of terrorism.

Whether India has the second or third largest Muslim population in the world (depending on the exact numbers in Pakistan), there is no doubt that India's is by far the largest Muslim minority in the world, both in numbers and as a proportion of the population. At the same time, Islam is deeply rooted in Indian soil, with few

Indian Muslims—even those who claim relatively recent Persian, Afghan or Arab descent—having links, or owing allegiance, to the lands of their forebears. Though conservative Islamist doctrine has sprung from Indian minds (the Deoband School, whose doctrines inspired the Taliban, is situated in India),[231] none of the dozens of prominent Islamic seminaries or theologians in India has ever advocated armed insurrection against the Indian state.

The migration to Pakistan, upon Partition, of a significant proportion of the Muslim elite and its educated middle class, meant that India's Muslims were always disproportionately poorer and less educated than their counterparts in other communities. Successive governments have tried to address this problem with only a modest degree of success, and many Muslims objectively suffer from unfavourable socio-economic conditions—which some ascribe to discrimination against them. If a narrative of injustice and discrimination gains ground across the community, it can provide propitious conditions for terrorists to exploit. It is all the more in the interests of the Indian state to ensure that the economic development of India fully embraces its Muslim minority.

An India led by rational, humane and open-minded ideas of itself must develop a view of the world that is also broad-minded, accommodative and responsible. Prime Minister Modi has shown signs of understanding this in his many 'U-turns', from embracing the Bangladesh Land Boundary Agreement to shelving his party's irresponsible line on Article 370 in the election campaign in Kashmir. A policy of inclusion and respect for India's Muslims must follow. That would be in keeping with the aspirations that the predecessor he prefers to disown, Jawaharlal Nehru, launched us on when he spoke of our tryst with destiny.

---

[231]Celia W. Dugger, 'Indian town's seed grew into the Taliban's code', *New York Times*, 23 February 2002.

chapter six

THE DANGERS OF A NATIONAL
HOLY BOOK

Hand in hand with the victimization of minorities goes another aspect of the majoritarian project—trying, in every way possible, to endow the country with overt trappings of Hindutva, a precursor to its ultimate goal of making India a Hindu Rashtra. One of these initiatives is the advocacy of the Bhagavad Gita as a 'rashtriya granth', or 'national holy book'. This was most prominently proposed by Sushma Swaraj, the external affairs minister, with whose overt support of this idea I have publicly disagreed.[232] Let me enumerate a few of my concerns.

The first is that to cite no less a source than Prime Minister Narendra Modi himself, we already have a national holy book: it's called the Constitution of India.

The second is that we are a land of multiple faiths, each of which has its own holy books; on what basis would we pick any one of them in the capacity of a national holy book? Which Sikh would put the Gita ahead of the Guru Granth Sahib, for instance?

And if the answer to that question is, as Sushma-ji suggests, that it is the holiest book of the overwhelming Hindu majority of our population, the proposition is contestable, like most things in Hindu philosophy. As a practising (and reasonably widely-read) Hindu myself, I find a lot of ideas in the Vedas, Upanishads and Puranas that are not in the Gita. I see Hinduism as a pluralistic faith of many holy books and many ways of worshipping the divine.

You don't have to agree with those Hindu scholars who argue that the Gita, being Smriti (that which is heard and remembered, orally), is inferior to the Vedas and the Upanishads, which are Sruti

---

[232]'Sushma Swaraj Pushes for declaring Gita as National Book', *NDTV*, 7 December 2014.

(memorized and recorded divine revelation). But arguments about superiority and inferiority apart, there is no doubt that there are many views of the relative merits of several Indian holy books.

Sushma-ji, like Gandhi-ji before her, may be inspired by the Gita, but other, equally devout, Hindus might have other preferences. Why not the *Rig Veda*, for instance, the primordial revelation text of the Hindu faith? Why not the Smriti text known as the *Srimad Bhagavatam*, or *Bhagavata Purana*, which is recited for an entire week (saptaham) every year in many Hindu temples and homes? The quest to anoint a national holy book will not just divide Indians—it will divide Hindus as well.

But it's the fourth problem that's most relevant to a political discussion of the issue. For a government minister to raise the idea of a national holy book serves to ignite not just controversy, but fears—fears of a majoritarian project that will slowly but surely erode India's 'pluralist' identity and replace it with an overtly Hindu one.

Sushma-ji's statement may well have been relatively innocent— she was speaking, after all, at an event to celebrate the Bhagavad Gita, and was recalling a recommendation she had made in Parliament a few years ago, when the Russians had banned the Gita and India had protested—but her comment adds to a long list of statements and actions by our new rulers that cumulatively have stirred disquiet across the country.

Just as investors tend not to come to war zones—which is why peace on our borders is in our national interest—so too do investors prefer to risk their capital in harmonious societies that are focused on the future rather than divided by the past. The BJP and its government should heed one simple dictum: leave religion to the personal space and preference of every Indian. Let us have no national holy book, just as our Constitution does not permit us to have a national religion.

chapter seven

CHANGING THE CONSTITUTION

With the BJP now in direct or indirect control of twenty-one states, and in the process of creeping up to majority status in the Rajya Sabha to add to its overwhelming numbers in the Lok Sabha, the question of what the party intends to do with its dominance assumes urgent importance. A close reading of the works of its principal ideologues, notably Deen Dayal Upadhyaya, a Modi hero, suggests that amending the Constitution is likely to be high on the ruling party's priority list.

Whether or not the BJP goes full tilt at rewriting the entire Constitution to establish the Hindu Rashtra of its dreams (which may still require numbers it doesn't have in the Rajya Sabha), an obvious first step in that direction is probable. The easy target our ruling party may aim at is to reverse the 42nd Amendment of the Constitution, which in 1976 added two words the BJP doesn't like—'secular' and 'socialist'—to the preamble.

During the constituent assembly debates, Prof K. T. Shah had tried and failed on 15 November 1948 to achieve inclusion of the words 'Secular, Federalist, Socialist' in the Preamble.[233] In the eventual compromise, the majority of the assembly took the view that the Indian state would indeed be secular but that it was not necessary to use the word in the Preamble.

The word 'secularism', after all, was explicitly Western in origin, emerging from the political changes in Europe that accompanied the Protestant Reformation and the era called the Enlightenment. But many twentieth-century leaders outside Western Europe were attracted to the concept, notably Kemal Ataturk in Muslim-majority Turkey and Jawaharlal Nehru in

---

[233]Adrija Roychowdhury, 'Secularism: why Nehru dropped and Indira inserted the S-word in the Constitution', *Indian Express*, 27 December 2017.

Hindu-majority India, both of whom saw a secular state as a crucial hallmark of modernity. In India's case, secularism also seemed to Jawaharlal Nehru the only way to avoid the religious and communal antagonisms that had partitioned the country when the British left.

The constituent assembly debates show the extent to which this logic was accepted by our founding fathers. 'I accepted this secularism in the sense that our State shall remain unconcerned with religion, and I thought that the secular State of partitioned India was the maximum of generosity of a Hindu dominated territory for its non-Hindu population,' said Lokanath Misra in the debate on 6 December 1948.[234]

But was it necessary to include the word itself in the Constitution? The chairman of the Drafting Committee, Dr B. R. Ambedkar, thought not. Dr Ambedkar said 'what should be the policy of the State, how the Society should be organized in its social and economic side, are matters which must be decided by the people themselves according to time and circumstances. It cannot be laid down in the Constitution itself because that is destroying democracy altogether.'[235]

Still, the adoption of Articles 25, 26, 27 and 28 of the Constitution, guaranteeing freedom of conscience and the right to profess, practise, and propagate one's religion, to manage one's own religious affairs and to enjoy the freedom of religious worship, confirmed that the concept of secularism was unarguably implicit in India's constitutional philosophy. It isn't the word 'secular' that makes ours a secular Constitution, but rather the various provisions that ensure equal rights to people of all faiths and creeds. But India's wasn't Western-style secularism. Rather, secularism meant, in the Indian tradition, a multiplicity of religions, none of which was espoused by the state.

The theory of secularism, as Prof R. S. Misra of Banaras Hindu

---

[234]Ibid.
[235]Ibid.

University has argued, is based on dharma-nirpekshata ('keeping apart from dharma'), which is impossible for any good Hindu to adhere to. BJP politicians like Rajnath Singh and Yogi Adityanath have argued that Indian governments cannot observe dharma-nirpekshata but should follow the precept of panth-nirpekshata (not favouring any particular sect or faith). In this they are not far removed from my argument—which I have made for several years before my entry into Indian politics—that 'secularism' is a misnomer in the Indian context of profuse religiosity, and what we should be talking about is 'pluralism'. As I have long argued, I believe the roots of India's pluralism can be found in the Hindu philosophy of acceptance of difference: ekam sat vipra bahudha vadanti—there is one truth, but the sages call it by many different names.

No matter whether it's called secularism or pluralism, it is something Hindutva-minded Sanghivadis do not like, as it does not privilege Hinduism. They are therefore determined to do away with the concept as a significant step towards the Hindutva project of transforming India into a Hindu state, or at least a state with a distinctively Hindu identity. To hear their point of view is to take in a litany of complaints—the uncritical acceptance by the Indian establishment of regressive practices among the Muslim community while demanding progressive behaviour from Hindus, the support for minority education while denying such aid to Hindus, the promotion of 'family planning' among Hindus but not among Muslims, the cultivation of 'vote banks' led by conservative Muslim leaders but the disparagement of their Hindu equivalents, and so on.

The result is a widespread denunciation of the 'appeasement' of Muslims, which seems bizarre when one looks at the statistical evidence of Muslim socio-economic backwardness and the prevalence of discrimination in such areas as housing and employment. Muslims are under-represented in the nation's police forces and over-represented in its prisons. Yet Hindutva leaders have successfully stoked a perception that government benefits are skewed towards minorities, and thus justified their campaign for Hindu self-assertiveness.

It is for such reasons that Hindutva ideologues like K. N. Govindacharya want the word secularism removed: in his words, it 'implies opposition of Hindus and appeasement of Muslims or other minorities. We should get rid of this word as soon as possible. It is completely irrelevant in the Indian context.'[236]

One can credibly argue that the 42nd Amendment merely put a word into the Constitution whose spirit was always deeply embedded in it, and reified in governmental practice. The loss of the word 'secularism' will not necessarily make the country less secular, since successive Indian governments had practised the peculiar Indian variant of secularism anyway before the 42nd Amendment. Nor can we protest a further amendment to a constitution we have already amended a hundred times before. As Anantkumar Hegde, minister of state in the Modi government, has unambiguously declared: 'the Constitution...will change in the near future. The Constitution has changed many times before. We are here and have come to change the Constitution.'[237] But this would be no ordinary amendment—it would attack something fundamental and intrinsic to the way our Constitution-makers intended India to be.

Hegde, a blunt-speaking politician who has a long record of preferring valour to discretion, was merely voicing one of the fundamental dreams the Hindutvavadis have long had—the reshaping of the Constitution to suit their own ends.

Deen Dayal Upadhyaya, who is honoured and exalted daily by the BJP government today, identified the fundamental flaw: by adopting a concept of territorial nationalism, India had written a Constitution imitative of the West, divorced from any real connection to our mode of life and from authentically Indian ideas about the relationship between the individual and society. Deen

---

[236]Vishwadeepak, 'We should remove secularism, socialism from the Constitution: Govindacharya', *National Herald*, 2 October 2017.
[237]Apurva, 'We are here to change the Constitution: MoS Anantkumar Hegde', *Indian Express*, 26 December 2017.

Dayal Upadhyaya felt the Constitution should embody a Hindu political philosophy befitting an ancient nation like Bharat, that reducing the Indian national idea to a territory and all the people residing on it was fallacious. Instead, he argued, a nation is not a territory but a people, and the people of India are the Hindu people; the Constitution should have embodied this notion of Hindu nationhood.[238] The RSS's founder leader, Dr K. B. Hedgewar (whose Marathi biography Upadhyaya translated) had pointed to the 'ideological confusion' created by the secular approach. Muslim communalism, in his and Deen Dayal Upadhyaya's view, had become more prominent and aggressive, while Congress leaders bent over backwards more and more to accommodate them.

In building his case for a Hindu Rashtra, Deen Dayal Upadhyaya specifically disavowed the existing Constitution of India. But in Deen Dayal Upadhyaya's view, the failure of the founding fathers to conceive properly of the nation led them into error when it came to drafting the Constitution. 'We aped the foreigners to such an extent that we failed to see that our inherent national ideals and traditions should be reflected in our Constitution. We satisfied ourselves with making a patchwork of theories and principles enunciated by foreign countries... The result was that our national culture and traditions were never reflected in these ideologies borrowed from elsewhere and so they utterly failed to touch the chords of our national being.'[239]

Having rejected its premise, Deen Dayal Upadhyaya was scathing about the Constitution's drafting and adoption: a nation, he argued, 'is not like a club which can be started or dissolved. A nation is not created by some crores of people passing a resolution and defining a common code of behaviour binding on all its members. A certain mass of people emerges with an inherent motivation. It is,' he added with a Hindu analogy, 'like the soul

---

[238]Shashi Tharoor, *Why I Am a Hindu*, New Delhi: Aleph Book Company, 2018, p. 159.
[239]Pavan Kulkarni, 'Deendayal Upadhyaya, Bigoted "Guiding Force" of a Hindu Rashtra', *The Wire*, 30 October 2017.

adopting the medium of the body.'

Deen Dayal Upadhyaya asked three questions: were the people who framed the Constitution endowed with qualities of selflessness, an intense desire for public service and a deep knowledge of the rules of dharma as the rishis were? Or did they formulate this Smriti of a free India under the influence of the unsteady circumstances prevailing at the time? Did these people possess originality of thought or did they have a tendency to primarily imitate others? Deen Dayal Upadhyaya's implicit answers to these questions were in the negative: the Constitution-makers were not figures imbued with selflessness and dharma, they were overly under the thrall of the turbulent politics of that era, and their minds had been colonized by Western ideas. The founding fathers of the Republic of India were largely Anglophile Indians schooled in Western systems of thought; their work revealed no Indianness, no *Bharatiyata*. The Constitution, therefore, was to him a flawed document, one incapable of guiding India towards the path of raj dharma. In fact, it condemned Hindus to slavery: 'Self-rule and independence are considered to be synonyms. A deeper thinking will bring home to us the fact that even in a free country, the nation can remain in slavery.'[240] The Hindu nation had been enslaved by inappropriate Westernization.

The Constitution's core conception of the nation, in his view, was fundamentally not Indian at all. The absence of the Hindu Rashtra idea in the Constitution was unacceptable for him, as it is to those who revere him. So what might they do about it?

The more conformist of the two BJP prime ministers India has had, the late Atal Bihari Vajpayee (in office from 1998 to 2004), took a moderate approach to constitutional change, arguing that 'even in the mightiest fort one has to repair the parapet from time to time' (while V. P. Singh cautioned that the 'tenants' should not go for 'rebuilding in the name of repairs'). His rule saw no

---

[240]C. P. Bhishkar, *Pt. Deendayal Upadhyay Ideology & Preception–Part–5: Concept of The Rashtra*, New Delhi: Suruchi Prakashan, 2014, p. 63.

dramatic change in India's constitutional arrangements, though his government did conduct a constitutional review that produced a 1,979-page report, largely unread.

There has so far been no dramatic challenge to the Constitution under the second BJP prime minister, Narendra Modi. Indeed, Deen Dayal Upadhyaya, who rejected the Constitution of India in conception, form and substance, would be astonished to find his supposed acolytes extolling its every line and holding special commemorations in Parliament with grandiloquent speeches to mark the anniversary not just of its adoption—which, after all, is Republic Day—but even of its passage by the constituent assembly in a newly anointed 'Constitution Day'. What would Deen Dayal Upadhyaya have made, I wonder, of a prime minister, who swears by him, saying that this Constitution—the very document that Deen Dayal Upadhyaya found fallacious, Westernized, un-Indian and devoid of chiti and virat shakti—is his 'holy book'?

It is, of course, difficult to know whether we should take the Hindutvavadis' claims to be admirers of the present secular, liberal, Western-influenced Constitution of India to be as sincere as their professions of devotion to Upadhyaya. Will Modi and his tribe, after consolidating their hold on both the Lok Sabha and the Rajya Sabha, and after taking over most of the state governments, feel emboldened to tear up the very Constitution to which they have so far so enthusiastically pledged allegiance?

There are already hints that the Constitution in its present form cannot long survive unscathed. K. N. Govindacharya has declared that the Constitution must be transformed: 'We are doing it very silently. Discussions and debates have been taking place for some time... There may be many gaps which need deliberations, and a cool, calm, dispassionate discussion needs the right atmosphere and a mechanism. However, this is just not possible in the media glare.'[241]

[241]Vrinda Gopinath, 'RSS Ideologue Govindacharya: 'We Will Rewrite the Constitution to Reflect Bharatiyata', The Wire, 20 June 2016.

Would a Hindutva-inspired revision of the Constitution, for example, move the issue of cow slaughter from the Directive Principles of the Constitution, where it is linked specifically to the preservation of milch cattle and scientific principles of animal husbandry, to somewhere more binding, and anchored more explicitly to religious sanction? Mr Govindacharya is clear: 'The cow is part of our civilizational past and it reflects those values, it should be a civilizational continuity in the preamble. The cow, environment protection, all this requires constitutional protection. It is part of Hindu ethos, culture—like Bishnois who embrace death by hugging those trees, this is all "Bharatiya" culture. Instead of assuming man is conqueror of nature, it is the duty of humans to protect nature, and all this must be incorporated in the Constitution.'[242]

Environmentalists may well approve, but the key question remains whether a Hindutva-modified Constitution, assuming that it ever comes about, will retain the core principle of independent India, that all adult Indians are deemed equal, irrespective of religion. Or would it consciously embrace the central theme of Hindutva, which would discriminate against non-Hindus? If it did so, it would be true to Hindutva as expounded by V. D. Savarkar, M. S. Golwalkar and Deen Dayal Upadhyaya, but not to the Hinduism of Swami Vivekananda or Mahatma Gandhi, who did not define citizenship or Indianness in terms of the gods one worshipped, what one ate, the way one dressed or where one went for pilgrimage. But if it did not do so, it would betray a century's worth of political philosophizing in the name of Hindutva, surrendering its tenets to the dominant nationalist stream it had long derided as 'pseudo-secular'.

This will be a crucial dilemma for the Hindutva ideologues. Do they take the opportunity given to them by their crushing political majority—which might not endure if they wait too long—to remake the Constitution as their principal thinkers had advocated? Or do

---

[242]Ibid.

they accept that the reality of ruling a multi- ethnic, multi-lingual and multi-religious polity makes their goal of a Hindu Rashtra unattainable?

Another litmus test would lie in whether a revised Hindutva Constitution would mandate a Uniform Civil Code for all the citizens of India. Leaders subscribing to Hindutva have long argued that differential laws based on religion—essentially the personal laws governing marriage, inheritance and divorce for Muslims, and also for other religious minorities—violate Article 44 of the Indian Constitution and have sowed the seeds of divisiveness between different communities; if we are all Hindus (albeit 'Hindu Muhammadans', 'Hindu Christians' and so on) why should we not all be subject to one civil code? Secular Congress leaders from Jawaharlal Nehru onwards have argued that while a Uniform Civil Code might be a desirable objective, it could only be adopted with the consent of the affected communities. This could not be obtained by pressure or by legal coercion; it required persuasion. Since minority leaders, especially Muslims, showed no inclination to be persuaded, seeing a uniform civil code as the imposition of majoritarian Hindu sensibilities, the idea needed to be deferred indefinitely, until the time was ripe. Hindutva leaders have long mocked this approach as caving in to minority prejudices; accepting Islamic personal law, they argue, violates the human rights principles of gender equality by discriminating against Muslim women and allows unelected and in some cases self-appointed religious personalities to interpret religious dictates and so 'lay down the law'. Could they now concede the permissibility of religious personal laws without losing credibility?

And would a Hindutva Constitution preserve the anomaly of Article 370, which grants a special status to the state of Jammu and Kashmir, to the extent that no law passed by the Parliament of India can apply to that state without being also passed by the constituent assembly of Jammu and Kashmir? Would the advocates of Hindutva allow the state to continue to restrict landholding to 'state subjects', a status a woman would lose, under Article 35A of the Constitution, if she married a man from outside the state?

India's constitutionalists have long argued that it is a living document, susceptible to amendment in keeping with the evolving demands of time, subject of course to judicial interpretation, which has decreed that its 'basic structure' cannot be tampered with. Would transforming an egalitarian and secular Constitution into a document infused with the principles of Hindutva not violate its basic structure? And yet, can the advocates of Hindutva—the intellectual legatees of Veer Savarkar, M. S. Golwakar and Deen Dayal Upadhyaya—afford not to try?

One more Modi paradox here: the very Constitution he swears by is in the crosshairs of the most devoted of his followers. During the huge national outcry in mid-2018 over my public statement that, if re-elected, the Sanghivadis would turn India into a mirror image of the majoritarian state next door—a 'Hindu Pakistan'—I challenged the prime minister and his acolytes to end the controversy by disavowing their avowed goal of a Hindu Rashtra. None did. I put the proposition to a Modi government minister with whom I shared a stage at a media-organized conclave; he evaded the question. I tried on television as well: 'Let the prime minister say,' I declared, 'that he admires Deen Dayal Upadhyaya but disagrees with him on the Constitution.' The prime minister said no such thing. It is clear that whatever their lips enunciate about the Constitution, their heart remains with the Hindutva doctrine that is antithetical to it. All of us who care about the spirit of Indian pluralism and religious freedom, which are enshrined in our Constitution, must resist attempts to change its fundamental character. For the Constitution as it currently exists is a reflection of India's pluralist soul. To destroy that would be to dismember the very idea of India that animated our struggle for freedom. A Sanghivadi India would no longer be the India that Gandhi, Nehru, Dr Ambedkar and Maulana Azad fought to free. It would merely be a Hindutva imitation of Pakistan.

chapter eight

HONOURING OUR WOMEN

BJP rule has been appalling for women. It is a telling detail that the party has the highest number of lawmakers accused of crimes against women. According to a study by the Association for Democratic Reform (ADR) and National Election Watch (NEW), as many as fifty-one BJP MPs and MLAs have had cases filed against them for crimes against women, including those alleging rape and abduction.[243]

(It must however be stated, for the record, that accusations do not necessarily amount to convictions, and that some charges may be unfounded. The Delhi Police, functioning under the central government's control, have accused me of the crime of abetting my wife's suicide; I am contesting their charge vigorously, as one who believes there was neither suicide nor abetment. My profound personal conviction remains that there is nothing more contemptible than a man assaulting a woman or child, whatever the provocation.)

To return to the political facts: the ADR/NEW study further said that among the major parties, over the past five years, the party that had given the highest number of tickets (forty-eight) to candidates who had been accused of assaults and other crimes against women was the BJP.[244] With such a record, is it any wonder that Modi's sarkar has seen the incidence of attacks on women and girls escalate sharply on its watch? It has responded to this national shame with a combination of denial, defiance, blaming-the-victims and attempted censorship, even as foreign countries increasingly issue advisories to female tourists not to travel unaccompanied in the country.

---

[243]'BJP has highest no. of MPs, MLAs with cases of crime against women: ADR study', *Hindustan Times*, 31 August 2017.
[244]Ibid

Every single day, the media have a new horror story to report. The tragic rape and murder of the student, Jyoti Singh (dubbed 'Nirbhaya' or Fearless One) in December 2012 seemed to have crystallized public opinion on the issue and given birth to a new national determination to deal effectively with crimes against women. A law was passed, increasing the punishment for rape. But the moment passed, and the country relapsed once more into its disgraceful ways. Worse, the ruling party's stalwarts tripped over themselves to minimize the impact of the stories, and in some cases even to justify them.

According to the NCRB, in 2016 the rape of minor girls increased by 82 per cent compared with the previous year.[245] In 2018, two new cases galvanized national attention: the repeated gang-rape and murder, in Jammu & Kashmir's Kathua, of an eight-year-old Bakerwal Muslim girl, apparently to drive her nomadic people away from grazing grounds in a Hindu-majority area; and the rape of a sixteen-year-old woman by a BJP legislator in Uttar Pradesh to whom she had gone seeking help. The specific details of each case were horrific enough—especially Kathua, where the nature of the atrocity defied the most basic notions of humanity—but what made them worse was the attitude of the ruling party. In Kathua, BJP ministers were deputed to address a rally denouncing the police for proceeding against the perpetrators; in Uttar Pradesh, the accused legislator brazenly blamed the victim as a willing participant in her own humiliation. Public outrage finally brought about ministerial resignations and the MLA's arrest, but the initial attitudes were revelatory of a problem the BJP has proved incapable of addressing.[246]

We have often heard it said that the mark of a healthy society is the treatment that is meted out to its women. Unfortunately, the BJP government embodies a culture that either deifies or maternalizes

---

[245]'Crying for help: 82% rise in child rape cases needs urgent attention', *Times of India*, 2 December 2017.
[246]Shuja-ul-Haq, 'Kathua rape case: 2 BJP ministers attend rally in support of accused', *India Today*, 4 March 2018.

women—as goddesses and mothers, both to be worshipped and protected—but has no concept of how to deal with women who are neither. In this, and in other chapters of the book, I will explore some of the more horrifying examples of the present government's attitude towards women in particular and sex and sexuality in general. The intelligent, autonomous, aspiring young woman with a mind of her own, her own wishes, desires and ambitions, is an individual most Indian men cannot come to terms with.

That has to change. Because if we don't understand the nature and scale of the problem of rape and violence against women in our country, and we don't change some of our own attitudes and responses to it, we will never solve it.

Understanding it means acknowledging that some of the remarks made by politicians about rape are simply wrong. It is wrong to claim that 'rapes take place in cities and not in villages', as RSS supremo Mohan Bhagwat did.[247] Some of the most horrific rapes have taken place in rural India, especially of women who have gone out into the fields at night to relieve themselves. Rural attitudes are often more backward, as numerous pronouncements by khap panchayats and village councils have proved. In 2014, a Santhal woman was raped by thirteen men for the 'crime' of having fallen in love with a man from another community. This happened on the orders of a tribal 'court' called a salishi sabha. While the Supreme Court has been expanding the rights of women in a series of recent judgments, traditional bodies without constitutional sanction have been narrowing their freedoms. We politicians must stand on the side of women and not with the khaps.

It is wrong to blame rape on the victims. Too many BJP politicians blame the way women dress or behave for the violence inflicted upon them. It is wrong to say, as Bhagwat did, that 'women should refrain from venturing out with men other than their relatives. Such incidents happen due to the influence of

---

[247]'Politicians tell us why rape is a woman's fault', *The Quint*, 7 January 2017.

Western culture and women wearing less clothes.'[248] Equally wrong was Haryana Chief Minister Manohar Lal Khattar's view that 'if a girl is dressed decently, a boy will not look at her in the wrong way.'[249] Why do politicians place the onus on the girl to dress in a certain way rather than the boy to behave properly? T. Babulal Gaur, a BJP leader from Madhya Pradesh, went further: 'The rate of crimes against women depended on how completely dressed they are and how regularly they visited temples. Rapes in the state of Chennai are comparatively less as their women are always completely clad and visited temples regularly.'[250] Sigh. Ironically, such comments seem to share the perspective of one of the convicted rapists in the Nirbhaya rape-murder, Mukesh Singh, who claimed the deceased victim was to blame for wearing the 'wrong clothes' and being out with a boy late at night.[251] But horrifyingly, a woman politician said the same thing, explaining rape as a result of 'a woman's clothes, her behaviour and her presence at inappropriate places... Did Nirbhaya really have to go to watch a movie at eleven in the night with her friend?' asked Maharashtra's Nationalist Congress Party leader Asha Mirje (a woman herself), adding: 'Take the Shakti Mills gang-rape case [in which a freelance photojournalist was gang-raped]. Why did the [victim] go to such an isolated spot at 6 p.m.?'[252]

Our government does not seem to have realized that our job as politicians is to work to create a safe society where a woman can go anywhere at any time without having to fear assault. It is not to excuse the criminals who prey on women in under-policed areas of our towns and villages.

---

[248]Shailaja Neelakantan, 'Indian politicians' revolting comments about rape', *Times of India*, 2 August 2016.

[249]Shibaji Roychoudhury, 'Manohar Lal Khattar, who blamed women for India's rising rapes, is new Haryana CM', *Scroll.in*, 22 October 2014.

[250]'Fully dressed Chennai women safe as they visit temples: M.P. Minister', *The Hindu*, 10 January 2014.

[251]Kounteya Sinha, 'Nirbhaya gang-rape convict blames victim for the fatal assault', *Times of India*, 3 March 2015.

[252]'India outrage after woman politician blames women for rape', *BBC*, 29 January 2014.

It is also wrong to suggest that 'child marriage is a solution to rape and other atrocities against women'.[253] The political leader who said this, former Haryana CM Om Prakash Chautala, is currently in jail, where I am sure he has been told that child marriage is against the law, as is rape.

It would be wrong to blame the BJP alone; we politicians in general must also stop making excuses for rapists. It is wrong to suggest [as Gaur did] that rape 'depends on the man and the woman.[254] It is sometimes right and sometimes wrong.' No, Gaur sahib, rape is always wrong. Mulayam-ji, I hope you didn't mean it when you said: 'Boys will be boys, they make mistakes. Two or three have been given the death sentence in Mumbai. We will try and change such laws... We will also ensure punishment of those who report false cases.'[255] The law should be supported, Mulayam-ji, not changed. And 'boys' should be responsible citizens of our society, not just 'boys'.

Rape is not an acceptable response to changing social mores. Much though I admire Mamata Banerjee, I cannot agree with her that 'Rapes happen because men and women interact freely.' And I disagree even more vehemently with BSP leader Rajpal Saini, who averred: 'There is no need to give phones to women and children. It distracts them... Why do women need phones? My mother, wife and sister never had mobile phones. They survived without one'.[256] Phones do not make women more vulnerable, Rajpal-ji; they empower them, and perhaps that is what you are afraid of. But turning back the clock on progress never actually changes the time.

All these comments point to the real problem: India's politicians have not fully been able to come to terms with the growing emancipation of women in our society, the increasing freedoms they

---

[253]Shailaja Neelakantan, 'Indian politicians' revolting comments about rape', *Times of India*, 2 August 2016.
[254]Ibid.
[255]Ibid.
[256]'Ten excuses for rape in independent India', *DailyO*, 13 August 2015.

are enjoying, their autonomy from male control—on everything from how they dress to where they go and when, and with whom. When some criminal men react to unfamiliar circumstances with violence and assaults on women, some political leaders are reluctant to condemn and punish them, because at heart some of them share the same resentment the rapists feel.

At the same time, many politicians, even the women amongst us, express patriarchal attitudes to women. Our outrage at rape reflects our perception that it is not just a physical assault but also a respect-depriving tragedy; the trauma of rape is compounded by the level of social stigma attached to the crime. The victim is made to feel that she has been defiled, violated and shamed before the public at large, and that she is no longer fit to lead a normal life—even a woman minister, Sushma Swaraj, lamented that a rape victim was a 'zinda laash' (a living corpse).[257] This is a form of social control of female sexuality that we must not encourage. The BJP government must not reinforce the sense of male sexual entitlement that pervades our society; but it does precisely that when, for instance, it opposes criminalization of marital rape. Rape is not about sex: it is about violence. Politicians have a duty to reiterate that message.

And though the government's job is to protect women, leaders sometimes act as if sexual violence is a not a priority for us. 'You are safe, why are you bothered?' a former Uttar Pradesh chief minister asked a reporter who questioned him about rapes increasing in the state. BJP leaders across the board have tended to behave as if the issue of women's safety is beneath them, since they have so many more important things to deal with.

There is also a national tendency to dismiss rape as 'a women's issue'. It's not. It's an issue that affects all of us, male or female, because it affects all of society. The BJP government has done nothing to set an example; its ministers have never spoken out

---

[257]Lakshmi Chaudhry, 'Everyone's favourite Mataji: Sushma Swaraj's big bindi politics', *FirstPost*, 16 January 2013

against social attitudes that, by diminishing women's value in our society, could one day prompt or justify violence against them. A 2011 survey found that 65 per cent of Indian men believed that sometimes a woman deserves to be beaten; 37 per cent of men had physically assaulted their intimate partner at least once; 24 per cent had committed an act of sexual violence against someone in society and 20 per cent had committed sexual violence against their partners.[258] Such attitudes start in the home, and those in public life must speak out against them.

Here's a prescription that all political leaders, particularly those in government, must consider. We must deplore preferential treatment given to boys over girls in our homes and workplaces. We must introduce gender-equality lessons in our classrooms at an early age so that little boys are taught that girls have just the same rights as they do. We must condemn the abuse of women on social media and attacks on women journalists and writers. We must seek an end to sexist portrayals of women in popular culture that legitimize male harassment, whether the songs of Honey Singh or movies that glamorize men stalking women (singing 'tera peechha na chhodoonga'[259] all the way). We must stop confusing our idea of a family's honour with confining women behind a lakshman rekha which they must not cross. And believing that if a woman transgresses it, she deserves what she gets. Such attitudes must be fiercely opposed, and we are uniquely placed, by virtue of our place as leaders, to challenge them.

Sadly, the answer does not lie in the one thing we lawmakers can easily do, which is to write laws. Laws already exist. The law on rape and sexual assault, in its amended 2013 version, is a strong one, but its implementation still has a long way to go. Women are often reluctant to report rapes, and policemen to record them. Successful rape prosecutions are all too rare. Sexual violence in rioting is lost in the clamour around the riot itself. I

---

[258]Vasundhara Sirnate, 'Good laws, bad implementation', *The Hindu*, 1 February 2014.
[259]'I shall never stop chasing you', a Bollywood hit song of the early 1970s.

myself have introduced a Private Member's Bill to make stalking a non-bailable offence so as to reduce the vulnerability of women who find the courage to complain to the police but find their stalkers immediately free on bail but twice as angry at them. We politicians know that while we can make laws that protect women, we have to also ensure that law enforcement agencies actually enforce them. Too many politicians seek to undermine law enforcement, rather than support it. This is where a responsible government can set an example; the BJP's, alas, does not seem to be doing so. Instead, it seems bent on worsening the situation. Rather than acting firmly, it seeks to justify crimes or brush them under the carpet. Take for example, a BBC documentary about violence against women that the BJP government tried to ban a few years ago on specious grounds.

I haven't seen *India's Daughter*, Leslee Udwin's film on the tragic rape and murder of Nirbhaya. With YouTube having been coerced into removing the film from that site, I am unlikely to be able to see it now in India. But my arguments relate to issues of principle and policy, not to the merits of the film. After all, bad or mediocre films are screened every day in India. What justifies a ban?

I have read the few reasonable objections to the film. Some are legal: that such a film would prejudice the appeals process and the accused's case for a mercy petition. (Judges can weigh that consideration on merits, but it does not seem to me an overwhelming one, given the saturation of coverage the case has already had in our media.) Some are moral: that no one should give a media platform to someone guilty of such a heinous crime. (That's worth debating, but the choice is that of the filmmaker and the organization that chooses to screen her work—just as we are all free not to watch it.)

But the government's and the ruling party's arguments were, frankly, a disgrace. We had the then parliamentary affairs minister, Venkaiah Naidu, delivering the mother of all political clichés:

'This is an international conspiracy to defame India.'[260] The BJP's Meenakshi Lekhi protested that 'this will certainly affect tourism'.[261] The 'this' she meant was the film, not the reports of previous rapes of tourists, nor the advisories issued by every Western country warning female tourists against travelling alone or after dark in India. Home Minister Rajnath Singh's statement invoked 'the dignity of women' and fulminated that the government would 'not allow any attempt by any individual, group or organization to leverage such unfortunate incidents for commercial benefit.'[262] Indeed, to add hypocrisy to wrong action, the restraining order obtained by the authorities against the BBC specifically stated that one of the accused, Mukesh Singh, 'had made offensive and derogatory remarks against women, creating an atmosphere of fear and tension with the possibility of public outcry [affecting the] law and order situation.'[263]

In sum: it's not the fact or prevalence of rape in India that bothers the government. It's not even the persistence of offensively misogynistic attitudes across the establishment, also brought out in the documentary, where aside from Mukesh Singh's assertion that his victim was asking for it, his lawyers put the onus for rape squarely on women's behaviour, clothes and social freedoms (one of them even declared that he would douse his daughter or sister with petrol and set her alight if she 'engaged in pre-marital activities'[264]). No, it's not the truth of such attitudes and practices in our country that upsets the government. It is, instead, that if this truth were shown by the BBC, India would be disgraced and tourists wouldn't visit our country.

---

[260]Tara Conlan and Maseeh Rahman, 'India's Daughter: BBC brings forward airing of Delhi rape documentary', *BBC*, 4 March 2015.
[261]'India's daughter: Chronicle of a death foretold by Udwin', *Bangalore Mirror*, 7 March 2015.
[262]'Govt plans legal action against maker of documentary on Nirbhaya', *Times of India*, 4 March 2015.
[263]Nirnimesh Kumar, 'Court stay on telecast to continue', *The Hindu*, 5 March 2015.
[264]Yvonne Roberts, 'India's Daughter: "I made a film on rape in India. Men's brutal attitudes truly shocked me"', *The Guardian*, 1 March 2015.

This is exactly the attitude we witnessed half a century ago when Satyajit Ray was condemned by Nargis and others for showing India's poverty to the West in his masterpiece, *Pather Panchali*. It wasn't our poverty that shamed us, but its depiction to the outside world. On that issue, fortunately, the Congress government of the day didn't ban Satyajit Ray's work. Nehru positively supported it: 'What is wrong about showing India's poverty?' he asked. 'Everyone knows we are a poor country. The question is: are we Indians sensitive to our poverty or insensitive to it?' With Ray, Nehru declared, there was the most profound sensitivity. He understood that truth is its own justification and that we need mirrors turned on us to understand ourselves better. History has shown that such self-examination has only made the world better.

The horrific rape was the cause of nationwide protests and media outrage, calling for change in our society's attitudes towards women that underlie crimes like rape. How can we bring about that change if we don't see and share the reality around us and bring people together to transform that reality for the better? We can bring in any change only if we understand the roots of the problem we want to change; if not, we will continue to be its victims. Awareness is the first essential step towards transformation.

But our government, as usual, prefers to ignore the message and shoot the messenger. In the case of *India's Daughter,* the home of the BBC co-producer in Delhi was ringed by police; the order of an Indian court was sought to be imposed on the freedoms of other societies; and people worldwide decried the thin-skinned intolerance of a supposedly democratic government. And of course, far more people rushed to see the film than would have been the case if the Indian government hadn't reacted with such juvenile petulance. So the government's intolerance was actually self-defeating: their conduct brought about the national disgrace they claimed they were trying to prevent.

In the 2014 election campaign, India's television screens were flooded with BJP advertisements in which a female voter called for a BJP government because she wanted to live in a country that would be safe for her daughter. The BJP's campaign cynically exploited the public outrage at crimes against women. But as has become obvious over the last four years of rhetoric divorced from results, the BJP government cares much more for appearances than reality. Its budgets have cynically ignored women's needs, aside from slogans. Successive BJP budgets have savaged allocations for women; to take just one example, funding for the national rape crisis centres, which were set up in the aftermath of the Nirbhaya case, was slashed from ₹244.48 crore to a mere ₹18 crore in 2015.[265] Five years after the centre had proposed 660 such crisis centres, funds had been allocated for only 151, and were further reduced to permit the establishment of just two! In the national capital, which reported the highest cases of crimes against women in 2016, as per government data, only nine such centres were operational in 2018.[266] These cuts, though the BJP government would pretend otherwise, are far more unkind than any made in the BBC's editing rooms.

Nirbhaya's father, Badrinath Singh, openly attacked the patriarchal mindsets of the Indian establishment. 'How will we protect our daughters if we don't tell our sons what is wrong and should not be done? Isn't it time to admit that there are both good and bad people everywhere and that certain ways of thinking have led to the death of our daughters?' he asked the BBC.[267] And he added, to the *Economic Times*, 'Many men, even from good families and with good degrees, seem to think like this. How can our daughters study and work freely if society thinks like this?... We ask parents to treat their daughters as they treat their sons. Educate them but at the same time make them strong and, more

[265]Ananya Sengupta, 'Rape centres cut, 660 to 36', *The Telegraph*, 24 February 2015.
[266]'Rape crisis cell: Centre says no proposal from Delhi, West Bengal', *Indian Express*, 6 September 2017.
[267]'Ban wasn't needed. For truth to be known, filth has to come out, says Nirbhaya's father Badrinath Singh', *Economic Times*, 5 March 2015.

importantly, teach your sons to respect women.'[268]

This is the kind of wisdom our society sorely needs. A website called 'The Political Indian' lists statements by seven respectable, 'mainstream' politicians, many of whom are members of parliament, on women, and they make chilling viewing or reading. The attitudes they reveal about women's place in society and to rape itself are the real problem reflected in the documentary. The BBC shows a defence lawyer saying, 'We have the best culture. In our culture, there is no place for a woman.'[269] That encapsulates the challenge, and it can only be met by a sustained campaign of education, from childhood onwards, of our boys to make them into real men—men who respect women.

The controversy over the film contributed in making us aware of the mindsets in our midst, the attitudes and ways of thinking that enable and legitimize rape. It is sadly not such a long leap from condemning girls' clothes and believing a woman's place is in the kitchen and the bedroom, to assaulting them sexually and torturing them with iron rods. The fact that such opinions are widespread, and the dangers they pose, are what films like *India's Daughter* reveal starkly to us. Rape, after all, is not about sex, but about the violent assertion of power over women. How will denial, or burying our heads in the sand, prevent Indian rapists with such views from claiming new victims? Has the BJP government's 'see no evil' attitude eliminated evil from our country?

The government and political leaders need to speak of zero tolerance for rape and sexual assault, and extend their rhetoric to concrete action to make this a reality. Prime Minister Modi has spoken of his pride in India's 'matru shakti' and declared that 'women's empowerment is very crucial for our development'.[270] If the prime minister and the government set the example through their own actions and not just words, the nation will follow. The

[268]Ibid.
[269]'Delhi rapist says victim shouldn't have fought back', *BBC*, 3 March 2015.
[270]'Narendra Modi full speech today at GES 2017: PM says women empowerment vital for India's future', *Financial Express*, 28 November 2017.

BJP leaders are much given to empty slogans like 'Bharat Mata ki Jai'. They need instead to give Indian women a decent and safe country to live in: only this would honour Bharat Mata and truly ensure her 'jai'.

chapter nine

SECTION 377—THE SUPREME COURT SAVES THE DAY

Over seventy years after adopting one of the world's most liberal constitutions, India was able to finally celebrate the expunging of a nasty colonial-era provision in its penal code, Section 377, which criminalized 'whoever voluntarily has carnal intercourse against the order of nature with any man, woman, or animal.' The Supreme Court ruling of 6 September 2018[271] was not so much about sex as it was about freedom—the freedom of Indian citizens to enjoy the rights of equality, dignity and privacy in their personal lives, without government interference.

Section 377 made any sex apart from penile-vaginal intercourse between a man and a woman—any sex the authorities in power decide is 'against the order of nature'—to be illegal. The Supreme Court ruling made it clear that the personal sexual preferences of adults was indeed as nature made them, and that it was lawful for them to be themselves.

Obviously this was great news for the LGBTQ community, whose idea of what is 'natural' reflects their sexual orientation. But it also impacted married heterosexual couples since, theoretically, an act of oral sex between a husband and a wife is also illegal. And if you were not married to each other, of course, it was worse. If Bill Clinton had been an Indian, he might have survived impeachment after the Monica Lewinsky affair, but he'd have ended up in jail under Section 377.

Though not widely used—there were fewer than a thousand arrests a year under Section 377[272]—the law was a tool for the

---

[271]'"Gay sex is not a crime", says Supreme Court in historic judgement', *Times of India*, 6 September 2018.
[272]Shibu Thomas, '14% of those arrested under section 377 last year were minor', *Times of India*, 29 September 2016.

harassment, persecution, and blackmail of sexual minorities within India. Beyond forcing millions of gay men and women to live in fear and secrecy, Section 377 undermined HIV-prevention efforts and contributed to depression and suicides. A 2014 study by the World Bank revealed that India suffers a loss of between 0.1 per cent and 1.7 per cent of GDP because of such homophobia.

The Supreme Court's decision recognized that by giving the state the authority to control what Indian adults do, consensually, in their bedrooms, Section 377 violated the constitutional rights to dignity, privacy, and equality enshrined in Articles 14, 15, and 21, respectively. Its decision meant that all consensual sex between consenting adults, irrespective of gender and sexuality, was now legal. This did not imply, as ill-informed critics on social media were alleging, that in the process it legitimized forced sex, sex with animals, paedophilia or pederasty.

In 2013, the Supreme Court had overturned a liberal Delhi High Court ruling which struck down Section 377 in 2009.[273] The heavens did not fall after the High Court ruling; Indian society did not collapse. Yet bigots petitioned to reverse that decision, ultimately succeeding in turning back the clock for gay rights in India in 2013, when the Supreme Court overturned the High Court's decision.

Like many Indians, I found the Supreme Court's 2013 ruling antithetical to India's commitment to pluralism and democracy, which provides for the embrace of a multitude of identities, including those based on sexual orientation. So, in December 2015, I sought to introduce a Bill that would have amended Section 377 and decriminalized all consensual sex between adults, irrespective of their gender and sexuality, but a vocal section of homophobes from the ruling party defeated my attempt even to introduce my Bill in Parliament. The same thing happened when I tried again in March 2016. Sneering comments were made about my alleged

---

[273]J. Venkatesan, 'Supreme Court sets aside Delhi HC verdict decriminalising gay sex', *The Hindu*, 11 December 2013.

personal interest in the Bill, to which I responded that one does not need to be a cow to defend the rights of animals.

The BJP's vote was incongruous on several levels, but most glaringly in its rejection of millennia of Indian practice in favour of a British colonial law (which the British themselves have outgrown). The Indian ethos toward sexual difference has historically been liberal, with neither mythology nor history revealing the persecution or prosecution of sexual heterodoxy. In fact, the Hindu epics are dotted with characters like Shikhandi in the Mahabharata, who was born female and became male; many Hindus venerate the half-man, half-woman Ardhanarishvara; and temple sculptures across India depict homosexual acts. Yet the BJP, the party of Hindu chauvinism, chooses to ignore this Hindu tradition.

In its 2013 judgment that reaffirmed Section 377, the Supreme Court said that legislators, not judges, must decide its fate. Unfortunately, Parliament proved itself unequal to the task; the bigotry and homophobia in the ruling party and the indifference and prejudice in much of the Opposition, had rendered the institution a temple of hypocrisy on this issue. Indeed, legislative recourse for the injustice of Section 377 would not have been available as long as the BJP was in power.

When I gave up my unsuccessful attempts to remove or amend Section 377 through legislative channels, I expressed the hope that good sense would prevail in the judiciary and that this provision would eventually be struck down by the courts. After all, whereas change via legislation would require political courage—a quality sorely lacking in the current Indian government—the judiciary is not hampered by such considerations. Still, one of the judges hearing the case was moved to comment on the abdication of political responsibilities to the 'wisdom of the judiciary'.[274]

The landmark judgment of September 2018 confirmed that India's Supreme Court has an exemplary record of interpreting

---

[274]Pritam Pal Singh, 'Why do politicians sometimes hand power to court: Justice Chandrachud on Section 377', *Indian Express*, 9 September 2018.

statutes in a way that expands human rights in the country. The
hope remains that the Supreme Court will consistently uphold an
idea of India in which the law embodies constitutional values of
privacy, equality, dignity, and non-discrimination for all citizens.
During the case, the words of Justice Rohinton Fali Nariman, one
of the justices on the bench hearing the petitions against Section
377, were especially heartening: 'The whole object of fundamental
rights is to give the court power to strike down laws which a
majoritarian government, swung by votes, will not repeal. We
don't wait for majoritarian governments to repeal laws. If a law
is unconstitutional, it is the duty of the court to strike it down.'[275]

The alternative—allowing Indian law to continue to serve
as an iron cage for some of our people—would have directly
undermined the freedom of identity and expression that constitutes
the backbone of Indian democracy. What is more, it would have
left India out of step with much of the rest of the international
community, a country embarrassed before the world's other
democracies.

The Modi government deserves no credit for the abolition of
Section 377. It allowed its MPs to twice thwart my attempts to
raise the issue on the floor of the House; it showed absolutely no
inclination to address the issue itself; and when the Supreme Court
finally took up the question of the constitutionality of Section 377,
it failed to take a stand when invited to do so, pusillanimously
leaving the matter to the judiciary. Bigotry sadly runs deep in the
veins of the votaries of Moditva.

---

[275]'Court's duty to strike down law if it violates fundamental right: Supreme Court'
Hindu BusinessLine, 17 July 2018.

chapter ten

NO SEX, PLEASE, WE'RE INDIAN

In a manner worthy of a regressive society, where women are objectified, their sexuality constrained and the sex lives of their citizens policed, the BJP's leading lights, rather than sorting out the myriad problems afflicting the nation, have decided to occupy themselves by policing the moral standards of the country's youth. The monk-turned-politician, Yogi Adityanath, leads the pack. In 2017, 'anti-Romeo squads' in Yogi Adityanath's state, UP, questioned 21,37,520 people for being out with girls.[276] This has offered a sobering reminder of how far moral policing has gone in today's India. Worse, it turns out that of those questioned, 9,33,099 have been officially 'warned' and 1,706 FIRs issued against 3,003 persons.[277] All this happened in less than nine months after his inauguration; more recent figures are hard to come by.

So this is what a once-free society has been reduced to: multiple police squads, each consisting of a sub-inspector and two constables, patrolling Uttar Pradesh's university campuses, college yards, cinema theatres, parks and other public places, looking for 'Romeos'. The term seems to be loosely defined, entitling the cops to stop and question any young couple. While it may have once been intended to curb harassment by louts loafing in public places to 'eve-tease' unwary women, the sheer numbers reported confirm that the harassment is now coming mainly from the authorities and not from their targets.

The term 'anti-Romeo squad' is itself telling. It traces its origins to the 'Roadside Romeos' of my own youth—raffish fellows in drainpipe pants, wavy locks and rakish moustaches, usually unemployed, who lounged about whistling at, or singing snatches

---

[276]Karan Thapar, 'Love in the time of anti-Romeo squads', *Hindustan Times*, 10 February 2018.
[277]Ibid.

of Bollywood film songs to, passing women. They were usually ignored, and mostly harmless. Today's UP police have a far broader target: a Romeo is any young man aspiring to woo his own Juliet. Shakespeare's Romeo, after all, defied convention and evaded his disapproving parents to pursue his love for a woman from the wrong family. That is precisely what Chief Minister Adityanath does not want Romeo's twenty-first century imitators to do.

The anti-Romeo squads are merely the latest sign of the continuing assault on any cultural practice deemed to be insufficiently Hindu by the self-appointed guardians of Indian culture. As Valentine's Day approached, CM Adityanath's squads doubled their vigil. Until he became CM of the state, policing Valentine's Day lovers was a task undertaken by lumpen activists of assorted senas and dals; now, in a sort of reverse of privatization, it is a task that has been taken up by the BJP-run state. And what of the freelance anti-romance troublemakers? After years of attacking couples holding hands on 14 February, trashing stores selling Valentine's Day greeting cards and shouting slogans outside cafes with canoodling couples, Hindutva activists changed tactics. The Hindu Mahasabha announced that it would send out squads to catch any unmarried couples out for a tryst on Valentine's Day and promptly cart them off to a temple to be married. (And, if the Hindutvavadi MP and Godse admirer Sakshi Maharaj has his way, they will be lectured on the virtues of producing between four and ten children forthwith, in order to give his fantasies a voting majority.) The Shiv Sena conducted a 'lathi puja' a few days before Valentine's Day this year, declaring that the sticks would be useful to discipline couples engaged in public displays of affection.[278] They warned restaurants not to organize special events to commemorate the day, arguing that Valentine's Day promoted 'love jihad', or Hindu girls falling prey to the romantic attentions of Muslim men. Lucknow University issued a circular banning students from

---

[278]Moh Delshad, 'Shiv Sena conducts "lathi puja", says will use sticks against lovers on Valentine's Day', *Times of India*, 13 February 2018.

campus on the day, purportedly on account of Mahashivaratri, while also advising them not to celebrate Valentine's Day as it was 'Western culture'—and threatening disciplinary action if they were seen on campus.[279]

The police-uniform-clad face of intolerance might be amusing if it weren't for the fact that all involved are deadly serious. The nativists argue that Valentine's Day is an imported celebration, which it is (but so is Christmas, or Eid-ul-Nabi, or International Women's Day, for that matter, and they don't have the nerve to attack those). They also argue that it is un-Indian because it celebrates romantic love, and there they're completely wrong. Historians tell us that there was a well-established Hindu tradition of adoration for Kamadeva, the god of love, which was only abandoned after the Muslim invasions in medieval times. But then no one in the Hindu Mahasabha has any real idea of Hindu tradition—their idea of Indian values is not just primitive and narrow-minded, it is also profoundly anti-historical.

In fact, what young people today call 'PDA' or 'public display of affection' was widely prevalent in ancient India. As late as the eleventh century, Hindu sexual freedoms were commented upon by shocked travellers from the Muslim world. Today's young celebrants of Valentine's Day are actually upholding India's ancient pre-Muslim culture, albeit in a much milder form than is on display, for instance, in Khajuraho. In a sense, 14 February is their attempt at observing Kamadeva Divas. How ironic that they should incur the disapproval of the self-appointed custodians of Hindu culture!

But let's face it: this is less about teenagers dating than about yet another aspect of the ruling dispensation's political project of transforming secular India into their idea of a Hindu state. Tradition is sought to be upheld in the name of culture: traditionalism benefits those who want to uphold the social order,

---

[279]'Why Lucknow University has declared Valentine's Day a holiday', *Times of India*, 12 February 2018.

ensure discipline and conformity, and prevent radical change. Love affairs, which may after all cross caste or religious lines, are to be disapproved of for threatening this social order. Worse still, they reflect the autonomy of the individual and her right to choose, which is anathema to those who would prefer to make faceless cow-worshippers of us all.

All this is being done in the name of a notion of Indian culture whose assertion is based on a denial of India's real rather than imagined past. India's culture has always been a capacious one, expanding to include new and varied influences, from the Greek invasions (which taught Hindus to make temples to worship their gods) to the British (who created our censorious penal code). The central battle in contemporary Indian civilization is that between those who, to borrow from Walt Whitman, acknowledge that as a result of our own historical experience, we are vast, we contain multitudes, and those who have presumptuously taken it upon themselves to define—in increasingly narrower terms—what is 'truly' Indian.

The Constitution is the only bedrock of true Indianness. All who cherish the freedoms engraved in our Constitution must resist the pernicious menace of the anti-Romeo squads.

'Wherefore art thou?' Shakespeare's heroine asked. Wherefore are we? We must stand up for Juliet.

chapter eleven

THE ATTACK ON SCIENCE

Among the many ailments inflicted upon India by the BJP, the most cringe-inducing (in a rather long list) must be its leaders' boastfully ignorant atavism. Not only do they claim credit, on behalf of their ancient Hindu forebears, for every invention of the modern era; they assert their point of view with a certitude that is immune to ridicule, or even common sense.

For example, the chief minister of the tiny northeastern state of Tripura, Biplab Deb, cheerfully declared that Indians had invented the Internet some two millennia ago.[280] The proof of this particular hasty pudding, he insisted, lay in the fact that in the ancient epic the Mahabharata, one of the characters, Sanjaya, was able to provide a detailed narrative to the blind king Dhritarashtra of a battle that was taking place many miles away. This proved, Mr Deb averred, that in ancient times India had invented and used both satellite technology and the Internet.

The ridicule was swift in coming. American historian Audrey Truschke asked wickedly why Sanjaya had bothered to narrate the story when he could have used Siri instead—and why Lord Krishna hadn't streamed the Bhagavad Gita on Facebook Live. Another social media user hoped that ancient Indians had better Internet bandwidth than their spectrum-starved descendants enjoy today. One said the longevity of the Internet in India, no doubt, explained why the country had the largest number of trolls in the world. A third dubbed the ancient invention the 'Indra-Net', a reference to the Vedic god Indra, and explained that the GPS used those days must have been the God Positioning System.

The unfazed chief minister remained defiant. 'Narrow-minded

---

[280]'India had internet and satellites during Mahabharata, claims Tripura CM Biplab Deb', *Indian Express*, 18 April 2018.

people find it tough to believe this. They want to belittle their own nation and think highly of other countries. Believe the truth. Don't get confused and don't confuse others,' he told the press. [281] The political uses of his claim were never far from his mind; the BJP has been pressing ancient 'achievements' as an integral part of its hyper-nationalism. 'I feel proud that I am born in a country with such an advanced technology', the chief minister added.

India's Constitution calls for the promotion of 'scientific temper, humanism, and the spirit of inquiry and reform' amongst the populace. This is the state's responsibility, and also the constitutional duty of every citizen. India's first prime minister, Jawaharlal Nehru, was a passionate advocate of science who argued that while religion tends to close the mind and produce 'intolerance, credulity and superstition, emotionalism and irrationalism', and 'a temper of a dependent, unfree person', a scientific temper 'is the temper of a free man', and therefore indispensable in free India.[282]

It seems, however, that such ideas are no longer fashionable in an India ruled by the BJP. Its leaders and acolytes are busy attempting to keep the theory of evolution out of school curricula, and insisting that the ancients had already discovered or invented every scientific accomplishment in the Vedic age, including jet aircraft (pushpak viman) and atomic weaponry. The underlying message is that ancient India had all the answers, and that traditional and indigenous practices and ways of life are vastly better than imported modern scientific ideas.

The reverence for the past that is integral to the ruling ideology is also reflective of a fear of rejecting the past, since the promotion of a faith-based communal identity is central to the Hindutva project, and faith is seen as emerging from the timeless wisdom of the past. Traditionalism benefits those who want to uphold the social order, ensure discipline and conformity, and prevent

[281]'Tripura CM Biplab Deb says narrow-minded people won't believe internet existed since Mahabharata era', *Indian Express*, 18 April 2018.
[282]Jawaharlal Nehru, *The Discovery of India*, New Delhi: Penguin Books India, 2004.

radical change. Science and rationality threaten such conformism.

This is why the ruling dispensation's political project of transforming secular India into a Hindu state requires the supremacy of religion over science, and the assimilation of science into the Hindutva project as merely something ancient India had had all along. Religion is no longer just a question of your personal beliefs, a form of stretching out your hands to the divine; it is part of the assertion of a politics of identity built around faith. This requires an assault on science, since science challenges the established verities as religion does not.

Another BJP stalwart, Rajasthan's education minister, Vasudev Devnani, dealt science another body blow by claiming that the cow was the only animal that inhaled and exhaled oxygen.[283] As we have seen, the veneration of the cow is something of an obsession for the BJP, whose followers have assaulted human beings in the name of cow protection, but this was a step too far even for many of its sympathizers among the educated public.

No greater proof of the BJP's religion-trumps-science agenda can be found than the prime minister himself. Narendra Modi likes to be portrayed as a technology-friendly twenty-first-century leader, but as I have mentioned earlier in this book, Mr Modi startled the world at the inauguration of a Mumbai hospital with the claim that the elephant-headed Hindu god Ganesh was proof of ancient India's knowledge of plastic surgery.

This was not the prime minister's only offence. Before heading off for the Paris climate change negotiations, Mr Modi told schoolchildren on Teachers' Day in 2014 that climate change was a myth because it was actually human beings whose capacity to cope with heat and cold that had changed, rather than the environment. Global warming, he explained on national television, 'is just a state of mind'. What made it worse was that this came as an answer to a schoolchild's question about climate change. 'That's because as you grow older you are less able to withstand

---

[283]'The myth and reality of India's heritage', *Economic Times*, 21 April 2018.

heat and cold. The climate isn't changing,' he said, 'we are.'[284]

The disease is catching. In May 2017, Justice Mahesh Chandra Sharma of the Rajasthan High Court, reportedly a science graduate himself, told a television channel that India's national bird, the peacock, 'is a lifelong celibate' who 'does not indulge in sex' but impregnates the peahen by shedding a tear. He cited Lord Krishna's use of a peacock feather as proof of its celibacy.[285] The idea of a peacock reproducing through tears may seem laughable, but there is nothing lachrymose about the ruling dispensation's dominant Hindutva ideology, which has helped propagate an astonishing amount of pseudoscience across the country. Narendra Modi associates like the yoga teacher and Ayurveda entrepreneur Baba Ramdev are regular offenders. Ramdev pronounces his pseudo-spiritual wisdom to the world, seeking, for instance, to sell medicines to 'cure homosexuality'.[286]

There's more in a similar vein. Junior education minister Satyapal Singh said that Darwin's theory of evolution was 'unscientific'—on the grounds that 'no one has ever seen an ape turn into a man'.[287] This is a minister of state responsible for higher education in the Government of India. More worryingly, Mr Singh is an educated man (he is a Chemistry graduate) as are most of the others whose examples I've cited. But then of course, we must understand that Mr Singh's statement had very little to do with the quality of the science education he received, and more to do with the ruling party's ideology.

To reiterate the point I made earlier in this chapter, the ruling dispensation's political project of transforming secular India into a Hindu state requires the supremacy of religion over science.

---

[284]Suzanne Goldenberg, 'Is Narendra Modi a climate sceptic?', *The Guardian*, 9 September 2014.
[285]'"Peacocks don't have sex": Raj HC judge's comment gets Twitterati chirping', *Indian Express*, 1 June 2017.
[286]Poonam Agarwal and Abhirup Dam, 'Curing homosexuality, Baba Ramdev way: *The Quint's* sting operation', *The Quint*, 1 February 2017.
[287]PTI, 'Darwin theory wrong; no one has seen ape turning into man, says MoS Satyapal Singh', *The Hindu*, 20 January 2018.

When an education minister questions Darwin or another minister asserts the miraculous powers of the cow, he is not merely offering a choice between a scientific theory and a faith-based one, he is reminding the public of their allegiance to a total world view. That world view embraces a larger political project that prescribes a set of beliefs and behaviours incompatible with science, scepticism and enquiry.

Science and rationality threaten such conformism, because they encourage scepticism, free enquiry, and testing of the traditional perspectives that the BJP is so eager to entrench. That is why, as the BJP attempts to transform secular India into a Hindu state, it must weaken the role of science.

It is difficult to overstate the tragedy that this trend represents. The obscurantist and atavistic state that Narendra Modi's BJP wants to create would look nothing like the one that made India the scientific superpower of the ancient age. It is enough to make one shed a tear. One can only hope that there are no peahens around.

chapter twelve

THE TAJ BY ANY OTHER NAME

In a country where in recent times toxic politics has led to everything—from festival firecrackers to animal husbandry (in this case, the care and protection of cows)—taking on a 'communal' religious colouring, it shouldn't be too much of a surprise that its most famous monument hasn't been exempt.

The Taj Mahal is India's most magnificent piece of architecture. Built nearly four centuries ago by the Mughal Emperor Shah Jahan as a mausoleum for his beloved wife, who had borne him thirteen children and died in the process of producing the fourteenth, it attracts tens of millions of tourists and is by far the country's most-photographed building. The exquisite marble monument to love was hailed by India's only Nobel Prize-winning writer, Rabindranath Tagore, as 'a teardrop on the cheek of Time'.

But this time the Taj has other reasons for tears. Its gleaming white surface is yellowing as a result of rampant air pollution from factories and cottage industries around it. Repairs are needed so frequently that scaffolding often obscures its famous minarets. There has been a 35 per cent drop in foreign tourists from the 743,000 who visited there in 2012 to the 480,000 tourists who came in 2015.[288] The crowded and grimy town of Agra, which hosts the Taj, puts visitors off: American basketball player Kevin Durant sparked a row with his graphic descriptions of the awful conditions around the Taj Mahal after a visit there in 2017.

And worst of all, the ruling party in Uttar Pradesh, Prime Minister Narendra Modi's BJP, has decided that far from being proud of its most famous edifice, it wants as little to do with it as possible.

---

[288]Annie Gowen, 'Is India neglecting the Taj Mahal because it was built by Muslims?', *Washington Post*, 3 October 2017.

Chief Minister Yogi Adityanath began the controversy by deploring that his government used to give models of the Taj as gifts to visiting foreign dignitaries. Declaring that the monument did not 'reflect Indian culture', Yogi Adityanath announced the government would be handing out copies of the Hindu holy book, the Bhagavad Gita, instead.[289]

It got worse. The Uttar Pradesh Tourism Department issued a brochure listing the state's principal attractions—and omitted the Taj Mahal altogether.[290] The state's (and the country's) biggest tourism draw was denied any cultural heritage funding in the allotments for the 2017–18 fiscal year.[291]

Domestic tourists have also decreased significantly. Indian tourists reportedly prefer the attractions of the holy city of Varanasi in the same state, Uttar Pradesh. This mirrors and reinforces the monument's neglect by the state government in favour of Hindu religious tourism.

But the objection to the Taj is more basic. One extremist BJP legislator, Sangeet Som, labelled the tomb 'a blot' on the fair name of his state, a relic that had been 'built by traitors'. The Taj Mahal 'should have no place in Indian history,' he said, demanding that India's history be 'changed' to remove it.[292]

The ruling party's campaign against the Taj Mahal might seem bizarre; after all, why would anyone undermine a universally admired architectural marvel that is such a revenue generator? But those familiar with the tortured prejudices of the ruling BJP would be less surprised. The attacks on the Taj are part of their politics of hate towards anything associated with the history of the centuries of Muslim rule in India.

---

[289]'Taj Mahal doesn't reflect Indian culture: Yogi Adityanath', *Indian Express*, 16 June 2017.

[290]Omar Rashid, 'Taj Mahal missing in U.P. tourism booklet', *The Hindu*, 2 October 2017.

[291]'Taj Mahal left out of UP budget heritage plan, Adityanath govt draws ire', *Hindustan Times*, 13 July 2017.

[292]'Taj Mahal, built by traitors, a blot on Indian culture, says Sangeet Som: supports UP govt move to remove it from tourism booklet', *FirstPost*, 16 October 2017.

That this is an unduly simplistic black-and-white rendition
of a complex history, in which there was far more assimilation
and coexistence than religious conflict, is irrelevant to Hindu
chauvinists who constitute the bulk of the BJP's support base. To
them, the Taj is an enduring symbol not of love, but of conquest
and humiliation.

Resentment that a monument built by a Muslim emperor
is Hindu-majority India's most recognizable monument was, in
the past, an obsession of the extreme right-wing fringe. But the
fringe is now in power in Uttar Pradesh and its enablers rule the
roost in Delhi.

Before becoming chief minister in a surprise appointment by
his party, Yogi Adityanath was best known for his incendiary
anti-Muslim speeches, laden with toxic rhetoric, and for leading a
volunteer squad of hoodlums who specialized in attacking Muslim
targets.[293] He spent eleven days in jail in 2007 for fomenting
religious tension through hate speech, earned notoriety by calling
India's most beloved film star, Shah Rukh Khan, a terrorist, and
urged his party's government in New Delhi to emulate Donald
Trump's travel ban on Muslims.[294]

But even he has been obliged by public and political opinion
to surrender to national outrage over the latest controversy. After
stoking it in the first place, the chief minister was forced to visit
Agra officially to assure an anxious public that his government
was committed to protecting the Taj. 'What is important,' he
conceded grudgingly, 'is that it was built by the blood and sweat
of India's farmers and labourers.'

This acknowledgement is only partly reassuring. It opens
the door to another divisive fringe view of the Taj, that of the
chauvinist historian, P. N. Oak, who argued that the monument

---

[293]Hugh Tomlinson, 'Hindu who urged death to Muslims gets top state job', *The
Times*, 21 March 2017; Ajit Sahai, 'The UP Government's Colossal Cover-Up
Attempt to Protect Adityanath', *The Wire*, 27 July 2017.
[294]Michael Safi, 'Hardline Hindu nationalists campaign against Taj Mahal', *The
Guardian*, 30 October 2017.

was originally a Shiva temple named 'Tejo Mahalaya'.[295] Some misguided Hindutva elements have already been caught trying to perform a Shiva puja in the mausoleum.[296] The RSS, the parent body of the 'Sangh Parivar' of organizations that includes the BJP, has called for Muslims to be prohibited from praying there as well.[297]

To many of us, in these circumstances, the BJP's new-found love for the Taj might be as alarming as its well-expressed hate for it.

The Taj Mahal is merely the latest victim of a political campaign over Indian history that, as we have seen, seeks to reinvent the idea of India itself. This 'cultural nationalism' by the Hindu right, stoking long-buried resentments and promoting hatred for the Muslim minority, is not just deeply divisive; it undermines the country's soft power in the world and fragments its political and social discourse at home.

The past should not be a blunt instrument to score petty political points in the present. The BJP is yet to learn that one cannot avenge oneself upon history: history is its own revenge.

---

[295]Aditya Dev, 'Claims to Taj, based on nothing at all', *Times of India*, 9 December 2014.
[296]Hemendra Chaturvedi, 'Hindu youths chant Shiva chalisa on Taj Mahal premises', *Hindustan Times*, 23 October 2017.
[297]Anand Patel, 'Ban namaz at Taj Mahal or allow Shiva prayers too, demands RSS history wing', *India Today*, 27 October 2017.

chapter thirteen

TRIAL OF AND BY THE MEDIA

I

One of the hallmarks of a vibrant, thriving democracy is a free and healthy press. The state of our media is yet another indicator of the poor job Prime Minister Narendra Modi and his government are doing. As already mentioned, in this year's World Press Freedom Index Report by the organization Reporters Sans Frontières (Reporters Without Borders or RSF), India is ranked 138th out of 180 countries, a disgraceful score. The reasons for the poor ranking are clearly visible—the murder and coercion of journalists, fake news, hate speech and the intimidation of editors and owners.

In its 2018 report, RSF said that among the reasons for India's poor score were the following—'At least three of the journalists murdered in 2017 were targeted in connection with their work. They included the newspaper editor Gauri Lankesh, who had been the target of a hate campaign on social networks... In India hate speech targeting journalists is shared and amplified on social networks, often by troll armies in Prime Minister Narendra Modi's pay.' The organization's secretary-general, Christophe Deloire, also said: 'Political leaders who fuel loathing for reporters bear heavy responsibilities because they undermine the concept of public debate based on facts instead of propaganda. To dispute the legitimacy of journalism today is to play with extremely dangerous political fire.'[298]

As Narendra Modi's government took power at a time of great change in the media, in this chapter I intend to take a look

---

[298]'Media-bashing by politicians a threat to democracies, RSF warns', Reuters, 25 April 2018.

at both the organic change that has taken place, as well as the toxic influence the BJP and its army of trolls have brought to bear on various forms of media.

Let's start where everyone seems to end up these days, social media. While there are invaluable benefits to the reach and transformative power of social media, unfortunately, in recent times, one can't but be alarmed by its growing toxicity. The vilification to which Indian Foreign Minister Sushma Swaraj was recently subjected by members and supporters of her own party was a stark indication of the darker side of India's social media space.

Ms Swaraj, who has developed something of a reputation for responding to citizens' appeals for her ministry's services on Twitter, was viciously attacked for the punitive transfer of a passport official who had made bigoted remarks to an inter-faith couple when they applied for a passport. Her party members, who through their unseemly protest showed they shared the anti-Muslim bigotry the official reportedly expressed, blamed her for his administrative punishment (a decision taken when she was out of the country). They expressed their rage in a flood of excoriating tweets, including referring to her disparagingly as 'begum' (a Muslim honorific) and urging her husband to beat her for getting out of line.[299]

In the last decade, the BJP has developed a powerful band of cyber goons to propagate its message of Hindu chauvinism, contempt for minorities and hyper-nationalism, coupled with a capacity for Rottweiler-like attacks on political opponents. The social media 'troll' has become a vital foot soldier in the party's political campaigns.

This extremism began at a time when the party was in the Opposition and felt its point of view was marginalized in the mainstream national media, but it has developed into a well-organized machine with a formidable presence on Twitter, Facebook, and WhatsApp.

Cyber cells of well-paid 'trolls' were set up in India and

---

[299]Apoorvanand, 'For whom the bells troll', *Indian Express*, 10 July 2018.

abroad to flood the social media space at all hours, taking on 'sickulars' [secularists], 'libtards' [liberal 'bastards' or 'retards'], 'Khangressis' (an allusion to the allegedly pro-Muslim leanings of the Congress Party) and responding ferociously to any statement or action deemed inimical to the BJP's interests. 'The reward for these non-official soldiers,' Santosh Desai observed, 'is a dizzying rise from obscurity and in some cases, the promise of official recognition and rewards.'[300] Several are 'followed' by the prime minister himself, a fact they advertise with pride.[301]

A 2016 exposé, *I Am A Troll: Inside the Secret World of the BJP's Digital Army*, by Swati Chaturvedi,[302] bared the details of the well-oiled and scurrilous machinery that has been set in motion. A virtual army of paid political pawns operates multiple accounts geared to attacking anyone deemed inimical to the BJP's political interests or hostile to its Hindu-chauvinist, anti-Muslim ideology.[303] The BJP's cyber hit squads are indeed so pervasive that it is difficult to express a liberal opinion on Indian social media without being assailed by a flood of insults and abuse.[304]

As a regular victim myself, I have experienced the daily mortification of opening my timeline to be assaulted by a flood of vile negativity. But for Ms Swaraj, a leading member of the BJP herself, it was a new experience to be trolled by her own side. She rashly conducted a Twitter poll to seek her followers' support against the textual harassment; a startling 43 per cent

[300]Santosh Desai, *Times of India*, 3 September 2018, *op.cit.*
[301] 'PM Modi follows a number of the chief offenders on Twitter, the BJP social media cell has waged battles against prominent actors for voicing concern against intolerance, student leaders from opposition parties have been thrown into jail because of doctored videos, verified accounts within the government have tweeted communal and hate speeches, and prominent ministers have begun to use some of this offensive language in public', from Swati Chaturvedi, *I Am A Troll: Inside the Secret World of the BJP's Digital Army*, New Delhi: Juggernaut Books, 2016, p. 140.
[302]Ibid.
[303]Nehal Ahmed, 'Anti-Muslim bigotry has been normalized under PM Modi', *Al Jazeera*, 12 April 2018; 'Communalism remains cornerstone of party's ideology', *Business Standard*, 24 February 2018.
[304]Swati Chaturvedi, 'General Modi and his Troll Army', *The Wire*, 8 September 2017.

supported the trolls instead.[305]

Ms Swaraj had merely discovered what the rest of us had long known: that her party has poisoned the social media well with posts of such toxicity that entering the social media space in India has become like stepping into a mud-wrestling pit. As Dr Frankenstein discovered, you can create a monster, but you can't always control what it does.

Abuse of women journalists and political activists is particularly widespread; not only are their morals called into question and aspersions cast on their looks and sexual conduct, but rape threats are routine. A recent threat on Twitter by a BJP activist to rape the ten-year old daughter of a Congress party spokeswoman led to his arrest.[306] Many hope that this will discourage future threats from similar social media misogynists.

But it may be too much to hope that the tide has turned. The Internet is particularly fertile ground for abusive behaviour because of the anonymity it often affords and the safe distance the perpetrators keep from their targets. This, coupled with the sense of righteousness that pervades all true believers in a political cause, seems to empower social media users to say anything they like.

It's not just sensibilities they disregard; it's also facts. The 'fake news' phenomenon has taken over the social media world; falsehoods are routinely asserted without the most elementary fact-checking. Sadly this has cost lives, as rumours forwarded on social media, especially on WhatsApp, have led to mob lynchings of innocent people wrongly suspected to be child-kidnappers, cow-slaughterers or worse. Tens of thousands of Indians from the northeast fled their homes and jobs in major Indian cities after fake social media posts used pictures of victims of a Myanmar cyclone to claim they were Muslims butchered in the northeast; Muslim activists, in revenge, started threatening Northeasterners

---

[305]'On Sushma Swaraj's Twitter poll, 43 per cent approves trolling', *Indian Express*, 1 July 2018.
[306]'BJP's "accounting assistant" arrested over threat to Priyanka Chaturvedi', *National Herald*, 5 July 2018.

elsewhere in India.[307] Things have reached such a state that even
Amit Shah has had to publicly ask supporters to avoid making
the 'mistake' of posting fake news on social media.[308]

It is in the nature of social media, which thrives on sensationalism
and unverified information, that falsehoods go viral faster than
sanity can be restored by disseminating the truth. But attempts
to regulate it should be resisted, because regulating content on
the Internet opens the door to censorship of free expression on
other media. There is no easy solution to the conundrum. But it
took a BJP leader to be trolled for the ruling party to realize the
horrors it has unleashed on the rest of us.

II

Social media constitutes the relatively new media frontier but
massive change has overtaken the rest of the industry, not always
for the better. I am, in a sense, a child of the Indian newspaper. My
late father, Chandran Tharoor, started in the newspaper business
when barely out of college, representing a pair of Indian papers in
post-war London, and spent his working life as a senior advertising
executive for some of our country's better-known mastheads. His
world fascinated me. My childhood in the 1960s and early 1970s
was replete with stories of editorial meetings and battles between
the editorial and the advertisement departments, for my father
injected newspaper ink into my veins at a young age. I literally
grew up with newspapers: from about six or seven years of age,
I can remember sitting with my father at 6.30 every morning
drinking chai and reading multiple newspapers, a daily ritual that
gave me an early and abiding passion for the Indian press.

Those were more innocent times, when no one expected to
find sex scandals in the daily news, and editors always knew far
more than they shared with their readers. But those were also days
when the papers were filled with dull accounts of worthy events,

---

[307]'India's north-east: A neglected crisis', *The Economist*, 25 August 2012.
[308]'Avoid posting "fake" items on social media, BJP chief Amit Shah to party
workers', *DNA*, 21 June 2018.

and the front pages regurgitated ministers' speeches with little context, explanation or analysis. There was no real engagement with the substance of what politics means to the Indian people. Investigative journalism was unknown and revelations about errant conduct on the part of our elected officials would only appear if they had first been unearthed by the government.

Obviously newspapers have come a very long way since the days in which I grew up with them. Technology is the most obvious change: today, almost everything is done on computers. No one knows what compositors are any more. Journalists do their own proofreading. Presentation and layout have also dramatically improved. With colour, with newspapers so attractively designed and presented, with lifestyle supplements and multiple sections, anyone who remembers those days knows we are looking at a different product being sold in a different environment.

The economics have also changed: newsprint is more affordable. A twelve-page paper, the norm in those distant days, would be considered a joke; multiple sections are now de rigeur. Circulations have shot up along with literacy and disposable incomes, so that the *Times of India* today can call itself the world's most widely-read English-language broadsheet, and Hindi newspapers boast readership numbers that would exceed the wildest fantasies of any editor in the world outside Japan. This is happening when newspapers in the developed West are falling by the wayside, unable to resist the challenge of the Internet. Our *Times* is read by some 13.4 million people daily, while the best-selling American paper, *USA Today*, has 2.5 million readers. According to the Indian Readership Survey (IRS) 2017, *Dainik Jagran*, in Hindi, had 70.37 million readers.

India now has the world's largest number of paid newspapers, and the number continues to grow, from 5,767 in 2013 to 7,871 in 2015.[309] (Over those same two years, fifty newspapers ceased publication in the US, which has less than a quarter of India's

---

[309]Rishi Iyengar, 'Newspapers are thriving in this country', *CNN*, 11 May 2017.

print papers). According to the 2017 IRS, the total newspaper readership in India shot up by 110 million, an impressive 39 per cent, over three years. Newspaper readership in rural India, which was 143 million according to a 2014 survey, had increased to 214 million by 2017.[310]

This increase in newspaper readership can be attributed to our country's rising literacy rate, which has climbed to 74 per cent, owing largely to the 'cow belt' of the northern states—the Hindi-speaking heartland. In the 1950s and 60s, when Hindi speakers were overwhelmingly less literate than those who read in English, Malayalam, and Bengali, Hindi newspapers had low circulations. Today, Hindi newspapers are on top and experienced the fastest growth—from 121 million readers in 2016 to 176 million readers in 2017—a 45 per cent surge in readership.

Along with this growth have come other, more substantive, changes, both good and bad. On the positive side, our newspapers are more readable, better edited, better laid out and usually better written than they were. Investigative stories are frequent and occasionally expose wrongdoing before any official institution does so. The role of newspapers in rousing the social conscience of the Indian public about apparent miscarriages of justice, most notably in the Jessica Lall, Ruchika Girhotra and 'Nirbhaya' cases, has been remarkable. Equally, their boosting of Narendra Modi's image has served the prime minister well.

Printed newspapers are a more reliable source of news than the Internet in a country where access cannot be guaranteed all the time, owing to still-patchy electricity supplies and weak broadband connectivity. So advertisers in India have remained loyal to the appeal of newspaper ink over the flickering cursor, and India's newspapers are in no danger of becoming financially unviable. There are still 280 million people yet to become literate.[311] And

---

[310]Dibyajyoti Sarma, '39% of Indians read newspapers: IRS 2017 Report', *PrintWeek*, 19 January 2018.
[311]'India's illiterate population largest in the world, says UNESCO report', *The Hindu*, 30 January 2014.

when they get there, they will want their own newspapers, too.

But still our newspapers also seem conscious that they have to compete in a tight media environment, where it is not they, but TV and social media that set the pace. They know that every morning they must reach readers who have watched TV and read WhatsApp messages the previous day. So newspapers too feel the need to 'break' news in order to be read, to outdo their TV and social media competitors. Most are led by the nose by TV's perennial ratings war, and seek to reach TV-exposed readers each day with a banner headline that stimulates prurience or outrage rather than increases awareness.

III

TV news has far too many channels competing 24/7 for the same set of eyeballs. Once dominated by government programming, India's visual media landscape is now brimming with numerous private offerings, with over a hundred 24/7 TV news channels in multiple languages—the medium-sized state of Kerala alone has thirteen all-news channels in Malayalam. TV news has long since given up any pretence of providing a public service, with the 'breaking news' story privileging sensation over substance. Indeed, Indian TV epitomizes that old crack about why television is called a 'medium'—because it is neither rare nor well done. The result of this evolution of TV, print and online media is that most of our media, in their rush to air the story, have fallen prey to the inevitable rush to judgement: they have too often become a willing accomplice of the motivated leak and the malicious allegation, which journalists today have neither the time nor the inclination to check or verify.

The damage is done in a blaze of lurid headlines—and rectification, if it comes at all, comes too feebly and too late to undo the irreparable damage to innocent people's reputations.

After three-and-a-half years of facing this myself, my patience finally snapped, and I have sued the most lurid of the TV news channels for defamation. But justice in our country moves at a

stately pace far removed from the breathless breaking news speed
of television, and one's character can be assassinated before a
judge has even scheduled a date for the next hearing of a case
aiming to prevent such character assassination.

We have had countless spectacles of unnaturally long drawn-
out media trials, fuelled by motivated leaks, with discussion shows
on the voyeuristic Indian TV channels debating accusations and
imputations with zero evidence or even elementary research behind
any of the statements aired. In the process justice itself is ill-
served; not only is the climate prejudiced for a fair trial, but even
judges consume media, and they are human—they are bound to be
influenced by what they have seen, heard and read in the news.

And the standards and filters for what gets into the news
have weakened or disappeared in the chronic quest for sensation.
Manipulated and malicious claims are reported uncritically,
without editors asking even the most basic questions about their
plausibility. One egregious BJP politician has spent years saying
the most outrageous things about matters he has absolutely no
clue about, and his absurd exaggerations are always reported
uncritically by a complicit media. No one even asks him the
elementary question, 'How do you know what you claim to know?'
I once asked a journalist friend about this, and she replied, abashed,
'Well, he always makes good copy.' So that's all it takes today—
make things up and assert them with confidence, and the press
will report you because it's good copy. It's hardly surprising that
trust in the media is eroding.

This should be a matter of serious concern to all right-thinking
Indians, because free media are the lifeblood of our democracy.
Media and journalism provide the necessary information that
enables a free citizenry to make the choices of who governs them
and how, and ensures that those who govern remain accountable
to those who put them there. Government needs a free and
professional media to keep it honest and efficient, to serve as
both mirror and scalpel; if instead we have a blunt axe, then
society is not well served.

IV

With rapidly changing technology, journalists now work across a multitude of news distribution platforms. While many venerable publications now have a multi-media existence—the *Times of India*, for instance, has three print newspapers, two television channels and multiple Internet sites as well as social media accounts—others are digital-only, including new entrants to the news business such as *The Quint*, *The Wire* and *Scroll.in*. Of course, print, radio and television also continue to flourish and require reporting. As a result, these days, a journalist's skill-set is not limited to just one medium, and constantly needs to be enhanced to keep pace with the new ways of news production and distribution.

Social media platforms, such as Facebook, Twitter and WhatsApp, are increasingly becoming the younger generation's first port of call for news coverage. With over 200 million users for WhatsApp, 241 million Facebook users and close to 25 million active Twitter users in India,[312] it is no surprise that a number of the leading news agencies across the country now push content to their audiences through these channels. The media is increasingly sourcing news stories directly from the public domain, from people's Twitter feeds and Facebook posts. (Mr Modi's BJP too has discovered the benefits of getting his messaging through to the Indian public on these platforms, which are increasingly flooded by memes and jokes boosting the prime minister and denigrating his opponents—though his critics have now also woken up to the same possibilities.)

Today's smartphones have made everybody a potential journalist. We are all familiar with the major stories, usually of assault and violence, which were filmed on a personal mobile phone and then made it onto our television screens. Other such snippets bombard us on WhatsApp. If every citizen is a source of news input in this way, the media business itself has changed

---

[312]'No, Facebook user base in India does not beat the US; still at number two', *Indian Express*, 14 July 2017.

beyond recognition.

This has wider consequences, raising new ethical challenges in journalism. How can we get at the truth when flooded by unverified information, whether through a phone call, a tweet or even a message on Facebook or WhatsApp? How do we preserve journalistic objectivity, which is cherished all the more in India because so few media outlets possess it?

The pressure of keeping up with the relentless 24/7 breaking news cycle, and now the rise of social media, prompts mainstream journalists to publish without the traditional recourse to fact-checking. Indian media has found it increasingly difficult to maintain a clear distinction between opinion and reporting, commentary and speculation, unverified rumour and certified fact—categories too often blurred in news coverage today.

Journalists must function as independents, and present news in an objective fashion. However, their salaries are paid by the owners, whose agenda must necessarily prevail. And it's not just the commercial agenda: more than a third of news channels in India are owned by politicians or political affiliates, who use their channels to pander to the political interests or ideology of the owner.[313] The new Republic channel, which claims to now be Number 1 in English-language prime-time television news, trumpets its muck-raking credentials but has never taken on a single misdeed of the ruling BJP, whether the Vyapam scandal or the medical college bribery scam revealed in Kerala. If that's your only source of news, you would never know these scandals have even occurred.

Couple this with the fact that we are currently ruled by a government that has been accused of intimidating the media by, among others, RSF, the organization with which I began this chapter, and you can understand India's embarrassingly poor performance in the World Press Freedom Index. However, there

---

[313]Vanita Kohli-Khandekar, 'When politicians own the media', *Business Standard*, 24 January 2013.

is often no need for overt censorship, when a discreet phone call can serve as a word to the wise. Much of the mainstream media is owned by investors with other business interests, that make them vulnerable to government pressure, whether in the way of inducements or threats relating to their other ventures. Curbing their media outlets or dismissing journalists and editors is a small price to pay for their businesses not getting on the wrong side of a strong-willed government.

V

What can be done to make our media and the environment it operates in better? A lot of the problems stem from a lack of a proper regulatory authority in the press. The Press Council of India, a statutory body with quasi-judicial powers, lacks any actual punitive power, rendering it a toothless watchdog. The Broadcast Standards Authority is no less ineffective.

The free press is both the mortar that binds together the bricks of our country's freedom, and the open window embedded in those bricks. No Indian democrat would call for censorship, or for controls on the free press: what we want is not less journalism, but better journalism. But before I get to suggesting how we might get there I'd like to mull briefly over a suggestion made by one of Narendra Modi's appointees to the Information & Broadcasting Ministry, the ministry that oversees our media and runs the state-owned media organs, among them Doordarshan and All India Radio (AIR).

Speaking on television, Prakash Javadekar said that both 'philosophically and ideologically' he believed his ministry ought not to exist, adding for good measure that I&B 'has no place in a democracy', echoing what his one-time predecessor, L. K. Advani, had said in 1977.[314]

Mr Javadekar added, in the same interview, that he would

---

[314]'Ideologically, I favour abolition of I & B Ministry: Prakash Javadekar', *Economic Times*, 7 June 2014.

consider appointing a professional editor-in-chief for Doordarshan and AIR with full freedom to cover the news as he or she thinks fit. He promised not to interfere in appointments, transfers and promotions in Prasar Bharati, which he said for good measure he wanted to make accountable to Parliament and not 'only' to himself. If he had followed through on those intentions, he could certainly have taken a meaningful step towards the withering away of his own ministry. But when he left the job a year later, he had not even begun such a process. His successors have ensured that the I&B Ministry remains firmly under the control of government.

So what does I&B do that would no longer be done if it ceased to exist?

It would no longer run the government's PR arm, the Directorate of Audio-Visual Publicity (DAVP); presumably the government would have to decide whether it needed a PR arm at all, or whether it would simply hand out contracts to private sector PR agencies when it needed paid publicity. (This could be done through the e-tendering route trumpeted by the Modi government in the president's address in 2014.)

It would also stop running Doordarshan and All India Radio (once dubbed All-Indira Radio by the critics of that formidable prime minister in the early 1970s), leaving that task to an autonomous, public-sector Prasar Bharati; even Mr Modi's most passionate acolytes have not taken his faith in minimal government to imply that our venerable public service broadcasters would be privatized. Some BJP ideologues want the Modi government to deregulate news and public affairs on radio, which would give us the same cacophony on FM that we currently get on TV. But the public-service duties of a government-funded broadcaster— notably relaying information in the border states and getting out authoritative and authentic official messages in times of national emergency—would be lost if Prasar Bharati were privatized.

There's a case, therefore, for keeping Doordarshan and AIR in the public sector, but not necessarily for preserving I&B to oversee them. If I&B were abolished, an autonomous Prasar Bharati would no longer have a political boss to be accountable to—but as long as it is even partly funded by taxpayers, it needs political oversight. The solution is to make it answerable to a committee of Parliament, which is also the body that votes its funding.

The I&B Ministry also plays a key role in the world of Indian cinema. It appoints and runs the Film Censor Board, of which more in the next chapter, conducts national and international film festivals, and funds and runs such worthy institutions as the National Film Development Corporation, the Film Finance Corporation, the Film and Television Institute of India and the National Film Archives. These are all things that need to be done, but there is absolutely no reason why, in the twenty-first century, they must be done by the government. Why not oblige the film industry to do the job itself, by creating a Cinema Corporation of India or a National Motion Picture Association as in the US, with regional versions for each language in which films are made in our country? The government could transfer its assets to these bodies in return for equity, and ask the industry to finance itself thereafter. Can the film industry be trusted to censor itself responsibly? Other democracies have proved that it can, because the market is often a more sensitive barometer of public tastes and of what society will tolerate than a bureaucrat or politician might be. One area where the industry might be less willing to do what the government has been doing is to finance and encourage the making of experimental or innovative films with limited commercial appeal. It could either be obliged to do so by law, or these functions—and these alone—could be retained by the government under the rubric of the Ministry of Culture.

One task we haven't discussed is that of the I&B minister himself, as the principal spokesperson of the government and boss of the Press Information Bureau, which diligently puts out press releases daily about whatever the government is up to (or says it is up to). The government obviously needs a spokesperson, but this role could be performed by a minister in the PMO instead, with the PIB assigned to his or her supervision. Or if that makes the PMO too heavy, park the task in the cabinet secretariat, which after all has the responsibility for coordinating the work of all ministries, and which could easily house the government spokesperson too.

In other words, I&B could indeed be abolished, with other ways of ensuring that its essential functions are still performed inside or outside the government.

VI

But to get back to the ways in which the media in our country can be better, here's a checklist:

First, we must engender a culture of fact-verification and accuracy that the industry currently appears to lack. Journalists should not feel pressed by their employers to 'break the news', but empowered to hold stories until they are sure their facts and accusations are accurate. The rush to judgement on the basis of partial information must stop.

Second, we must insist on better journalistic training at accredited media institutes that emphasize values of accuracy, integrity and fairness in their students. These standards should extend to media organizations: when false claims or intentionally misleading statements are published or broadcast, TV and print news outlets should issue retractions with equal prominence.

Third, we must welcome different perspectives in our newsrooms and not allow them to become echo chambers forcing an opinion onto their viewers in the guise of 'the nation wants to know'. Newsrooms must be required to maintain a more diverse journalistic environment. Every story plugging a point of view must be required to provide some space for the alternative view, or for a refutation.

Fourth, journalists must welcome comments and feedback from their viewers and readers, to generate both an environment of trust between the consumers and the media, and the feeling on the part of the public that they are not merely passive recipients of a point of view. *The Hindu* is perhaps unique in India in having a Reader's Editor who serves as a sort of ombudsman for the newspaper and acknowledges mistakes of fact or emphasis in the newspaper's coverage. This helps drive a natural cycle of loyalty and engagement between the paper and its readers.

Fifth, government must introduce laws and regulations that limit the control of multiple new organizations by a single business or political entity, thereby encouraging an independent and robust press in the country. A powerful business interest, vulnerable to government pressure, will usually override ethical journalistic concerns. India is one of the few major countries where no restrictions currently exist when it comes to media ownership by our own citizens. Too many capitalists own media outlets with a view to using them to shore up their business interests. As Arun Shourie recently observed by recalling a Zulu proverb, 'A dog with a bone in its mouth can't bark.'[315] Succumbing to government pressure is often a business necessity.

Finally, a single overseer for print and television news companies, as recommended by the Telecom Regulatory Authority of India, would help limit the power of corporate and political behemoths over our media and help promote media standards.

The free press is like the parrot in a cage being sent down a mineshaft to see if there is enough oxygen at the bottom; if it comes back dead, or choking and spluttering for air, you know it is not safe for miners to go down. If the media is choking or suffocated, that is a clear indication that society is no longer safe for the rest of us.

The aim of journalism in times of change, especially when some changes in society may be considered for the worse, is to offer us the most meaningful record of how it would have felt to live during our era and how humane values were kept alive—even if they couldn't prevail over political repression, intimidation or violence.

---

[315]"A Dog With a Bone in Its Mouth Can't Bark": Arun Shourie on Mainstream Media', *The Wire*, 4 September 2018.

In an India assailed by gau-rakshaks and assorted vigilante squads, where intolerance and bigotry have been unleashed across the land and seemingly condoned by those who are in power, at a time when morality is tossed aside and ethical values are sneered at, there has never been a more urgent need for a journalism of principle and courage.

We do not have enough of that. Instead, the media's current obsession with the superficial and the sensational trivializes public discourse, abdicates the watchdog responsibility that must be exercised by free media in a democracy, and distracts the public from the real questions of accountability with which the governed must confront the government.

chapter fourteen

STANDING UP TO CENSORSHIP

I

Censorship has a peculiar status in India. When it comes to news media, print or broadcast, censorship is utterly unacceptable, even unthinkable. Yet all films produced by India's prolific film industry must be reviewed and approved by the Central Board of Film Certification (CBFC), which has the authority to demand that scenes be cut or language changed before a film can be screened publicly.

The discrepancy is a matter of elitism. Decades ago, the supposed guardians of India's public morals decided that those with the education and good taste to read a newspaper could handle its contents, but ordinary people seeking diversion would have to be protected from the pernicious effects of the 'wrong' kinds of entertainment.

To be sure, violence often makes it past the censors. But sexuality is another story. While images of nudity appear in urban glossy magazines to titillate the bourgeoisie, city-based censors make sure that villagers do not see a woman's bare breast on a movie screen. Until recently, not even a kiss could appear in a Bollywood movie; instead, as the man and woman tilted their heads towards each other, the camera would pan to two birds pecking or two flowers touching onscreen.

Other perceived threats to Indian culture include offensive language, gay themes, and unconventional views, especially on socially and politically sensitive topics. Sentiments that we take for granted in the opinion pages of newspapers rarely find their way into Bollywood blockbusters.

Even on television, entertainment is subject to rules that don't apply to news. A fashion show, for example, would be rigorously reviewed to ensure that no non-conformist attire that shocks the sensibilities of Indian culture's custodians makes it onscreen. Fashion channels have been taken off the air for showing models in revealing clothes.

India's film industry has long suffered stoically under the pressure of the paternalistic censors. But it was perhaps at its worst under Pahlaj Nihalani, an appointment blessed by the prime minister's more rabid followers (Mr Nihalani had made a campaign video, 'Har Har Modi, Ghar Ghar Modi', for Narendra Modi before the 2014 elections), who was chief censor from January 2015 to August 2017.

To get an idea of the scale of the Nihalani-led review board's moral policing, a kiss in the James Bond movie *Spectre* was deemed too long (and therefore trimmed). A sex scene in the superhero hit *Deadpool* got the same treatment. Mr Nihalani went so far as to declare that engaging in a long kiss 'means you want to do sex in your house with your door open, and show to people the way you are doing sex.'[316] Needless to say, that comment attracted considerable derision.

Gay themes also met with Mr Nihalani's disapproval, with the film *Aligarh*, about the persecution of a gay professor, receiving an 'A' rating, which restricted the film to adults, despite the lack of nudity or sex. The board demanded that the word 'lesbian' be removed from another film.

Mr Nihalani's reign of cultural terror came to a head with the review board demanding 72 cuts from the big-budget Bollywood film *Udta Punjab* ('Punjab on a High'), a gritty tale centred on the drug culture that is prevalent in the eponymous northwestern Indian state. That decision was, it seems, entirely political.

At the time, Punjab was controlled by the BJP, in alliance with a powerful regional party, the Shiromani Akali Dal, neither of which was pleased by the film's portrayal of the state they

---

[316]'You want to "do sex with your door open"': Pahlaj Nihalani on censor board cuts in Spectre', *FirstPost*, 23 November 2015.

ruled. And, unsurprisingly, the cuts largely targeted scenes and dialogue highlighting the government's failure to curb—and some politicians' complicity in promoting—Punjab's widespread drug abuse. To add insult to injury, the censors asked the filmmakers to remove all ninety-four references to Punjab in the film, including from its title.[317]

'All the characters are negative,' Mr Nihalani reportedly said. But when he declared that the film would 'hurt the whole community', what he really meant was that it would hurt the BJP and its allies.[318] The fact that the cuts would have gutted the film—as would have happened if Woody Allen were forced to remove Barcelona from *Vicky Cristina Barcelona*—was apparently irrelevant.

But Mr Nihalani failed to reckon with *Udta Punjab*'s feisty producer, Anurag Kashyap, a luminary of Bollywood's avant-garde. Anurag Kashyap launched a Twitter attack on Mr Nihalani, calling him a 'dictatorial man' and an 'oligarch'—and not stopping there. 'I always wondered what it felt like to live in North Korea,' Kashyap tweeted. 'Now I don't even need to catch a plane.'[319]

Anurag Kashyap continued his resistance offline, taking the almost unprecedented step of suing the review board—and winning. The Mumbai High Court ordered that the film be shown with only one scene cut. It was promptly released, and went on to break many of India's box-office records.

But even with Pahlaj Nihalani gone (lyricist and screenwriter Prasoon Joshi, who had played such a crucial role in Modi's image management and makeover in 2013–14, was appointed CBFC chief in August 2017), the review board went back to its old ways. India remains a modern democracy engaged in the thoroughly undemocratic practice of limiting freedom of speech,

---

[317]'How censor board made Udta Punjab bleed: Here are all the 94 cuts', *Hindustan Times*, 9 June 2016.
[318]Vasudha Venugopal, 'Udta Punjab, if released will bring a bad name to the Punjabi community: Pahlaj Nihalani', *Economic Times*, 8 June 2016.
[319]'Udta Punjab censor row: Anurag Kashyap compares India with North Korea', *Hindustan Times*, 7 June 2016.

if only in the film industry.

The practice of film censorship is yet another relic of a bygone colonial era, the values of which Indians have too readily internalized. Over seven decades after independence, Indians must recognize that our democracy is mature enough to end censorship.

II

Towards the end of 2017, Modi's India was torn apart further by another cultural controversy—this time over the film *Padmavat*. *Padmavat* tells the story of an eponymous Rajput queen believed to have died, together with 16,000 other women of the Rajput warrior caste, by self-immolation in 1301, in order to avoid being captured alive by the invading Delhi sultan Alauddin Khilji. Even before its release, *Padmavat* (originally known as *Padmavati*) had already inspired countless front-page stories and debates on the evening news, hysterical threats of violence, and a ban in four states governed by India's ruling Bharatiya Janata Party.[320]

The historical accuracy of Padmavati's story is dubious: no contemporary account of Khilji's attack on Chittorgarh, including by historians accompanying his forces, mentions the queen. Yet Padmavati has been a figure of legend since 1540, when the Sufi mystic poet Malik Muhammad Jayasi devoted his lyrical epic *Padmavat* to her story.

It has been suggested that Jayasi did not intend his tale to be taken literally, and that his work, instead, represented the Persian mystical-poetic tradition of using romance to represent humanity's search for the divine. By this interpretation, the poem is an allegory for the union of mind and soul, under attack from external forces. Jayasi may have chosen Khilji's attack on Chittorgarh as a setting for his epic because its name includes the word chit (consciousness).

But literature, once published, acquires a life of its own. Jayasi's tale was retold countless times, by Bengali bards, Rajasthani

---

[320]'Gujarat Becomes Fourth BJP-Ruled State to Ban "Padmaavat"', *The Wire*, 15 January 2018.

folk-tellers, and even the English Colonel Tod, who included Padmavati's tale in his compilation, *Annals and Antiquities of Rajputana*. Through those retellings, her self-immolation (jauhar) became a noble act of resistance against the lustful Muslim, making her an exemplar of unsullied Hindu womanhood.

Over time, Padmavati was effectively deified. The reputed site of her suicide became a tourist attraction. The head of the Karni Sena, a Rajput organization, claimed to be her direct descendent. (When confronted with the view that she was fictional, he replied, 'I am 37th in her direct line of descent. Am I a ghost?'[321])

With so much riding on Padmavati's image as a symbol of female honour and purity, Sanjay Leela Bhansali, the Bollywood filmmaker who set out to make a film of her story, unwittingly became a target of historical passions. The Karni Sena trashed the film set at Jaigarh Fort in Jaipur, and disrupted further shooting in a new (less 'authentic') location at Kohlapur, accusing Bhansali of filming a love scene between the Hindu queen and the Muslim invader. The Rajput community is also rumoured to have delayed the release of the film on the grounds that it 'distorted history,' though Mr Bhansali denied this.

The film's detractors, including the four BJP chief ministers who instituted the preemptive bans (with not a murmur emerging from their leader, the prime minister), did not even see the film before condemning it.[322] That is how defensive some Hindus in India have become over the version of history to which they subscribe—even when, as in Padmavati's case, that history may well be nothing more than a figment of collective imagination.

No less an ardent secularist than India's first prime minister, Jawaharlal Nehru, summed up the phenomenon seven decades ago: 'Facts and fiction are so interwoven together as to be inseparable, and this amalgam becomes an imagined history, which may not

---

[321]'Padmavati: Rajput Karni Sena chief claims he's a descendant of Padmini and says the film must be burned', *Times of India*, 24 November 2017.
[322]'Padmavati row: Bihar, UP, Gujarat and other states where Sanjay Leela Bhansali's film faces hurdles', *Hindustan Times*, 29 November 2017.

tell us exactly what happened but does tell us something equally important—what people believed had taken place, what they thought their heroic ancestors were capable of, and what ideals inspired them.'[323] This 'imagined history'—'a mixture of fact and fiction, or sometimes only fiction'—becomes 'symbolically true.'

This explains, in a nutshell, the opposition to *Padmavat*. For some Hindus, the difference between historical fact and cultural myth does not matter; what is remembered and believed is as important as what is verifiable. And in today's climate, where 'taking offence' is the name of the game and 'hurting the sentiments of a community' is the name of the crime, that perspective is particularly relevant. The old Hindu boasts of expansive tolerance and acceptance of difference—the very tenets that underlie India's remarkable diversity—are wearing thin these days.

But there is precedent for this response. A decade ago, hairdressers objected to the film *Billu Barber*, arguing (absurdly) that the term 'barber' is an insult to their profession. So they threatened to protest the film everywhere it was shown—threats that forced the Bollywood star and producer to drop the second word, renaming the film simply *Billu*.

While it may seem alarmist to suggest that freedom of expression in India is in peril, the atmosphere of intimidation by inflamed mobs, to whom governments surrender all too willingly, is palpable. By permitting these intolerant bullies to get away with their lawless acts of intimidation, we are allowing them to do violence to something vital to India's survival as a civilization.

I saw the film myself in a theatre in Thiruvananthapuram. Among the fellow cine-goers who inevitably asked for selfies was a young family from Rajasthan who regretted that the film could not be shown in their own state, whose glories the filmmaker had done so much to promote in his film. The government, they told me, should not have surrendered to the mob. As we spoke,

---

[323]Jawaharlal Nehru, *Discovery of India*, New York: Oxford University Press, 1989, p. 101.

it emerged that they had voted for Mr Modi: they wanted a 'strong leader'. Shouldn't a strong leader, I asked, denounce the thugs who want to deny you the right to watch a film like this in your hometown? They agreed that maybe on some issues, Mr Modi was not such a strong leader after all.

chapter fifteen

THE PUSH FOR HINDI

The arrival of Modi on the national scene has seen his government pushing Hindi with more enthusiasm than judgement. I got caught up in the undertow of the new zeal for Hindi when in reply to a question on Twitter, in all innocence, I asserted that Hindi was not our natural language. I was accused of being anti-national, of being a slave to a foreign language—as if the British had excreted their language on us as pigeons might spatter us with their droppings. Unfortunately for them, I was right: the Constitution of India provides for no 'national language'. But being wrong rarely bothers a troll.

The ugly exchanges did, however, reveal two more essential truths about our country. The first is that, whatever the Hindi chauvinists might say, we don't have one 'national language' in India, but several. The second is that the Hindi zealots, including their recent Southern converts like Venkaiah Naidu, whose assertion 'Hindi hamari rashtrabhasha hai' had provoked the recent debate, have an unfortunate tendency to provoke a battle they will lose—at a time when they were quietly winning the war.[324]

Hindi is officially the mother tongue of some 41 per cent of our population; the percentage has been growing, thanks to the spectacular failure of population control in much of north India. It is also spoken by several who claim primary allegiance to other languages, notably Punjabi, Marathi and Gujarati. It is not, however, the mother tongue of the rest of us.

When Hindi speakers emotionally decry the use of an alien language imposed on the country by British colonialists and demand that Hindi be used because it speaks for 'the soul of

---
[324]"When did we get a national language?": Venkaiah Naidu criticised for calling Hindi "rashtra bhasha"', *Scroll.in*, 25 June 2015

India', or when they declare that 'Hindi is our mother, English is a stranger', they are missing the point twice over.

First, because no Tamil or Bengali will accept that Hindi is the language of his soul or has anything to do with his mother—it is as alien to him as English is. And second, because injecting anti-English xenophobia into the argument is utterly irrelevant to the issue at stake for those who object to the idea of a national language.

That issue is quite simple: all Indians need to deal with the government. We need government services, government information and government support; we need to understand easily what our government is saying to us or demanding of us. When the government does so in our mother tongue, it is easier for us. But when it does so in someone else's mother tongue with which we are less familiar than our neighbour, our incomprehension is intensified by resentment. Why should Shukla be spoken to by the Government of India in the language that comes easiest to him, but not Subramaniam?

The de facto solution to this question has been a practical one—use Hindi where it is understood, but use English everywhere and especially in the central government, since it places all Indians from all parts of our country at an equal disadvantage or advantage. English does not express Subramaniam's soul any more than it does Shukla's, but it serves a functional purpose for both, and what's more, it helps Subramaniam to understand the same thing as Shukla.

Ideally, of course, every central government document, tax form or tweet should be in every one of India's languages. Since that is not possible in practice—because we would have to do everything in twenty-three versions—we have chosen to have two official languages, English and Hindi. State governments complement these by producing official material in the language of their states. That leaves everyone more or less happy.

Since the BJP came to power, however, they have not been content to let sleeping dogmas lie. The move to push Hindi has required governmental file notations to be written in that language, even where that undermines comprehension, accuracy and therefore efficiency.

Obliging a south Indian civil servant to digest a complex argument by a UPite subordinate writing in his mother tongue is unfair to both. Both may write atrocious English, for that matter, but it's the language in which they are equal, and it serves to get the work done.

Language is a vehicle, not a destination. In government, it is a means, not an end. The Hindi-wallahs fail to appreciate that, since promoting Hindi, for them, is an end in itself.

This is what sustains the government's futile efforts to make Hindi a seventh official language of the United Nations. PM Modi's Foreign Minister Sushma Swaraj dramatically declared that her government was willing to spend hundreds of crores of rupees to achieve this objective.[325] Now in the United Nations, there are six official languages (used for formal speeches and translations of documents) and two working languages (in which the organization's work is conducted daily). Similarly, in India, we have no single 'national language': Article 343 of the Constitution makes it very clear that Hindi is an official language. The Official Languages Act of 1963 says that Hindi and English are both official languages of India and the Gujarat High Court ruled in 2010 that Hindi is not the national language of India. So for India to be spending significant government resources in seeking to promote Hindi as a UN language has more to do with misplaced Hindi chauvinism than with constitutional principle.

It also has little to do with practical efficiency. Six languages have been made official languages at the United Nations because a number of countries speak them. Arabic does not have more speakers than Hindi, but Arabic is spoken as an official language by twenty-two countries, whereas Hindi is only used as an

---

[325]'"India Ready To Spend Up To 400 Crore To Make Hindi An Official Language Of UN": Sushma Swaraj', *NDTV*, 3 January 2018.

official language by one country, India. When I questioned her in Parliament, Ms Swaraj claimed disingenuously that Hindi is spoken in Mauritius, Fiji, Surinam, Trinidad and Tobago, and Ghana. But she failed to acknowledge that it is not the official language of any of these countries, and therefore not a means of official communication with any of them.

Indian diplomats using Hindi at the UN would, in other words, be speaking to themselves and to the Hindi-speaking portion of their domestic audience. This narrow, essentially political objective, does not justify expending vast sums of taxpayers' money. If India were to have a prime minister or a foreign minister who prefers to speak Hindi (as we do currently), they can do so and we can pay for that speech to be translated at the UN. But that is not the same time as making it an official language. Why should we put our future foreign ministers and prime ministers who may be from Tamil Nadu or West Bengal in a position where they are condemned to be speaking a language they are uncomfortable with, merely because we are paying for it?

The irony is, as I observed earlier, that the Hindi chauvinists should realize they were winning the war. The prevalence of Hindi is far greater across India today than it was half a century ago. The Parliament has become a bastion of Hindi; you hear the language now twice as often as you hear English, and three times as often as you did in the previous Parliament, when stalwarts like Pranab Mukherjee and P. Chidambaram refused to speak anything but English on the floor of the House. Our present prime minister speaks only in Hindi, and his ministerial colleagues, with only a handful of exceptions, try to emulate him.

But the inevitable triumph of Hindi is not because of Mr Modi's oratory, or Mulayam Singh Yadav's imprecations, or the assiduous efforts of the parliamentary committee on the promotion of Hindi. It is, quite simply, because of Bollywood, which has brought a demotic conversational Hindi into every Indian home. South Indians and Northeasterners alike are developing an ease and familiarity with Hindi because it is a language in which they are entertained. In time, this alone will make Hindi truly the national language.

But it would become so only because Indians freely and voluntarily adopt it, not because some Hindi chauvinist in Delhi thrusts his language down the throats of the unwilling.

III

MODITVA AND MISGOVERNANCE

Narendra Modi rode to power on promises of good governance and assured his followers that his raj would witness the advent of achhe din. Instead, the country has been given a succession of bad initiatives like demonetization or good ideas that have been poorly executed, such as GST and Swachh Bharat. Further, in various chapters in this section, I show how this government has assailed institutions such as Parliament and meddled with the judiciary and educational institutions and dishonoured the armed forces. The conclusion this section arrives at is clear—misgovernance has been the hallmark of Moditva and almost everything he has turned his hand to hasn't quite worked.

chapter sixteen

MAXIMUM GOVERNMENT, MINIMUM GOVERNANCE

Many voters chose to give Narendra Modi the benefit of the doubt when it came to governance. They had the misleading figures of his performance as Gujarat chief minister to support their hope that here was a man who would propel India into the front ranks of the higher performing countries and economies. Sadly, Mr Modi has flattered to deceive, as we will see in this section and the next.

Let's start with the most basic unit of governance, the PM and his cabinet. At first, being an unabashedly old-fashioned liberal, I confess to being rather attracted to PM Modi's oft-repeated maxim, 'minimum government, maximum governance'. I had no illusions about the fact that the prime minister's talent for sound bites was not often accompanied by matching action. But his expansion of his cabinet in the course of his prime ministership has confirmed that his definition of 'minimum government' is rather stretchable.

When Modi began his innings in government with a council of ministers of just forty-four, including the allocation of several related portfolios to select ministers, it seemed he might actually be serious about reducing the size of our central government. According to our Constitution, 'there shall be a Council of Ministers with the Prime Minister at its head, to aid and advise the President who shall, in the exercise of his functions, act in accordance with such advice'. But the Constitution is silent on the size of such a council. Ministers are appointed by the president on the advice of the prime minister (Article 75.1) and the PM decides not only how many ministers he or she wishes to have, but what portfolios they will be allocated. There is nothing immutable about the specific ministries of government, which can be created, merged or dissolved by a PM at will.

While this has made for varying sizes of councils of ministers over the years, the Administrative Reforms Commission has regarded 10 per cent of the total membership of the Lok Sabha (that is, fifty-four ministers, including cabinet ministers, ministers of state, and deputy ministers, the three recognized categories of ministerial office) to be the ideal size.[326] But this has been exceeded in practice by every Government of India since Indira Gandhi's day.

Still, the question of the optimum size has never been properly addressed in Delhi. A law passed during the tenure of Atal Bihari Vajpayee limits the size of the council of ministers in state governments to 15 per cent of the strength of the lower house of the state assembly. An informal convention has sprung up that such a percentage should also be adhered to in the central government, so that the council of ministers is not too large in relation to the lower house of Parliament. Since the Lok Sabha has 543 members, that suggests an upper limit of 81 ministers. The last government of Prime Minister Manmohan Singh came closest to that number, with seventy-eight ministers, but did not breach it. Mr Modi has exceeded his predecessor's total.

The reasons for the ballooning size of ministerial councils have nothing to do with administrative logic; the calculations involved are unabashedly political.

In a large and diverse democracy like India's, ministerial appointments need to reflect the range and diversity of the country: all regions of India must be represented, whether or not the ruling party or coalition has worthy candidates from all regions, and this being India, the same logic applies to all religions and castes. Appointments are also made to reward long political service, to quell brewing dissidence, to test mettle, to grant rewards and to send a signal to the appointee's state in advance of assembly elections. Whether or not the recipient of such ministerial honour is actually capable of doing the work allotted is often beside the point. It is accepted that the country is really run by the

---

[326]Mohan Guruswamy, '91st Constitutional Amendment: Not quite adequate', *Hindu Business Line*, 20 July 2004.

bureaucracy and by a key group of top ministers handpicked for powerful positions by the prime minister.

Over the years, the tendency to use the council of ministers to offer political rewards to MPs meant that other practices developed which moved the government away from administrative efficiency in the interests of distributing ministerial rank to as many beneficiaries as possible. The position of parliamentary secretary used to reward young MPs, usually first-termers, who worked as understudies to their ministers, was discontinued. More surprisingly, the slots of deputy ministers, commonly filled in the Jawaharlal Nehru governments, fell into disuse as well. The intermediate level of ministers of state (MoS) became the de facto deputy ministers, devaluing the rank. Over successive governments, many MoS's complained of having no work allotted to them, and no authority over the work that did come their way. While, as MoS for external affairs, I benefited from a genuine division of responsibility and served as de facto minister for Africa, the Middle East and Latin America, as well as for passport and consular matters, policy planning and for the Haj, as MoS in the Ministry of Human Resource Development (MHRD), no files stopped their journey at my desk except on their way to the cabinet minister, with whom ultimate decision-making on all issues resided.

This meant my role was limited to influencing and articulating policy, but not to making it. (I could not resist tweeting, as the Modi government was being sworn in, that 'being MoS is like standing in a cemetery: there are a lot of people under you, but no one is listening'.)

As I have mentioned at the outset, Narendra Modi's first council of ministers, which was the smallest one for decades, seemed a refreshing change from this usual practice. It seemed he was determined not to worry about giving ministerial office to his own party's experienced seniors, many of whom were sidelined, or to touching all political bases or even to stocking his council with the right number of minorities, lower castes and so on. Many of us grudgingly acknowledged that streamlined government might

well mark a major departure for a political class overly fond of
the perks of ministerial office—the cars with red beacons, the
offices and extra staff—rather than their ministerial duties. We
looked forward to seeing what fewer ministers could accomplish,
apart from reducing traffic congestion in Lutyens' Delhi.

But after his first pair of cabinet reshuffles, Prime Minister
Modi increased his council of ministers by more than 50 per cent,
from forty-four to seventy-six; by 2018 this had reached eighty. If
his initial cabinet gave him bragging rights over his predecessors
in speaking of 'minimum government', especially thanks to his
placing some related ministries (coal and power, for example)
under the same minister, now his government looks little different
in size from the last several governments, all of which had between
seventy and eighty ministers. And despite that the south is still
under-represented in his ministry, as are minority groups (other
than in the Minority Affairs Ministry). But PM Modi's minimum
government has reached the maximum permissible size.

So has Narendra Modi missed a trick here? I'd argue that he
has, and offer an alternative vision that really could deliver the
'minimum government' he used to speak of.

What are the existing ministries that simply cannot be done
without and so should remain intact? The four 'big ones'—home,
finance, defence and external affairs—brook no argument. Since
agriculture still engages ('employs' would be a disingenuous word)
more than 40 per cent of our population, an Agriculture Ministry is
indispensable.[327] The core needs of our people—health, education,
transport, law and justice, and environment follow; so do some
of the core responsibilities of government, to provide our nation
with energy, and to steward our domestic commerce (including
foreign trade) and industry.

That gives us twelve indispensable ministries. But the list can't
stop here: in a developing country, the government has to undertake

---

[327]Employment in agriculture (percentage of total employment) (modelled
International Labour Organization estimate), WorldBank.org, updated November
2017.

to help the nation grow and develop its urban infrastructure as well as meet the range of its rural development challenges, as well as promote tourism and build tourist infrastructure. Then we need a strong PMO to help keep the whole lot in line.

That's sixteen ministries we absolutely can't avoid retaining. Give each a cabinet minister and one or two MoS (or deputy ministers), and you could have a council of ministers totalling no more than forty to forty-five, with the PM and a fifteen-strong cabinet at the helm.

So why do we have so many more today, and in earlier governments of the last few decades? Simple—as I have noted, the more ministries you create, the more political interests you placate. So functions that really belong together were divided up amongst different political heavyweights, not because they warranted a separate governmental machinery but because the individual in question had to be given a chance to exercise authority over something tangible, however undemanding that share of the pie might be.

So though we have a Ministry of Industry, we have managed, over the years, to create separate ministries for heavy industries, micro-, small- and medium-enterprises, steel, mines, textiles, chemicals and fertilizers, and food processing, all of which, properly speaking, are merely different kinds of industries. The heavy hand of regulatory and licensing authority in each of these industries was then exercised by a different minister in each case, spreading the clout (that comes from having the authority to grant permissions) to many hands.

That's anything but 'minimum government', and if PM Modi meant it, he could have put a stop to it.

He seemed to have recognized this principle when he clubbed together the separate ministries for power, and new (or 'alternative') and renewable energy under one minister (but still as different ministries located in different buildings). But coal sits with the railways minister, atomic energy is under a minister of state and the largest source of India's energy—petroleum and natural gas—

stands as a ministry by itself. Wouldn't it have been more logical to have one all-inclusive Ministry of Energy to ensure that the nation has a comprehensive and coordinated energy policy—one that sees multiple sources of energy as elements in one national energy mix, needing policy direction from one minister? Instead of a single minister deciding, for instance, to alter the proportions of that mix, increasing the national output of solar, for instance, in preference to petroleum imports or incentives for coal production, we have different government policies on coal, alternative energy (wind and solar), and of course on the pricing of gas, petrol and diesel. Mr Modi has foregone an obvious win here.

Similarly, shouldn't the Agriculture Ministry subsume Food and Public Distribution, while Consumer Affairs goes to Commerce and Industry? Yet, currently these are three ministries (and Food Processing is a fourth). Forty years ago all of them came under one food and agriculture minister.

Mr Modi's decision to place the Ministry of Overseas Indian Affairs under the MEA was wise, especially since the former relies almost entirely on the latter to get its work done overseas, where its 'clients' are. The same logic does not seem to have been applied, however, in keeping the Ministry of Law and Justice separate from those of Social Justice and Empowerment, Minority Affairs, Women and Child Development, and Tribal Affairs. Surely a justice minister's job is to ensure justice for all? Some functions of the present ministries could then be placed in more logical departments—for instance, maternal health issues could go from the Women's Ministry to the Health Ministry, minority education to MHRD, and so on. Where an issue is of sufficient importance, the PM could always declare a national mission that subsumes two or more ministries, and take the coordinating lead himself, as he has done with the Swachh Bharat Abhiyan. That could be the case with Ganga Rejuvenation, for instance, which could be an abhiyan rather than a ministry.

I have already argued in Chapter 13 that the I&B Ministry can be abolished, and that Prasar Bharati could be given genuine autonomy. We also have a plethora of small ministries exercising functions that belong outside government, or in specialized institutions not requiring ministerial intervention. These include Science and Technology (for which few ministers are qualified anyway) and Earth Sciences (which usually ends up in the PMO, where it is understandably neglected). Couldn't the latter just go to the Geological Survey of India and the former to MHRD?

Indeed, the Ministry of Human Resource Development was conceived by Rajiv Gandhi as an omnibus ministry, but over the years it has been whittled down to just managing education. Why does PM Modi need separate ministries of Skill Development, Labour, Culture, Youth Affairs and Sports, all of which were once under a single MHRD minister?

I am not seeking to diminish the importance of the tasks being undertaken, at least in some cases, by the separate ministries. But the answer lies not in creating more silos that make for inefficiencies in policy coordination and convey an impression of policy incoherence. The answer lies in giving real work to the ministers of state to handle these portfolios under the overall direction of powerful coordinating ministers. Give real departmental power to ministers of state, and you solve two problems in one; but also revive the post of deputy minister, and use it for the younger and less experienced MPs to work under cabinet ministers and MoSs.

There, PM Modi, you would have 'minimum government, maximum governance'. But as with pretty much all he stands for, the phrase is not an agenda for action, but little more than a slogan for the sound-bite era. What he should have really said, as we will find out in the chapters in this section, is that his administration really only stands for 'maximum government, minimum governance'.

chapter seventeen

THE ATTACK ON INSTITUTIONS

Mahatma Gandhi once said: 'The truest test of a democracy is in the ability of anyone to act as he likes, so long as he does not injure the life or property of anyone else.'[328] In order for this to happen, every institution that upholds a healthy and vibrant democracy needs to be fostered and cared for by the government of the day. The independence of these institutions needs to be protected so they are able to dispense neutral decisions in the interest of every citizen of India. A list of such institutions would include the judiciary, headed by the Supreme Court; the Election Commission, which organizes, conducts and rules on the country's general and state elections; the Reserve Bank of India, the nation's central bank; the armed forces; the national exam-conducting bodies that test tens of millions of schoolchildren every year in highly competitive examinations that could make or break their futures; the investigative agencies (notably the Central Bureau of Investigation, India's equivalent of the FBI); the elected legislatures; and the free press. Every one of these priceless institutions has come under threat in the last four years, as an assertive Hindu-chauvinist BJP government moves to consolidate its power in the world's largest democracy.

The judicial system, traditionally above the cut-and-thrust of the political fray, came under withering scrutiny in January 2018, when the four senior-most judges of the Supreme Court held an unprecedented press conference to question the decisions of outgoing Chief Justice Dipak Misra in allocating cases to his favourite judges as 'master of the roster'—their criticism seemed to imply that this would lead to outcomes to favour the government.[329]

---

[328]M. K. Gandhi, *Young India*, 1 August 1920, p. 4.
[329]R. Balaji, 'CJI is "master of roster": CJI bench', *The Telegraph*, 12 April 2018.

Chief Justices of India are supposed to be free of political interests, but in April several Opposition parties circulated an equally unprecedented impeachment motion against the Chief Justice in the upper house, the Rajya Sabha. Though this was rejected by the Rajya Sabha chairman, the vice president of India, two MPs moved the Supreme Court itself to challenge his rejection, only to find the Chief Justice naming a bench favourable to him to hear their appeal.[330] They then withdrew their case, but the image of the judiciary has taken a beating from all this, from which it will not easily recover.

India's Election Commission has also enjoyed a proud record of independence and boasts decades-long experience of conducting free and fair elections, despite its members usually being retired civil servants appointed by the government of the day for fixed tenures. While in the past, election commissioners have largely enjoyed a reputation for integrity, this took a severe blow last year, when a BJP-appointed chief violated the convention of announcing election dates for all impending state elections at the same time. A quarter century ago, the commission had introduced a Code of Conduct that prohibits government expenditure to impress voters once election dates are announced. With the BJP, which is in power in both the centre and in Gujarat state, scrambling to impress voters in Gujarat through last-minute schemes and pre-election freebies, it was alleged that the EC came under pressure to delay the election announcement there as long as possible.[331] Surprisingly, it declared the dates for elections in Himachal Pradesh, a state that normally goes to the polls at the same time as Gujarat, thirteen days before the latter, ostensibly in order to permit flood relief work in Gujarat (which the Code of Conduct would not in fact have disallowed).[332]

---

[330]Bhadra Sinha, 'On move to remove Chief Justice, Congress withdraws SC plea and protests', *Hindustan Times*, 8 May 2018.
[331]'"Election Commission acted under moral pressure"', *The Hindu*, 26 October 2017.
[332]Sanjay Singh, 'Different dates for Gujarat, Himachal Pradesh Assembly elections is EC's missed opportunity to try simultaneous polls', *FirstPost*, 12 October 2017.

Former election commissioners condemned the decision unanimously, even as the Gujarat government and the prime minister himself took advantage of the delay to announce a series of pre-election giveaways.[333] It does no good to Indian democracy to see a shadow fall over the very institution that guarantees free and fair elections, especially at a time when reports of data manipulation by the likes of Facebook and Cambridge Analytica have begun to raise doubts over the security of the electronic voting machines (EVMs) on which ballots are cast.

The concern that, under BJP rule, the Election Commission was behaving like a government department, became more acute when the Delhi High Court threw out an EC decision to disqualify twenty Aam Aadmi Party (AAP) MLAs of the Delhi Legislature on technical grounds, an action that could have benefited the BJP had by-elections to their seats followed.[334] The court termed the decision 'bad in law', 'vitiated' and a failure to 'comply with principles of natural justice'. How had an institution widely hailed as the impartial custodian of India's democratic process allowed itself to be brought to such a sorry pass? The answer lay clearly with the ruling party at the centre, which was seen by many as pressuring the institution to act according to its wishes.

The Reserve Bank of India (RBI), the nation's central bank, was thoroughly discredited over the BJP government's disastrous demonetization of November 2016, when it was widely denounced for failing to perform its fiduciary duties. The RBI, which did not appear to have been fully consulted on the political decision, conspicuously failed to exercise its autonomy, to anticipate the problems of Mr Modi's scheme, to prepare its implementation better, and to alleviate its impact. During the shambolic demonetization process, the goalposts kept shifting: the RBI issued

[333]Meghdoot Sharon, 'It's Raining Freebies in Gujarat Since Himachal Poll Dates Were Declared', *News18*, 26 October 2017; 'Delay In Gujarat Poll Date Announcement Creates "Ground Of Suspicion", Says Former Chief Election Commissioner', *Huffington Post*, 13 October 2017.
[334]Aniruddha Ghosal, 'Office-of-profit case: Delhi HC strikes down disqualification of 20 AAP MLAs, says EC order is bad in law', *Indian Express*, 24 March 2018.

multiple notifications on demonetization—some seventy-four in fifty days, each intended to tweak an earlier announcement.[335] It seemed as if the Reserve Bank had been reduced to a puppet on a string for the Indian government. Many began to refer to this once-respected institution as the 'Reverse Bank of India' for its frequent reversals of stance on such matters as the amounts of money permissible to withdraw, the last legal date for withdrawals, and even whether depositors would have their fingers marked with indelible ink so they could not withdraw their money too often.

Demonetization caused serious and seemingly lasting damage to India's most important financial institution. The United Forum of Reserve Bank Officers and Employees wrote to the government in January 2017, pointing to 'operational mismanagement' which has 'dented RBI's autonomy and reputation beyond repair'.[336] The inexplicable silence of its governor, Urjit Patel, reduced him to a lamb. But this 'silence of the lamb' was cannibalizing the RBI itself.

The Modi government has also not hesitated to politicize the armed forces, not just bypassing time-honoured principles of seniority in appointing the army chief, but by repeatedly using the army in its political propaganda. The shameless exploitation of the 2016 'surgical strikes' along the Line of Control with Pakistan, and of a military raid in hot pursuit of rebels in Myanmar, as a party election tool—something the Congress had never done despite having authorized several such strikes earlier—marked a particularly disgraceful dilution of the principle that national security issues require both discretion and non-partisanship. As I've mentioned, the 2018 Karnataka state elections saw the prime minister, no less, falsely denouncing India's first prime minister for allegedly having insulted two army chiefs from the state.[337]

[335]'Demonetisation: 50 days, 74 notifications', *Indian Express*, 31 December 2016; T. K. Arun, 'View: 59th circular by RBI, how many more to come?', *Economic Times*, 20 December 2016.
[336]'"Humiliated" RBI employees write to Governor Urjit Patel, say bank's image "dented beyond repair"', *India Today*, 14 January 2017.
[337]'Karnataka polls: Modi accuses Congress of insulting Cariappa and Thimayya', *Business Standard*, 4 May 2018.

The principle that the army should be kept out of politics, and that the military are above regional or religious loyalties, was disregarded in his flagrant exploitation of the Indian military for short-term purposes.

A controversy over leaked exam papers for an important national school-leavers' examination cast doubt on another cherished national institution, the Central Board of Secondary Education (CBSE), which conducts the test. The faith of millions of schoolchildren in the competitive examination system is vital for India's social peace; in an environment where job seekers vastly exceed jobs available, unimpeachable exam results are fundamental to any perception of fairness. That the exam, which could make or break their futures, might have been leaked in advance to a favoured few casts a doubt on the entire culture of meritocracy that millions of young Indians aspire to.

Under the BJP, the federal investigative agencies (notably the Central Bureau of Investigation) are widely seen as instruments of the government; the CBI has even been described as a 'caged parrot'.[338] Its investigations and indictments, once seen as the gold standard of Indian crime-fighting, are now too often seen as purely politically motivated.

As for the 'temple of democracy', the Indian Parliament, its work has been reduced to a farce as allies and supporters of the ruling party brought the Lok Sabha's Budget session to a standstill through disruptions orchestrated by the government. With the BJP-appointed speaker claiming she could not count heads in the din, a motion of no-confidence moved by Opposition parties was initially not debated, citing 'lack of order'.[339] It seemed as if the government was willing to destroy the temple rather than permit prayers against its misrule to be heard there. (The motion was eventually permitted to be introduced in the following session,

---

[338] Ashhar Khan, "'BJP called CBI a caged parrot, but now it has become its long arm'", *Asian Age*, 21 May 2017.
[339] Jatin Gandhi, 'Parliament disruptions drown no-confidence motion again', *Hindustan Times*, 2 April 2018.

but the damage was done.)

As we have seen, India's free press, which ought to be calling the government's actions to account, has seemingly been cowed by the overweening power of the government. In the chapters that follow I will go deeper into the way in which our institutions are being assailed by the Modi sarkar. If the deinstitutionalization of Indian governance proceeds like this, the greatest danger facing India will be that of the public losing faith in the system altogether— with incalculable consequences for the country's biggest asset, its democracy.

chapter eighteen

CONDUCT UNBECOMING

When I was elected to the Lok Sabha in April 2009 and invited to join the UPA government, I was coming off not just an extensive United Nations career but a short stint in private life, during which I had served a number of institutions in an advisory capacity. No sooner had I taken up my MoS position in the Ministry of External Affairs than a request came from the PMO, asking me to inform them of all such commitments and affiliations.

I duly listed them in a memo to the cabinet secretary. There were nine such positions in all, mostly a legacy of my earlier international life. They included serving on the board of trustees of my last alma mater, the Fletcher School of Law and Diplomacy; as an honorary adviser to the International Committee of the Red Cross; as a fellow of the New York Institute of the Humanities; and as the patron of an Indian school in Dubai. Within a few days the cabinet secretary, K. M. Chandrasekhar, called. I would have to resign from all of them.

When I expressed curiosity, since these were unremunerated advisory positions in prestigious institutions whose activities and principles were totally compatible with those of the Government of India, the cabinet secretary sent over a document that explained his request. This was the Code of Ethical Conduct for the council of ministers, adopted decades earlier—I believe in the 1950s—and most recently reissued in the 1970s. The code required ministers to relinquish not only their business activities, if any, but also affiliations to other institutions, including charitable ones.

I accepted without demur, but sought further clarification of the way in which the code was interpreted. The cabinet secretary was frank: no minister of the government ought to risk being associated with an institution's action or position by the mere fact of his association with it. This applied to charitable and philanthropic bodies too, even those engaged in a social purpose with which the Government of India had no problem. After all, my extending my patronage to one school would put me in an invidious position vis-à-vis other schools; serving as the trustee of one institution could imply favouritism in relation to other institutions.

And even if the position were honorary, he pointed out, if those institutions did any fund-raising to conduct their work, the presence of a minister's name on their masthead could be misused. If someone donated money to a charity in which a minister was involved, for instance, there could be the expectation of a quid pro quo from the minister in his official capacity. Even if the minister refused to provide any favours in return, the mere perception could be damaging. A member of the council of ministers, he explained, had to be above any suspicion of a conflict of interest, however trivial.

The key provision of the code in this respect was Article 3.1, which forbade a minister to 'personally, or through a member of his family, accept contributions for any purpose, whether political, charitable or otherwise'; and denied him the right to 'associate himself with the raising of funds'. There was in fact a loophole, though: a minister could be associated with such efforts 'for the benefit of a registered society, or a charitable body, or an institution recognized by a public authority'.[340] Exceptions would have to be authorized by the prime minister.

I did not seek an exception. It was clear that on Dr Manmohan Singh's watch, his cabinet secretary was going to be a strict constructionist. I duly resigned from all my positions, informing the institutions concerned that my appointment as a minister required me to do so.

This was why I was all the more curious when a controversy arose in November 2017 over four ministers (Nirmala Sitharaman,

---

[340]'Code of conduct for ministers (both Union and State)', Ministry of Home Affairs, Government of India.

Suresh Prabhu, Jayant Sinha and M. J. Akbar) serving on the board of the India Foundation, a body closely associated with several luminaries of the ruling establishment.[341] Like me, as foundation head Shaurya Doval pointed out, they had been associated with the foundation before they became ministers. Unlike me, however, they had not been asked to resign.

It is not my place to question the Modi-era cabinet secretary's performance of his own duties. But the basic issue arises: has the prime minister of India granted his ministers an exemption from the rules of the code to continue serving the India Foundation? Was this explicitly sought and approved through the cabinet secretary? And if not, has the government in effect abandoned its own code—and with what authority?

The issue of conflict of interest is, in fact, a fairly simple one. In the classic definition, a conflict of interest arises from 'a set of circumstances that creates a risk that professional judgement or actions regarding a primary interest will be unduly influenced by a secondary interest'. The primary interest of any minister is, of course, meant to be his ministerial responsibilities. Conceivably the ministers concerned could argue that there is nothing in the work of the India Foundation that would influence their professional work as ministers. But what about the other way around?

When the India Foundation raises funds for its conferences, publications and other activities, doesn't the presence on its masthead of a pair of ministerial names prompt donors to be more forthcoming than they might be to another foundation? When they invite foreign dignitaries to attend their events, is it not possible that these foreigners accept because they are attracted by the possibility of proximity to these ministers? And is it ethically right for the India Foundation to benefit in these ways from the association with it of ministers who are being paid by the Indian taxpayer?

---

[341]Swati Chaturvedi, 'Exclusive: Think-Tank Run by NSA Ajit Doval's Son Has Conflict of Interest Writ Large', *The Wire*, 4 November 2017.

Dr Manmohan Singh and his cabinet secretary had one kind of answer; it seems Narendra Modi and his PMO have another.

In a country where we tend to be obsessed with corruption scams in multiple crores, this kind of ethical dispute may seem somewhat precious, the political equivalent of the old theological dispute about how many angels can dance on the head of a pin. But in a polity where there's a desperate need to uphold the standards we do have, it is only fair that the issue should be faced. The Code of Conduct for ministers, after all, has not been modified; it still figures on the MHA website. Shouldn't it, then, be applied?

The marvellous thing about conflict of interest in India is how blissfully our political class is completely unaware of it. We are all reared in a culture where a good and upstanding pillar of society is identified by his fulfilment of his duty to his family, clan and caste before anything or anyone else. In a classic exchange in Haryana a prominent politician, criticized for favouring his son in an appointment, retorted: 'Of course I favoured my son! Then whose son should I favour, yours?'[342]

We have seen earlier in the book how the External Affairs Minister Sushma Swaraj thought nothing of intervening with a foreign government in favour of an absconding Indian citizen, wanted by the law enforcement agencies of our own country.[343] In any other democracy, even if such a matter had come to her desk, she would have been expected to recuse herself from all involvement because her husband and daughter happened to be the legal representatives of the person concerned.[344] I doubt the thought of recusal even occurred to her. Favours, after all, are done for one's friends; why step back from an opportunity to do one?

---

[342]Attributed to Devi Lal, former chief minister of Haryana, in Shekhar Gupta, 'Poll-bound Haryana flaunts its assets, liabilities, glory and muck like no other', *India Today*, 9 October 2014.
[343]'Helped Lalit Modi with travel papers on humanitarian grounds, Sushma Swaraj says', *Times of India*, 14 June 2015.
[344]Utkarsh Anand, 'Sushma Swaraj's daughter part of Lalit Modi's legal team in passport case', *Indian Express*, 15 June 2015.

A conflict of interest exists when any official's fiduciary responsibility to the obligations of his or her official position clashes with a personal interest, e.g. a sense of duty towards a friend. The Sushma Swaraj case fits so obviously within that definition that it could almost be a classic example for a case study on conflict of interest.

Or take Vasundhara Raje Scindia. It turns out the chief minister of Rajasthan (then the once and future holder of that designation) also supported the same individual's residency application to the British authorities on the 'strict condition that my [i.e. CM Raje's] assistance will not become known to the Indian authorities'![345] The individual in question had transferred ₹11.63 crore to CM Raje's son's company by valuing ten-rupee shares at a thousand times their worth.[346] Could that imply a conflict of interest that would explain the extraordinary 'unattributable' support for his 'leave to remain' beyond the reach of Indian law enforcement in the UK? Conflict of interest? Perish the thought!

The home minister of India, no less, made it clear that such mundane considerations as conflict of interest do not apply to the exalted panjandrums of the NDA. 'Resignations? That's for the UPA government, not for us,' he declared.[347] 'There will be no resignations over such issues in the NDA.' Conflict of interest is something that happens to other people—those who have a conscience. Not to us, who have been divinely ordained to rule as we see fit.

I hope some intrepid soul will take the entire issue to the Supreme Court and seek a direction that spells out conflict of interest duties and obligations. These must be enforceable, unlike the existing code of conduct for ministers, which was strongly upheld by the UPA but cheerfully ignored by the current government.

---

[345]'Vasundhara Raje "pushed Lalit Modi plea, said keep it secret", documents purportedly show', *Indian Express*, 17 July 2015.
[346]Pradeep Thakur, 'Lalit Modi invested ₹11.63 crore in CM Vasundhara Raje's son's company', *Economic Times*, 17 June 2015.
[347]This is not UPA; Smriti Irani, Sushma Swaraj won't quit: Rajnath Singh', *Times of India*, 24 June 2015.

As I have mentioned at the beginning of this chapter, when I joined the government in May 2009 I was told by the cabinet secretary that I must relinquish every one of my advisory board positions—every single one of them honorary—because of a possible conflict of interest. I wonder whether the new cabinet secretary has found occasion to enlighten the current external affairs minister about her obligations under the existing code of conduct for ministers and public servants.

But the real problem, of course, is implicit in the home minister's defiant stand that NDA ministers don't resign. It's part of an overall pattern we have seen from this government. They have taken no steps to appoint a Lokpal or ensure that the institutions created by the Lokpal Bill start functioning. They have refused to comply with a record number of applications for information under the Right to Information Act (RTI) which has been hollowed out under four years of the Modi regime, with vast numbers of questions awaiting replies. They kept the post of Chief Central Vigilance Commissioner vacant for several months before finally filling it with an appointee who has yet to find any grounds for action in the conduct of the BJP's ministers. It's not a pretty picture.

The only hope is that the media exposure of wrongdoing will prompt public interest litigation that in turn might give us a Supreme Court directive on conflict of interest. But how sad it is that our democracy needs the judiciary to do what any honest government ought to be able to do for itself.

Unfortunately ours is a government that proclaims its own virtue from the rooftops, but declines to spell out the standards it holds its own leaders to. Perhaps because it doesn't have any. The BJP's answer to charges of conflict of interest appears simple enough: self-interest will always prevail over the national interest. Then where's the conflict?

chapter nineteen

DESTROYING PARLIAMENT

I

The BJP government's undermining of Parliament is one of the most striking examples of misgovernance apparent in the Modi era. Under his regime, the government will propose. The Opposition will oppose. If matters come to a head and a vote is called, the government's brute majority will dispose.

The merits of the issue will matter little. There will be no reasoned attempts to persuade the other side; or rather, when such attempts are made by the well meaning, they will prove futile, since persuasion, reflection and exchange are not the purpose of the exercise. Increasingly, parliamentary debates have become a ritual, the obligatory airing of opposing views, until the whip is cracked and MPs duly vote on party lines.

Even sensible suggestions by the Opposition—with which the treasury benches do not in fact disagree—are never adopted, since to do so would admit the possibility of flexibility into government legislation in the Lok Sabha. The only time that Opposition views are taken into account is when the outcome of the vote would otherwise be uncertain—in the Upper House. And now, as we have seen, even that is changing, as BJP control of state assemblies gradually assures the government a majority in the Rajya Sabha as well.

But in the Lok Sabha, secure in its overwhelming majority, the government simply chooses not to listen, or to listen with a closed mind. The idea of Parliament as a forum for collective deliberation and agreed outcomes has ceased to have any meaning.

I had a taste of this myself in 2017's monsoon session, on a routine and non-controversial Bill on labour rights, which my party (having initiated the reform itself in the UPA days) had agreed to support. The Bill merely required that employees in companies of a certain size had the right to be notified of their rights, in writing. During its passage, I suggested that, given that nearly a fifth of Indian men, and more than a third of Indian women, were illiterate, two words should be added: '*orally and* in writing'. My logic, as I explained to my fellow MPs, was that while the Bill's objectives were laudable—in giving labourers knowledge of their rights in writing, so they could be legally enforceable—the substance of those rights should also be conveyed orally, so that illiterate workers could understand what they were entitled to. This suggestion was entirely within the spirit of the Bill.

I saw several BJP MPs nodding their heads affirmatively at this common-sense suggestion. But when the amendment was put to a voice-vote, the ruling party erupted raucously in a vociferous chorus of 'No'. My proposal was negatived. The whip was to vote in a certain way—common sense be damned.

This is a small example of how little real give-and-take there is in our parliamentary system, especially when the government in power rules by brute majority. Enabling such an authoritarian way of conducting itself is the Anti-Defection Law, 1985, which inaugurated a practice of party whips on all issues, making receptivity to the ideas of the other side punishable with expulsion from the House.

There was nothing about my idea that need have upset the ruling party, or that went against its ideological interests or the substantive purposes of the Bill. But the debate that was scheduled on the Bill was never intended to influence the terms of its adoption. It was just a ritual. The outcome was preordained: the Bill would be passed without change.

What, one might ask, is the point of such debates at all, other than to nail one's colours to the party mast? Why should a serious MP exercise his grey cells to come up with constructive suggestions, if they are never going to be considered, let alone adopted?

This was not how it was meant to be. Parliament, in the classic

British conception, was supposed to be a forum where individual MPs of ability and integrity met to discuss common problems and come to agreed solutions. Edmund Burke, in his famous speech to the Electors of Bristol on 3 November 1774, articulated most brilliantly and clearly the logic of parliamentary representation. Burke was addressing the issue of MPs being asked to advocate the wishes of their constituents, rather than themselves, but his logic applies also to the issue of MPs parroting their party lines. He is worth quoting in his own words:

> It ought to be the happiness and glory of a representative to live in the strictest union, the closest correspondence, and the most unreserved communication with his constituents [or here, if you prefer, read 'Party']. Their wishes ought to have great weight with him; their opinion, high respect; their business, unremitted attention. It is his duty to sacrifice his repose, his pleasures, his satisfactions, to theirs; and above all, ever, and in all cases, to prefer their interest to his own. But his unbiased opinion, his mature judgment, his enlightened conscience, he ought not to sacrifice to you, to any man, or to any set of men living. These he does not derive from your pleasure; no, nor from the law and the constitution. They are a trust from Providence, for the abuse of which he is deeply answerable. Your representative owes you, not his industry only, but his judgment; and he betrays, instead of serving you, if he sacrifices it to your opinion.[348]

In other words, an MP betrays himself and his voters if he surrenders his own better judgement to the dictates of either his constituents or his party leadership. As Edmund Burke explains, 'government and legislation are matters of reason and judgment, and not of inclination; and what sort of reason is that, in which the determination precedes the discussion; in which one set of men deliberate, and another decide; and where those who form

---

[348]*The Portable Edmund Burke*, New York: Penguin Books, 1999.

the conclusion are perhaps three hundred miles distant from those who hear the arguments?'[349]

His final point is the clincher: 'Parliament is not a *congress* of ambassadors from different and hostile interests; which interests each must maintain, as an agent and advocate, against other agents and advocates; but parliament is a *deliberative* assembly of *one* nation, with *one* interest, that of the whole; where, not local purposes, not local prejudices, [one might add today, "not party lines"] ought to guide, but the general good, resulting from the general reason of the whole. You choose a member indeed; but when you have chosen him, he is not a member of Bristol, but he is a member of *parliament*.'[350]

This goes to the nub of the entire issue. What is our conception of what Prime Minister Modi has called 'the temple of democracy'? Is it merely a place to ratify decisions made elsewhere in party cabals or cabinet meetings, whose adoption is rendered inevitable by the previous general election results? Or is it a chamber where the representatives of the Indian people assemble to express their considered opinions and thoughtful disagreements, before coming to an outcome in the interests not of a party but of the country as a whole?

The Anti-Defection Law was passed with good intentions—the same good intentions with which, the proverb tells us, the road to hell is paved. It was intended to stop the aaya Ram–gaya Ram practice of legislators crossing the floor in pursuit of power and pelf, which saw state governments (and two central governments) between 1967 and 1985 rise and fall like skittles. The idea was noble, and rested on sound principles: governmental stability matters; people must stay loyal to the party on whose platform they contested; the intent of the voters must not be betrayed by defections. When the law was first explained by its proponents, there was widespread support, even enthusiasm, for its passage.

---

[349]Ibid.
[350]Ibid.

But how has the Act worked in practice? It has dramatically reduced defections, but not eliminated them, as we have seen in Uttarakhand in 2017 and Manipur, Gujarat and UP in 2018. What it has done most effectively is to stifle the voice of the individual legislator. Since every single vote in Parliament sees a whip being issued, however trivial the subject of the Bill, there is no room for honest differences of opinion. Disobeying a whip offers grounds not just for disciplinary action by the party, but expulsion from Parliament altogether. No MP who has struggled and strived (and spent) to get elected to his seat lightly places it in jeopardy. His convictions become secondary to the party line. The 'argumentative Indian' is often on display in both Houses, but only when he is arguing strictly according to his party's position.

As a result, the Anti-Defection Law has reduced each MP to a cipher during every vote, a number to be totted up by his party whip rather than an individual of ability, conviction and conscience. This outcome has other effects: it reduces the need for each MP to study an issue thoroughly and come to a position on it, since his position no longer matters unless he is part of the party leadership. In my experience, most MPs only study the Bills they are assigned to speak on; the rest sees them dutifully voting as their whip tells them to.

This is, in many ways, a travesty of the parliamentary process. In the UK, where the system originated, no whip was issued even on so fundamental a vote as to whether to authorize the government to proceed with the Brexit negotiations. Earlier, no whip was issued on whether the UK should support the US in the Iraq war. Dissent was freely and honestly expressed on both sides of the aisle. Such freedom is unknown to the Indian MP after the passage of the Anti-Defection Law.

Ironically, the underlying logic of the Indian approach has been called into question by the Election Commission itself offering a 'None of The Above' (NOTA) option on the ballot for the recent vice-presidential election. Every MP voting in that election was subject to a party whip; would not voting NOTA violate his whip? If a NOTA vote was cast, then, would it be grounds for disqualifying the voter from Parliament? If NOTA embodies a constitutional right, then isn't punishment under the Anti-Defection Law for exercising that right itself unconstitutional?

At least in the vice-presidential election, there was a secret ballot. Some cross-voting appears to have occurred. Votes in Parliament, however, are out in the open. A dissenting vote is an act of defiance; under the Anti-Defection Law, it will automatically attract sanction.

Part of the problem is that the main provisions of the Constitution regarding the legislature were silent about the party system; the later addition of the anti-defection clause in the schedule in 1985 was patently illogical since it sought to punish the undermining of an institution which was itself not mentioned in the main provisions. Surely the schedule cannot override the main provisions of the Constitution? Did the founders ever intend the party system to be paramount over the individual parliamentarian, obliging him to subordinate his conscience to the party whip?

These are questions to which there are no real answers in today's India. But the right ones, in the words of the 2016 Nobel laureate for Literature, are 'blowin' in the wind'. We just have to grasp them firmly and bring them indoors into Sansad Bhavan.

One such answer might be to amend the Anti-Defection Law to ensure that party whips can only be issued for specific kinds of issues—those involving the survival of the government, perhaps, and money bills. That would lead to more open discussion on other subjects, but it is doubtful that any MP would openly vote against his party line even on a minor issue. Even if such a vote no longer attracts disqualification, it would attract the disapproval of his party leadership, and that is disincentive enough for most parliamentarians.

One of the consequences of the crisis of representation I have diagnosed here is that Parliament itself has become less and less seminal an institution in our democracy. Prime Minister Modi occasionally shows up to deliver rodomontade speeches in

Parliament, but he does not take questions, and has refused to
subject himself to any kind of parliamentary cross-examination
of his policies or statements. That junior ministers respond for
him is also, in a way, an effort to preserve an aura around him—
something that takes him beyond and 'above' such lowly concerns
as Parliament and its squabbles—and establish him, visually and in
the general perception, as a PM who is no longer just first among
equals. In the process, the 'temple of our democracy' has been
devalued to little more than its proscenium stage, with ministers
and MPs little more than sacerdotes hovering around with ritual
offerings for the head priest. Whereas in the early days a prime
minister could even be challenged by MPs from his own party—
think of Jawaharlal Nehru being attacked by Feroze Gandhi,
Finance Minister T. T. Krishnamachari being forced to resign by
his own backbenchers, or Mahadev Mishra challenging his prime
minister's China policy—today conformity, even unquestioning
obedience, rules the roost. So why give Parliament an importance
its performance does not warrant?

The result of this kind of thinking is apparent. The first three
Lok Sabhas saw as many 140 sittings a year; we are now at
about half that number, and it is reducing every year, since the
BJP government clearly has very little time for the distractions
of Parliament. In the 15th Lok Sabha, 25 per cent of the Bills
were passed with scarcely any discussion at all and only 20 per
cent witnessed discussions of three hours or more. (These figures
are almost certainly lower in the current 16th Lok Sabha, which
has met only for a grand total of 287 days over a span of four
years.)[351]. In the Modi-era Lok Sabha, only 26 per cent of the
Bills introduced have been referred to committees.[352] Barely 15 per
cent of the Union Budget is discussed in detail; our government is

---

[351]http://www.prsindia.org/media/articles-by-prs-team/parliament-logjam-part-
2-examining-legislative-avenues-available-to-keep-govt-accountable-exercise-
necessary-oversight-5300/
[352]http://www.prsindia.org/media/articles-by-prs-team/while-in-session-good-
parliament-productivity-weak-examination-of-bills-5349/

spending taxpayers' money without the taxpayers' representatives having a meaningful say in how it is spent. (State assemblies are even worse: many sit for fewer than thirty days a year, and in Haryana the average is twelve days!)[353]

Once Bills are passed in a hurry, they become Acts, and Acts are implemented through the promulgation of Rules, which are drafted by the government and supposed to be placed on the table of each House. The Rules really govern how the Act works in practice, and in theory are subject to parliamentary scrutiny. Guess how many Rules have been discussed in the current Lok Sabha? Precisely zero.[354]

Such practices are destroying the role of the Indian parliamentarian as the legislator he was envisaged to be by our founding fathers in the Constitution. Our prime minister spoke of introducing minimum government, maximum governance. In Chapter 16, we saw that transmorgified into maximum government, minimum governance. And here we have a system of minimum Parliament, maximum government. The judiciary is eagerly stepping into the breach, taking initiatives that should have been Parliament's to take—unelected judges substituting themselves for the people's representatives. It's nobody's fault but our own— but it's not the democracy Dr Ambedkar and his colleagues in the constituent assembly envisaged.

II

The other aspect of the functioning of Parliament today that deserves to be reiterated here is parliamentary disruption, which has become a frequent and ubiquitous feature of our democracy in the Modi era.

I am a conscientious objector to parliamentary disruptions. Sadly, my belief that Parliament is a place where the elected representatives of the people work uninterruptedly for the benefit

---

[353]M. R. Madhavan, 'Put the houses in order', *The Week*, 25 December 2016.
[354]Ibid.

of the people, doesn't seem to be shared by too many of my fellow parliamentarians. I think back to an occasion when the House was in bedlam but the Opposition legislator was unrepentant. 'The disruption we have started in this session will be taken to the people till we are able to restore fairness and some degree of accountability,' he said. 'If parliamentary accountability is subverted and a debate is intended to be used merely to put a lid on parliamentary accountability, it is then a legitimate tactic for the Opposition to expose the government through the parliamentary instruments available at its command.'[355]

He was righteous in his indignation at the suggestion that by disrupting Parliament he was not doing the work he was elected to do. 'Disrupting does not mean not doing work. What we are doing is in fact very important work.'

Asked whether Parliament should not be used to debate rather than disrupt, the Opposition MP was categorical. 'A national debate is on. Every aspect is being debated, yet not in Parliament. This debate rages on elsewhere, while the government runs Parliament. Our strategy does not allow it to be debated in Parliament, that is all.'[356]

'In a debate, you talk the issue out,' he said dismissively to *Open* magazine. 'Sometimes, disruptions bring greater gains to the country.'[357]

Another senior Opposition figure, already then a former union minister, was asked about the losses to the national exchequer from the disruption of Parliament, which was wasting crores of taxpayers' rupees. Yes, she agreed, 'when Parliament ends this way, there is criticism—we are told that there is a loss since the Parliament wasn't allowed to function... By losing ₹10-20 crore from loss of Parliament proceedings, if we can build pressure on

[355]Anita Katyal, '"Disrupting Parliament is important": BJP's words from opposition days come back to haunt it', *Scroll.in*, 24 December 2014.
[356]Jatin Gandhi, 'Who Needs Parliament?', *Open*, 30 August 2012.
[357] Ibid.

the government, then that is acceptable.'[358]

Veteran leaders of the Opposition agreed. A former prime-ministerial candidate of the party declared that, sometimes, blocking legislative action 'yields results'.[359] A former finance and foreign minister added: 'Because the government has been silent on the issue we have decided to rake up the issue... I would like to strongly demand that the government announce right now a probe. If there is no announcement of a probe, then how can we let the House function?'[360]

Were these Congress leaders defending the disruption of recent sessions of Parliament? No, perish the thought. These are verbatim quotes from BJP stalwarts (in the order quoted) Arun Jaitley, Sushma Swaraj, L. K. Advani, and Yashwant Sinha. Except they were spoken in 2011–13, as the BJP paralysed session after session with its clamour for resignations, for a joint parliamentary committee on the telecom allocations, and for probes into assorted alleged misdemeanours of the UPA government.

In a final irony, Vice President Venkaiah Naidu, in a speech on the importance of legislatures, advocated the immediate suspension of legislators who invade the well of the House. An admirable sentiment, especially for a former parliamentary affairs minister of the current dispensation. Except that just four years ago, the same Venkaiah Naidu, when asked about BJP legislators doing the same thing, and asked if these were not unparliamentary tactics, replied unapologetically: 'Let us invent new tactics so that the principle of accountability is not sacrificed. We will not keep quiet. We will take the fight to the people.'[361]

Turnabout, it is said, is fair play. These were the arguments used, with eloquence and even legalese, by the BJP leadership

[358]Sabyasachi Dasgupta, 'Prime Minister blames BJP for "wasted session of Parliament"; BJP hits back', *NDTV*, 7 September 2012.
[359]'Sonia Gandhi lambasts India's opposition', *BBC*, 13 September 2010.
[360]'BJP disrupts LS demanding probe, House adjourned for day', *FirstPost*, 11 December 2012.
[361]Raman Iyer, 'BJP justifies disruption of Parliament over coal blocks allocation issue', *TopNews*, 9 January 2012

when, for the ten years of UPA rule, they disrupted Parliament with impunity. More than 60 per cent of the time of the previous Lok Sabha was lost to BJP-led disruptions.[362] It was hardly surprising that—faced with the stubborn refusal of the government to accept that the conduct of their external affairs minister and two chief ministers warranted their resignations or at least a serious investigation—the UPA members decided to emulate their predecessors in Opposition.

Those of us who attended missionary schools learned the golden rule: 'do unto others as you would have them do unto you'. The new golden rule of Indian politics has become: 'do unto others what they did unto you'.

In a startling turnaround, the poachers have now become the gamekeepers. The very politicians who had argued the case for disruption—who had used sophistry and morality to obstruct the work of Parliament for years in the cause of the higher principle of accountability—suddenly decided that on this issue, where you stand depends on where you sit. Now that they are sitting on the treasury benches, disruption is wasteful, even anti-national.

I am sorry, but it won't wash. Of course, two wrongs don't make a right. But it was the BJP who had set the standards of parliamentary conduct they are now deploring. It was they who had declared 'resignations first, discussions later'.

Well before I entered politics, I had been invited by then-speaker Somnath Chatterjee to a round table of eminent citizens (Narayana Murthy and Shyam Benegal among them) to discuss the functioning of Parliament. We had all called for strict enforcement of the rules to ensure higher standards of decorum and debate, and been disabused by the speaker of our illusions. Disruptions, he said, occurred because an outnumbered Opposition saw them as part of their democratic rights; to thwart them by invoking the rule book would be condemned by all parties, including the ruling Congress, as undemocratic. So suspending, let alone expelling,

---

[362]G. Pramod Kumar, 'Parliament Logjam', *FirstPost*, 25 July 2015.

MPs was not an option he could easily exercise.

Matters got worse under the next speaker, Meira Kumar, whose decency and gentility were shamefully abused by a belligerent BJP. Still, she echoed the Somnath Chatterjee line: it would be wrong to expel unruly Opposition members without an all-party consensus on doing so. So disruption continued.

Whatever the merits of this method of parliamentary protest—and personally, it is not something I have ever cared for—it has become part of the convention of Indian parliamentary practice. So the shock when Speaker Sumitra Mahajan expelled twenty-five of the Congress's forty-four members for five days in 2015, invoking Rule 374A, which had only been used three times in the entire sixty-seven-year history of independent India (at the time), was palpable.[363] Seven Opposition parties announced they were joining the Congress in boycotting the Lok Sabha in protest against this deplorable decision.

Certainly, let us create new standards of acceptable parliamentary conduct, but by consensus with all parties. Expelling your Opposition is not democracy. But Mr Modi knows that: he has done exactly the same thing, repeatedly, in the Gujarat Assembly, passing laws with almost the entire Opposition suspended from the House.[364]

In his 2014 election campaign, Mr Modi had boasted that he would apply the Gujarat model to the rest of India. We just have to ensure he doesn't start with Parliament.

---

[363]'25 Congress MPs suspended for five days for disrupting Parliament, Sonia says "black day"', *Indian Express*, 4 August 2015.

[364]"He once got 12 laws passed in 17 minutes in 2009 after getting the Opposition suspended from the House. Under him, the Assembly would be convened once every six months just to meet the constitutional requirement", from Anita Joshua, 'The one-man show', *The Hindu*, 22 May 2015.

chapter twenty

GOVERNING GOVERNORS

Over the past four years the NDA government has repeatedly elicited the resignations of several UPA-appointed governors and appointed its own candidates. This prompts a number of interesting questions. Predictably, UPA supporters have raised the issue of constitutional propriety (and a non-UPA critic, CPI(M) leader Sitaram Yechury, has called it 'politically unethical and constitutionally incorrect'[365]) while NDA supporters have cited precedent, not least pointing to a similar action by the UPA in removing four NDA-appointed governors in 2004. There have also been allegations that the replacement of governors is among the steps being taken to saffronize the country's institutions. Battle has been joined over an issue that ought to be, ideally, beyond the realm of contention.

First, let's get the blame game out of the way. If we go back far enough, the practice of turfing out governors appointed by the defeated government started in 1977, when the victorious Janata Party defenestrated a number of Indira Gandhi appointees. Changes of government have often seen a recurrence of the practice by all sides, though it is also true that many governments have left governors appointed by their predecessors in place. But what is happening today has happened before.

However, what is different this time is that since the last round of gubernatorial musical chairs in 2004 (when Haryana's Babu Parmanand, Uttar Pradesh's Vishnu Kant Shastri, Goa's Kidar Nath Sahani and Gujarat's Kailashpati Mishra were replaced by the UPA government), the Supreme Court has weighed in. Earlier decisions had been justified (though justifications had not earlier

---

[365]'Exodus of UPA-era governors: PM Modi begins mass clean-up', *FirstPost*, 17 June 2014.

been deemed necessary) by a principle advanced in October 1980, when Tamil Nadu Governor Prabhudas Patwari was dismissed on the basis of the argument that governors serve at the president's 'pleasure' under Article 156 (1). At the time, given the precedent of 1977, it was generally accepted that the prime minister of the day could dismiss any governor for political reasons, and without giving any explanation, since the PM alone decided when the president would grant or withdraw his 'pleasure'. But in 2010 the Supreme Court differed, concluding, on a petition moved by one of the governors dismissed in 2004, that the government cannot arbitrarily transfer appointed governors without 'compelling' reasons. It declared: 'Nor can he be removed on the ground that the Union government has lost confidence in him. It follows, therefore, that a change in government at the Centre is not a ground for removal of governors holding office to make way for others favoured by the new government.'[366]

What reasons could the government advance that would be so compelling as to pass the Supreme Court's test? The BJP today is making the same argument that the UPA did before the Supreme Court in 2004—that a governor appointed by a defeated government would have a different view of national policy than the new government, giving rise to conflict between the governor's views and the government's. It is on this basis that UP Governor B. L. Joshi and Kerala Governor Sheila Dikshit resigned, as did Governor of Nagaland Ashwani Kumar, West Bengal Governor M. K. Narayanan, Maharashtra Governor K. Sankaranarayanan, Goa Governor B. N. Wanchoo and Karnataka Governor H. R. Bharadwaj. Assam Governor J. B. Patnaik was said to have faced pressure to turn in his papers, but he served until the end of his term.

But this argument had explicitly been rejected by the Supreme Court, which wanted evidence of such conflict to be cited before

---

[366]Maneesh Chhibber and Utkarsh Anand, 'In 2010, SC ruled govt change not a ground to remove Governors', *Indian Express*, 18 June 2014.

a governor was dismissed or even transferred. It is safe to assume that the Modi government would consider such a requirement to provide evidence an inadmissible interference in its executive prerogatives. Yet one could also make the counterargument that the very same principle could, by the same logic, be extended to a president of India elected under the previous dispensation, yet no government has dared suggest the president should leave office when 'his' government loses an election. Any conflict between the president's views and the government's simply has to be resolved in favour of the latter; that is what our democracy requires. Why can't governors be told that, whoever appointed them, they must now follow the directives of the new government? Surely that would end the issue of any potential conflict?

But the truth is that this really isn't about a conflict of principles or policies at all; it's really all about jobs—jobs for 'our' people rather than 'theirs'. Various defeated or superannuated BJP leaders need to be accommodated in comfortable sinecures, and it galls them to see the Congress party's favourites enjoying the perks of palatial Raj Bhavans around the country while they languish in semi-retirement, itching to be appointed. So when Congress leader Ghulam Nabi Azad calls the NDA's decision 'arbitrary and capricious', using the Supreme Court's words, the fact is he's right. It's about emptying chairs for BJP people to occupy—nothing more and nothing less.

As Congress leader Kapil Sibal has pointed out, the Modi government's idea of constitutional merit does not look beyond the Sangh Parivar.[367] He provides a detailed list of Prime Minister Narendra Modi's appointees to substantiate his argument: Kalyan Singh, governor of Rajasthan; O. P. Kohli, governor of Gujarat; Vajubhai Vala, governor of Karnataka; Ram Naik, governor of

---

[367] A look at the credentials of those appointed as governors after 2014 suggests that many of them are committed RSS functionaries, or sympathizers, who are, without being cognizant of the high constitutional office they hold, involved in politics within the state they represent. This vitiates the environment in the state'; from Kabil Sibal, *Shades of Truth*, New Delhi: Rupa Publications, 2018, p. 51.

Uttar Pradesh; Kesri Nath Tripathi, governor of West Bengal; Balramji Dass Tandon, governor of Chattisgarh; Tathagata Roy, governor of Tripura; P. B. Acharya, who held the additional charge of governor of Assam till August 2016; and V. Shanmuganathan, former governor of Meghalaya, who resigned from his post in January 2017 following allegations of sexual harassment against him—have all been associated with the RSS. Indeed, some of them have gone to the extent of saying that their loyalty to the RSS comes before their other responsibilities[368]—a far cry from the quasi-monarchical political detachment expected of governors in India's federal democracy.

Ghulam Nabi Azad found the removal of governors to be 'against the very grain of democratic traditions and constitutional propriety'. If taken forward, he warned, the move would be 'fraught with serious repercussions and have a debilitating impact on our constitutional democracy'.[369] So what can we do to ensure we don't go through the same problems after every election?

There are two alternatives. The first is to insulate the office of governor from politicization altogether, by various measures that I suggest below. The second alternative is the more radical one: to abolish the post of governor altogether, as a colonial relic that democratic India can dispense with. Except in the increasingly rare resort to president's rule, the governor has little of substance to do, and his few substantive and mainly ceremonial tasks could easily be divided between the chief minister and the chief justice of the state.

But that would mean depriving the ruling party of twenty-nine comfortably provisioned freebie positions to hand out to its loyal supporters. And what are the odds of that happening?

I considered the first option in depth when Sheila Dikshit's resignation as governor of Kerala brought to eight the number of

<hr/>

[368]Ibid., p.52; Sanjay Singh, 'How to be a governor in the Modi sarkar: Be an obedient RSS loyalist', *FirstPost*, 15 July 2014.
[369]'It's political vendetta, says Congress, as Modi government asks UPA-appointed Governors to go', *Indian Express*, 17 June 2014.

UPA-era gubernatorial appointees who had been coerced by the BJP government into demitting office prematurely.[370]

As the MP for Thiruvananthapuram, I didn't conceal my disappointment at seeing her go. Sheila-ji brought to her office a wealth of political experience and administrative ability, as well as the indefinable qualities of style and grace.

Her tenure as governor lasted barely six months, but it was marked by swift and impressive decision-making in the few areas under her direct authority, as well as a genuine interest in Kerala and its cultural heritage.

Her decision to demand the resignation of the vice-chancellor of Mahatma Gandhi University, against whom charges had been pending on her predecessor's desk for nearly a year, was one of several examples of the former. Her active involvement in the promotion of the arts, and her regular attendance at performances of Kerala dance and music, including at the Raj Bhavan, confirmed the latter. She adorned her office, and was missed.

But 'The Sad Case of Sheila Dikshit' need not be the title of a tragic opera if we use the situation her case epitomizes to review the entire problem of governors, their appointment and what one may, not entirely jocularly, call their dis-appointment.

Isn't it time we developed an all-party consensus on a code of conduct regarding governors, so that we can put an end to the unseemly and unedifying spectacle we have all been forced to witness in recent years—the slow-motion assassinations of some of the highest constitutional authorities of our land?

Though the suggestion that the very post of governor be done away with is tempting, it is going to be far more difficult to evolve a political consensus on amending the Constitution to achieve that, than to reform the process and criteria by which governors are appointed.

The governor represents in each of our states what the president of India does in the country as a whole. The president is universally

[370]'Kerala Governor Sheila Dikshit resigns', *The Hindu*, 26 August 2014.

considered to be above politics; even when a government changes, a president elected under the previous dispensation remains above controversy, and, as I've said, no government has dared suggest that a president should leave office when 'his' government loses an election. It doesn't need to; the president clearly understands, both as matter of constitutional principle and political reality, that he may be the nation's First Citizen for protocol purposes, but it's the popularly elected government that calls the shots. Indeed, what is known as the President's Address to Parliament is merely the performance of a figurehead reading out a script given to him or her by the elected government of the day. And that, in our parliamentary democracy, is exactly how it should be.

It is true that the president is elected by MPs and MLAs, whereas governors are appointed. But what the governor, as the president's representative in the state, must be is a carbon copy— just as apolitical as the president, equally subordinate to the elected government (in his case that of the state as well as that of the centre), owing primary allegiance only to the Constitution of India.

Such an institution of governorship should ideally, like the presidency it mirrors, be beyond the realm of contention. But we all know it's not: the practice of the last several decades has sometimes, though not always, dragged the institution into disrepute. Amongst the reasons for the plummeting stature of the office have been: the appointment of political time-servers who conducted themselves in office as agents of their parties; the profusion of decrepit sinecure-seekers long past their use-by-dates, who brought neither energy not distinction to their posts; the elevation of a number of active politicians who used Raj Bhavans as a rest-stop on their way to resuming their political careers; and the occasional misuse of governors by a party at the centre at loggerheads with one in the state to dismiss elected governments on spurious (or at least contestable) grounds. If all these practices span the range of evident transgressions of the intent of the framers of the Constitution, there have also been men and women of integrity and class who served their states, and the country, ably as governors.

How do we ensure that we get more such men and women to be governors in the future? There is a crying need for an all-party consensus, to be embodied in law, to achieve this.

The consensus would require agreement on insulating the office of governor from politicization by adopting these principles, or something very like them:

1. Anyone appointed governor must:
    renounce primary membership of any political party;
    be ineligible for future appointment as office-bearer of any political party;
    be disqualified from election or appointment to any post, bar that of president or vice-president of India, or Lokpal.
2. In turn, a governor shall be immune from being removed from office till the completion of his or her term;
    being transferred to another state, except by mutual consent;
    receiving instructions from any functionary of the government other than the president of India.
3. A governor may, of course, be impeached for gross misconduct or dereliction of duty, but only through a procedure akin to that currently governing the impeachment of members of the country's senior judiciary.

If such a code were to be adopted, it would elevate the office of governor to the status intended by the founding fathers, which it no longer enjoys. It would ensure the position attracts men and women of integrity and ability, while simultaneously ending the spectacle of politicians taking a breather in some Raj Bhavan before returning to the electoral fray for their parties, and so conducting themselves in office with an eye on their own political future.

There should be no bar on former politicians becoming governors, as some are advocating: it would be a pity to lose their political experience in such an office. But these rules would ensure that upon appointment, they cease to be politicians. Their lifelong allegiances would not disappear overnight, but they would be empowered, and expected, to transcend them.

If the Modi government had ever been serious about reform, and about working with the Opposition, fixing the institution of governor would have been a good place to start. But as we have seen over the past several years, the timeless and irresistible appeal of 'jobs for the boys' has ensured that the BJP too, has carried on the practice of using Raj Bhavans as retirement homes for their apparatchiks.

chapter twenty-one

MATTERS OF JUSTICE

The judiciary is the third branch of government, besides the legislature and the executive, which the Constitution has invested with powers to run the country. Given the authoritarian tendencies and general dysfunction that appear to be the hallmarks of this administration, the importance of the judiciary to the well-being of the nation and the safeguarding of the Constitution has risen even further. In earlier chapters in this section I wrote about the crisis of many aspects of the legislature and the executive and touched upon an issue that showed the judiciary in a poor light. In this chapter I'd like to look at two key issues affecting the judiciary, on both of which the government has been shown up. Both these problems affect the efficient functioning of our courts, so it is critical that they are addressed fairly and competently.

The first has to do with the appointment of judges to the higher courts of the land. The process is simple. A collegium of the Chief Justice and the four most senior judges decides on the appointments and sends its list to the government for approval. Once this approval is given, the appointments are made. In recent times, the smooth functioning of this process has been interrupted on more than one occasion, with the government sitting on nominations or questioning the collegium's recommendations. One of the ruling party's most contentious actions was its holding up of the appointment of Uttarakhand Chief Justice, K. M. Joseph, to the Supreme Court. To its credit the judiciary stuck to its guns and several months of delay later, the government gave in and appointed him, albeit with reduced seniority as a result of the delay. But the widespread perception that Justice Joseph was victimized because of his unfavourable verdict on a case directly affecting the BJP's political interests in Uttarakhand did no credit to the Modi government.

It is not the business of the government to hold up the appointment of judges at a time when the judiciary is buckling under the strain of the huge number of cases clogging the courts. At least half the high courts in the country are functioning at 50 per cent of their strength—there are over 500 vacancies in the high courts alone.[371] Some of this has to do with delays within the judiciary in coming up with nominations to fill existing vacancies, others to do with dilatory government processes. Pointing this out, the incoming Chief Justice of the Supreme Court, Justice Ranjan Gogoi, said while addressing a gathering of judges in July 2018 that it was imperative that the vacancies be filled as soon as possible. 'If we are unable to fill [the vacancies] I do not blame the government for embarking upon the idea to centralize the recruiting system,' he said.[372] At the same time, any attempt by the government to block or influence the hiring of judges should be strenuously resisted. On this depends the strength and fairness of our democracy.

The horrendous backlog of cases in all courts of the land underscores the old dictum that justice delayed is justice denied. At the moment there are more than 3 crore pending cases in various courts—over 2.84 crore cases in district courts, over 40 lakh cases in high courts and 57,987 cases in the Supreme Court.[373] It is clear that something needs to be done to tackle this crisis on a priority basis and the Modi government has missed a great opportunity to help fix the problem, despite former Chief Justice T. S. Thakur breaking down and weeping in front of the prime minister at the resultant judicial crisis.[374]

It would help, of course, if the judiciary got its own house in order, refusing to admit frivolous cases (such as the recent

---

[371]Abhishek Anshu, '24 High Courts short on judges by 43.6 per cent with 50.5 lakh pending cases', *Outlook*, 13 January 2017.
[372]Bhadra Sinha, 'Chief Justices of all high courts must speed up process of hiring district judges: Justice Gogoi', *Hindustan Times*, 28 July 2018.
[373]'3.3 crore cases pending in Indian courts, pendency figure at its highest: CJI Dipak Misra', *Business Today*, 28 June 2018.
[374]'An overworked Chief Justice TS Thakur breaks down in front of PM Modi', *Times of India*, 24 April 2016.

petition to outlaw Sikh jokes) and transparently mala fide ones (like
the four-year-long persecution of me for placing my hand across
my heart during a rendition of the national anthem, rather than
standing stiffly to attention as the rules dictate). The admission
of a bewildering range of cases unworthy of the name, and their
repeated procedural adjournments, have added to the clogging
of the judicial system, resulting in interminable prosecutions that
drag on for years. Some of this can be remedied by the judges
themselves; others clearly require the government to exercise both
imagination and political will.

One way to take the pressure off the courts is to set up
an efficient Alternative Dispute Resolution system (ADR) to sort
out business disputes and the like. No wonder foreign investors
have shown great reluctance to set up offices in India, citing our
tedious legal system. Arbitration is an excellent mechanism for
speedy resolution of conflicts, but to our shame, international
businesses operating in India prefer to arbitrate abroad in places
like Singapore and Hong Kong. So inadequate is the Indian judicial
system seen to be that even Mauritius is offering itself as a place
to settle disputes affecting businesses in India!

To take Singapore as one example, apart from a strong legal
framework, it offers hefty tax breaks to law firms on income from
arbitration cases and has eased restrictions to enable foreign law
firms to practise in Singapore. Singapore is therefore attracting
arbitration business from our country (India is the country with
the most number of cases at the Singapore International Arbitration
Centre). This is a standing reproach to our failure to deliver an
effective arbitration mechanism in India. We cannot urge businesses
to 'make in India' without encouraging them to arbitrate in India.

Mahatma Gandhi mentions in his autobiography, *The Story of
My Experiments with Truth*, how it struck him one day 'that the
true function of a lawyer was to unite parties riven asunder'.[375]

---

[375]M. K. Gandhi, *The Story of My Experiments with Truth: An Autobiography*,
New Delhi: Om Books International, 2009.

This is perhaps the best argument for arbitration, which has been an alternative system of justice since ancient times. One doesn't have to recall examples of arbitration in Roman law, when even in ancient India disputes were often resolved by a single headman or a village panchayat.

The economic reforms of 1991 ushered in an era of globalization and created a need for an alternative forum to resolve disputes involving international commercial transactions. The Arbitration and Conciliation Act, 1996, was introduced by the then Congress government to consolidate the law on domestic arbitration and provide for international commercial arbitration on the basis of the United Nations Commission on International Trade Law model. But India has resisted adopting this practice widely, and though the Act has been in force for nearly two decades now, the practice has not kept up with the law.

When the BJP government finally promulgated the Arbitration and Conciliation (Amendment) Ordinance, 2015, it was too little, too late. It did not do enough to minimize the supervisory role of courts in arbitration proceedings. Under Clause 15 of the Ordinance, for instance, arbitration proceedings have to conclude within a period of eighteen months, or else the mandate of the arbitrator will be terminated unless the court extends the time period. But arbitration proceedings in our country take a minimum of two years to conclude and vary depending on the nature, complexity, and stakes involved in different disputes. For arbitration proceedings that exceed this time period, the parties will have to apply to the court for an extension of the mandate of arbitral tribunals. This has created an unnecessary interference of the court and will defeat the very objective of arbitration by delaying the arbitration process.

While the government wants to allow high courts in India to pass interim orders for international commercial arbitrations seated outside India, it has failed to specify the criteria for determining the jurisdiction of the high court. Ideally the jurisdiction of a civil court or a high court is determined on the basis of the place or territory of the subject. But when you are talking about international commercial arbitrations seated abroad, involving transactions conducted abroad, how do you decide which high court will have jurisdiction? If we do not address this loophole, parties in dispute will have to wait for the courts to decide the criteria—which will bring in more delays in arbitration.

Additionally, the new law should have had a provision for recognizing emergency arbitrators and their decisions. Decisions of emergency arbitrators are now recognized in arbitration rules of most international arbitral institutions to assist parties who want urgent relief. Countries such as Hong Kong and Singapore have recently amended their arbitration laws to enforce the decisions of emergency arbitrators. Our new law doesn't do this.

The arbitration practice in our country should encourage academicians or lawyers as arbitrators instead of only retired judges of the Supreme Court and high courts. This is the practice in countries with successful arbitration mechanisms, such as the US. While a judge would bring judicial experience to a proceeding, arbitration doesn't have to resemble a judicial hearing. There is a need to create a pool of experienced professionals in arbitration who can be formally trained and certified as arbitrators by a specialized body. In that regard, the law also overlooks the need for a specialized body such as an Arbitral Commission of India to encourage and create awareness of the practice of arbitration as an alternate method of dispute resolution.

The objective of the law is supposed to put in place an updated and modern practice of Alternative Dispute Resolution. Yet there are no provisions that encourage the use of technology during arbitration proceedings. Use of teleconferencing and video-conferencing to replace formal sittings of the arbitral proceedings would save time and aid in a smoother and more efficient conduct of arbitration proceedings.

While I welcome the government attempting to promote arbitration through an amended law, I feel that it could have done more to modernize arbitration in our country, especially when India is favourably placed to take advantage of the shift in global trade and investment from the West. Instead of taking the challenge from Singapore and Hong Kong head on, the government has missed a golden opportunity to address and resolve issues plaguing our dispute resolution system.

We need to reform our arbitration regime to bring it into the twenty-first century. Sadly, the government's new law doesn't come close enough. Instead of creating the legal equivalent of a bullet train, the Modi government has simply missed the bus.

chapter twenty-two

JUVENILE (IN)JUSTICE

The Modi government enacted the Juvenile Justice (Care and Protection of Children) Act in January 2016. By changing the law to ensure that 16 to 18 year olds can now be tried, convicted and sentenced as adults to twenty years in prison for 'heinous offences', it has regressively plunged our nation into the darkness of nineteenth-century jurisprudence.

The Juvenile Justice Board will now have discretionary powers to transfer a child in the age group of 16–18 years, accused of rape, murder, kidnapping, robbery, dacoity, and other offences which are punishable with imprisonment for a minimum term of seven years, to an adult criminal justice system for trial and conviction. An excuse for this barbarism is not hard to find. It is a reaction to the horrific Nirbhaya case of 2012, which shocked the national conscience, especially when it was claimed in the media that the most heinous acts in that criminal episode were allegedly the doings of a juvenile. When the media suggested that it was likely he would get away with minimum punishment, and that the system might leave a predator free on the streets, there was understandable uproar in all quarters. Someone close to me, naturally agitated and emotional, said: 'If he is old enough to rape, he is old enough to hang.'

The problem with such an approach is twofold. It treats children as adults, which is wrong morally, legally, ethically, emotionally, and constitutionally. A 16-year-old may physically be a man but does not have the mental maturity of an adult. During the immediate aftermath of the Nirbhaya tragedy, the UPA undertook extensive consultations in 2013, which confirmed that the arguments for punitive action were based on fear, moral outrage, misinformation, and ignorance. This is why we did not give in to popular demand for such a change. And secondly, entire laws, which apply to the cases of all juveniles across the board, cannot and should not be determined on the basis of one bad example, no matter how horrifying or terrible it might be. Laws should be studied instruments of justice; they cannot be based on a specific instance alone, and it is the duty of the government of the day to ask itself whether good law and good justice can ever be born out of an impulsive reaction to emotional headlines.

This law defies all logic. International examples show that transferring children to the adult system has failed to prevent repeat offences, failed to reduce the juvenile crime rate and failed to promote public safety. In fact, it will increase the risk to public safety because convicting a child in an adult criminal trial will not just deny the child the fulfilment of his basic rights and his physical, emotional and intellectual development—twenty years in jail will eventually churn out hardened criminals rather than reformed adults, defeating its declared purpose. A US study has established that 80 per cent of the juveniles released from adult prisons go on to commit more serious offences.[376] So jailing more children will be neither in the best interests of the child nor of society as a whole.

Of the 446 million children in our country, only 0.008 per cent actually committed cognizable crimes in 2016.[377] The number of children who committed 'serious and heinous crimes' was miniscule. In 2016, of all the children apprehended for crimes under the Indian Penal Code, 2.4 per cent were accused of murder and 5.3 per cent were accused of rape. That is 2.4 per cent of 0.008 per cent—a tiny figure for whose crimes we are turning our system of justice upside down. These figures of the National Crime Records Bureau account for the FIRs registered and not the children who were actually found guilty. They do not justify this stringent and completely retrograde step.

Worse, this law will predominantly affect the country's poor

---

[376]Kanimozhi Karunanidhi, 'A bill for juvenile injustice', *The Hindu*, 27 April 2015.
[377]'Crime in India 2016 Statistics', National Crime Records Bureau, Ministry of Home Affairs.

and marginalized sections of our society—OBCs, SCs, STs and minorities. A majority of the children in conflict with the law come from illiterate families and poor homes. Statistically, in 2013, 77.55 per cent of the arrested children came from families with a monthly household income less than ₹4,200, and 87 per cent of the offenders had not even received a higher secondary education.[378] Such socio-economic conditions only reiterate the urgency to develop better reformative facilities for educating and reintegrating children with criminal tendencies into mainstream society, rather than subjecting them to a harsh justice system and twenty years' jail, especially when such children lack adequate legal representation. This would never succeed as a deterrent: it will simply make them unfit for normal life after they are freed. The government could have raised the punishment for heinous crimes by kids from three to a maximum of seven years rather than taking the extreme step of considering a child no longer to be a child.

It is really the government's job to implement the existing provisions for rehabilitating children in conflict with the law. It cannot shrug off its responsibility by holding the children accountable for failures of the juvenile rehabilitative system of our country. The government should fix the juvenile justice system, not bypass it and victimize our children. Instead, it is trying to brush the real issue under the carpet, to put behind bars the problem we face. Political convenience for the BJP has trumped justice for India's children.

The selective and unequal treatment of children between the age group of 16–18 years clearly violates the fundamental rights guaranteed under Article 14 and Article 15(3) of the Constitution. While Article 14 extends equal protection of law and equality before the law, Article 15(3) allows the state to enact special provisions for protecting children, for they are vulnerable and

---

[378]Danish Raza, 'Kids accused of heinous crimes to be tried as adults: Will the law be misused?', *Hindustan Times*, 31 May 2015.

require special care and protection. The existing juvenile system recognizes that 16–18 years is a sensitive age, which requires greater emphasis on reformation and rehabilitation than on punishment. The new law goes in the opposite direction.

The law also creates a trial before the trial by giving the Juvenile Justice Board one month for a preliminary assessment of whether the child should be tried as an adult—a period so short that it could lead to a presumption of guilt, which itself violates the Constitution. As the Justice Verma Committee observed in 2013 while rejecting the case for a draconian new law, 'We cannot hold the child responsible for a crime before first providing him/ her the basic rights given to him by the court.'[379]

Ironically we can't even be sure the child we're trying really is the age he appears to be. Our courts rely on the matriculation certificate of a child or his birth certificate from a school or a municipal corporation. However, many government and municipal schools often record age on the basis of the physical appearance of a child, and in many cases parents give an earlier age just to get the child into school (ask Gen V. K. Singh!)[380] The children who would be immediately affected by this legislation were born at a time when the level of birth registration was just 58 per cent (in 2001).[381] Since the estimated age can have drastic repercussions on the life of a child, the presumption should in fact be that the child is younger than the date mentioned in his school certificate. The law makes no allowances for this Indian reality.

This government may not be embarrassed to shame us before the world, but the law violates India's undertakings under the United Nations Convention on the Rights of the Child of 1989, the

---

[379]Bindu Shajan Perappadan, '"Juvenile Justice Act has failed miserably"', *The Hindu*, 24 January 2013.

[380]Gen Singh, as Chief of the Army Staff, waged an unsuccessful campaign (that included taking his own government to court) to rectify his official recorded date of birth, which he said perpetuated an error made at the time of his admission to school.

[381]'Birth registration—the picture in India', UNICEF, http://unicef.in/Story/1133/ Birth-Registration-the-picture-in-India

United Nations Standard Minimum Rules for the Administration of Juvenile Justice, 1985, or the Beijing Rules, and the United Nations Rules for the Protection of Juveniles Deprived of their Liberty, 1990—all of which require a child or a young person, accused of an offence, to be treated differently from an adult. This law is an equal-opportunity offender: it violates every principle it can possibly violate. Condemnation by the UN Committee on the Rights of the Child may well follow.

Okay, forget the UN—what about India? There are no special provisions or guidelines for either a female juvenile in conflict with the law or a juvenile sex offender. Misuse is likely: if children are found indulging in consensual sex, it is possible that the male can be charged with rape and sent to the adult crime system.

Even though the law could bring about some much-needed reforms in adoption and foster care, it disappoints in its inability to justly treat children in conflict with the law. An important principle of jurisprudence that all law students learn is 'Lex iniustanon est lex': 'an unjust law is no law at all'. Instead of passing such laws, the government should have focused on actually protecting children.

In our country, child protection under the law has been marred by insufficient investments, lack of adequate number of Juvenile Justice Boards (JJB) and Child Welfare Committees (CWC), lack of institutional services such as Shelter Homes, Special Homes, and Observation Homes, and the absence of an effective monitoring and coordinating mechanism.

The BJP government has shirked its responsibilities to finance such essential work. Budgetary allocations for the development of children have faced drastic cuts over the years. The total allocations for children in 2018–2019 remained stagnant at 3.23 per cent of the Union Budget.[382] In fact, the Integrated Child Protection Scheme (ICPS), the primary scheme for creating a safe environment

---

[382]Komal Ganotra, 'Budget for children: The story doesn't change', *Down to Earth*, 5 February 2018.

for children in need of care and protection, was allocated just ₹400 crore in the Modi government's first Budget, though this sum has mercifully been increased in successive years.[383] Child Welfare Officers have not been appointed in police stations across the country. Even though the law now provides for a National Commission for Protection of Child Rights and a State Commission for Protection of Child Rights for monitoring the implementation of the provisions of the law, they could become as redundant as the existing institutions, especially if this government starves them financially.

The Juvenile Justice (Care and Protection of Children) Act, 2015, despite a few positive provisions, makes one cardinal error: it forgets that our justice should be about rehabilitation, not retribution. We must not sacrifice our values and our children for political gain. That is what the BJP has done, and the nation must rise against it. This is one law that must be amended the moment Mr Modi is out of office.

[383]Ibid.

chapter twenty-three

ABOLISHING THE DEATH PENALTY

Besides its failure to govern effectively, and uphold the institutions it has been charged with safeguarding by the Constitution, the Modi government has also missed the opportunity to do something good for the country by repealing bad laws or refraining from promulgating new laws or Acts that aren't in the nation's best interest. One law it could have done away with was the one that allows the state to put convicted criminals to death. Let us examine the law through the example of one of the most high-profile cases in which it was used in the recent past.

On 30 July 2015, Yakub Memon, a chartered accountant and the brother of a notorious gangster now living in self-imposed exile, was hanged for complicity in the planning and execution of serial bomb blasts that killed 257 people in Mumbai in 1993. The hanging, India's first for years, prompted reactions ranging from dismay to scarcely concealed bloodlust. And it has intensified the domestic debate over the death penalty.

To be sure, no one suggests that India's judicial system did not function properly in Mr Memon's case. He was convicted according to the due process of law, and his punishment was in accordance with valid statutes. During his twenty-one years behind bars, Mr Memon exhausted every possible appeal available to him, including one for presidential clemency. The Supreme Court even held an emergency hearing at 2.30 in the morning, just hours before the execution was set to occur, before deciding to allow it to proceed.

But the question remains: should capital punishment be on the books at all?

As an Opposition legislator, I attracted considerable opprobrium for voicing my opinion, on the morning of Mr Memon's hanging, that it should not be. I expressed my sadness that our government had killed a human being, whatever his crimes might have been. State-sponsored killing diminishes us all, I added, by reducing us to murderers, just like those we are punishing.

My view is not popular in India, and my own party disclaimed my statement. But my position is based on ample evidence that the death penalty does not actually deter the crimes it punishes. Data collected by the Death Penalty Project at Delhi's National Law University demonstrates conclusively that there is no statistical correlation between applying the death penalty and preventing murder.[384] This evidence echoes similar findings in other countries.

My statements were also motivated by problems with the way capital punishment is imposed in India. The Supreme Court has declared that the death penalty should be applied only in the 'rarest of the rare' cases. And, indeed, the last three executions in the country stemmed from terrorist offences that threatened or took a large number of lives.[385]

But the decision to impose capital punishment remains highly subjective. Indeed, whether the death penalty is meted out depends on a number of variables, beginning with judicial and social biases. Public outrage—potentially fuelled by inflammatory media coverage—can push for a harsher sentence, especially in cases relating to terrorism or crimes against women. Economic status also comes into play, with poor criminals being executed much more often than wealthy ones, not least because they cannot afford high-quality legal representation. And the president's decision to commute a sentence is subjective.

A 1980 case held that one way to determine whether a crime meets the 'rarest of the rare' requirement is whether the community's 'collective conscience' has been 'so shocked' that it expects those wielding judicial power to inflict the death penalty,

---

[384]Amrith Lal, 'Most on death row are poor, from backward caste groups, minorities: Law University report', *Indian Express*, 7 May 2016.
[385]Chaitanya Mallapur and Devanik Saha, '10 years: 1,303 death sentences, 3 executions', *IndiaSpend*, 29 July 2015.

regardless of their personal opinions.[386] This leaves much room for the arbitrary and disproportionate application of capital punishment.

Currently there are 477 people in the country who have been sentenced to death. Lower courts hand down around 132 death sentences every year, but the Supreme Court upholds barely three or four of these.[387] Many cases are likely to remain in limbo for decades, with the tedious process of appeals and approvals. As for the death sentences that have already been carried out—three in the last decade—it is impossible to ascertain the objective criteria that made the crimes in question more heinous or 'rarer' than those that did not merit execution.

Ambiguity and subjectivity have no place in matters of life and death. Yet, when it comes to the imposition of capital punishment, both are prominent. That makes it all the more difficult to justify the practice.

Just a couple of weeks before Mr Memon's execution, India's Law Commission, a government body composed of retired judges and legal experts that works for legal reform, organized consultations to assess the effectiveness of the provisions governing the death penalty in India and the purpose of the penalty itself. Unsurprisingly, based on the evidence and the opinions presented at the Law Commission's hearings, there was a general consensus that the courts are unable to adopt a fair and non-discriminatory approach to the death penalty, and support for its abolition was overwhelming. In August 2018 I introduced a Private Member's Bill in the Lok Sabha calling for the abolition of the death penalty in India.

That will not happen any time soon. The Indian public overwhelmingly supports the death penalty, especially for convicted terrorists. The debate over Mr Memon's hanging was often

---

[386]'What happens after a court hands down the death penalty in India?', *Scroll. in*, 14 March 2017.
[387]Coreena Suares, 'In India, death row cases dealt extremely slowly', *Deccan Chronicle*, 11 July 2018.

emotional, with media interviewing survivors of the Mumbai blasts.

Moreover, it has been suggested that the alternative to the death penalty—life imprisonment—would make India vulnerable to hijackings and other assaults by terrorist groups attempting to free their jailed comrades. In the face of such security concerns, my argument that taking a human life is wrong, and that the state should not compound criminal wrongdoing with its own, found little resonance.

Globally, India is part of a dwindling minority. More than 130 countries have abolished the death penalty. Twenty-five countries have it on the books, but have not executed anyone for decades. That leaves roughly thirty countries that still apply it.

India's membership in this group has international repercussions; for example, European Union countries will not extradite criminals to countries where they may face execution. But the real problem is deeper: capital punishment is, at its core, about nothing more than retribution.

It may be tempting to declare that anyone who kills (or participates in killing) innocent people does not deserve to live. But is revenge a worthy motive for a state's actions, especially towards its own citizens?

India's greatest son, Mahatma Gandhi, observed that 'an eye for an eye makes the whole world blind'. For now, India remains blind to the case for abolishing the death penalty. One day, I am sure, it will see the light. Until then, the lonely battle for its abolition must continue.

chapter twenty-four

DISHONOURING THE ARMED FORCES

Besides the three formal arms of the government, the load-bearing pillars of our democracy, there is a fourth institution that is responsible for ensuring the safety, integrity and well-being of our country, our armed forces. Our soldiers give their all in the service of the nation—up to and including their own lives—something that is not expected of the rest of us. This is one of the reasons why it angers me to see the army treated shabbily.

The BJP government came to power talking big about its commitment to the defence of our country and the armed forces, but it has fallen short of providing one of the country's most important institutions the support and honour it deserves. To go through all the ways in which the army, navy and air force have been short-changed by Narendra Modi's government would require a book to itself—a revolving door of ineffectual defence ministers, shortage of equipment, outdated ammunition and technology, confused signals and dangerous war talk, a dysfunctional procurement process and much more. I will therefore limit myself to just two issues in this chapter on which the government could have done a great deal more than it has done.

I

The first has to do with the One Rank One Pension (OROP) issue that led to an unprecedented 320-day long agitation by armed force veterans, which was eventually suspended in April 2016, when the ex-servicemen decided to continue their battle in court.

What is OROP? This can be stated simply as the provision of pensions that have not been indexed to inflation—a brigadier who retired twenty years ago gets a lower pension than a captain who leaves the force this year. This is what our retired military personnel are fighting to change.

Although the government finally decided to implement OROP in 2017, the veterans were unsatisfied. Their main complaint is that instead of giving the highest pension at any one rank, the government has decided to give the average pension at that rank which 'nullifies' the meaning of OROP. Earlier this year, Col Anil Kaul (retd), a spokesperson for the protesting ex-servicemen, said 'The protest will continue...and legal options will be exercised.'[388]

I believe that it is a crying shame that Modi's government is not prepared to accede to the legitimate demands of our veterans, and I think it is reprehensible for his ministers to make statements like the one former Defence Minister Manohar Parrikar did at a media conference in 2014. He maintained that the ex-servicemen would get 80 per cent of the promised pension, gratuitously adding that '100 per cent satisfaction to everyone is never given in real life.'[389] This is insulting. Would PM Modi say during his election campaigns in 2018 and 2019 that we should not believe anything he promises, but that he will try to deliver 80 per cent of it? If the Kargil War had happened on his watch, would we have to be content with getting 80 per cent of the heights back? For soldiers who give more than is asked of practically any other citizen of this land, this is rather too much. Our soldiers do not make an 80 per cent effort when performing their duties, they routinely give 100 per cent; it would only be fitting for the government to return the favour with 100 per cent of what they legitimately seek.

The government says that to give in to the veterans' demands would cost too much. Yes, it will cost the exchequer thousands of crores of rupees but when PM Modi blithely says he will construct a statue of Sardar Patel at a higher cost than OROP would amount to, it puts the whole issue into perspective.

When the men and women of our armed forces have never

---

[388]'One Rank One Pension: Ex-servicemen vow to continue agitation', *NDTV*, 4 February 2016.
[389]'At a recent Aaj Tak conclave, Defence Minister Manohar Parrikar said ex-servicemen would get 80% of OROP and then added "100% satisfaction to everyone is never given in real life"', from Karan Thapar, 'They defend us but there's no one to defend their rights', *Hindustan Times*, 28 December 2014.

counted the cost of serving the nation how can we quibble about the cost of paying their pensions, and humiliate them by making them sit in protest at Jantar Mantar, where their dignity and rights are trampled upon? It is time to ask the government of Messrs Modi and Finance Minister Jaitley: gentlemen, have you no shame?

The government must fully honour the debt to our ex-servicemen. Not to do so is an act of dishonour. It dishonours the nation and the flag these men have fought to defend. And it thoroughly discredits those who would treat the well-being of our jawans and officers as one more election promise to be lightly cast aside.

II

With all the understandable (and justified) focus on OROP, the media appears to have missed another major development in the Ministry of Defence—a decision to extend Short Service Commissions for fourteen years.

The issue of recruitment and the shortage of officers in our country is widely known. But the army appears to be addressing this by extending the duration of Short Service Commissions in a way that is doing an injustice to the officers concerned. In the old days, you would have a five-year commission. You would then leave and you would still be in the prime of your life; you would be able to find a job and move on. Today, they are making these Short Service Commission officers stay for ten years, eleven years, even fourteen years. These are people who have no pension; they have no benefits. They leave the army late and, as a result, they are not in a position thereafter to actually resume life in the civilian sector. In December 2014, I had raised the question in Parliament, asking the then Defence Minister Manohar Parrikar, to explain what the government's policy was on Short Service Commissions. If they were going to do extend them for so long, would it not be fairer to give them all the benefits that a normal officer would be entitled to, pensions included?

Parrikar replied as follows (this is a verbatim transcript from the parliamentary proceedings):

> Madam, I entirely agree with the Hon. Member. Whatever
> was the original concept of the Short Service Commission
> is being totally put upside down by extending it to fourteen
> years. In fact, I had a discussion on this issue. We are trying
> to address this issue very shortly. We will definitely take
> care of this concept. There was 17 per cent shortage of
> officers by the year 2012. As of now, we are recruiting more
> officers. Every year, we are addressing one per cent. So, we
> are coming down by one per cent every year. I expect that
> by another ten years, we should be able to ultimately fill up
> the vacant posts. As far as the Short Service Commission is
> concerned, I will definitely address this issue because I am
> also concerned with the same issue. I have asked for more
> details. There is some reasoning given by them. Give me
> some time. I think, in a couple of months, I should be able
> to address this issue. I understand your concern. The same
> concern was expressed by me. You are virtually suggesting
> to convert them into a regular Commission by taking it to
> fourteen years. The original idea was different.

That's the point. The original idea behind the Short Service
Commission was a good one: it kept the armed forces young, gave
men and women in their twenties an opportunity to experience
military life, while allowing them to have the satisfaction of serving
our motherland in their youth and going on to pursue other
careers thereafter. Those Short Service Commission officers who
sought it could seek a Permanent Commission, but few got one
and the vast majority was supposed to move on to other careers
outside the Forces.

This is why the Short Service Commission was genuinely
short—five years in your twenties added to your experience without
making a major dent in your life or career plans. But there has
been a gradual extension of the five-year period to seven, ten,
and now fourteen. As a former officer who brought the problem

to my attention observed to me, 'The SSC ceased to be short when it was made minimum seven years. It became exploitative when made minimum ten years. Now that the minimum service is fourteen years, it is just abuse of the youth.' As this former officer, Mr Balakrishna, argues, 'Anything more than seven years should be treated as a career option. And a career cannot end abruptly after ten or fourteen years.'

The charge of exploitation or even abuse is not exaggerated. I recently received a heart-rending email from a navy lieutenant on a Short Service Commission, who shall remain nameless since he is still in service and I do not want him to be open to reprisals. I am quoting from it in his own language (without editing the English) to convey his genuine anguish: 'The charter of duties are same for SSC officers as of PC officers. If duties are same then why there is a huge difference in benefits. We SSC officers will be out from the service at ten or fourteen yrs. At that stage we will be at critical stage we don't have any further exposure of outside world. We SSC are neither entitled for pension, ECHS and membership of any club... All benefits is only for permanent commission officer and the other ranks who does minimum fifteen yrs of service and gets all facilities. If we are also relieved at the same age bracket then why this discrimination. Dear sir it is a sad state of affairs, all veterans are busy in asking OROP, but they left their brothers behind who had also spent their prime young time with them... Most of us has just started our families. Few are about to become fathers. Sir we are also human being and did nothing wrong while joining service enthusiastically but some where it is getting diminished... Our future is at stake.'

It is time that, as a nation, we thought about the human beings who don uniforms to keep us safe. After fourteen years of service, SSCOs would retire at the age of around 36–40 years, the time when job/financial security matters the most. By this age, most would have married and have school-going children; this is likely to be the case also for those released after ten years. The chances of a Permanent Commission are minimal for most of the

SSCOs; indeed the policy on granting Permanent Commission is very vague and decisions are left to the discretion—sometimes the whim—of the senior officers concerned. Those in the executive branches of the navy and air force are not granted Permanent Commissions even if their performance has been better than their fellow officers who are permanently commissioned. It is a criminal waste of India's human resources that young officers, well-trained, qualified, medically fit, and willing to serve, are simply let go because they were hired under one category rather than another.

In fact many choose to extend their service to fourteen years because of the uncertainty of a second career. And where can they go? There are no special provisions for them, and the existing rules don't help. Former SSCOs who are 36–40 years old will not be eligible to most of the Group A equivalent positions in the civil services or in public sector undertakings, as the age limit at entry is 30 years (a relaxation of five years is sometimes granted for ex-service personnel, but at 35 that prospect also disappears).

As young officers who joined the services in the first flush of idealistic enthusiasm wake up to these realities, disenchantment sets in. Our country cannot afford demoralization among SSCOs after a few years of service. Worse, the government is beset with a large number of ongoing legal cases and representations against the evident discrimination in terms of grant of financial and other benefits on release.

The solution is simple. Keep Short Service Commissions short: in and out in five years, no further obligations on either side. But for those who wish to continue further in service—and whom the armed forces consider good enough to keep—they should be converted to a status that gives them the same benefits and entitlements as Permanent Commissioned officers of equivalent experience. This would make the SSCO both a platform to give motivated young people an opportunity to experience military life, and an alternative route to filling the ranks of military officers and curing the chronic shortages our armed forces are suffering from.

Those who quit after five years (typically in the age group of

27–30 years when the pressures of family are much lower and the appetite for risk is higher) will not find it difficult to embark on a second career; indeed the experience will stand them in good stead in landing a job. And these officers can be ambassadors of the armed forces in their second career and attract more youth to join the services.

As for those who stay on for ten and even fourteen years, the government should pay a pro-rata pension and related benefits, based on the length of service. The government should also consider making arrangements for lateral entry into the civil services, the central armed police forces, or public sector undertakings, relaxing the rules that prevent this from being an option.

It has been four years since the then Defence Minister Parrikkar asked in Parliament for 'a couple of months' to address the issue I had raised. The Modi government's failure to do so is yet another indication of the fecklessness with which it has dealt with its responsibilities to the defence services. These brave young women and men protect our nation with their lives. We cannot let them down.

chapter twenty-five

FAILING AT EDUCATION

I

As is well known by now, India is set to be the world's youngest country, with an average age of twenty-nine. The demographic dividend that awaits our nation from its youthful population can only be reaped if we train and educate our young people to be able to take advantage of what the world has to offer them in the twenty-first century.

But the Modi sarkar's performance in education does not inspire confidence. For example, the overall education budget in 2015–16 came down from ₹82,771 crore to ₹69,074 crore.[390] Whereas under the UPA, the plan allocation went up by 18 per cent in 2012–13 and by 8.03 per cent in 2013-14, the BJP government reduced the plan allocation for 2015-16 by 24.68 per cent. There were savage cuts across the board: the flagship Sarva Shiksha Abhiyan (SSA) was reduced by 22.14 per cent, funding for the Mid-Day Meal Scheme by 16.41 per cent, the Rashtriya Madhyamik Shiksha Abhiyan for secondary education by 28.7 per cent and the Rashtriya Uchchatar Shiksha Abhiyan, to support state colleges, by 48 per cent.[391] Moreover, important bodies like the SSA, which funds schools across the country, were hollowed out—MHRD had asked for ₹50,000 crore in 2015-16; it received ₹22,000 crore from the Modi sarkar's 2015-2016 Budget.[392]

What is even more striking is that instead of investing in our future through strengthening our higher education, what have we seen in the share of budgetary outlay towards education? In

---

[390]Zoya Hasan, 'No acche din for higher education', *The Hindu*, 20 May 2015.
[391]'Modi-Smriti chemistry dangerous: Cong', *Daily Pioneer*, 25 May 2015.
[392]Tarun Cherukuri and Shijoy Varughese, 'Budget 2018: India needs to focus on inclusive education for development', *Business Standard*, 31 January 2018.

the 2017 Budget, it was stagnant at only 3.71 per cent and only
a meagre 1.5 per cent had been allocated to higher education
altogether,[393] even though the need has risen year after year,
the population is growing year after year and inflation is also
reducing the value of the amounts year after year. The Standing
Committee Report in March 2017, which discussed the Demands
for Grants of the Department of Higher Education, made very
strong and pertinent observations and noted that though the
government claims to have increased the expenditure for IIMs and
IITs, these institutions have been dealing with a chronic shortage
of resources and funds that deters them from competing with the
global institutions against which we must benchmark institutions
like the IIMs. Only three of our IIMs feature in the list of the
hundred best management schools in the world as per the 2017
Financial Times' ranking.[394]

Considering the quality of students that we get in the IIMs—we
have very rigorous selection procedures in place in our country and
strong competitive examinations—it is clear that we are failing our
young minds if we cannot offer them access to the best universities
of the world in our country. These are young men and women
who have to go out and compete with the world where in a
globalizing economy, Indian companies must hold their own with
multinational corporations and against the best that the world
has to offer. Why can we not offer them the best or even better
educational facilities than are available in some of these western
countries? I believe that having only three out of a hundred is
a travesty, and I think that it reveals that the government is not
doing enough to bolster their development.

Let's probe deeper into the existing state of affairs at the
IIMs and the IITs. Apparently, 26 per cent of faculty posts in
the IIMs and 35 per cent of faculty posts in the IITs are lying

---

[393]Subodh Verma, 'Share of spend in government expenditure, GDP on education
falling for 3 years', *Times of India*, 6 February 2017.
[394]"Global MBA rankings 2017', *ft.com*.

vacant.[395] Now, the race to create more institutions in numbers, which is definitely necessitated by our population growth, must not overshadow the aspects of quality of education. We cannot make up in mindless numbers the glaring lack of quality in higher education in India, but for quality we need resources; we need money; we need facilities; and we need faculty. This is where I am sorry to say that the government is collectively lacking.

However, let me say that despite all the problems facing institutions of higher education in this country, brand 'IIM' has truly come into its own and it is synonymous with world-class management education with a distinctively Indian flavour. The story of our country's economic resurgence would be incomplete without acknowledging the critical role collectively played by the IIMs in providing our country with an amazingly talented, motivated and highly successful pool of managers who have gone on in many ways to transform every area of our society and our economy with their exceptional leadership. In my view, they have largely realized the hopes of the man who established the IIMs—Pandit Jawaharlal Nehru—who had the vision to realize that India needed management education and brought it into this country. As in many other areas of our nation building, we must pay homage to his far-sightedness in realizing that if India is to meet its tryst with destiny, India would need world class leaders for business and industry as well.

But much more needs to be done to improve and extend the excellence of the IIM brand. The BJP (in a step I welcomed in Parliament) has given the IIMs autonomy, it has stipulated that there should be at least three women on the board of governors of each institution, but it needs to do more. It needs to insist that the IIMs recruit a lot more faculty from the weaker sections of society, which are very poorly represented at the moment. Moreover, the government needs to take a look at how it can

---

[395]Kritika Sharma, 'Many IITs, IIMs, CUs without full-time heads', *DNA*, 1 October 2017.

regulate the fees of the IIMs going forward so that students from poorer families wouldn't have to undertake the burden of very heavy loans just to be able to study in a government institution, which is what an IIM is. There are several other aspects of the IIMs that should be carefully thought about, such as the right to award degrees, the tabling of the annual report of the IIMs in Parliament and so on and so forth.

To move to the IITs: in 2014, the Modi government announced the creation of five new IITs and IIMs with a grand total investment of ₹500 crore—but the government's own Detailed Project Report specifies that the cost of establishing an IIT is ₹2,200 crore over a period of seven years! In other words, each new IIT needs an annual expenditure of around ₹310 crore a year.[396] The Modi government's allocations fell dramatically short of that—and this excludes any amount which may be needed for completing the construction of previously announced IITs. Inadequate funding has compromised the quality of education in all newly established IITs and IIMs, with the government rolling out more such institutions without strengthening the existing infrastructure.

When it comes to higher education in the country, the BJP government has shown complete disregard for the principle of quality in its quest for mere quantity. It has created a profusion of universities with the stroke of a pen but paid scant attention to whether they would actually be worth attending. In July 2016, the motion for consideration of the National Institutes of Technology, Science Education and Research (Amendment) Bill, 2016 was discussed in Parliament. The house was informed that a new NIT in Andhra Pradesh, with 900 students, was functioning out of a temporary campus.[397] There were no laboratories; no libraries; no high quality IT or engineering tools for training; not to mention an acute shortage of infrastructure in terms of accommodation as well. Can you imagine an engineering college

---

[396]'Budget 2014: Finance Minister proposes 5 new IITs, IIMs and 4 AIIMS', *Indian Express*, 10 July 2014.
[397]'Education is beyond politics, says Javadekar', *Indian Express*, 22 July 2016.

without a functioning laboratory or library books? We had a situation where we created an institution which was not ready to be launched, but in a haste to erect the foundation-stone as announced, they went ahead.

The NIT was permitted to commence activities, but do we want shells of institutions, or path-breaking resource centres that would truly make a difference? In contrast, around the very same time that this discussion took place in Parliament, a fully functioning central polytechnic, the best-known in Kerala, which was established in 1949, was derecognized by the AICTE for not fulfilling a list of conditions that they deemed had to be fulfilled. If that same list were applied to the NIT in Andhra Pradesh, it would have been derecognized by the same AICTE.

Similarly, why can we not get more private sector money into higher education? In the OECD countries, about 75 per cent of research and development funding in the OECD countries comes from the private sector, whereas in India, it is only 15 per cent from the private sector. Why does everything in India have to be dependent upon the government's largesse? Having heard our prime minister's speeches, we should expect that this government would be infusing much more funding into our NITs and IITs. Pending, when the UPA government left office, was our Research and Innovation Bill which would have allowed the setting up of some fourteen universities purely for research and innovation, including in the private sector or funding on a PPP mode, or even on a sole ownership mode.

II

Moving from higher education to primary education, while the enrolment picture is somewhat encouraging, it is offset by an alarming level of dropouts. Our Gross Enrolment Ratio at the primary level is high (over 101 per cent) but so is the dropout rate—about 17 per cent drop out by the secondary level Class IX–X.[398] You can't educate children if they're not in school. The

---

[398]'Trends in school enrolment and dropout levels', *LiveMint*, 2 October 2017.

government has also released figures of 60 lakh out-of-school
children; according to the ministry's 'Education for All' report to
UNESCO in 2012, this had declined to 30 lakhs just two years
ago, which suggests that the trend is reversing.[399]

While on the subject of school enrolment and schools in general
it would be appropriate to talk about the Right to Education Act
(RTE) which was enacted about a decade ago. How is it faring?
The truth is shocking.

Five states (Goa, Manipur, Mizoram, Sikkim and Telangana)
have not even issued notifications regarding admissions under
the RTE.[400] Section 12(1)(c) of the Act mandates private unaided
schools to reserve 25 per cent of seats for children from
economically weaker sections (EWS), in the age bracket of six
to fourteen years. This would enable economically marginalized
communities to access high quality private schools, at the expense
of the state. While Telangana may be excused due to its recent
formation, it is unjustifiable that the other states have failed to
undertake the most basic steps to implement Section 12(1)(c) of
an Act passed over eight years ago.

States have to notify per-child costs to pay the private schools,
on behalf of the children admitted under this provision. However,
out of thirty-six states and union territories, only fourteen of
them have notified their per-child costs. The provision does not
apply to J&K and there are no private schools in Lakshadweep;
therefore, as per the data provided, a shocking twenty states/UTs
have still not notified the per-child costs, a blatant violation of
the letter and spirit of RTE.

It is also shocking to note that in 2017–18, out of the fifteen
states which submitted their reimbursement claims to the central
government, only six were approved.[401] Many of the claims of
the states were not provided funds by the centre, as they had not

---

[399]Oommen C. Kurien, 'Still too many children out of school', *Hindu BusinessLine*,
28 October 2015.
[400]Shashi Tharoor, 'Marginalised from school', *The Hindu*, 20 April 2018.
[401] Ibid.

notified the per-child costs. In response to my query regarding the number of children admitted, per state, under Section 12(1)(c) in the last three years, eighteen states have claimed that the question is not applicable to them, without giving any reason for this response. This could mean that in eighteen states, poor children are not even benefiting under this Act. If there is no data to record the number of students being admitted, it begs the question as to how states are reimbursing private schools. The respective state governments and the centre should clarify this specific point.

According to Indus Action, an organization which works in ten states across India specifically on this provision, while there are higher order issues like the methodology used by states to calculate the per-child cost and lack of coverage of ancillary costs in the reimbursements, the absence of a streamlined disbursement framework both at the central level and the state level is one of the biggest reasons that reimbursements are not processed.[402] If the states are not provided sufficient funds, the private schools would be forced to bear the costs of the children. Civil society activists have informed me about instances of schools refusing to admit children under the RTE provision, citing non-payment of dues by the state governments.

The data regarding the number of children admitted under Section 12(1)(c) of the Act, in states which provided the figures, is also distressing. The number of children studying under this provision increased by 6,12,053 from 2014–2015 to 2015–16, and by 5,02,880 from 2015–16 to 2016–17. This means that there was a reduction of one lakh beneficiaries under this provision during this period. The State of the Nation 2015 report by IIM Ahmedabad, based on official data obtained from the District Information System for Education, puts the total number of seats under this provision as 1.6 crore over the next eight years.[403] This

---

[402]Ibid.
[403]State of the Nation: RTE Section 12(1)(c)—2015 (Provisional) Report by RTE Resource Centre at IIM Ahmedabad, Central Square Foundation, Accountability Initiative (Centre for Policy Research) and Vidhi Centre for Legal Policy.

means that 20 lakh seats should be available annually for EWS children in private schools under the Act; however, according to the answer of the minister, only 5-6 lakh seats are being filled on an annual basis.

The preamble to the Constitution of India states that the democratic Republic of India shall secure social, economic and political justice. Education is undoubtedly the most important element in the movement to secure this end. Although the Directive Principles of State Policy mandate the state to provide children the right to access education, and the 86th Constitutional Amendment and the RTE dictate its implementation, it will be only be fulfilled if sincere efforts are made by the states under the guidance and prodding of a committed centre.

The executive is responsible for the implementation of RTE and the legislature has the duty to hold the executive accountable. Neither—judging by the evidence—has done its job properly.

III

Of particular concern to me where our schooling system is concerned is the way in which children from SC/ST communities and other disadvantaged sections of society are being treated. It is clear that they are not taking sufficient advantage of schemes like the Kasturba Gandhi Balika Vidyalayas (residential schools in which 75 per cent seats are reserved for SC/ST/OBC/minorities). The Modi government also says it will no longer support states in building 6,000 model schools in educationally backward districts.[404] Announcing central objectives and expecting the states to fund them has been a peculiar hallmark of the Modi regime. But it is not going to transform this country in any domain, least of all education.

Take Kendriya Vidyalayas. Demand for KVs has been going up: most Indians want quality education that's also affordable.

---

[404]Prashant K Nanda, 'Model schools: centre opts out, onus on states', *LiveMint*, 4 March 2015.

But again, more central investment is required in the scheme. For the six KV seats I was entitled to allot under the MP's quota in 2011, I had 459 requests from constituents; when it went up to ten seats I could allot in 2018, I got 923 requests! The increase from six seats to ten hasn't come close to overcoming the demand/supply mismatch. The only answer lies in creating 500 more KVs across the country, as UPA wanted to do. The BJP has given no resources for this. Nor does it plan to enhance the Jawahar Navodaya Vidyalayas, highly sought-after residential schools for the mainly rural poor. It should ideally create JNVs for specially disadvantaged groups, like the fishing community in the coastal areas, but my proposal in this regard has been quietly buried.

We have a shortage of trained teachers as well as training institutes. There are 6 lakh posts of teachers vacant under the SSA.[405] Even in the KVs, 9,749 out of 42,640 sanctioned teaching posts are vacant; so are 50 per cent of positions in teacher-training institutions.[406] Most teacher training colleges, as the Justice Verma Commission report observed, are so bad they should be closed down.[407] If we train teachers badly, they will teach children badly. A serious initiative by MHRD is needed: urgent recruitment, more teacher eligibility tests, remedial training. Instead we have a level of governmental inattention to the crisis that matches our notorious culture of teacher absenteeism.

The picture is even worse in higher education, as I have mentioned earlier in this chapter. Central universities, IITs, NITs, IIMs, are all suffering crippling shortages of teachers. According to the government's own figures, it is about 35 per cent in the IITs, but in the NITs, the shortage is now in the glaring vicinity of 50 per cent of the authorized faculty. There are no teachers

---

[405]Mihika Basu, 'SSA: 63.44% teachers' posts vacant in state', *Indian Express*, 14 March 2014.

[406]'More Than 3 Lakh Teachers' Posts Vacant In KVS Schools, Reveals RTI Reply', *NDTV*, 17 May 2017.

[407]The Justice Verma Commission (JVC) was constituted by an order of the Supreme Court and, in 2014, submitted its almost 500-page report which analyses and gives recommendations on teacher training colleges.

and students are being herded into half-built campuses with half the faculty strength to receive an education that can only be called half-baked. Frankly, this is inadequate. We cannot run education like this.

On top of that, employers across the board are complaining about the unemployability of Indian graduates. A FICCI survey showed that 62 per cent of employers were dissatisfied with the quality of our engineering graduates. Infosys and Tatas, among others, have set up their own campuses to train the people they have already hired after an engineering degree, not for on-the-job training, but to make up for the deficiencies of the education we are giving them in our engineering colleges. They are getting nine months to one year of new education because their actual college education is not good enough. Of course, they are also paying teachers better, so that many teachers are leaving and going to Tatas and Infosys and companies like that, rather than staying in the NITs or the IITs.

A UGC survey of 1471 colleges and 11 universities found that 73 per cent of the colleges and 68 per cent of the universities were of a standard that the HRD/UGC considers to be medium or low quality. As a result, the quality of education continues to suffer. Learning outcomes in our school system, too, remain weak. The National Achievement Survey, PISA and other measurements show that not even half the children in Class V can read a Class II text. The government seems bereft of ideas to remedy this.

One of the areas the government should be able to have a direct impact upon is infrastructure. But construction delays are affecting 177 KVs (including Pangode in my own constituency). Only 52 per cent of schools have a playground; only 83 per cent have a girls' toilet. (MHRD's own figures show 2 lakh schools without toilets and 5.2 lakh without playgrounds.)

Performance indicators make dismal reading. Take the scheme to set up girls' hostels in all Educationally Backward Blocks: 3453 were approved, only 536 are functional. Only 69 per cent of the kitchens-cum-stores sanctioned for the mid-day meal programme have been constructed; the quality of food served remains a widespread concern, and not only because of the Bihar tragedy of July 2013 in which dozens of children died. Teachers remain reluctant to supervise the cooking or taste the food. These are all issues the government could fix, but it will take resources, including more honoraria to the cooks/helpers. Instead, the mid-day meal budget has been cut by the Modi government.

IV

What is worse is that instead of improving the education system, this government seems bent on saffronizing our universitites and institutes of higher and secondary education by removing the heads of several of these institutes and replacing them with others, who owe their advancement to their allegiance to a particular ideology or to this government.[408]

Worse, the BJP has tried to subvert Indian universities through its irresponsible use of one of the most punitive weapons in its armoury—the sedition law.

The freedom of speech and expression under Article 19 of the Constitution is indispensable to our democracy. But sedition under Section 124A of the Indian Penal Code infringes upon this right by harassing citizens who simply disagree with the government.

This archaic and oppressive provision is a legacy of our colonial masters, introduced in pre-independent India. Even Pandit Jawaharlal Nehru had stated that 'the sooner we get rid of this provision, the better'. The constituent assembly abstained from including it as an exception to Article 19.

Section 124A of the Indian Penal Code, a remnant of British colonialism, is in desperate need of revision. The ambiguities in Section 124A have led to its misuse as a means of silencing dissent, with police arresting a variety of victims from cartoonists to student agitators, ignoring the Supreme Court's stricter interpretation of sedition as requiring more than just sloganeering.

---

[408]Praful Bidwai, 'How the Sangh Parivar is taking over education and culture institutions', *Scroll.in*, 25 December 2014.

The Hon'ble Supreme Court has also ruled that acts of sedition should be put through a test of 'tangible evidence of actual harm', to establish a direct link between the 'action' and the 'reaction' before punishing individuals. In December 2015, I introduced an amendment to Section 124A as a Private Member's Bill in the Lok Sabha to clarify and restrict the use of the law to instances in which there is a direct and immediate incitement to violence, as has been interpreted by the Indian Supreme Court as well as judiciaries across the democratic world. This is, sadly, still pending, undiscussed.

The law was back in the news in early 2016 when hysteria was whipped up following the arrest of student leader Kanhaiya Kumar and others from JNU accused of shouting 'anti-national' slogans on campus. Two fundamental issues were overlooked in the national uproar that followed. First, universities are where young people find themselves—in many cases through engagement, political passion, ideological fervour and personal involvement—in causes larger than their own academic careers. Many—perhaps most—students grow up in the process, and outgrow the more extreme views they adopted out of youthful zeal. Two of my most obdurately leftist classmates at St. Stephen's, for instance, are now conservative pundits who were both long associated with the BJP, though one has left them after two terms as a BJP MP in the Upper House. They would undoubtedly be embarrassed to be reminded of the fervour with which they espoused positions that they would dismiss with scorn today.

Second, and perhaps more important, the Indian state is not so feeble that a few irresponsible slogans shouted by misguided students can destroy it. But undermining the democratic ethos of the Indian republic can destroy the essence of the state, and of the grand national experiment our nationalist leaders embarked upon nearly seven decades ago. By branding dissent as 'anti-national' and so illegitimizing it, our BJP rulers are betraying the founding idea of the India that Mahatma Gandhi fought to free.

The events at JNU highlighted that the sedition law will need to be amended. But the events of the past few years reveal that amendment alone will not be enough to curtail today's troubling tendencies. The BJP's larger political project to bring Indian universities to heel extends far beyond JNU. Their apparent strategy involves a number of troubling behaviours: silencing students who criticize the government's policies, removing dissenting teachers from their posts, and appointing, as I have pointed out earlier, leadership at universities who are friendly to their political interests while disregarding legitimate academic merit.[409]

The use of the sedition law against Kanhaiya Kumar is but one example of the BJP's subversion of Indian universities and schools. From Dinanath Batra's RSS-supported curriculum in Haryana and Gujarat on 'moral science' (which, of course, is neither particularly 'moral' nor 'scientific'[410]) to the politically-driven harassment of Rohith Vemula in Hyderabad and the sacking of Prof Sandeep Pandey for his dissenting views at Banaras Hindu University, a deeply disturbing pattern emerges which points to an ominous political project.

Dattatreya Hosabale, joint general secretary of the RSS, declares that 'All universities must be purged of all kinds of anti-national elements.'[411] Mr Hosabale's regrettable use of the word 'purge' in reference to squashing dissent is eerily reminiscent of Stalin's infamous 'Great Purge' of the Soviet Union and Hitler's 'purge' of Jewish elements in Nazi Germany. What's next—the burning of books the RSS doesn't agree with?

The university is often the first and foremost target of campaigns that seek to derail democracy. Mao Zedong shut down universities entirely as he launched his Cultural Revolution. The sorry history of twentieth-century authoritarianism is pockmarked with examples of autocratic rulers recognizing that universities

[409]Ibid.
[410]'Dinanath Batra's moral science and verse will enter Haryana textbooks', *Indian Express*, 28 September 2015.
[411] Mohammed Ali, 'Universities must be purged of anti-national elements: RSS', *The Hindu*, 14 February 2016.

threatened the legitimacy of their rule. To control the universities is to capture the mind of the nation. In my earlier book, *An Era of Darkness* (2016), I argued that colonialism was also a colonization of the mind, from which Independence liberated Indians. But what we see today is an Indian variant of 'internal colonialism', where a patriarchal state, acting paternalistically, is trying to police thought and abridge action.

Today's market pressures focus our attention on the role of universities in promoting access to economic opportunity. But we cannot forget the supreme purpose of the university in our republic: to create well-formed minds which can participate in a democracy whose future depends on citizens' capacity to scrutinize their elected officials. The purpose of the university is to help us expand our minds in service of that democracy. In a deliberative democracy, universities are meant to be hotbeds of argument, debate and dissent rather than centres of conformity.

While our universities are the battlegrounds—the theatre of protests and the target of arrests and censorship—Indian democracy is the real victim of the government's assault on intellectual freedom. Indian nationalism and Indian democracy are inextricably linked. An attack on one is an attack on the other. One can criticize the government of the day and be loyal to the nation. To define dissent as anti-national is to betray the nationalism of a freedom struggle that was itself built on dissent.

To make India's democratic experiment work, we must embrace a wider idea of our nation than the narrow conception put forth by chauvinists who are attacking our universities. The wider and more robust notion of an India that accommodates, rather than abandons, dissent and disagreement, can take a few allegedly 'anti-national' slogans in stride. Democratic freedom includes the freedom to be wrong.

V

There is much more I can go on about when it comes to this government's ham-handed and sometimes sinister actions in the field of education, but to talk about all that is wrong would require much more space than a chapter gives me, so let me wrap up my enquiry into education under Mr Modi with just a couple more issues that deserve brief consideration.

The MHRD's directive to educational institutions to observe 25 December as Good Governance Day, requiring the physical presence of students on the Christmas holiday, was an anti-national step.[412] So was the instruction to set up separate vegetarian canteens at the IITs.[413] (I am vegetarian myself, but my intellectual contact with my fellow students was never, and should not be, limited by what they eat.) We need an assurance from the government that it will uphold the integrity of educational attainment in India beyond religious considerations.

The supposedly autonomous University Grants Commission (UGC) has become a poodle, being instructed to issue a directive to Delhi University to withdraw its four-year undergraduate programme abruptly, and to disqualify all other universities from offering such courses. (The UGC's craven political expediency in reversing its own previous decisions on laughable grounds was another embarrassment.) In 2018, there was also an abortive proposal floated to abolish the UGC altogether, replacing it with a grandly-named Higher Education Council that would actually do less, surrendering its grant-disbursal functions to the ministry's own bureaucrats.[414] That was placed in abeyance after a public outcry, but the need to rethink our regulatory institutions for higher education remains urgent. I would personally have welcomed the creation of a genuine Higher Education Council that subsumed the myriad regulatory institutions in the field of higher education, and that relinquished the UGC's onerously intrusive bean-counting

[412]Abishek Choudhari, 'Govt wants schools to observe "good governance day" on Christmas', *Times of India*, 15 December 2014.

[413]'HRD ministry suggests IITs get separate canteen for vegetarian students', *Business Standard*, 31 October 2014.

[414]Neelam Pandey, 'HRD ministry to scrap UGC, replace it with new Higher Education Commission to improve academic standards' *Hindustan Times*, 28 June 2018.

role in favour of an emphasis on the quality of learning outcomes.

Our educational system is over-regulated and under-governed. I had hoped the BJP government would rethink the disastrous course upon which it had embarked, and revive the UPA proposal to abolish UGC and AICTE and create an overarching Council of Higher Education to facilitate, rather than restrict, educational autonomy. Excellence can only thrive amid freedom. Sadly, the BJP government does not appear to believe either in promoting freedom or financing excellence.

If further evidence were needed for this proposition, there was the dismaying MHRD instruction that the ministry must be informed before any MoUs with foreign universities are signed. This is contrary to the Acts governing institutions like IITs, NITs, and central universities, which give them the power to enter into academic collaborations with other educational institutions, including foreign ones. The previous NDA government had done the same thing; in August 2004, the UPA withdrew that requirement, saying it was 'unnecessary interference in the autonomy of institutions'.[415] With the BJP back in power, autonomy once again became history.

Earlier in this chapter, I lamented the fact that only three IIMs featured among the world's best management schools; even worse, not a single Indian university featured in the global rankings. One of the surveys was conducted by the Times Higher Education World University Rankings in 2014–2015. In a presentation by its team about the weightage given to various aspects in their rankings, they mentioned that 30 per cent weightage each is given to research and citations (which are, of course, of published research).[416] Since India's universities are largely teaching institutions where little research is done, and research is done in small institutions where there is very little teaching, India starts off with 60 per cent of the weighting against us—an obvious disadvantage in the global

[415]Ruhi Tewari, 'HRD to institutes: Follow MEA, inform us on foreign MoUs', *Indian Express*, 20 January 2015.
[416]World University Rankings 2014-15 methodology, www.timeshighereducation.com

university rankings.

While these rankings remain a matter of debate, we clearly need to create, across India, an ecosystem of research and teaching around related disciplines. If we can bring several such institutions to life, we could also be in a position to attract the best minds from abroad to work in our laboratories and research think tanks and produce solutions which could answer the foremost questions of the world.

Ironically, India has one of the largest higher education systems in the world and ranks second in terms of student enrolment, exhibiting a healthy growth in the number of institutions and enrolment over several decades since Independence. India now has 864 universities and 40,026 colleges,[417] but only a few world-class institutions, including notably the globally renowned Indian Institutes of Technology, which I have touched upon briefly. But these are still islands in a sea of mediocrity.

But let's look beyond the rankings. They're a symptom of something far more important to diagnose: what ails our higher education? There are many maladies we could talk about, but the one we always gloss over is the basic one of capacity. How do we create enough quality institutions to meet the demand?

Given the size and potential of our population, foreign universities are now showing a keen interest in creating institutions in India. But whereas countries in the Middle East, and China, are going out of their way to woo foreign universities to set up campuses in their countries, India's regulatory framework turns away the many academic suitors who have come calling in recent years. Harvard and Yale would have both been willing to open branches in India to offer quality education to Indian students, but have been obliged to stay away.[418]

Those Indians who choose to study abroad easily get

---

[417]All India Survey on Higher Education (2016-2017), Ministry of Human Resource Development, www.aishe.nic.in
[418]Prashant K. Nanda, 'Government puts on hold plan to let in foreign universities', *LiveMint*, 15 August 2017.

opportunities to do so—currently there are over 100,000 of them in the United States alone. We made a huge fuss about Indian students getting beaten up in Australia. They would not need to go abroad—nor their parents to spend an estimated $3 billion a year in sending them afar—if we opened up the higher educational space in our country to institutions of international repute, and authorized the setting up of double the number of universities as we currently have.

There is no question that the need exists, the demand is huge, and that our growing and youthful population could easily fill several hundred new campuses. Nor is there a shortage of able and willing institutions ready to come into India. But many of these would not brook the interference of our unimaginative and over-directive UGC, made worse by the political diktats of the BJP government, which, as we have seen, has taken a hatchet to what little autonomy our universities enjoyed.

And there's another problem: foreign universities would offer stiff competition to the vested interests, well-represented in our Parliament, who have made the higher education sector their chasse gardée, a closed source of largely illicit revenue flowing from a supposedly non-profit vocation. This is one of the reasons we have university places available to barely 15 per cent of those who clamour for them. Meanwhile, ordinary Indians would scrape and save to buy their children the best possible education, but it's simply not available.

VI

Before I end, I'd like to touch upon a poignant and tragic consequence of the crisis in education. In March 2018, Nikhil, a medical aspirant, ended his life by jumping from the Chambal Bridge. In April, Rishabh, an IIT aspirant, hung himself inside his hostel room. This was the eighth suicide in 2018.[419] In 2017,

---

[419]'17-year-old IIT aspirant commits suicide in Kota', *Hindustan Times*, 19 April 2018.

seven students had committed suicide in Kota, sixteen ended their lives in 2016, seventeen in 2015 and forty-five in 2014.[420] More than sixty student suicides have taken place in this coaching hub in the past five years.[421] In fact, the coaching institutions in Kota preparing students for the IIT Joint Entrance Examination (IIT-JEE) are a symptom of a larger problem hinted at by the city's senior administrator, District Collector Ravi Kumar Surpur, in an emotional letter he wrote in response to some of the deaths in 2016. Addressing parents directly, Surpur pleaded with them not to subject their children to excessive stress in an attempt to live vicariously through them.[422] (A memorable cartoon I posted on social media summarizes the problem brilliantly: a grey elephant telling a baby elephant, 'I expect you to do all that I could never do. I was never able to learn to fly. You must make me proud, my son.' This is precisely the kind of unreasonable pressure most Indian parents place upon their children.)

Indian parents are known for demanding academic excellence from their children. They know that a professional degree in the right field is a passport to social and economic advancement, so they push hard to ensure that their children get one—something that India's higher-education system does not make easy. Given this deeply entrenched culture of academic ambition, the planned administrative enquiry into conditions at the Kota coaching institutes is unlikely to result in remedial action.

The toll this culture takes on young people is obvious. Students are forced to pass brutally difficult examinations—only about 10,000 of the 500,000 who take the IIT-JEE each year score high enough to be admitted—in subjects they often detest. And Indian students are far more likely to push themselves until they crack than to drop out.

[420]Snigdha Poonam, 'Why 57 Young Students Have Taken Their Lives In Kota', *Huffington Post*, 1 June 2016.
[421]Ibid.
[422]'After reading many suicide notes, Kota District Collector writes a moving letter to the parents of IIT aspirants', *India Today*, 4 May 2016.

Engineering and medicine remain the subjects of choice for middle-class Indian parents. As I have mentioned earlier, the country graduates far more engineers than actually find jobs commensurate with their qualifications. But, in a throwback to the mid-twentieth century, Indian parents view engineering as the gateway to modernity, and continue pressing their children to study it. Students who do not make it to an IIT end up in institutions of varying quality, many of which do not equip their graduates for today's labour market.

But at least there are enough engineering colleges in India to meet demand. Medicine, by contrast, is a frustratingly crowded field—and for no good reason.

India's medical profession is controlled by the Medical Council of India, an opaque and self-serving cabal that has intentionally limited the supply of available medical college seats. Medical colleges must be recognized by the MCI, which has seen fit to permit only 497 to exist.[423] That leaves only 60,530 slots each year in a country of over 1.3 billion people—enough space for fewer than 1 per cent of Indian students aspiring to attend medical school.

As if that were not bad enough, some of the seats are awarded against 'donations,' with the wealthy essentially purchasing positions that their marks do not merit. Meanwhile, high-achieving students who just barely missed the cut-off have to find alternatives—or pursue another field altogether.

Those whose families can afford it often end up studying medicine abroad. Many do not return to India, depriving the country of their much-needed expertise. Some return after having attended obscure colleges in countries like Georgia or China, only to have the MCI refuse to recognize their degrees and block them from practising.

Yet India desperately needs doctors. According to the World Health Organization, the country has just 0.7 doctors per 1,000

---

[423]www.mciindia.org/CMS/information-desk/for-students-to-study-in-india/list-of-college-teaching-mbbs

people.[424] In the United States and the United Kingdom—two countries to which Indian doctors often emigrate—the rate is 2.5 per 1,000 and 2.8 per 1,000, respectively.[425] The crippling lack of capacity means that lives are lost every day—particularly in rural areas—for want of medical attention.

India could be graduating four or five times as many capable doctors as it does each year. Yet the MCI has been allowed to pursue its restrictive approach, depriving poor Indians of adequate healthcare, while augmenting the already huge pressure on students to gain a seat in a medical college.

It is in this context—with a huge population competing for a tiny number of seats in professional colleges—that coaching institutes like those in Kota thrive. When succeeding in tough entrance examinations is the only way to fulfil one's educational goals, test preparation becomes the be-all and end-all of schooling. Eager to satisfy pushy parents, young people sacrifice their own interests at the altar of a false god. The dozens of pyres lit in Kota over the last few years are a tragic testament to how damaging this conception of academic excellence can be.

The Modi government and those that follow should recognize that over the next twenty years, India faces the challenge and opportunity of growing at a rate of 8 per cent and more, with a youthful, productive working-age population that vastly outnumbers those available in the rest of our ageing world. A well-educated, highly skilled workforce will be an essential prerequisite for driving this momentum. We know that the price of failure is too high: the Naxalite movement shows what might become of frustrated, undereducated and unemployed young men. We have to get it right; India's future depends on it. But that means taking far-seeing and courageous decisions. Is that too much to expect from our system?

---

[424]'Density per 1000, Data by country', *WHO.int*, updated on 21 August 2018.
[425]Ibid.

chapter twenty-six

MESSING UP SWACHH BHARAT

The PM picks up a broom, it is news; the country pays attention. By launching his Swachh Bharat (Clean India) campaign on the occasion of Gandhi Jayanti in 2014, the prime minister grabbed the nation's attention. But he simply hasn't done enough with it—and the attention is, inevitably, fading.

Nearly a year later, at the end of his lunch for the visiting Sri Lankan prime minister, Mr Modi asked me, 'Swachh Bharat kaisa chal raha hai?' (How is the Clean India mission progressing?) I replied that though it had raised awareness, action on the ground was lacking and he would need to provide much more central funding. 'Karoonga,' he responded. 'Karoonga' (will do).

Unfortunately, as with the vast majority of Prime Minister Modi's initiatives, this too has failed to happen, and Swachh Bharat just hasn't taken off. This is a real pity as a clean India would benefit all of us, and I had been pleased, at some political cost to myself, to support the prime minister's initiative when he asked me to be one of its original nine patrons or goodwill ambassadors. At the same time, as I also said in accepting his invitation, I am not a fan of tokenism, and I was worried the campaign would descend to symbolic photo opportunities for grandees who would pick up a broom for the cameras on Gandhi Jayanti, and never touch a broom again till the cameras came back the next October 2nd. Clean India is a great campaign idea, the kind of agenda-setting our prime minister excels at, but the real challenge, as I said then, will be to sustain it beyond a week of photo ops. The photo ops and speeches have continued, and yet India is no cleaner than it was when Mr Modi first announced his scheme.

This is not the first time there has been a central government effort to clean up India. What Swachh Bharat is trying to do, in its half-hearted way, is give a fillip to a national effort by successive governments to make our country a cleaner place. Congress gave the nation a Rural Sanitation Programme, which in 1999 was changed by the first NDA government to a Total Sanitation Campaign, with equally modest results. The UPA government in 2012 subsumed that into a Nirmal Bharat Abhiyan, with the objective of making the nation Open Defecation Free by 2022.[426] Mr Modi, who acknowledged the work of previous governments, advanced the UPA's deadline by three years. But there is no guarantee that it will succeed any more than its predecessor programmes. The fundamental problem is not just that funding has been limited; Mr Modi has actually spent less on sanitation than UPA, but five times more on publicity. The problem lies in our people's ingrained behaviour patterns—and mindsets are the hardest things to change.

The government announced that it would spend about ₹2 lakh crore on building more than 111 million toilets, and invited contributions to a new 'Swachh Bharat Kosh' (Clean India Fund) to attract contributions from corporates and well-heeled individuals. (The government has given no indication of the total sums in this Kosh and according to its very modest website, it has made just six disbursements each in 2015 and 2016, and two each in 2017 and 2018.)[427] The UPA named swachhata preraks or sanitation coordinators who would work in the rural districts. The Clean India effort should have make swachhata preraks of us all. Instead, it seems to revolve around Mr Modi. The PM's personal involvement, his websites and Twitter feeds, his walkathon and the reach-out to nine Indians (who were each supposed to reach out to nine more, and so on) were intended to enhance national awareness of the campaign. That it has done. It reminded me of the mass movement that brought Kerala to full literacy, as volunteers fanned out to remote hamlets, leper colonies and tribal hutments to reach the unreached. That's the kind of sustained

---

[426]'Making India an open defecation free country', *Press Information Bureau, Government of India*, 18 February 2014.
[427]http://sbkosh.gov.in/swb_sanction.html

effort that was needed to make India clean. Sadly, however, that has not taken place.

Moreover, our government has discovered that even when toilets are built, people continue to defecate in the open, some because the toilets do not have water, or have rapidly become too filthy to use, but most out of sheer habit. An estimated 53 per cent of Indians still do so: one survey across several north Indian states learned that 47 per cent found open defecation 'pleasurable, comfortable or convenient'.[428] Litter is everywhere because we are used to discarding things in public places—roads, pavements, beaches—and because there are few public garbage bins anywhere. An attempt to install wastebaskets at every street corner in Delhi and Mumbai found they were being stolen; when they were replaced by iron or concrete bins that could not be removed, those became tempting targets for terrorists to drop lethal explosives into, or so the security-wallahs claimed. Thus ended our very brief attempt at abolishing littering. As one who habitually carries everything from used chewing gum to discarded wrappings in his pocket till I can throw them into a bin, I can testify from personal experience how difficult it is to find a public dustbin on the streets of India.

We also have a cultural problem: we are a nation full of people who live in immaculate homes where we bathe twice a day, but think nothing of littering public spaces, spitting on walls, dumping garbage in the open and urinating and defecating in public, because those spaces are not 'ours'. It is this individualistic mindset and lack of civic consciousness that makes our country a land of private cleanliness and public squalor. Educating Indians about public hygiene must start in schools and be drummed into the minds of adults through information campaigns, exhortations and warnings—as well as fines and punishments for wilful disobedience. If we can fine people for exceeding the speed limit or not wearing a

---

[428]'53 per cent of Indian households defecate in open: World Bank', *NDTV*, 19 November 2013.

helmet—on the grounds that such behaviour is a menace to others and a cost to society—we should fine litterers and despoilers of public spaces on the same grounds.

I am growing increasingly discouraged that any real progress will be made. It is not just that the government needs money to actually build the toilets, instal the dustbins, and improve the drainage facilities it is supposed to establish. It also needs money to ensure that there is water in the toilets it builds, so the toilets are worth using. As I have noted, studies suggest that most of the toilets built since Mr Modi announced his scheme are unused or unusable because they have no water to clean them.

If you clean up a street, or a park, or a beach (as I did), you need to create viable alternative places for dumping the garbage and waste that people have got used to dumping on the street, park or beach. If you don't create those alternatives, people will dump their garbage once again in the place you've just cleaned up. Those alternative places should incorporate comprehensive waste management systems, from collection to processing, perhaps conversion to biogas or other products. A clean-up, in other words, can't be an end in itself, but a mere first step in a comprehensive effort to improve public sanitation. This simply hasn't happened under the Swachh Bharat Abhiyan.

After fulfilling my own cleaning drive in October 2014, I wrote to the prime minister about why his government needed to do more to fulfil the objectives of Swachh Bharat. I took the example of the Parvathy Puthenaar Canal in Thiruvananthapuram, a once-beautifully-flowing water body where boats plied, people swam and even drank the water from, till the 1930s or 40s. Now, however, the canal is choked with garbage, sewage and weeds; the idea of stepping into it, let alone swimming in it, is unthinkable. I pointed out that the canal could be cleaned, at considerable cost. But if it was not to become a sewage dump again, steps would have to be taken to construct effective sewage systems for the people living on both sides of the canal, so their effluents didn't flow into it; waste disposal systems would have to be created so they didn't have to throw their garbage into the canal. Otherwise the crores spent cleaning it would prove a total waste.

But this would require a mammoth effort, which an MP or even a local government would never be able to afford. It would need central funding, the kind of thing that perhaps a Swachh Bharat Kosh—or even a larger NDA sanitation budget—could have financed. It was a classic example of the kind of substance that needed to lie beyond the slogans of Swachh Bharat.

Mr Modi's response? The PM still hasn't even acknowledged my letter, let alone replied to it. The detailed project proposal prepared by the district collector is presumably gathering dust somewhere in the Prime Minister's Office. Meanwhile, the canal remains choked up and filthy. And the Swachh Bharat photo ops go on.

I don't mean to imply that money is everything. There's also citizen involvement. When I cleaned up a section of Vizhinjam beach in my constituency, I involved the local community as volunteers, because as the local residents, they were the obvious stakeholders in the exercise, with most at stake in the cleanliness of their immediate environment. Since it was a largely Muslim community, I involved the mosque and the leadership of the local Jama'ath (as well my local Congress party workers). With their blessings, it became something everyone in the area could participate in and could share the benefits of—the opposite of a few leaders sweeping a street and disappearing.

My fear is that Swachh Bharat will again be reduced to one of those empty rituals, a label without content, a slogan devoid of substance. If that happens, it will be far worse than if Mr Modi had never devised Swachh Bharat in the first place. Nothing corrodes a nation's spirit more than empty cynicism—but raising hopes without taking the basic steps to fulfilling them produces the most cynicism of all.

chapter twenty-seven

OUR FUNDAMENTAL RIGHT TO PRIVACY

India has little oil, no coltan or rare earths, and inadequate water. What it does have, of course, is people—over 1.3 billion of them and counting. Which means it is potentially rich in something that, in the twenty-first century, has been described as the 'new oil' of our times: data.

India is generating valuable data at a dramatic pace. The country has led an ambitious effort to issue every one of its residents a Unique Identification Number, or Aadhaar, linked to your biometrics. Aadhaar was initiated in 2009 as a project to link a biometric-based unique identity with eligible beneficiaries of various government schemes. It was envisaged, by the previous Congress party-led government, as a method to eliminate the number of 'ghost beneficiaries' of government subsidies and to reduce the pilferage of state funds.

Ironically, the then chief minister of Gujarat, Narendra Modi, who vociferously opposed the project and pledged to scrap it if elected, has now, as prime minister, become the greatest proponent of the scheme. Worse, he has enlarged it to an extent never imagined by his predecessors, ordering Aadhaar to be linked to virtually everything under the Indian sun—from birth to death (hospital admissions and crematorium certificates), and from mobile connections to bank accounts to school admissions to travel, all of which now require an Aadhaar number, despite the government having assured the Supreme Court that the use of Aadhaar would not be made mandatory.

This has raised serious concerns that the entire scheme is unconstitutional. The very statutory foundation of the project is flawed, as the government avoided the oversight of the Rajya Sabha by pushing through the Aadhaar (Targeted Delivery of Financial and Other Subsidies, Benefits and Services) Act, 2016, as a 'money bill'.[429] It did so even though, in the opinion of most analysis, the Act failed to meet the requirements for a money bill under Article 110 of the Constitution.

The fact is that the Act states that every resident of India shall be entitled to obtain an Aadhaar number. Its language also indicates that obtaining an Aadhaar number is voluntary in nature. Even the Supreme Court, while hearing the batch of petitions challenging Act, had noted that the Aadhaar card scheme is 'purely voluntary' and it cannot be made 'mandatory'.[430] However, the government appears to have blithely disregarded that order as it continues to try to link Aadhaar with virtually everything.

The Act limited the purpose of authentication to establish the identity of an individual in relation to the receipt of a subsidy, benefit or service incurred from the Consolidated Fund of India. It begs the question as to how services provided by private banks and telephone operators fall within these categories. Why should we link our bank accounts and mobiles to Aadhaar, then, in order to be able to use them? Yet phone companies and banks insist we must.

The linking of Aadhaar with various services also raises the question: what compelling interest does the State have to know whether an individual has travelled by flight or by a train, whether an individual has opened a bank account or whether she has a mobile connection?

By linking biometric data and other sensitive information of an individual to a central database without providing adequate security to such a database (judging by the data leaks reported in the media), one can argue that such actions in effect violate the fundamental right to privacy. The right to privacy can of course be limited by a compelling state interest. However, where the state has a compelling interest, it must choose the least restrictive

---

[429]Shruthi Radhakrishnan, 'Is the Aadhaar Bill a money bill?', *The Hindu*, 10 May 2016.
[430]'Govt cannot "belittle" SC order holding Aadhaar voluntary', *Times of India*, 5 May 2017.

method to achieve such goals.

But such fundamental concerns clearly do not matter much to this government. It likes collecting data: biometric devices are being used to identify the office attendance of government employees and the absenteeism from school of students and teachers.[431] In the wake of Mr Modi's disastrous demonetization scheme, which I will explore in Section IV of this book, he has urged Indians to make digital payments instead of cash, even for small transactions. As prime minister he has led an enthusiastic drive for digital governance, hailing its efficiency and extolling its capacity to transform the country. He has unabashedly declared that data is 'real wealth' which would enable 'whoever acquires and controls' it to attain 'hegemony'.[432]

But if Narendra Modi's India is a country where Big Government meets Big Data, it hasn't handled the intersection very well. There have been numerous incidents reported in the media where machines meant to authenticate Aadhaar number holders have failed to do so, due to lack of internet connectivity, electricity or other adequate facilities in rural parts of the country. This has denied many poor people their Public Distribution System (ration) supplies, in violation of their rights. A scheme meant to help the poor is depriving people of their entitlements.

To make matters worse, Aadhaar leaks like a sieve. An intrepid investigative journalist of *The Tribune* newspaper was able to purchase 5 million ID numbers for a mere 500 rupees.[433] A government oil and gas company site made it possible for anyone with basic technical skills to uncover the names, bank details and Aadhaar numbers of over 500 million Indians.[434] Nearly 13.5 crore Aadhaar numbers were accidentally exposed on government portals run by the national Ministry of Rural Development and

---

[431] Amit Gupta, 'Biometric watch before pay', *Telegraph India*, 8 June 2015.
[432] 'Data is real wealth: PM Modi in Davos', *Business Standard*, 23 January 2018.
[433] Rachna Khaira, '₹500, 10 minutes, and you have access to billion Aadhaar details', *The Tribune*, 4 January 2018.
[434] Alison Saldanah, 'Aadhaar security lapse could allow major chunk of information to be stolen, says data security expert', *FirstPost*, 30 March 2018.

the Andhra Pradesh government.[435] The Modi government reacts to each revelation with a combination of denial, complacency and cover-up. But cumulatively, Aadhaar is more compromised than Facebook, which allowed Cambridge Analytica unauthorized access to 87 million users' data.

The inability to protect data starts with the PM himself. In 2015, Mr Modi invited his followers 'to receive messages and emails directly from the prime minister' by downloading the 'Narendra Modi mobile app' onto their phones. 'No intermediaries, no media, no officials, no red tape,' he promised.[436] The Android version of the Modi app was downloaded over five million times.

But there was a catch that didn't appear in the fine print: the details the prime minister's followers trustingly uploaded when they signed up for his app were shared, without their consent, with a US firm. According to the *Indian Express*, these details were hardly insignificant: the Modi app sought permission from its users to access their cameras and photographs, contacts, locations and microphones. A lot of data changed hands that's now in the hands of Americans; who knows what they might use it for?[437] The app's privacy policy has since been changed.[438]

The problem's only going to get worse. At our current pace, it is estimated that 2.5 quintillion bytes of data is generated every day and 90 per cent of the world's data was generated in just two years. In India, the percentage may even be somewhat higher. As Indians get online in record numbers, the increasing ubiquity of 4G services and the nose-diving prices of the cheapest Internet-enabled smartphones means that millions are offering up their personal information to obtain apps, play games, make purchases

---

[435]Mayur Shetty, '13.5 crore Aadhar accounts compromised', *Times of India*, 3 May 2017.
[436]'Narendra Modi App: Here's why you should always have it on your phone', *Narendramodi.in*, 1 November 2016.
[437]'Narendra Modi Android app sharing personal info of users without consent: Researcher', *Indian Express*, 26 March 2018.
[438]Krishn Kaushik, 'Narendra Modi App asks for sweeping access: Camera, audio among 22 inputs', *Indian Express*, 26 March 2018.

and obtain online services.

India will clearly be the land of Big Data. Right now, it also looks like the land of the Big Leak. The country lacks strong data privacy and protection laws; my own attempt to introduce one in a Private Member's Bill has been repeatedly thwarted by disruptions that have stalled Parliament.

II

So why do I believe data protection is of paramount importance? For that, let's start with a statement made by the then Attorney General of India, Mukul Rohatgi, to the Supreme Court. On 22 July 2015, he argued that the right to privacy is not guaranteed as a fundamental right under the Constitution of India. While the Supreme Court formed a constitutional bench to determine the nature of the right to privacy in India, I had submitted the Data Privacy and Protection Bill, 2017, a Private Member's Bill which I had drafted, on 4 July 2017, to the Lok Sabha for introduction and consideration.

My Bill envisages a comprehensive framework to protect the right to privacy of all, in furtherance of the recommendations of the Justice A. P. Shah Committee and international best practices. Nearly two months after the Bill was submitted, the nine judge bench of the Supreme Court in its landmark judgment in *Justice K. S. Puttuswamy v Union of India*, unanimously and unambiguously held that the right to privacy is a fundamental right guaranteed under Articles 14, 19 and 21 of the Constitution. While that should simplify matters for all of us—since privacy is now recognized as a constitutional right—there is an urgent need to enact a comprehensive data protection law to implement it. The Justice Srikrishna Committee is looking into the matter and its final report has just been released as this book goes to press. Meanwhile, it is important for policy makers to be clear on certain essential principles on privacy, which I have incorporated in my Bill.

The law must be clear on what it seeks to protect, which in this context is the personal data of each Indian citizen. Personal data is the type of data which, if linked to other information, can be used to identify the concerned individual. Within the sphere of personal data, the law must recognize and distinguish sensitive personal data, which encompasses information relating to a person's sexual preferences, political and religious views, ethnicity, race, financial information, DNA, biometric data and so on. The level of protection for sensitive personal data should be more stringent than in the case of other personal data.

Consent is the cornerstone of any comprehensive framework on data protection and it must be obtained by the data-controller or processor before collecting, processing, using and disseminating personal data. The underlying principle for a consent-based mechanism is that personal data is owned by the subject—the person who generates the data. It is important to understand that privacy, which arises out of the right to life and liberty, is not a creation of the Constitution; instead 'these rights are recognized by the Constitution as inhering in each individual as an intrinsic and inseparable part of the human element which dwells within', as the Supreme Court has succinctly explained.[439] So every one of us whose personal data is collected has the right to be informed of the particular purpose in collecting the data, the duration for which the data will be stored, the manner in which it has to be obtained and how our consent can be withdrawn.

Once the consent to use the personal data is withdrawn, the data collector should destroy any record of the data collected. There should be a general bar on disclosing data except to the person to whom it pertains. The consent of the subject should be required to transfer any personal data. The subject should also have the right to access her own data at all times so that she may check and update it as necessary. The law must prescribe fines or even imprisonment for the handling or collection of data in contravention to the standards prescribed under the data protection framework.

---

[439]V. Shivshankar, 'Privacy an essential aspect of human dignity, says Supreme Court in historic ruling', *The Wire*, 24 August 2017.

Consent should be meaningful. We must ensure that the subject can make an informed choice and still retain control over the data collected, unlike the prevailing scenario in which websites merely intimate the user that they use cookies, or where they interpret the scrolling of a website or the clicking of a banner as an act of giving consent. At the same time, the law must be flexible to allow for exceptional circumstances due to which data may be collected without prior consent, such as the prevention of commission of a cognizable offence or a reasonable threat to the security of the State. It is essential that the exceptions to the consent-driven regime are strictly and narrowly defined, without leaving any elbow room for the crushing of dissent under the guise of 'national security'.

Facebook founder Mark Zuckerberg has grudgingly accepted that maybe his company's activities should be regulated.[440] To ensure the effective implementation of a data protection regime, the law must create an independent regulatory body—let's call it a Privacy Commission. The Privacy Commission should be empowered to investigate complaints of any breach of the data protection framework I have described above. The Commission should be enabled to issue orders to those collecting data (like Facebook) on activities that may be in contravention of the law, as well as to take necessary steps to implement the law. All forms of interception and surveillance should only be permitted if authorized by the Privacy Commission, and they should be carried out strictly to the extent necessary for the purpose of the surveillance or interception.

Industries dependent on data for their businesses may fear that a regulatory body may end up as an overburdening behemoth, and therefore may be in favour of a law which prescribes general principles of privacy for self-regulation by companies. But we must not give in to their fears. We can define the scope of powers of

---

[440]Josh Horwitz, 'Mark Zuckerberg says Facebook should (maybe) be regulated', *Quartz*, 22 March 2018.

the regulatory body to reduce the risk of misuse of its powers.

Since earlier laws (such as the Information Technology Act, 2000, and the Aadhaar Act, 2016, as well as older laws) impact an individual's right to privacy, any proposed Bill on data protection must specifically require that all existing laws relating to this subject should comply with the provisions of the Bill.

The admirable Justice Chandrachud, while delivering his judgment on the right to privacy, noted that a constitutional democracy can survive only when citizens are provided an 'undiluted assurance' that the rule of law will protect their rights and freedoms against any intrusions, and judicial remedies are provided for the redressal of any unwarranted intrusion or violation of a right.[441] That's what a data protection law should do.

The citizens of India deserve a strong and comprehensive statutory framework to supplement the fundamental right to privacy as part of the 'undiluted assurance' of the State to uphold the rule of law. The way things are going, my Bill may never see the light of discussion in Parliament, but the government can surely prepare a law that does everything I have suggested. I have offered them my draft in the hope that they will incorporate its provisions into the Bill they say they will present to the country before the end of the year.

The ball is squarely in the government's hands. Let us hope that, unlike the Australian cricket team, they do not scuff it so badly that it reverses the direction the law should take.

[441] Anurag Bhaskar, 'Key highlights of Justice Chandrachud's judgment in the Right to Privacy case', *The Wire*, 27 August 2017.

chapter twenty-eight

NORTH VS SOUTH

One of the big achievements that Mr Modi and Amit Shah and the rest of the BJP leadership never fail to shout about is the fact that the BJP won an unassailable majority at the centre and now controls the vast majority of states. It is strong at the centre and strong in the states, something that would help it, you'd imagine, work out a clear-headed, sensible way of dealing with centre-state relations, as well as sensitively balancing the needs of the various states within the Indian union. Prime Minister Modi has spoken of propping up 'co-operative federalism'. But being the BJP, they have been making a hash of things here as well: there has neither been much co-operation nor any tangible federalism.

It is not often that a seemingly technical issue points towards a potentially grave challenge for the survival of our nation itself, but that is exactly what happened in early 2018 when a letter sent to ten chief ministers and the prime minister by DMK leader M. K. Stalin, questioning the 'ill-conceived' terms of reference of the Fifteenth Finance Commission, revealed how a thoughtless decision by the Modi government had opened a Pandora's box with incalculable consequences for the country.[442]

The Finance Commission is one of the less well-known institutions of our governing system. It is appointed every five years to review and decide how the country's revenue from taxation will be apportioned between the states. The Finance Commission uses various criteria to determine this, including each state's percentage of the national population. But for more than four decades, it has based itself on population figures from the 1971 census.

That may seem odd, since we have had four censuses since

---

[442]Anna Isaac and Ragamalika Karthikeyan, 'Stalin calls Centre's allocation of funds to states a "travesty of justice", writes to 10 CMs', *News Minute*, 21 March 2018.

1971 and new numbers have been available to successive Finance Commissions. But the reason for this is very simple, and it was made explicit in relation to a far more vital issue—that of political representation in our Parliament. In 1976, the omnibus 42nd Amendment to the Constitution decided to freeze the allocation of Lok Sabha seats to our states for twenty-five years to encourage population control, by assuring states that success in limiting population would not lose them Lok Sabha seats. In 2001, the NDA government of Prime Minister Vajpayee extended this arrangement for another twenty-five years; its proposal, which became the 91st Amendment, was unanimously adopted by all parties in both Houses of Parliament.[443]

The reasoning behind this policy was clear: it was based on the sound principle that the reward for responsible stewardship of demography and human development by a state should not be the cause of its political disenfranchisement. While there is some logic to the argument that a democracy must value all its citizens equally—whether they live in a progressive state or one that, by failing to empower its women and reducing total fertility, has allowed its population to shoot through the roof—no federal democracy can survive the perception that states would lose political clout if they develop well, while others would gain more seats in Parliament as a reward for failure.

This is the carefully balanced arrangement that the Modi government has so carelessly undone. The rather abstruse Terms of Reference of the Fifteenth Finance Commission (which was constituted on 27 November 2017 and will submit its report on 31 October 2019) has deepened existing fault lines. In March 2018 it was reported that the Modi government had instructed the Finance Commission to use the 2011 census figures instead of the 1971 figures[444], which had the southern states up in arms as they felt that states that had failed to improve their governance,

---

[443]'Freeze on LS seats till 2026', *Times of India*, 24 August 2001.
[444]Janane Venkatraman, 'The Hindu explains: why the 15th Finance Commission has riled some states', *The Hindu*, 29 March 2018.

empower women and curb population had been unfairly rewarded. An even bigger danger, as I have pointed out, looms if the same logic prevails when the current arrangements freezing political representation at 1971 population levels expires in 2026. If at that time, new population figures are used, the South would face political disenfranchisement to go along with its sense of financial victimization. This would have serious implications for national unity.

It was Mr Modi's instruction to the Finance Commission to use the 2011 census figures now that caused Mr Stalin to erupt. He was not alone. Then Karnataka CM Siddaramaiah, in tweets and a Facebook post, also articulated a strong case; and Pawan Kalyan, the former film star who has founded a political party in Andhra Pradesh, did so as well. 'Is the success of south Indian states going to be used against them by Union of India?' he tweeted, expressing 'genuine concern that population based formula for sharing tax revenues between states & Centre would hurt south Indian states.'[445]

Former CM Siddaramaiah's post went much further, raising a whole host of issues relating to Indian federalism, from Karnataka's ancient history and its right to its own flag, to the importance of honouring the Kannada language and the unfairness of the current tax distribution system: 'Historically, the South has been subsidizing the north... For example, for every one rupee of tax contributed by Uttar Pradesh, that state receives 1.79. For every one rupee of tax contributed by Karnataka, the state receives 0.47. While I recognize the need for correcting regional imbalances, where is the reward for development?' He added his concern that population is an important criterion for the apportionment of central taxes. 'For how long', he asks, 'can we keep incentivizing population growth?'[446]

---

[445]Pawan Kalyan, *Twitter*, 18 February 2018 <https://twitter.com/pawankalyan/status/965064871426445313?lang=en>.
[446]Siddaramaiah, 'Regional identity & federalism', Facebook, 14 March 2018 <https://www.facebook.com/Siddaramaiah.Official/posts/602181456793987>.

These are important questions that the rest of India can ill afford to ignore. The states of the Hindi-speaking heartland—once called the BIMARU states—have comprehensively failed to improve their development indicators, notably relating to female literacy and women's empowerment. As a result, their population growth has outstripped that of the southern states. And thanks to the Finance Commission's new formula, that makes them eligible for a larger share of tax revenues.

While the furore raised by the Finance Commission has died down due to some skilful bureaucratic compromises, the country should pay attention to the greater dangers. While northern states like Bihar, Jharkhand, Madhya Pradesh, Rajasthan and Uttar Pradesh had a decadal population growth rate over 20 per cent between 2001 and 2011, southern states like undivided Andhra Pradesh and Telangana, Kerala, Karnataka & Tamil Nadu grew at less than 16 per cent in the 2001–11 period. My own state of Kerala has the country's lowest growth rate (4.9 per cent in 2001–11, and dropping, it is estimated, to negative growth by 2021).[447] That is one-fifth of Bihar's growth rate. Why should Kerala be punished for its impressive performance by losing seats in Parliament and thereby being forced to dilute its voice in national affairs?

The answer, of course, is that those are the rules of democracy: one-person-one-vote means the more people you have, the more political clout, and tax rupees, you get. But in a country like India, whose diversity is held together by a sense of common belonging but constantly under strain from regional, religious and linguistic tensions, such an answer risks rupturing the fragile bonds that hold us all together.

As it is, the politics of Mr Modi's BJP is very different from the conciliatory coalition-building of the Vajpayee era. Their blatant majoritarian triumphalism, the brazenness of the Hindi supremacism that infuses their discourse, and the culture of Aryavrat domination that infects their attitudes, have already

---

[447]'What explains the obsession with the 1971 Census?', *Newslaundry*, 8 June 2017.

raised disquiet among many southern politicians.

The only remedy is to acknowledge that we need a more decentralized democracy, one in which the central share of tax resources is not so crucial and the political authority of New Delhi not so overwhelming. That could make the concerns raised by the new census figures less relevant.

But as long as our system is what it is, we need to run it sensitively. That is something that, on this occasion again, the Modi government has failed to do.

Already some hotheads are calling for serious consideration of secession, and some in the environs of Chennai have begun reviving the case for a 'Dravida Nadu'.[448] Such an idea may have little appeal beyond a few limited circles in Tamil Nadu, but that does not mean the underlying concerns behind it should be ignored. How can we flesh out what a decentralized democracy would mean? Former Karnataka Chief Minister Siddaramaiah argued that India is evolving from a 'union of states' into a 'federation of states'.[449] This may, to some degree, be wishful thinking for now, in an era in which a glib phrase like 'co-operative federalism' masks a reality of over-centralization; but there is no reason for us not to consider how to take India in that direction, even though we are not there yet. In our 'quasi-federal' system, there is no doubt that the union currently enjoys the upper hand: after all, in India the union created the states, rather than the states coming together to create the union, and new states have been created in recent years by Acts of Parliament. But that does not mean that the dominance of the union need extend to the point where the states have little or no autonomy and feel themselves the playthings of New Delhi. It is that perception that has stirred the current unrest and made the seemingly technical correction of the Finance Commission's TORs such a major political issue.

But what would a more federal India look like? The first fear

[448]B. Kolappan, 'Dravida Nadu: from political oblivion to centre-stage', The Hindu, 19 March 2018.
[449]Siddaramaiah, 'Regional identity & federalism'.

to set at rest is that a more substantive federalism would loosen the bonds that tie all Indians together in a shared nationality. When Karnataka approved its own official state flag, alarms went off, and the cry arose that such a flag would constitute a de facto challenge to the Indian flag.[450] But many other federal nations have state flags and state symbols without their national governments feeling in the least threatened. Indeed, recognizing strong regional identities is a mark of a strong and confident state. It is only the weak who are reluctant to empower their subordinates.

India has also been distinguished by its capacity to promote and celebrate multiple identities. The great Malayali poet Vallathol wrote: 'Bharataam ennu kettaal, abhimaana pooritham aavanum antharangam; Keralam ennu kettalo, thilakan choara namukke njerambaglil.' ('If one hears the name of India, one's heart must swell with pride; if one hears the name of Kerala, the blood must throb in one's veins.') Similarly the Kannada poet Kuvempu composed 'Jaya Bharatha Jananiya Tanujathe', hailing Karnataka as the daughter of Bharata, the Indian nation.

So the southern states are not really interested in secession; they want a more genuine federalism. Siddaramaiah has argued the case for a system where states receive a larger portion of the taxes collected from them; this would permit the relatively well-developed southern states to retain a larger portion of what they currently contribute to the centre. The difficulty with that suggestion, of course, is that it reduces the quantum of funds available to the central government to subsidize India's poorer states. Former CM Siddaramaiah argues that 'the share of centrally sponsored schemes must go down'. That could be the answer: yes, take some revenues from the more affluent states to finance central schemes in the poorer states, but apply those schemes more flexibly so that each state can judge whether it needs them, and also be empowered to tailor these schemes to their needs. This in turn would free more funds to be allocated to the states' own

---

[450]'Karnataka flag will not unfurl anytime soon', *Indian Express*, 4 July 2018.

priorities rather than to the centre's.

Former CM Siddaramaiah also laments that 'the states do not have a say in making of the country's economic policy'. He cites the example of the import of cheap pepper from Vietnam through Sri Lanka as the result of a Free Trade Agreement that states like Kerala and Karnataka had no say in negotiating, though it was their pepper farmers whose livelihoods would be most seriously affected. He proposes a body 'on the lines of the GST Council' to discuss 'trade policy and agrarian issues so that we have a better say in making policies that affect our farmers... We urgently need a mechanism where the states get a greater say in [the] making of the nation's policies.'

This proposal is worth considering. It is time for a second liberalization: just as the original liberalization of 1991 set Indians free from the restrictions of the licence-permit-quota raj, so also we need to liberate the states to grow according to their capacity and through good governance. 'The states need greater autonomy to run their economic polices,' writes Siddaramaiah, 'borrow internationally as long as they convince the lenders of their creditworthiness, build the infrastructure of their choice without depending too much for licenses from the centre, and design programs of their choice.'[451]

This may sound like a radical idea to those who have been working in recent years to pursue 'Hindi-Hindu-Hindutva' as India's *Volksgeist*. But for the rest of us, in Dr Manmohan Singh's famous phrase, it is an idea whose time has come.

---

[451]Siddaramaiah, 'Regional identity & federalism'.

chapter twenty-nine

THE CULTURE OF OPACITY

Historians and conspiracy theorists alike rejoiced when numerous files revealing details related to the death of Netaji Subhas Chandra Bose were declassified. In the excitement of the much-anticipated release of the files, the prime minister even launched a web portal at netajipapers.gov.in to publicize the released files. The files revealed many details related to the mysterious death of Netaji, including the location of his death, how his body was treated and how his death was received in the international community. The story—and all the ensuing conspiracy—dominated the news cycles during celebrations of Netaji's birthday in January 2016.

And yet, virtually no attention was paid to the structural barriers in the Indian government that prevented the release of such documents of public interest in the first place. The declassification of the Netaji papers was a much-needed step towards transparency. But the Netaji declassification demonstrated a larger problem: a culture of opacity in the Indian government. The measures taken by the prime minister in response to the decades-long Netaji controversy missed the forest for one set of trees. India still lacks comprehensive and accountable routines for maintaining accessible public records.

The wider lack of transparency across the government, which keeps important information outside the discriminating gaze of public scrutiny, harms India in two crucial ways. First, opacity undermines the democratic process, which requires that an informed citizenry acknowledge the successes and the failures of its governmental officials. Democracy demands transparency; secrecy is essentially undemocratic. For voters to keep their government accountable, they require access to critical information. Assessment requires access, lest such restrictions—intentional or otherwise—undermine the democratic apparatus. That is the principle behind the Right to Information Act, and it's ironic that the RTI exists alongside such a regressive policy on declassifying public records.

Second, public records are critical to understanding national history, culture and identity. Public records are the institutionalized embodiment of Indian history, codified in the form of documents, records and archives. Our understanding of yesterday's events also enables us to solve today's challenges. The American statesman Henry Kissinger said, '[History] teaches by analogy, not by maxims. It can illuminate the consequences of actions in comparable situations, yet each generation must discover for itself what situations are in fact comparable.'[452] Lacking access to yesterday's public records derails the current generation's ability to shed light on today's pressing issues.

Underlying all of this is a lack of clarity and public consensus of the purpose of public records. Public records currently function as the prerogative of a government bureaucrat who can use records to retain some level of tangible evidence of their industriousness in the event that their productivity comes under closer inspection.

Public records serve as evidence of transactions between two parties, serving a political purpose. For instance, an MP might write to a minister advocating a favour for a constituent. The record of this action can be paraded amongst the MP's constituents to solicit public support. But the private benefit of such records—i.e. the showcasing of personal activities—is dwarfed by the potential public benefit of making *all* such records, by default, part of the public domain. They are a living window to the historical actions of an entire democracy. The benefits accrue to a larger collective.

Accessible records are part of the debt we owe to history. Much of what we now know about the Soviet Union—a thoroughly undemocratic state—was only discovered after a mass release of Soviet records and files following its dissolution. The release of Soviet records in the early 1990s led to a new era of scholarship

---

[452]Quoted in Graham Allison, 'The key to Henry Kissinger's success', *The Atlantic*, 27 November 2015.

and updated our understanding of contemporary global affairs.

Indian law already governs the management of public records. The 1993 Public Records Act intended to accommodate the public's interest in maintaining records. However, many flaws in the original bill promoted opacity, making it near-impossible for a layman to obtain public records. And archaic classification rules allowed the government to keep records from public access, most notably Netaji's—but also material relating, for example, to the wars of 1962 and 1971, far past any reasonable declassification deadline in any other democracy.

The pending Amendment (2014) to the Public Records Act introduced by me mitigates the numerous shortcomings of the antiquated 1993 Act by introducing transparency and accountability to the management of India's public records. It redefines the role of the Public Records Officer from 'regulating' access to public records to *promoting* access. Transparency is the expectation, rather than the exception. Classified records are to be declassified by default within twenty years (reduced from twenty-five years). The Amendment updates the original Act's language to more comprehensively include twenty-first century forms of digital records; it will encompass every medium from parchment, palm leaves and birch bark to modern-day optical drives. It also increases the number of historians on the Archives' Advisory Board—the governing board of India's National Archives—to advocate for the public historical and cultural interest in the governance of India's public records.

The Amendment is a critical first step to a more open and accessible government. India remains critically behind some global standards in encouraging its citizens to engage with government data more broadly. The United States launched data.gov—a government website that improves public access to digitized data—over half a decade ago. The online repository, part of President Obama's 2009 Memorandum on Transparency and Open Government, resulted in a multitude of user-friendly apps that leverage government data in the public interest. The apps help people navigate college selection, dietary decisions and even consumer purchases based on government data about product recalls. Two years later, in 2011, India started data.gov.in as an open-sourced joint initiative between the United States and Indian governments. The platform boasts thousands of datasets for public use, but still faces a number of implementation problems, including a weak infrastructure to facilitate the collection and management of data in various government agencies and problems sharing the most recent data sets with the public.

The Public Records Amendment and data.gov.in seek to reimagine the ethos of how the government handles its data and records. Parliament must support the Public Records Amendment to honour the simple notion that democracy demands reasonable measures of accountability and transparency from public officials. India needs more than belated declassification: it needs an effective system of public oversight of the government's work. This is something the Modi government has throughout appeared reluctant to do. We must demand that Mr Modi, and whoever succeeds him, remember they exist to serve the public, not to hide whatever they are doing from them.

chapter thirty

CIVILIZING THE CIVIL SERVICES?

In Section I, I showed how PM Modi doesn't seem to value the services and abilities of his cabinet too much, preferring to operate through a cabal of trusted bureaucrats. But Narendra Modi being Narendra Modi, even bureaucrats are not safe from being buffeted by his whims and fancies. During his term as PM, he committed one of the worst acts of politicization of the civil service in living memory. This was the government's decision to disqualify those civil servants who had worked on the personal staffs of the previous government from serving in a similar capacity under the Modi government.[453] My own Private Secretary at MHRD, who had been recruited in a similar capacity by a new MoS in the Home Ministry, was abruptly transferred back to his parent cadre for this reason. This is a peculiar interpretation of the role of the permanent civil service in our democracy.

Ironically, early in its tenure the Modi government promulgated an amendment to the All India Services (Conduct) Rules, 1968, by inserting assorted sub-rules under the All India Services (Conduct) Amendment Rules, 2014.

Under sub-rule (1A), every member of the service shall maintain:

(i)   High ethical standards, integrity and honesty;
(ii)   Political neutrality;
(iii)   Promoting of the principles of merit, fairness and impartiality in the discharge of duties;
(iv)   Accountability and transparency;
(v)   Responsiveness to the public, particularly to the weaker sections;

---

[453]Rajeev Sharma, 'PM Modi's ministers defy orders on hiring personal staff from UPA regime', *FirstPost*, 2 January 2015.

(vi)   Courtesy and good behaviour with the public.

Under sub-rule (2B), every member of the service shall:

(i)   Commit himself [yes, good old linguistic sexism continues in the Government of India] to uphold the supremacy of the Constitution and democratic values;
(ii)   Defend and uphold the sovereignty and integrity of India, the security of State, public order, decency and morality;
(iii)   Maintain integrity in public service;
(iv)   Take decisions solely in public interest and use or cause to use public resources efficiently, effectively and economically;
(v)   Declare any private interests relating to his public duties and take steps to resolve any conflicts in a way that protects the public interest;
(vi)   Not place himself under any financial or other obligations to any individual or organization which may influence him in the performance of his official duties;
(vii)   Not misuse his position as civil servant and not take decisions in order to derive financial or material benefits for himself, his family or his friends;
(viii) Make choices, take decisions and make recommendations on merit alone;
(ix)   Act with fairness and impartiality and not discriminate against anyone, particularly the poor and the under-privileged sections of society;
(x)   Refrain from doing anything which is or may be contrary to any law, rules, regulations and established practices;
(xi)   Maintain discipline in the discharge of his duties and be liable to implement the lawful orders duly communicated to him;
(xii)   Be liable to maintain confidentiality in the performance of his official duties as required by any laws for the time being in force, particularly with regard to information, disclosure of which may prejudicially affect the sovereignty and integrity of India, the security of State, strategic, scientific or economic

interests of the State, friendly relations with foreign countries
or lead to incitement of an offence or illegal or unlawful
gains to any person; and
(xiii) Perform and discharge his duties with the highest degree of
professionalism and dedication to the best of his abilities.[454]

Phew! Quite a list. But is there, in fact, anything new about them?
Wasn't the civil service always supposed to behave this way? After
all, were our civil servants ever meant to be discourteous, partial,
corrupt or anti-national? There was a time when, as Jawaharlal
Nehru memorably observed, the colonial-era Indian civil service
was neither Indian, nor civil, nor imbued with any spirit of service;
but that was all supposed to have changed with the advent of
Independence and the creation by Sardar Vallabhbhai Patel of
an indigenous 'steel frame' for the Government of India. Very
clearly, all that these amendments do is to make explicit what
has always been implicit.

Perhaps it is a reflection of our times that the government
feels the need to spell out the obvious in such excruciating detail.

But that's hardly a crime, and the list of prescriptions
and proscriptions is in itself quite unexceptionable—what the
Americans call 'motherhood and apple pie', things that no one
can oppose. All Indians would want their civil servants to adhere
to the code spelled out in Mr Modi's nineteen commandments.
(Though nineteen does seem a bit much: as Clemenceau remarked
in a different context, 'even the good Lord only needed ten!')

But there's more than a bit of irony to the fact that it's
Modi's government that, under sub-rule (1A) point (ii), urges
'political neutrality' on the civil service. After all, it is this very
government that—in an action unprecedented in the history of
Indian democracy—issued a circular decreeing that any civil servant
who had served on the personal staff of a UPA minister was
ineligible to serve in an NDA government. While the UPA had

[454]Press Information Bureau, Government of India, 'All India Services (Conduct)
Rules, 1968 Amended', 8 August 2014.

earlier issued rules saying that no officer could serve more than ten years on any minister's personal staff, the NDA circular made length of service, or indeed competence, irrelevant in its instruction: any personal staff who had served the UPA government in such a capacity for any length of time had to be removed from the offices of NDA ministers.

As a result, many officers of unimpeachable integrity and impressive service records were rusticated from the personal staffs of NDA ministers. Their sin was not a negative performance report or excessive length of service on personal staffs—no, their only deficiency was that they had been tainted by association with the preceding government.

This overtly political way of dealing with our civil service was a betrayal of the fundamental principles on which our bureaucracy was constituted. After all, governments may come and go, but the civil service is meant to be permanent and immune to the vagaries of changing political fortunes. Some senior civil servants in the mid-1990s ended up serving four prime ministers in five years, without ever changing their own jobs!

As for myself, I had no hesitation in blessing my former aide's wish to serve an NDA minister: his duty was, after all, to the government, not to me or my party, and I did not begrudge him the recognition of his administrative talents by a different party. This was as it should be. In any government, ministers will naturally exercise their powers in a politically partisan manner, because that is what they have been elected to do—they arrive in their jobs on a platform that requires them to cater to their political constituency and voter preferences. But our system of democratic government, as the founder of the IAS, Sardar Patel, made clear, requires that laws and rules be administered without prejudice. Politicians make policies, but the actual application of laws or rules underpinning those policies is meant to be done by civil servants without any political bias.

That is the logic of our bureaucracy: a new government can announce a new benefit it has advocated politically, but once that benefit is established and funded by the Government of India, it must be given fairly to all eligible beneficiaries, whatever their political persuasion. That's why we are supposed to have politically neutral civil services which are only accountable to the Constitution and the laws for their execution of policies—and to their political masters, the ministers, for their conduct and their impartial functioning.

The NDA's decision to make service to UPA ministers the sole grounds for transferring officials is a disgraceful violation of that principle. It establishes a new principle, that bureaucratic service will henceforth be seen as evidence of political allegiance. When the NDA loses power, the bureaucrats who served them will, by the same logic, be seen as having been politically committed to the Modi government—because the NDA chose them on that basis.

How hypocritical of the very same government to mouth pious homilies about civil service neutrality!

These new rules appear to be a fresh example of the politicians' PR disease, 'watch what I say, not what I do'. What the NDA says is civil servants must be politically neutral; what it has 'done', in fact, is to move no fewer than seven senior civil servants from Gujarat to the Prime Minister's Office in New Delhi, presumably for having shown their political commitment to Mr Modi while serving under him there.

We have learned to get used to more and more examples of the gulf between proclamation and actual implementation in the Modi era. For a prime minister who professedly admires Sardar Patel, it is a pity that Narendra Modi has trashed one of the doughty Sardar's most invaluable legacies—the proverbial 'steel frame'—while issuing rules codifying his adherence to it. One can only hope that the bureaucracy will live up to the new amendments and not to the hypocrisy of those who have issued them.

chapter thirty-one

CAPITAL SPIES

One of the hallmarks of authoritarian governments and rulers everywhere is the increase in surveillance of innocent citizens by a paranoid state. The last time we had to deal with this sort of thing was during Indira Gandhi's Emergency about half a century ago, but Narendra Modi's government has shown that it can resort to blatantly unlawful snooping whenever it wants to.[455] Let's take one of the most egregious examples of this dangerous phenomenon as practised by this government.

On 2 March 2015, Assistant Sub-Inspector (ASI) Shamsher Singh of the Special Branch of Delhi Police Headquarters was found sniffing around the Tughlak Lane residence of then Congress Vice-President Rahul Gandhi in New Delhi, asking inane and suspicious questions. Confronted by the Special Protection Group (SPG), which protects the premises and the staff of Rahul Gandhi, to whom he was taken by the SPG, he produced a questionnaire he was carrying. This required him to obtain various particulars about Rahul Gandhi like the colour of his hair and eyes, birthmarks, any disabilities or preferences, the type of clothes he wears, his shoes, photographs and the names, addresses and phone numbers of his associates.

On 12 March, a beat constable came by the house, and on the 14th, two police officers, an Additional DCP and an ACP, again visited the residence of Rahul Gandhi at 12, Tughlak Lane, New Delhi. They spent about seven minutes at the residence enquiring about the whereabouts of various Gandhi aides.

The Congress party erupted in indignation at these developments, alleging that this was a misuse of the Delhi Police

---

[455]'BJP orchestrated "political espionage and snooping" on Rahul, says Congress', *Indian Express*, 14 March 2015.

SHASHI THAROOR

personnel by the government to obtain personal information about a prominent political opponent. Given that not long ago, the 'Snoopgate' scandal involved a brazen misuse of Gujarat state machinery for the surveillance of the movements of a private citizen, a young woman, the Congress's fear was that the same process might be at work at the Centre.[456]

The party dubbed the affair 'Snoopgate2' and demanded an explanation from the prime minister and the home minister. After all, Rahul Gandhi is protected by the SPG, and has been since his childhood; why would the Delhi Police need such information about an SPG protectee, and if for some innocent reason it did, why not just ask the SPG? And why did the police need the telephone numbers and addresses of Shri Gandhi's associates and friends?

Faced with this controversy, the then Delhi Commissioner of Police, Bhim Sain Bassi, held a press conference to state that this was a routine enquiry; a beat constable had gone not only to the residence of Rahul Gandhi but also to the residences of Veerappa Moily, P. C. Chacko and other political leaders.[457] The police commissioner argued that the information being sought was to prevent spontaneous demonstrations at the Congress leader's residence, to ensure his security and the maintenance of law and order. He explained that various vulnerable persons could not be easily identified by police officers, and it was for this reason that photographs and other descriptive details were being sought. He averred that there was no pressure from the prime minister or the union government to spy on Rahul Gandhi.

This seemed reasonable enough, on the face of it, except for a few inconvenient details. The beat constable's routine security visit to the homes of various political leaders was on 12 March, the Shamsher Singh episode was on 2 March. The Congress stressed that it was objecting to the latter, not the former. Why conflate a

'From snooping to suiting: the controversies around Modi', *The Hindu*, 5 May 2016.
'Cop's Visit To Rahul Gandhi's Home Was Routine Practise, Says Delhi Police Commissioner', *Huffington Post*, 14 March 2015.

routine visit on the 12th with a suspicious episode on the 2nd, if not to confuse and mislead the press? And can anyone seriously suggest in the Information Age that any sentient Delhi policeman would have difficulty identifying Rahul Gandhi without details of his hair, eyes and birthmarks?

That was not all. 'If spontaneous demonstrations against Shri Rahul Gandhi or other VIPs are to be prevented by police,' the Congress pointed out, 'information must be collected regarding those persons or organizations who are likely to conduct such demonstrations', not about Rahul Gandhi and his friends. In any case, what was the logic or rationale of seeking information regarding his associates or the colour of Rahul Gandhi's hair or eyes, and how did such information help in stopping spontaneous demonstrations?

For the commissioner of police to suggest that the enquiries were being made for the 'safety and security of vulnerable persons'[458] like Shri Rahul Gandhi was, to put it mildly, inconsistent with the fact that he has been an SPG protectee for nearly twenty years and is protected under the SPG Act, which leaves no role for the Delhi Police in ensuring his security and safety. How could the Delhi Police justify its spying on Rahul Gandhi in the name of assessing the security of an individual for whose security it is neither responsible nor accountable?

The statement by the commissioner of police that similar information was being also sought in regard to Veerappa Moily, P. C. Chacko, other senior Congress leaders and senior BJP leader Lal Krishna Advani further raised Congress hackles: why was the police collecting information about senior Congress and Opposition leaders, and also of BJP leaders known to be opposed to Prime Minister Narendra Modi? In any event, both Veerappa Moily and P. C. Chacko denied having received any security questionnaire from the police, weakening the authorities' alibi even further.

---

[458]Neeraj Chauhan and Raj Shekhar, 'Used same pro forma for PM Narendra Modi, Amit Shah, police say', *Times of India*, 15 March 2015.

When I issued a series of tweets raising just some of these questions, I received the inevitable invective-laden BJP backlash, but also some reasonable-minded criticism, along the following lines:

—if it's true the police came openly to the house, why is this snooping? Isn't objectionable surveillance supposed to be clandestine?

—if it's true that the same pro forma has been given to other political leaders, including Congressmen like Moily or Chacko, why is this snooping?

—how can the information sought be misused when it is so basic and routine?

The problem is that there were two different visits: one open, one clandestine; one as part of the routine work of the beat constable from the local police station, one from an ASI of the Special Branch. The former was fine, the latter objectionable. The ASI only revealed his questionnaire when confronted by the SPG and Rahul Gandhi's staff.

The pro forma reportedly given to other leaders had not been received by the leaders named, but in any case that was not the issue. The issue was the ASI's snooping, not the overt pro forma, even though that too was unnecessary for an SPG protectee (the SPG records all such details anyway and also tracks the protectee's movements). If it was routine information the police were after, why not send the basic questions with a formal letter from the commissioner of police and ask Rahul Gandhi and his staff to fill it in? Why ask an ASI to sniff around the house making enquiries?

Finally, the question of how the information sought could be misused is best left to the imaginations of those seeking it. Far more important is the principle at stake. India is a democracy with a fragile tradition of respect for personal privacy. Surveillance, telephone tapping and interception of communications, are all too easily misused for political purposes that lie well beyond law and order or national security. While previous governments, besides the aberration of the Emergency, have been more or less respectful of individual privacy rights, the track record in Gujarat of the progenitors of the original Snoopgate is hardly reassuring. The Congress party's concerns were therefore hardly overblown.

Intrusive surveillance of political leaders is something no law permits in India. As far as the Delhi Police is concerned, they should come clean and state under which law and under the provisions of which clause, they carried out this procedure of enquiry against Rahul Gandhi. To what purposes would the information being collected have been put? Would the names and addresses of all of Rahul Gandhi's associates and related information be then used to elicit further information about his whereabouts, location, visits, preferences and habits? To what end?

There are so many other issues in Delhi for the police to be concerned about, from widespread incidents of rape and violence to the daily challenges of law and order. Surely the Delhi Police has better things to do than snooping on political leaders? But the issue goes beyond the Delhi Police, which, after all, is only following orders (though whose orders remains an open question, since the home minister himself seemed unaware of the directive for the ASI's ill-advised expedition). It is the government that needs to explain why politicians' privacy is being invaded.

Our Constitution allows every Indian the right to disagree strongly with the government without being intruded upon, subjected to surveillance and enquired about intrusively in this manner. That Rahul Gandhi leads the principal Opposition party makes 'Snoopgate2' that much worse, but it would be a matter of concern to the Congress party even if he were just an ordinary citizen of India.

chapter thirty-two

TWO FABLES ABOUT FATALISM

As we look back at what Narendra Modi's government has been doing in the years it has been in power, I find myself thinking of what is happening to our country these days in the form of two parables that I am fond of recounting.

The first is an old story, from our ancient Puranas.

A man, the quintessential Indian one might say, is pursued by a tiger. He runs fast, but his panting heart tells him he cannot run much longer or faster. He spots a tree. Relief! He accelerates and gets to it in one last despairing stride. He climbs the tree. The tiger snarls beneath him, but he feels he has escaped its snapping jaws. But no, what's this? The branch on which he is sitting is weak and bends dangerously. That is not all; wood mice are gnawing away at it. Before long, they will eat through it and the branch will fall.

The man realizes this and sees the tiger waiting below him. But as the branch bends, it sags over a well. Aha! Escape? Our hero looks hopefully into the well, but it is dry. Worse, there are poisonous snakes writhing and hissing on its bed, waiting for prey.

What is our hero to do? As the branch bends, he perceives a solitary blade of grass growing out of a crack in the wall of the well. On the tip of the blade gleams a drop of honey.

What action does our Puranic man, the archetypal Indian, take in this situation?

He bends with the branch, and licks up the honey.

This story is at least 2,000 years old, but it could be told today. It speaks of what the Orientalists saw as Indian fatalism, our self-absorption in the face of impossible circumstances and our willingness to make the best we can out of those circumstances.

That is the Indian answer to the insuperable difficulty. One does not fight against that which one cannot overcome, but seeks instead to find the best way, for oneself, to live with it.

So, your life is messed up by demonetization, you spend hours in bank queues, your elderly neighbour collapses and dies while waiting for his pension money, no one can change the 2,000-rupee note you are stuck with, and your wife's life-savings in an atta tin cannot be encashed because you can't prove it isn't black money—but you console yourself, saying the rich have it worse. You find comfort in the belief that since the prime minister is a bachelor, his only thought is to serve the country, and he could not possibly be doing any of this for selfish purposes. In any case, what can you do about it? You may as well adjust to what you can't change.

You voted for Mr Modi hoping to get good governance, an efficient chief executive, strong economic growth and a multiplicity of jobs to choose from—but you got unemployment, lower growth, 120-rupee tomatoes, the gang rape of little girls and women and cow vigilantes lynching poor Muslims and Dalits. You ask yourself, 'What's the alternative?' It wasn't what you voted for, but it's what you are saddled with. At least the PM makes great speeches. You may as well lick up that drop of honey.

The second parable is more troubling. It's a modern one. If you throw a live frog into a pan of boiling water, it will leap out, scalded, and hop frantically to safety. But if you put a live frog in a pan of tepid water and gradually turn up the temperature, it will keep adjusting to the heat until it is cooked to death. [459]

I hope and pray that is not what is happening to my fellow Indians. Are we accepting each new sign of our new political reality like that Puranic man, adjusting ourselves to it as the 'new normal', till the last spark of life is snuffed out of us like the boiling frog's?

---

[459] This story may not be literally true: according to contemporary biologists the premise is false, and a frog that is gradually heated will jump out of the pan. See *Fast Company* Issue 01, October 1995. Still, it works effectively as metaphor!

IV

THE FAILURE OF MODINOMICS

In three successive terms, as chief minister of Gujarat, Mr Modi's relentless publicity machine extolled his virtues as administrator and chief executive of one of India's most prosperous states. Under him, the quality of life and economic status of all Gujaratis were supposed to have improved to unheard of levels. Mr Modi promised that if he were elected prime minister he would use the experience he had gained in Gujarat to magically dispel all the country's ills. The 'Gujarat model' would be applied to the rest of India and all would be well. As with all Mr Modi's promises, this one too was a sham. A rising economy was almost flattened by demonetization and the shocks caused by the improper execution of GST, his attempts to eradicate black money have been unsuccessful and his budgets and implementation of taxation have been disastrous. In this section, I delve deep into the multiple failures of what has come to be known as Modinomics—Narendra Modi's brand of economics.

chapter thirty-three

THE MIRAGE OF ACHHE DIN

As we know, the Modi government was elected in 2014 on a promise of 'achhe din' for the Indian people. As I have shown, although the core supporters of PM Modi's Bharatiya Janata Party belonged to the Hindu right-wing, there is no doubt that what tipped it over the threshold of victory was an upbeat economic message of imminent growth and prosperity. CM Modi was portrayed as the dynamic CEO of his home state, Gujarat, who had presided over unprecedented growth and development and who would be able to do for India what he had done for Gujarat. A vote for the BJP, it was said, would be a vote for rapid and effective economic development. 'Achhe din' would soon follow.

It didn't. As we come to the end of the Modi government's term, we have witnessed economic misgovernance on quite a spectacular scale, including the recklessly irresponsible overnight demonetization of the bulk of India's currency with hugely negative consequences for the economy, lost jobs (I go into this in detail later on in this section), closed businesses, extortionate tax-collection and the botched implementation of one genuinely reformist measure, the rollout of a nationwide Goods and Services Tax (GST), which I have looked at more closely in Chapter 36. As GDP growth has slowed dramatically, exports have declined, manufacturing has collapsed and agriculture stagnated, the government has stopped talking of 'achhe din'. Its new slogan is 'saaf niyat, sahi vikas'—clean intentions, true development. But in a democracy, voters and taxpayers are unlikely to reward intentions alone. Results matter, and the BJP has none to show.

Take demonetization, which I have excoriated in various forums, including on the Lok Sabha floor and in Chapter 35 of this book. It was sprung upon the nation as we were watching news of Donald Trump's US election win in November 2016.

Over twenty months later, none of its stated goals have been met: 'black' money is once again in circulation, 'cashlessness' remains a chimera, and even terrorists coming from across the Pakistan border have been found to be carrying the new notes. It is clear that demonetization has achieved nothing except causing immense inconvenience to ordinary Indians, and the deaths of some hundred citizens, many aged pensioners who collapsed in the interminable queues required to withdraw their own money from banks.[460]

As of 10 June 2018, the total amount of valid currency notes with the Indian public amounted to ₹19.3 lakh crore, higher even than the ₹17.013 trillion figure reported ten days before demonetization was announced to curb the menace of too many notes.[461] While credit and debit card usage is reportedly up, the Indian public seems to be using the latter mainly to withdraw record amounts of cash from ATMs. Though the number of ATMs has risen only marginally since demonetization, the number of ATM withdrawals and the amounts involved have increased to more than 22 per cent of the levels recorded in pre-demonetization months. Cash in circulation is at a record high, with the currency with the public doubling from ₹7.8 lakh crore before demonetization to ₹18.5 lakh crore in April 2018.[462] In a country where digital transactions are still to earn public trust (and where fees for using cards arouse considerable reluctance from spenders), cash is still king, whether for purchasing clothes or buying meals.

This is not a minor matter: it points to the failure of a key government policy initiative, the kind of dramatically disruptive move that Narendra Modi imagined would jump-start and modernize the economy.

Mr Modi campaigned in 2014 on the insincere but attractive

---

[460]Nishant Saxena, 'Demonetisation death toll: 90 people & counting as note ban takes tragic turn', *Catch News*, 9 December 2016.
[461] 'Currency with public doubles from demonetisation low; hits record at over ₹18 lakh crore', *Times of India*, 10 June 2018.
[462]Pragya Srivastava, 'In India, cash is still king! ATM withdrawals up 22%, higher than pre-demonetisation era', *Financial Express*, 20 June 2018.

slogan that 'government has no business to be in business'.[463] But for four years he has continued the government's role in every business it ought not to be in, from running hotels to making condoms. 'Divestment' consisted merely of selling part of the government's share of some public sector companies to other public sector companies; thus the government-owned Oil and Natural Gas Corporation bought the government-owned Hindustan Petroleum Corporation, with Mr Modi crowing about disinvestment.[464] And when the government finally attempted an important act of privatization—that of the loss-making state airline Air India— it hedged the sale offer with so many conditions, including the government's retaining a 25 per cent stake, that not a single bidder came forward.[465]

All of this, coupled with the sea of red ink listing bad loans at state-owned banks (now at a record breaking ₹85,370 crore in 2017–18, with a dozen major bad-loan defaulters in the bankruptcy courts), has dented the investment climate in India. The bond market is in a mess; bank lending to industry has declined to a mere 0.7 per cent growth rate, prompting industrial growth recession; the banks are groaning under sovereign debt (and don't want to acquire any more).[466] There is practically no major private investment by major Indian companies. And foreign investors are fleeing: since January 2018, they have dumped more than $4.5 billion in Indian government bonds.[467]

Inevitably, the rupee has sunk to record lows. This in turn has hugely driven up the cost of India's energy imports at the very time that global oil prices are increasing. As India's energy-

---

[463]'Government has no business being in business, PM Modi tells US investors', *NDTV*, 1 October 2014.
[464]'ONGC buys govt's entire 51.11% stake in HPCL for ₹36,915 crore', *Economic Times*, 31 January 2018.
[465]Mihir Mishra, 'No taker for Air India stake sale as bids close without a single offer', *Economic Times*, 31 May 2018.
[466]Pallavi Nahata, 'Growth in credit cards, unsecured loans holds strong for a fourth year running', *Bloomberg Quint*, 30 April 2018.
[467]'Vulnerability concerns: FPIs dump Indian bonds', *Financial Express*, 24 May 2018.

import bills rise, the current-account deficit, already 2 per cent, will increase.[468] Before he became PM, Narendra Modi saw any depreciation in the value of the rupee as an assault on national pride and honour. If the rhetoric he used then were used against him today, by his own logic, as the rupee tumbles to 72 to the dollar, he'd have to accept blame for squandering more national pride than any PM before him. The government is not on course to fulfil its Budget pledge to trim the fiscal deficit in 2018–19 to 3.3 per cent of GDP from 3.5 per cent last year (itself revised from earlier talk of 3 per cent).[469]

The things the government could do—and boasted it would—haven't been done either. In his election campaign, Mr Modi made almost a fetish of complaining about the crippling burden of regulation that was stymieing business growth in India; he promised to streamline the requirements for opening and running businesses, and to take India into the top fifty in the World Bank's Ease of Doing Business rankings. Today he celebrates India having risen from the rank of 131st in 2016 to 100th in 2017 instead.[470]

Mr Modi promised the youth of India he would create 2 crore jobs a year. He hasn't managed 1 per cent of that.[471] Modi's much-vaunted 'Make in India' initiative to boost investment in manufacturing has had rather poor results, with manufacturing actually shrinking as a proportion of GDP and new project investment declining; manufacturing is clearly not going to be the job-generator Narendra Modi had imagined it would be.[472] His close aide, BJP president Amit Shah, admitted in 2017 that 'it is impossible to provide employment through jobs in a country with

[468]Gayatri Nayak, 'Current account deficit widens to 2% of GDP on higher oil import bill', *Economic Times*, 17 March 2018.
[469]Asit Ranjan Misra, 'Budget 2018: Govt revises fiscal deficit target for FY19 to 3.3% of GDP', *Livemint*, 1 February 2018.
[470]'India jumps 30 places in ease of business, PM Modi says "historic": 10 Points, *NDTV*, 31 October 2017.
[471]'Modi's promise to double farmer incomes is "jumla": Manmohan Singh', *The Quint*, 18 March 2018.
[472]Prathamesh Mulye, 'More layoffs likely as India's manufacturing sales shrink', *IndiaSpend*, 27 February 2017.

125 crore people.'[473] As I have pointed out earlier in the book, the prime minister has been reduced to arguing that selling pakodas on the street—something that many unemployed graduates have been reduced to doing—is also a 'job'.[474] He has made the far-fetched claim in Parliament—during his reply to a July 2018 debate on a motion of no-confidence in his government, no less—that the real problem is lack of data on jobs actually being created; for instance, he claimed, every vehicle sold in the country creates two new jobs.[475] In any other nation he would have been laughed out of his own job by now.

Mr Modi is sounding increasingly desperate as he attempts to convince himself and the world that things are not all that bad. He told the annual general meeting of the Asian Infrastructure Investment Bank at Mumbai in June that India was projected to grow in 2018 'at 7.4 per cent', asserting that inflation was under control and that India's foreign exchange reserves of more than $400 billion 'provide us enough of a cushion.'[476]

The prime minister stressed that India had received $222 billion in Foreign Direct Investment in the last four years. But he did not mention that FDI in the last financial year had plummeted to a five-year low, despite the government significantly relaxing the FDI norms. For the first time since 2015, India was out of the AT Kearney list of the top 10 economies for global investors.[477]

In other words, Narendra Modi's India is heading towards precisely the kind of crisis of economic confidence it was elected to resolve. With elections looming, it is under pressure to increase minimum support prices for farmers, finance the ambitious social

---

[473]Kumar Uttam, 'Not possible to provide jobs to all, so we promote self-employment: Amit Shah', *Hindustan Times*, 31 May 2017.
[474]'No Prime Minister, earning ₹200 a day by selling pakodas is not employment', *The Wire*, 22 January 2018.
[475]'PM Modi junks criticism, says 1 crore jobs created in last 1 year', *Times of India*, 21 July 2018.
[476]'Address of the Prime Minister for the opening ceremony of the Third Annual Meeting of AIIB', Press Information Bureau, Government of India, 26 June 2018.
[477]'India slips 3 notches to 11th spot in AT Kearney FDI Confidence Index', *Economic Times*, 2 May 2018.

welfare schemes it had announced with much fanfare, lower the
hefty taxes it has been levying on petrol and diesel to balance
its books and show some genuine progress on infrastructure. It
hasn't a clue about how to do any of this. Instead of the promised
'good days', India is facing plenty of bad ones.

With elections looming in three BJP-ruled states in December
2018, one sign is telling: it seems the BJP is quietly abandoning the
mantra of 'vikas', since there has been none in four years. 'Vikas
Yatras' have been renamed in the poll-bound states: 'Ashirwad
Yatra' in Madhya Pradesh and 'Gaurav Yatra' in Rajasthan. After
all, 'Gujarati asmita' worked in Modi's home state; he is now
reduced to hoping it can do the trick everywhere else. When you
can't show development, talk of pride instead!

In the ultimate irony, the RSS-affiliated trade union, the
Bharatiya Mazdoor Sangh (BMS), launched a nationwide agitation
in September 2018 against the Modi government's modest labour
reforms—especially the extension of contract labour to various
sectors of the economy—that it says have led to 'extreme
exploitation and harassment' of the labour sector as well as caused
increasing unemployment in the country.[478] The principal Modi
labour reform has run up against his party's principal labour
organization and been found wanting. On the economy, Mr Modi
literally has no friends left.

---

[478]'RSS-backed trade union says Modi government causing "extreme labour
exploitation"', *Economic Times*, 4 September 2018.

chapter thirty-four

THE DARK TRUTH ABOUT BLACK MONEY

One of the more popular campaign promises of the victorious Narendra Modi campaign in 2014—and the most difficult to fulfil—was his commitment to 'bringing back' to India 'within 100 days' the billions of dollars of 'black money' reputedly stashed abroad by tax evaders, corrupt officials and the like.[479] No one in our country disagrees that black money is a serious problem or that the black money squirrelled away abroad should be identified and brought back, if possible. Black money is particularly pernicious for a developing country like India, because it siphons away resources that could be spent for much needed investments in health, education, roads and general public welfare. There were debates on black money in each one of the first eight Lok Sabhas, but despite learned judges like Santhanam and Wanchoo heading Committees that issued voluminous reports, the problem seems only to have got worse over the years.

Black money in India is generated by various practices: real estate transactions, diversion of government resources from welfare programmes, kickbacks on government contracts (especially those involving international procurement) and malpractices in international trade, especially under-invoicing.

What is the scale of the problem? Various numbers, including some fanciful ones, were flung about in the course of the political debate on the issue. One Internet and SMS allegation doing the rounds, and cited by the yoga guru and black-money crusader, Baba Ramdev, claims that there is about ₹500 lakh crore worth of black money.[480] This figure would be equivalent, even at today's

---

[479]I will bring back black money and distribute it to honest taxpayers': Modi, *Times of India*, 12 February 2014.
[480]'Indians have ₹500 lakh crore black money, says Baba Ramdev', *DNA*, 28 February 2011.

depreciated Indian exchange rate, to some $7 trillion, whereas our entire GDP is only $2.5 trillion; we should probably not learn our economics from a yoga teacher. The more realistic number of the many generally cited comes from a widely circulated report called 'The Drivers and Dynamics of Illicit Financial Flows from India 1948 to 2008', published in November 2010 by the reputable US-based organization Global Financial Integrity. It concludes that we have lost a total of $213 billion in illicit money since 1948, the present value of which in today's dollars would be about $462 billion or 20 lakh crore rupees, which is still serious money.

Even when it comes to Swiss banks, the burden of the BJP's song for some years now, official Swiss bank figures show that Indians hold only 1.01 billion Swiss francs (₹7,000 crore) out of 1.46 trillion Swiss francs (about 100 lakh crore).[481] We are not, therefore, the country with the largest Swiss bank deposits ('more than all the other countries combined,' one BJP MP had alleged while in Opposition). Even one illegal rupee in a Swiss bank is unpardonable. But the real dimensions of the problem should be understood accurately.

The Swiss banks are a red herring in the black money debate. Swiss banks pay less than 1 per cent interest at the most; it is highly unlikely that Indians with black money are leaving it there, and far more probable that the bulk is being reinvested more profitably elsewhere, including in our own country. Why not? In India, in the last decade, housing prices have risen ten times since 2000, the Sensex has gone up six times, and government bonds offer 8 per cent while the best terms abroad are at 3 per cent.[482] This makes India a very attractive investment destination for Indian money, which can be routed back to the country in a practice called 'round-tripping'—taking illegal money out but bringing it back as a legitimate investment, especially through

---

[481]'Money of Indians in Swiss banks rise 50% to over ₹7,000 cr', *Times of India*, 28 June 2018.
[482]'Home prices rose 14.5% a year since Jan 2011: RBI', *Economic Times*, 10 April 2017.

investment havens like Mauritius.

In our desire to facilitate foreign investment, we have unwittingly made 'round-tripping' easier through, for example, the anonymity guaranteed by participatory notes: in December 2017, investment in participatory notes rose to a six-month high at ₹1.5 lakh crore, despite the measures taken by the Securities and Exchange Board of India (SEBI) to check their misuse.[483] Whereas our domestic investors have to fulfil stringent 'Know Your Customer' (KYC) norms, these are much more lax for participatory notes. While we need productive investments from abroad, we must not allow them to become a contemporary equivalent of the old 'voluntary disclosure schemes' under which the government used to soak up black money.

At the same time, there are specific concerns. Forty per cent of the total FDI coming into India comes from Mauritius. We have been trying to renegotiate the Tax Treaty we have with Mauritius, but inevitably our strategic interests in that country will affect how far we can push its government to accede to our demands. The fact is, however, that there is no taxation on capital gains in Mauritius, so that if an entity sets up a paper company there, our Double Taxation Avoidance Agreement becomes, in fact, a double non-taxation agreement for us. Our income tax department had the power to examine and verify whether the resident status of a company in Mauritius was genuine or not. The NDA government, whose leading lights are today waxing indignant on the issue, withdrew that power by Circular 789 of April 2000, under which a simple certification from the Mauritius government is now accepted.[484] This has rendered 'round-tripping' from Mauritius much easier, because India no longer has the power to question the residential status of a company there.

---

[483]'Investment in participatory notes hits 6-month high of 1.5 lakh cr in December', *The Hindu*, 28 January 2018.
[484]'Clarification regarding taxation of income from dividends and capital gains under the Indo-Mauritius Double Tax Avoidance Convention (DTAC)', *Income Tax India*, 13 April 2004.

It is also mildly amusing that some of the BJP leaders seem to presume that the tax haven countries are just waiting to hand over information and money to us, if only our government is tough enough to ask. The opposite is true. Whatever India can do in relation to the banks of foreign countries is subject to the domestic laws of those countries and of course of international law, including treaties to which India is a party. Under the Indo-Swiss DTA Agreement, information on Swiss bank deposits cannot be revealed by them until we provide the names of the individuals we are investigating, of the banks where they have their money, and evidence of criminality; the Swiss have made it clear they will not support 'fishing expeditions' for names in their banks.[485] In addition, we are bound to secrecy clauses; releasing names (except for prosecution) would violate our undertakings and jeopardize future cooperation.

No wonder that Switzerland is ranked number one on this year's Financial Secrecy Index compiled by the Tax Justice Network.[486] Since 1934, breaking bank secrecy is a criminal offence in Switzerland, whereas tax evasion is not a crime under their law.

To suggest that the Government of India under the UPA was not strong in its efforts in this regard is particularly unfair because, since the Pittsburgh G-20 Summit in 2008, India led the push in the G-20 against banking secrecy and opaque cross-border financial dealings that protect black money. India joined the Financial Action Task Force and pushed the G-20 to restructure and strengthen the OECD's Global Forum on Transparency and the Exchange of Information for Tax Purposes. The head of the Global Forum on Tax Transparency rated India 'first in terms of promoting the standards, in terms of fighting tax evasion, and having the international community lining up behind it.'[487] Similar

[485]'Black money: No fishing expedition, says Switzerland', *Hindu BusinessLine*, 7 December 2014.
[486]'Financial Secrecy Index - 2018 Results', *Financial Secrecy Index* <https://www.financialsecrecyindex.com/introduction/fsi-2018-results>.
[487]'Initiatives taken by the government for unearthing and curbing black money: a fact sheet', *Income Tax India*, 10 August 2012.

praise came from the director of the OECD Centre for Tax Policy and Administration.

The UPA government had also taken a number of related steps. It enacted legislation incorporating countermeasures against non-cooperative countries, whose companies, for instance, must pay a 30 per cent withholding tax. It tightened provisions on transfer pricing. There is a provision in 30 of our DTAAs requiring assistance for collection of taxes, including taking measures of conservancy, and the government tried to put this into the other agreements as well. Eight more income tax overseas units were set up, more manpower was deployed to the transfer pricing and international taxation units, and a large number of officers were given specialized training.[488] With all its efforts, the UPA government was able to make specific requests in 333 cases to obtain information from foreign jurisdictions and obtained over 9,900 pieces of information regarding suspicious transactions by Indian citizens.[489]

Many speakers in the Lok Sabha debate on black money in 2011 referred to Hasan Ali Khan, the Pune stud farm owner with billions stashed abroad. But though the case is shocking, he did get caught: his prosecution is evidence of the government at work to pursue the holders of black money abroad. The fact is that there is a lot of domestic black money too—notably in politics. Election campaigns are awash in black money; most candidates are reputed to spend far more than the permissible limits, and the difference has to come in unaccounted (i.e. black) money. Root and branch reform is necessary.

While it is very easy to shout slogans or to clamour for political change, Mr Modi's extravagant campaign promises on retrieving and curbing black money have been revealed as hollow. Now the real question the country's political parties need to ask is what can we do together to resolve the problem of black

---

[488]'Government's white paper on black money', *Income Tax India*, 16 May 2015.
[489]'Probe on into black money deals by Indians: Pranab', *Hindustan Times*, 19 October 2011.

money. I would like to suggest a brief list: We have to tackle the problem of tax evasion, which would require cooperation with the government on tax reform and rationalization and on financial sector reform. We need to incentivize compliance. We have to tackle black money coming from real estate, which again requires cooperation on effective land titling, on reformed land revenue and land record systems, and the elimination of policy distortions, including rationalizing taxation, such as onerous stamp duties which promote evasion. We have to tackle black money in education, which means removing the scarcity of good education supply in our country, which permits some colleges to take black money to provide access to good education. We need effective implementation of government spending programmes, especially their financial management. Action to strengthen law enforcement and criminal justice will help eliminate terrorism-related funding, which also relies on black money. And we do need to tackle electoral reforms to ensure that politics does not remain a major locus of black money. The Lokpal Bill is one of several measures that could conceivably tackle corruption effectively, but four years after its passage, the Modi government is yet to appoint a Lokpal.

In other words, I would respectfully say to the BJP leaders who campaigned to bring the Modi government to power in the name of returning black money that it would be far better to work together to deal with the real problems facing this country. Instead of adjourning the House as the BJP repeatedly did over the issue, we need to use the House to create the policies and reforms that will enable us effectively to deal with black money here and abroad.

During his 2014 election campaign Mr Modi grandly promised that he would bring back all the black money stashed abroad by Indians and that each citizen of India would, as a result, find ₹15 lakh per person deposited in his bank account. No doubt this fanciful promise won him some votes, but like many of Mr Modi's promises it was never intended to be fulfilled. His party president,

Amit Shah, subsequently declared that the ₹15 lakh promise was only an election 'jumla' and we should not take this figure too seriously.[490] At the very least one must hope that Mr Modi will stop trying to use black money as a campaign issue in 2019.

[490]'What about 15 lakh in accounts promised by PM Modi, asked RTI. the reply', *NDTV*, 23 April 2018.

chapter thirty-five

INDIA'S DEMONETIZATION DISASTER

Change comes in many forms to different countries. Some embrace change, some resist change, and some have change thrust upon them. Take India, which was plunged into chaos on the night of 8 November 2016, when Prime Minister Narendra Modi, in a forty-eight-minute address, announced that some ₹14 trillion worth of ₹500 and ₹1,000 notes—amounting to 86 per cent of all the currency in circulation in India—would become illegal as of midnight. People would have until the end of the year to deposit them in bank accounts (and pay whatever taxes and fines the authorities decided to impose on them), but they were no longer legal tender.

This unexpected shock-and-awe announcement, Mr Modi said, fulfilled a declared campaign objective to fight 'black money' or, put another way, cash made from tax evasion, crime and corruption. The prime minister declared that his announcement would not only rid the nation of black money, it would render worthless the counterfeit notes that were reportedly printed by Pakistan to fuel terrorism against India.

The initial stunned reaction was followed by a panicky scramble to unload the expiring notes: the very night of the announcement, people rushed to petrol pumps to fill up their tanks, jewellers tripled their sales and loans were hastily returned. There were unexpected consequences too: housewives who had salted away their savings in biscuit tins for a rainy day found their years of thrift would soon be worthless. In most cases, even their husbands had not known how much their wives had saved.

But within days the real result of the Modi announcement became apparent—the severe disruption of normal economic activity. Inept implementation made a mockery of the initial shock-and-awe. Not nearly enough new currency had been printed before

334

the announcement (some estimates were that only 4 per cent of replacement currency was printed), so banks did not even have a fraction of the money needed to meet consumer demand for new notes. Long queues snaked in, outside and around banks, foreign exchange counters (including at the international airports) and ATMs to change the old notes and withdraw new ones.

But the ATMs were largely empty, since the new notes had been made in a different size from the old ones and did not fit the existing ATMs. These needed recalibration, a process that took tens of thousands of engineers several months to complete. The government had not thought of making the new notes the same size as the old to avoid this obvious problem.

An additional complication was the fact that there are not enough ATMs in India: the country has only 20 ATMs per 100,000 people, as compared to 77 in China, 114 in Brazil, and 279 in South Korea. Even South Africa has 70 ATMs per 100,000 people.[491]

In the meantime, thanks to the slow speed of the Mint's presses, cash was in short supply. Banks did not have enough money and so restricted withdrawals to small amounts of cash that most customers found insufficient. Though the permissible withdrawal limits kept changing, being raised and lowered confusingly, they went up with time—provided the bank had the cash available when one asked for it.

Such restrictions are arguably illegal—under which provision of law can an Indian citizen be denied access to the money in his or her own account? When, in Parliament, I asked the finance minister to name one country in the world that disallows people from withdrawing their own money from a bank, he could give me no reply.

Thirty days after the prime minister's speech (in which he had asked the public to bear with inconvenience for just fifty days), only 30 per cent of the currency in circulation had been

[491]Aashiq Hussain Lone, 'Demonetisation Drive: A colossal mismanagement', *Rising Kashmir*, 9 October 2017.

restored. The Reserve Bank of India (RBI) told the Public Accounts
Committee of Parliament on 18 January that it was up to 60 per
cent. The State Bank of India estimated that it would go up to 70
per cent by the end of February. The government's own annual
Economic Survey 2016–2017, released on 1 February, then claimed
that replenishing the cash supply would be complete by March
2017—but that target too slipped. Cash shortages remained for
months more; the rate of printing new ₹500 notes fell below target.
It took another three months to remonetize the banking system.

The initial replacement notes all came in the form of an
unusually high denomination (₹2,000) that most people did not find
useful—especially since the government's failure to print additional
quantities of smaller notes meant that for weeks no one was able
to make change for a ₹2,000 note. Since over 90 per cent of all
financial transactions in India are made in cash, and over 85
per cent of workers are paid their incomes in cash, the everyday
economy was brought to a standstill in the last two months of
the year.[492] The recovery in the new year was slow, and official
figures showed a marked slowdown in the country's growth rate
in the first quarter of 2017.[493]

If this points to an appalling lack of elementary planning on
the part of the government, the broader consequences have been
far worse. The economy plunged into chaos, and the decision
looks more like a miscalculation than a masterstroke.

The lack of cash reduced both consumption and demand across
the board. A booming economy that boasted the highest growth rate
in the world suddenly became a cash-scarce economy. Production
went down in all sectors. Small producers could not get working
capital to keep their businesses going, and many had to shut down.
Daily-wage workers (a large majority of India's labour force) lost
their jobs because firms did not have the cash to pay them.

[492]Wade Shepard, 'A cashless future is the real goal of India's demonetization
move', *Forbes*, 14 December 2016.
[493]Asit Ranjan Misra, 'India GDP growth rate slumps to 5.7% in Q1 in challenge
for economy', *Livemint*, 1 September 2017.

In November/December 2016, all indicators—sales, traders' incomes, production, and employment—were down; former Prime Minister Manmohan Singh estimated that India's GDP would shrink by around a full percentage point for the fiscal year.[494]

The Economic Survey 2016–2017 released by the Chief Economic Adviser to the government itself stated that demonetization was an aggregate demand shock, an aggregate supply shock, an uncertainty shock and a liquidity shock. It said that the cash crunch 'must have' affected the informal economy, which accounts for nearly half of the overall GDP and about 80 per cent of the employment economy—one which runs on cash.[495]

India's unemployment rate shot up to a five-year high of 5 per cent in 2015–16.[496] According to the All-India Manufacturers' Organization (AIMO), macro- and small-scale industries and traders incurred 60 per cent job losses and a 47 per cent revenue loss because of demonetization. Not only were small-and medium-sized enterprises shutting down; medium and large infrastructure companies surveyed by AIMO reported a 35 per cent drop in employment and a 55 per cent drop in revenue.[497]

Two years after demonetization, unemployment remains one of the biggest problems the country is facing. The Centre for Monitoring Indian Economy (CMIE) estimates that around 15 lakh jobs were lost between January and April 2017.[498] The Labour Bureau's Quarterly Employment Survey for October to December 2017 showed that about 1.25 lakh casual and 46,000 part-time workers were out of jobs. The ₹8 lakh crore construction industry,

[494]'Economics of note ban: Why this is Manmohan Singh's turn to laugh', *Economic Times*, 1 September 2017.
[495]*Economic Survey 2016–17*, Government of India, Ministry of Finance, Department of Economic Affairs, Economic Division, August 2017.
[496]'India's unemployment rate highest in 5 years in 2015-16', *Indian Express*, 29 September 2016.
[497]Arjun Janardanan, 'Demonetisation: 35 per cent job losses, 50 per cent revenue dip, says study by largest organisation of manufacturers', *Indian Express*, 9 January 2017.
[498]Mahesh Vyas, '1.5 million jobs lost in first four months of 2017', Centre for Monitoring Indian Economy, 11 July 2017.

which employs 30 million people, virtually ground to a halt after demonetization, with a drop of 80–90 per cent in income.[499]

Inventory piled up due to low consumer demand. Local industries—footwear in Agra, garments in Tirupur—suspended work due to a lack of money. Several enterprises are now struggling to their feet, whereas many have not been able to resume at all.

The informal financial sector—rural moneylenders who provide loans that amount to 40 per cent of India's total lending—has all but collapsed.

Rural India was affected badly by demonetization. The fishing industry, dependent entirely on cash sales of freshly caught fish, was one of the hardest hit. Demonetization even affected coastal security, as I pointed out during Question Hour in Parliament, because the cash shortage dramatically reduced the number of boats going out to sea to about 10 per cent of previous levels, thereby reducing the number of eyes and ears available to our intelligence agencies monitoring suspicious activities in our waters.

Traders lost perishable stocks and farmers began unloading produce below cost—since no one had the money to purchase their freshly harvested crops. Peas that Punjabi farmers sold at ₹30 a kilo only a year before the PM's announcement were brought down to ₹7 a kilo two months after demonetization.

The liquidity crisis deeply affected farm production, farm prices, and agricultural credit repayments. A study by two economists at Delhi's Indira Gandhi Institute of Development Research found that in mid-November 2016, deliveries of rice to rural wholesale markets were 61 per cent below usual levels, soybeans were down 77 per cent, and maize nearly 30 per cent. The winter crop could not be sown in time, because no one had cash for seeds, and the resultant harvest was lower than projected.

All this was hugely destabilizing in the short term. The prime minister asked people to be patient for fifty days, but those fifty days came and went and it soon became clear that the process

[499]Shweta Punj, 'Down and ouch', *India Today*, 24 November 2016.

would take much longer before normal money supply was restored. As for the long term, as former Prime Minister Manmohan Singh trenchantly observed, quoting Keynes, 'in the long run, we are all dead.'

The story of demonetization was of unnecessary suffering throughout the country. As ordinary people clutching their savings wasted hours standing patiently in queues that offered no assurance of money at the other end, fatalism battled with exasperation. Stories of individual tragedies were reported daily—of hospitals turning away patients who only had old notes, children not being fed, middle-class wage-earners unable to buy medicines for the sick, and, as I have noted, about a hundred people reportedly dying after collapsing in bank queues or committing suicide.[500] Ironically, the rich—more likely to hold credit cards and be 'cashless'—were relatively unaffected; the main victims were the poor and the lower middle classes, who rely on cash for their daily activities.

Thus, those at the bottom of the economic pyramid were the principal victims of this supposedly 'pro-poor' policy. Yet they reacted with stoicism, swayed by the government's assiduous public relations messaging that portrayed their difficulties as a small sacrifice for the nation. 'If our soldiers can stand for hours every day guarding our borders,' one popular, and hugely effective, social media meme asked, 'why can't we stand for a few hours in bank queues?'

The impact of the demonetization in terms of the cash deficit and its consequences was particularly severe in Kerala, the state I represent in Parliament, because of the distinct character of its banking sector, in which the cooperative sector and primary cooperative societies play a central role.

Overall, the cooperative banking sector is much more active and vibrant in Kerala than elsewhere in India. As a result, over 70 per cent of the deposits in cooperatives in India come from Kerala;

---

[500]Maninder Dabas, 'Here are 9 incidents during demonetisation that marked people's suffering', *India Today*, 13 January 2017.

over 70 per cent of the non-agricultural loans and advances made
in India are made in Kerala; and over 15 per cent of agricultural
loans and advances disbursed in India are disbursed in Kerala.
But the Reserve Bank of India prevented all 370 central district
cooperative banks and 93,000 primary agricultural credit societies
in the country from depositing or converting old notes after 8
November 2016. They were allowed to exchange old notes only
as late as June 2017.[501]

Keeping the cooperative banks and societies out of the note
exchange process was particularly damaging for Kerala. Dairy,
agriculture, and the market for fish were all severely affected.

Tourism, vital for India's economy, was hit hard, albeit briefly.
Foreigners were spared tragedy but not inconvenience, for they
were only allowed to cash a hundred dollars a day and often
had to go from bank to bank to get the money. In November
2016, for instance, tourists returned without seeing the Taj Mahal
because their notes were not accepted at the ticket window, and
travel plans were curtailed by lack of new money. Tourism works
by word of mouth: how will one regain the trust of foreigners
that have already spread the word of their harrowing ordeals in
demonetizing India?

While it is clear that the government had not done its homework
before launching the scheme—and in a manner typical of the Modi
administration, had consulted very few officials within it, and
bypassed his cabinet—it is not the prime minister's style to be on
the defensive. His propagandists boasted about a 'surgical strike'
on black money, corruption, terrorism and counterfeiting. Over
time, it became painfully clear that those objectives had not been
met. A 'surgical strike' is supposed to be precisely targeted, but it is
clear that the collateral damage is so extensive that the pain it has
inflicted outweighed any tangible gain, at least in the short term.

In the beginning of December 2016, new victims surfaced,

[501]'Govt allows district central cooperative banks to exchange old notes', *Times
of India*, 22 June 2017.

ranging from salary earners trying to get money out of their bank accounts and pensioners unable to receive their monthly allowances, to fathers and brides unable to finance long-planned weddings at the peak of the Hindu marriage season. As late as the end of January 2017, Indians were surviving on less than half the cash that had been in circulation at the beginning of November 2016.[502] Shockingly, this was all happening in a country where cash represented 98 per cent of all transactions by volume and 68 per cent by value.[503] While the cash is now largely back in circulation, memories of demonetization have shaken many people's faith in the currency. As recently as April 2018, India faced a shortage of cash with ATMs running out of money and banks placing restrictions on withdrawals.[504]

Indeed, the Modi government itself has effectively conceded that demonetization has failed and has had a severe adverse economic impact on India. In its list of achievements touted in the Economic Survey 2016–2017, the list takes note of assorted schemes continued from the previous regime, but fails to mention demonetization. The Survey also accepts that demonetization resulted in 'growth slow[ing], as demonetization reduced demand (cash, private wealth) [and] supply (reduced liquidity and working capital and disrupted supply chains), and increased uncertainty' and 'job losses, decline in farm incomes, social disruption, especially in cash intensive sectors.'[505] The RBI's Annual Report for 2016–2017 stated the cost of printing notes doubled to ₹7,965 crore in the 2017 financial year, from ₹3,421 crore in the previous year as a result of printing the new 500 and 200 rupee notes.[506]

[502]Gayatri Nayak, 'Post demonetisation: India running on half the cash', *Economic Times*, 12 January 2017.
[503]Mayank Jain, 'The Beginning Of The End Of The Parallel Economy In India?', *Bloomberg Quint*, 9 November 2016.
[504]Somesh Jha, 'ATMs run out of notes: Here's the reason behind the massive cash crunch', *Business Standard*, 17 April 2018.
[505]*Economic Survey 2016–2017*, Government of India.
[506]'RBI releases big demonetisation data; cost of printing notes doubled to ₹7,965 cr due to noteban', *Financial Express*, 30 August 2017.

Unfortunately, there is no evidence that any of the declared objectives of the scheme will be attained. In a largely cash-fuelled economy, all cash is not 'black money' and all black money is not cash. In fact, as I have explained in the previous chapter, most of India's black money has been invested in real estate and other forms of property, gold and jewellery, investments in property abroad, and 'round-tripping' that has seen the money return to India's stock market as 'foreign investment' via countries like Mauritius. The Modi move, therefore, touched only a small proportion of black money assets.

Worse, the government had hoped that the sudden move would eliminate a large portion of the black money holdings altogether from the government's liabilities, since it was assumed that many hoarders would destroy their money rather than attract the attention of the taxman by declaring it. Various agencies of the government had initially estimated that around 25 to 35 per cent of the demonetized banknotes would not be deposited by the stipulated dates. On 23 November 2016, the Attorney General of India told the Supreme Court of India that the government expected that notes worth four to five lakh crore rupees would be rendered worthless by not being deposited. But as has been noted in this book and elsewhere, the RBI's annual report declared that 99 per cent of the denominated 500 and 1,000 rupee bank notes had been returned by 30 June 2017.[507]

And since corruption seems to be a way of life in India, it will not be long before the old habits of under-invoicing, fake purchase orders and bills, reporting non-existent transactions and straightforward bribery all generate new black money all over again. The government's plan is therefore likely to be ineffective beyond the short term, since it does nothing to control the source of black money.

Indeed, in the first six weeks after demonetization, the

---

[507]'What was the purpose of demonetisation? RBI says 99% of banned ₹500, ₹1000 notes returned', *Business Today*, 30 August 2017.

Income Tax Department announced it had seized ₹3,185 crore in unaccounted cash from people hoarding currency they could not explain. Strikingly, ₹86 crore of their seizure happened to be in brand new ₹2,000 notes![508] Cases of corrupt officials, including bank managers, being caught red-handed in illegal transactions have been reported, all of which involved the new currency. Some bank managers worked from 9 a.m. to 5 p.m. telling people they had no money, and then from 5 p.m. to 9 p.m. gave money through the back door to money launderers for a fee.

Though I am by no means tarnishing all bank managers for the sins of a few, the fact is that in its drive against corruption the government has created new forms of corruption. Black money clearly continues to be generated—it has merely changed its colour and shape. Black money has become white by way of pink! And, of course, ₹2,000 notes will take up less space in the briefcases of the corrupt than ₹1,000 notes did.

The prime minister's other declared objectives have not been met, either. Demonetization is not a necessary exercise to achieve the objective of thwarting counterfeiting, and the government's citing of such an aim displays considerable overreach. Media reports confirm that counterfeit bills of our freshly designed currency notes are widely in circulation. This could, however, have been prevented by enmeshing strong security features with the design. It seems that the government has missed the opportunity of ensuring the adoption of such security features in the new ₹500 and ₹2000 currency notes that it launched post-demonetization. This indicates a lack of foresight and inadequate planning on the government's part. There appears to be no special new watermark, no security thread or fibre, no new latent image and certainly no nano chip, as BJP supporters were boasting on social media!

Will a mere change of colour and size render the notes safe? Shockingly, the RBI has admitted that two different versions of the

---

[508]'IT-raids uncovered Rs 3185 crore of undisclosed income since demonetisation', *FirstPost*, 22 December 2016.

₹500 note were printed in haste.[509] If both versions are authentic, one can reasonably assume that this is going to confuse the public and make it easier for counterfeiters to get away with their own fake versions.

But still, how big of a problem is this? A study conducted by the Indian Statistical Institute in Kolkata, under the supervision of the National Investigation Agency, estimated that the value of fake Indian currency notes in circulation was about ₹400 crore, which amounted to only roughly 0.03 per cent of the withdrawn currency.[510]

It also indicated that the ability of banks to prevent counterfeit notes being deposited was limited, since their machines often fail to identify fake notes and bank tellers—overwhelmed by the pressure of the astronomically high level of deposit activity in the fifty-day window period—could not make the manual effort to identify fake notes.

As a result, every indication suggests that several fake currency notes slipped through into the banking system and became legitimized. Thus, far from hurting counterfeiters, demonetization may have helped legitimize fake currency by having it exchanged, amid the chaos, for new notes.

Prime Minister Modi also cited among his objectives the undermining of terrorist and subversive activities. He even went so far as to say, on 27 December, that 'through the note ban, in one stroke, we destroyed the world of terrorism, drug mafia, human trafficking and the underworld.'[511]

But empirical evidence collated from data on terrorist strikes and fatalities from the Global Terrorism database and the South Asian Terrorism portal shows that it is very difficult to establish a causal relationship between the number of terrorist strikes on

---

[509]Chethan Kumar, 'Two variants of new ₹500 note surface, RBI says printing defect due to rush', *Economic Times*, 25 November 2016.
[510]Rahul Tripathi, 'Secret study pegs value of fake notes in circulation at ₹400 crore', *Economic Times*, 13 July 2018.
[511]Kavita Upadhyay, 'Terrorism, drug mafia destroyed by note ban: PM', *The Hindu*, 28 December 2016.

Indian soil and the absolute levels of currency in circulation. In any case, we are seeing reports of terrorists being caught or killed in Kashmir in possession of large quantities of new notes. So where is the claimed effect on terror financing?

Meanwhile, the goalposts kept shifting: the Reserve Bank of India issued 74 notifications in 50 days after demonetization.[512] Each of these was intended to tweak an earlier announcement. As I've noted, many began referring to this once-respected institution as the 'Reverse Bank of India' for its frequent reversals of stance on such matters as the amounts of money permissible to withdraw, the last legal date for withdrawals and even whether depositors would have their fingers marked with indelible ink so they could not withdraw their money too often.

Demonetization has caused serious and seemingly lasting damage to India's fledgling financial institutions, most notably the RBI, which conspicuously failed to exercise its autonomy, to anticipate the problems of Mr Modi's scheme, prepare its implementation better and to alleviate its impact. The United Forum of Reserve Bank Officers and Employees wrote to the government on 13 January 2017, pointing to 'operational mismanagement', which has 'dented RBI's autonomy and reputation beyond repair.'[513] The inexplicable silence of its governor, Urjit Patel, reduced him to a lamb, as I have said before, but the 'silence of the lamb' was eating India's citizenry alive.

In a late change of declared objective, the prime minister and finance minister started talking about moving India to a 'cashless society'—an idea and a phrase that was not mentioned even once in Prime Minister Modi's original 8 November 2016 speech. (This was hastily amended to a 'less cash' society when the absurdity of the proposition was widely pointed out.)[514] But they seem blissfully

---

[512]'Demonetisation: 50 days, 74 notifications', *Indian Express*, 31 December 2016.
[513]'"Feeling humiliated" by post-note ban events, RBI employees write to Urjit Patel', *Times of India*, 13 January 2017.
[514]'Instant recall: how Modi government kept changing demonetisation's goalposts', *The Wire*, 31 August 2017.

unaware of the fact that over 90 per cent of retail outlets do not even have a card reader at the point of sale, that half of India's population is unbanked[515]—India is home to 11 per cent of the world's unbanked adults—and that the overwhelming majority of their nationals still function in a cash economy.[516] In fact, 97 per cent of retail transactions in India are conducted in cash or by cheque. Only 6 per cent of Indian merchants accept digital payments.[517]

As columnist T. J. S. George asked: 'Are we to assume that daily wage earners, small-time farmers and sundry hawkers who don't even know what is a bank will be happy to see the country getting rid of cash, rather than vague things like illiteracy and poverty?'[518]

The plain fact is that the digital infrastructure for 'cashlessness' simply does not exist in India. The aforementioned Economic Survey acknowledges that digital transactions face significant impediments.

Though the government hopes many will use their mobile phones for cashless payments, the survey enumerates approximately 350 million people without cellphones (the 'digitally excluded'); 350 million with regular 'feature' phones, and 250 million with smartphones.[519] A mere 25 per cent of the country has Internet access, and there are around 200 million users of digital payment services.[520] A 2015 World Bank study of bank account usage and dormancy rates across different regions found that only 15 per

---

[515]Wade Shepard, 'A cashless future is the real goal of India's demonetization move', *Forbes*, 14 December 2016.

[516]'19 crore Indian adults don't have bank account: World Bank', *Times of India*, 19 April 2018.

[517]Sharad Raghavan, 'Ninety seven per cent of retail transactions still cash-based, says USAID report', *The Hindu*, 22 January 2016.

[518]T. J. S. George, 'The cash mess. Changing goalposts, new exemptions raise doubts about the government's intentions', *Indian Express*, 25 December 2016.

[519]'Eco Survey: Inter-operability of payments system key to success of digitalisation', *Hindu BusinessLine*, 31 January 2017.

520 'Despite talk of digital India, only 25% of Indians access the internet: study', *FirstPost*, 20 June 2018.

cent of Indian adults reported using an account to make or receive payments.[521]

In such an environment, a cash scarcity is economically crippling. Moreover, most mobile applications and internet banking websites are largely available in English, a language not understood by a majority of the people.

There are also appalling deficiencies in cyber security. Ours is a country where cybercrime flourishes; the government's drive for a cashless economy may be creating new vulnerabilities and new victims. Expecting India to become a 'less cash' economy at this point is like removing 86 per cent of a person's blood circulation and then asking him to dance.

Studies confirm that most Indians who use cards use them just to withdraw cash from ATMs; making payments by plastic is still something of a novelty. Multiple stories—which might have been hilarious, if they were not so pathetic—have been told of people patriotically trying to use plastic at the few outlets that do accept cards and being told 'the server is down'; of salesmen frantically rushing out onto the street from their shops with card readers in hand hoping to catch a better signal; and of single transactions taking a dozen minutes because the card reader keeps breaking down mid-execution.

India offers some of the slowest broadband speeds in the world, and at least a third of the population has no reliable electricity supply. It is all reminiscent of Marie Antoinette: 'if they do not have cash, let them use plastic!'

The government seems to be engaged in an exercise to furnish the penthouse of a building whose foundations it has not yet dug. As the *Harvard Business Review* noted, 'India's digital state (it ranked 42nd out of the 50 countries we studied in our Digital Evolution Index), does not engender the threshold of trust needed for cashlessness to take hold in a meaningful way.'[522]

---

[521]'175 million new bank a/c in India in three years: World Bank', *The Hindu*, 16 April 2015.
[522]Bhaskar Chakravorti, 'India's botched war on cash', *Harvard Business Review*,

Worse still, there is a transaction cost involved in each digital payment that is absent in any cash exchange—so using 'less cash' actually involves more expenditure for the payer. This obviously affects ordinary citizens who are used to cash, which involves no transaction costs for them. It is also expensive for merchants to adopt digital payments, which affects them adversely. Merchants highlight the high cost of even trying out these machines as a factor that is driving down interest in acceptance of digital payments.

The government is doing nothing to ensure point-of-sale machines are made available to traders, small retail outlets and small- and micro-enterprises, free of cost, as I suggested in Parliament, or to remove charges for all cashless transactions.

The financial implications of moving to a 'less cash' economy have raised related concerns. It has been said that the real beneficiaries of demonetization are the handful of companies that specialize in digital payments, especially by mobile phone. (The number of daily transactions through e-wallets surged up to 300 per cent after demonetization, from seventeen lakh on 8 November to sixty-three lakh a month later.[523]) In addition, digital transactions, by leaving a traceable record, add to the state's ability to monitor individuals' expenditures. As former Finance Minister P. Chidambaram asked, 'Why should a young adult be forced to disclose that she bought lingerie or shoes or he bought liquor or tobacco? Why should a couple be forced to leave a trail of a private holiday? Why should an elderly person leave a record that he bought adult diapers or medicines for his ailments? Why should the government or its numerous agencies have access to our lives through access to Big Data?'[524]

These are serious questions that call into account the government's insouciant announcement of objectives that were

14 December 2016.
[523]Pankaj Doval, 'Digital payments soar by up to 300% after demonetisation', *Times of India*, 10 December 2016.
[524]P. Chidambaram, 'Across the aisle | Cashless economy: A distracting mirage', *Indian Express*, 25 December 2016.

never presented to Parliament for approval until three months later, when the policy was irreversible and the damage had already been done.

Equally serious is the continuing concern about the legality of the government's action. The entire demonetization exercise had been conducted by the issuance of gazette notification no. 2652 by the joint secretary, finance, under Section 26(2) of the Reserve Bank of India Act of 1934.[525] This provision gives the union government the limited power to demonetize certain series of the country's currency through a notification. This provision does not, however, give the government the power to freeze bank accounts through limits on cash withdrawals, disrupt normal banking operations, and impose mandatory disclosure requirements (such as identity cards) while depositing cash into bank accounts or exchanging old notes.

The relevant provision of the aforementioned Act unambiguously states: '(1) Subject to the provisions of sub-section (2), every banknote shall be legal tender at any place in India in payment or on account for the amount expressed therein, and shall be guaranteed by the Central Government.'[526]

This means that the money every Indian holds in her hand or in the bank is a debt guaranteed by the government to her. Currency thus represents a 'public debt' owed by the government to the holders of banknotes. 'I promise to pay the bearer of this note...' vows the RBI governor on every Indian currency note. Every currency note is a contract between the bearer and the state, something that has been signed in good faith and ratified by the prevailing law of the land. The questions that then arise— and have still been left unanswered by the government and the courts—include: can this contract be repudiated unilaterally by the

[525]'Withdrawal of legal tender character of existing ₹500/- and ₹1000/- bank notes', RBI Instructions to Banks, Reserve Bank of India Circular dated 8 November 2016.
[526] Reserve Bank of India Act, 1934 (As modified up to February 28, 2009) <https://rbidocs.rbi.org.in/rdocs/Publications/PDFs/RBIAM_230609.pdf>.

state? On what legal grounds can the RBI write off notes that it
had promised to honour?

And while we are considering the issue of legality, why has
the RBI not placed in the public domain the minutes of the RBI
meeting of 8 November 2016 that was supposed to have requested
the prime minister to make the announcement he did? Is it for fear
that revealing the real nature of the meeting would only confirm
the Bank's surrender of its autonomy to the government? Only
eight out of twenty-one directors attended, and four of them were
officials. Only four independent directors were present.[527]

This entire decision-making process was a government exercise
trampling on the autonomy of the RBI, rather than a decision of
the institution meant to be in charge of India's monetary policy.

Among the longer-term effects of this monetary disruption
have been unemployment and severe dislocation of India's informal
economy; the collapse of many marginal businesses unable to
survive the ongoing loss of income; severe reductions in crop yields
and problems pertaining to agricultural credit; and the accelerated
flight of investment out of India.

Even more worrying is, as I have pointed out earlier in the
chapter, the prospect of a long-lasting decline in India's so-far
robust economic growth, and the danger that it will push more
Indians who were in the process of escaping poverty right back
into it.

The burden of demonetization has undoubtedly been regressive,
as it has most negatively affected the poor and the unbanked who
have had to lose their daily wages to stand in queues or have
lost their jobs because of non-functioning markets; and they are
the ones who are expected to transform their financial habits.
The truly cashless are the poorest Indians, who depend on cash
for their daily survival: as the *Harvard Business Review* puts it,
'this unfortunate crisis is a case study in poor policy and even

---

[527]Himanshu Mishra, 'RTI on demonetisation: RBI says it proposed note ban hours
before Modi's speech', *India Today*, 24 December 2016.

poorer execution. Unfortunately, it is also the poor that bear the greatest burden.'[528]

While many Modi fans are blaming the implementation rather than his intent, the fiasco was inherent in the design of the policy.

It is clearly a 'symbolic' policy—high ambiguity, high conflict, top-down, centralized and authoritarian. There was no 'policy skeleton' and, worst of all, no cost-benefit analysis, no evidence that alternative policy options were considered. It is clear no impact study was done, judging by the blizzard of new official notifications that appeared every day, tweaking and fixing the regulations.

The government has presided over a non-transparent policy environment that seems entirely unconducive to the creation of a cashless society. In his extravagantly emotional television address to the nation asking for fifty days to implement demonetization, Mr Modi had promised that 'if any fault is found... I am willing to suffer any punishment'. But all the faults I have enumerated above have been found, yet Mr Modi has escaped punishment. Instead, his party members have prevented Parliament's finance committee (in which the Bharatiya Janata Party enjoys a majority) from adopting and publishing a report on demonetization that reportedly criticized it as an 'ill-conceived' exercise that 'led to the lowering of the Gross Domestic Product (GDP) by at least 1 percentage point'.[529]

This debacle was a manufactured crisis. The government, for no public benefit anyone can understand, threw a spanner into the works of the Indian economy. It was indeed an ill-conceived scheme—ill-planned, poorly thought through, badly implemented and disastrously executed. Demonetization failed in its stated objectives. Deep-rooted problems, like corruption or terrorism, are not amenable to blunt, one-off policy instruments. Demonetization was the equivalent of an 'anti-stimulus' policy intervention, and

---

[528]Chakravorti, 'India's botched war on cash'.
[529]'BJP MPs stall adoption of contentious draft report on demonetisation', *Indian Express*, 26 August 2018.

the consequent drag on demand has been significant.

Narendra Modi came to power in 2014 promising to boost growth, create jobs for India's youthful population and encourage investment. These objectives lie in tatters with his ill-considered demonetization. He abolished the central government's Planning Commission to signal that the days of top-down statist control of the economy were over, but his demonetization decision brought back the worst days of government control. His reputation for being an efficient and competent manager was irremediably stained by the implementation disaster. How long it will take for India to fully recover is anyone's guess.

chapter thirty-six

GETTING A GRIP ON GST

In his 2017 Independence Day speech, the PM declared GST to
be a great success: 'The world is in awe,' he declared with his
customary grandiloquence, 'seeing how we implemented the new
tax system in such a short notice.'[530]

Flabbergasted might have been the more appropriate word.
Other countries had taken at least a year between the announcement
of a new tax system and its implementation; Mr Modi had not
even given Indians a month.

It is undoubtedly a relief that the farrago of some twenty-three
central and state sales taxes that had previously bedevilled Indian
businesses have nearly all been replaced by GST. But instead of the
promised 'One Nation, One Tax' the government has introduced
three GSTs (IGST, CGST and SGST) as well as seven slabs of
GST—'One Nation, Three GSTs, Multiple Tax Slabs'. India is the
only GST system in the whole world to have so many slabs. So,
instead of one nation, one tax, we have one nation, three taxes
and multiple slabs. The World Bank has dubbed it one of the
most complex indirect tax systems in the world, with the second
highest tax rate in the world among a sample of 115 countries
which use a similar indirect tax system.[531]

That is not a slogan that will trip so comfortably off the
tongue of our government propagandists. It also has created
massive confusion. When the GST came into force on 1 July
2017, many shops simply pulled down their shutters and did not
open for business: they did not know how to cope with the GST
that had been imposed upon them.

---

[530]'Key highlights of Prime Minister Narendra Modi's speech on India's 71st
Independence Day', *Economic Times*, 15 August 2017.
[531]Asit Ranjan Mishra, 'GST one of the most complex, has second highest tax
rate: World Bank report', *Hindustan Times*, 15 March 2018.

In fact this GST taxes different variations of the same product differently. Take the case of milk, for instance, something millions of Indians consume. There are actually four different rates for milk products. If we take flour, generic flour is not taxed, but if you put a brand on a packet of flour, it immediately attracts a tax of 5 per cent. Similarly, pastries, sweet biscuits and cakes are taxed at 6 per cent, but if they have a chocolate icing or coating, suddenly they go to 12 per cent. This is a recipe for chaos: for fudging, if one may be excused the pun, and irresponsibly complicated. And, on top of that, these tax slabs were only announced just as the tax was being rolled out, which left little or no time for a small trader to prepare himself for the changes that then became necessary in the accounting and filing of returns.

As a result, a simple business operating in only one state will now have to make 37 tax filings. If you have offices in three states, you have to file 111 tax forms.[532] What is going on in this country? The finance minister who told us that he was opposed to 'tax terrorism' has instead given us 'tax-form' terrorism.

The Congress party had asked for a flat rate, with an 18 per cent ceiling on GST, but the government, in its greed for revenue, adopted a maximum GST rate of 28 per cent.[533] This extortionate rate, instead of being imposed only on a few luxury items, applied to as much as 226 goods when GST was first rolled out, and will certainly promote tax evasion, corruption of tax officials and arbitrage between categories. (A year after its introduction, the government has rather sheepishly begun pruning the vast list of items that attracted 28 per cent tax)[534].

Businesses will also seek to have their goods assessed at the lowest possible tax rate, and if they don't get their way, the viability of their ventures might require them to go to court.

---

[532]'Bad news for small biz: GST forces you to file 37 tax returns instead of 13', *Business Standard,* 10 June 2017.
[533]'BJP government has imposed highest ever GST in world: Randeep Singh Surjewala', *Business Standard*, 1 July 2017.
[534]'Now, only 35 goods in highest tax bracket of GST', *Times of India*, 23 July 2018.

GST could generate thousands of lawsuits in an already backlogged system, with 3.3 crore pending cases choking the Indian judicial process.[535] Of these, 1.18 lakh already relate to indirect tax appeals, with a ₹3 lakh crore loss in tax revenue from direct and indirect tax cases stuck at litigation.[536]

But the problem with GST doesn't end with its complexity. It also requires firms to file about three online tax returns a month (up to 37 a year) into the GST Network (GSTN), a massive IT system, the backbone of GST, intended to process 3.5 billion invoices a month.[537]

About 1.03 crore taxable businesses have so far registered with GSTN, but the haste with which GST was rolled out raises legitimate concerns about whether the software for the new system is ready.[538] There was little time to test it. Reports showed that the system was not ready; it crashed repeatedly.[539]

Through the GST, the government has figured out how to get people to pay taxes they cannot afford, on services they do not need. 'The best things in life are free', goes the old saying, but I am sure the Modi government is working to fix that too.

There are other complications too. By extending GST to Jammu and Kashmir, the centre gained effective control of the taxation in the state. That was, of course, something reserved by the Constitution to the state government. A state like Jammu and Kashmir must be approached with sensitivity. There has not been much sensitivity in the Modi government's handling of Kashmir generally. J&K has been beset by terrorism and by violence. It has very many security issues. Its principal revenue generation

[535]'3.3 crore cases pending in Indian courts, pendency figure at its highest: CJI Dipak Misra', *Business Today*, 28 June 2018.
[536]'Pending cases: Over Rs three lakh crore tax amount stuck in litigation', *Indian Express*, 13 April 2018.
[537]Shruti Srivastava, 'GSTN to handle 3.5 billion transactions a month: Chairman Navin Kumar', *Livemint*, 27 April 2017.
[538]'Over 1.03 crore businesses registered under GST: Government', *Economic Times*, 9 March 2018.
[539]'GSTN glitches: Infosys asked to send more "technically qualified staff" to States', *Hindu BusinessLine*, 4 October 2017.

comes from tourism, which has been affected by terrorism; now GST will damage it further. The 28 per cent GST will affect all of the tourism in Jammu and Kashmir. The adventure camp operators and house boat owners have already protested. If this is not rolled back, it is likely to make Kashmir uncompetitive in tourism. An economy that loses a large chunk of its productivity to constant turmoil in Kashmir is now going to be burdened by the centre's over-enthusiastic experiments. And indeed, it is already making parts of India unviable. My state, Kerala, has become uncompetitive in tourism because the tax rate is driving up the cost beyond any of our neighbouring states and Sri Lanka.

GST has been moved by the government in extreme haste. When GST was introduced in Malaysia, the government gave the public and shopkeepers and others affected one year after the announcement to get used to the procedures before it came into force. India, a much larger country than Malaysia, did not get one year, we got only two weeks. (Despite all the preparation time, the Malaysian government abandoned GST in mid-2018).

Under the Modi government, GST is not applied to several items, notably petroleum products. The International Energy Agency estimates that India will account for 30 per cent of global energy demand growth by 2040 as booming manufacturing and a bigger, richer and more urbanized population will drive fuel growth.[540] It expects the country's oil demand to reach 10 million barrels a day in the next quarter of a century. The Parliamentary Standing Committee, considering this, pointed out that since crude oil and natural gas will be kept out of GST, upstream companies like ONGC and OIL cannot claim credit for their money spent towards VAT on services hired and goods used for the production of petroleum products.[541] Further, during the actual process of refining crude oil, it seems maddeningly inefficient that some of the manufactured products would be kept under the ambit

---

[540]'World Energy Outlook 2017', *International Energy Agency*, 14 November 2017.
[541]'Operational costs of petro products will rise under GST', *Hindu BusinessLine*, 20 March 2017.

of GST while some of them would not. There is a complete lack of consistency, which will result in distortions in pricing of petroleum products as well as an increase in the input cost of the oil companies. Industry experts have pointed out that this will inevitably have a negative effect on the oil, petroleum and petrochemical industries. The Modi government seems to expect the same industry to follow two tax regimes: the existing model as well as its successor, the GST. The present chaos would drive up the operational costs of manufacturing and there is likely to be a cascading effect across the supply chain, with either the customer or the manufacturer (or both) taking a hit. For the Modi government to trumpet the establishment of GST on the one hand while creating parallel taxation systems with the other points to how ill-considered their approach has been.

Mr Modi tried to sell GST to the nation as a 'Good and Simple Tax'.[542] If he had followed the UPA formula of a GST at one rate (around 15 per cent, up to a maximum 18 per cent), covering all goods and services including petroleum, alcohol and telecoms, and applicable in the same way everywhere in India, it would have been—and it would, as many industry associations suggested, have added 1 to 2 per cent to India's GDP right away. But the botched implementation of a good idea, so typical of the BJP government, has turned GST into a tax that is anything but good or simple. Instead, as Rahul Gandhi dubbed it, it is seen as a 'Gabbar Singh Tax'—a reference to the notorious dacoit in the blockbuster film *Sholay*.[543]

Many traders from across the country went on strike in protest over having to comply with GST, most out of fear that they would be badly affected. Most small business owners, as well as traders and shopkeepers, are not computer-enabled and have to scramble to acquire computer literacy and register online on

---

[542]'Modi calls GST Good and Simple Tax: 11 things prime minister said about India's landmark tax', *Economic Times*, 1 July 2017.
[543]Mahesh Langa, 'Note ban, GST ruined the nation, alleges Rahul', *The Hindu*, 23 October 2017.

GSTN. The self-employed informal sector, a major contributor to India's economy, already badly wounded by demonetization, was further affected.

The confusing tax rates, the excessive documentation, the inordinate number of tax returns a year and anxiety over the implementation of compliance requirements have prompted fears of a negative impact on livelihoods. And although there have been, from time to time, attempts to fix the GST, as I have said at the outset, this was an initiative that was badly planned, executed in extreme haste and extremely complicated to deal with, and has negatively affected a sizeable section of the business community. The Modi government's version of GST could turn out to be a second body blow to the economy, after the disastrous demonetization exercise. After its botched implementation, Mr Modi's reputation for managing the economy lies deservedly in shreds.

chapter thirty-seven

UNBALANCED BUDGETS

I

As soon as the Modi government's second Budget speech was over, mercifully in under two hours, the platitudes began to flow: 'a breakout budget', said the bhakts. 'A corporate-friendly budget', sneered the Left. I tweeted the latter charge, adding: 'corporate-friendly but little for the aam aadmi, and the poor completely forgotten.' One can point to the elimination of wealth tax and the phased reduction of corporate tax as evidence for the latter charge.

This is the sort of thing that happens every year. The Modi government issues an unremarkable Budget, bereft of vision or originality, and far from inspirational; it is hailed by its supporters (and the craven fawning spokesmen of industry) as if it were a revelation sent down from Mount Sinai; it is equally denounced by the Opposition and independent critics for its deficiencies and favouritism to special interests; the country adjusts to the new numbers, and life goes on. We have seen this BJP-produced movie five times already, and it never seems to improve in each retelling.

But this is well-ploughed ground: one must look beyond the obvious criticisms and see how each Budget will or will not change the lives of Indians for the better. Unlike the first year's underwhelming laundry-list, the second year's Budget did contain a vision for the future, albeit once again falling short of the 'big bold ideas' that Finance Minister Jaitley liked to insist upon when he was in Opposition. We had already been warned, in the government's Economic Survey, not to expect any of the big-ticket reforms the world had been hoping for: 'Big-Bang reforms as conventionally understood,' the Survey had argued defensively, 'are an unreasonable and infeasible standard for evaluating the government's reform actions.' Instead, it called for 'a persistent, encompassing, and creative incrementalism', which is more or less what we've got in the Narendra Modi-led central government.[544]

The finance minister's speeches are usually fine; as is too often the case with this government, words, rhetoric and sound bites are what they are good at. But in the face of a lack of adequate resources abetted by low tax collections, a dangerously high fiscal deficit and weak corporate spending, it's not enough. Implementation of the soaring vision of a growing, prosperous and just India is where the challenge lies. Here the auguries are less promising. Again and again, for instance, we hear a great deal about infrastructure and investment therein. But how exactly is more investment in infra going to transform India, at a time when incomplete projects costing around ₹18 lakh crore (about 13 per cent of GDP) have tied up public and private funds in stuck infra projects right now?[545] The only yardstick that matters is change on the ground, not good intentions in North Block.

Here, 'achhe din' haven't dawned yet. The decline in global oil prices was partially responsible for the slight improvement in the economic figures boasted about by the government for three years; once prices began to rise again, the Modi administration was clueless. Every year India spends almost 12 per cent of its GDP in importing commodities such as petroleum, gold, coal, vegetable oils, fertilizers and silver, which constitute 51 per cent of our country's total imports. A decrease in the global prices of these commodities has benefited our economy by improving our current account, controlling inflation and consequently increasing GDP growth. But when the prices go up, since nothing has changed in the underlying ground reality, the economy starts reeling. The government can hardly take credit for the earlier positive numbers when it shamelessly used lower oil prices as an opportunity to gouge the Indian consumer. It offset the declining oil prices by

---

[544]'Time for "Big Bang" reforms to accelerate growth: Economic Survey', *Economic Times*, 28 February 2015.
[545]'349 infrastructure projects show cost overrun of ₹2 lakh crore', *Economic Times*, 18 February 2018.

levying an additional excise duty of nearly ₹20 per litre at the pump, up from ₹2 under the UPA government[546], which directly hit the aam aadmi.

From a macro-economic perspective, there are some real worries about how the finance minister will achieve fiscal consolidation with his Budgets. Put bluntly, Mr Jaitley's tax numbers don't add up. The fiscal deficit keeps surpassing each year's Budget Estimate. The higher fiscal deficits are mainly because of the low revenue collections, which each year have in fact been much lower than the figures projected by the government in its overambitious maiden Budget for FY 2014–15. So where's the extra revenue going to come from? Mr Jaitley doesn't say. Meanwhile the current account deficit had risen to 2 per cent in the last quarter of 2017 and may well cross 2.5 per cent of GDP in Mr Modi's final fiscal year.[547]

And what happened to the Expenditure Reforms Commission he promised in his first Budget speech, in July? Where are the promised reforms? To get a measure of the gap between promise and achievement in the Modi era, one only has to contrast his finance minister's first Budget speech after his government was formed, with the stark reality of under-performance that followed it and the government's comprehensive failure to fulfil any of its own intentions.

The long-term debt of the government saw an increase of multiple billions each year, despite the government's continuous criticism of the long-term borrowings of the UPA. Where is the prudent financing that the government had claimed it would deliver?

To take a few examples of the 'successes' touted by the government in successive Budget speeches, Mr Jaitley regularly points to three 'major successes' of his government: the Pradhan

---

[546]The Modi government found the cess at ₹2 and gradually raised it to ₹20 per litre. The UPA's highest petrol cess was ₹3.90 per litre.
[547]Gayatri Nayak, 'Current account deficit widens to 2% of GDP on higher oil import bill', *Economic Times*, 17 March 2017 and 'India's current account deficit to widen to 2.5% of GDP in FY19: Moody's, experts', *Economic Times*, 19 August 2018.

Mantri Jan Dhan Yojana, the transparent auction of coal blocks, and the Swachh Bharat Abhiyan.[548] Let's take each in turn.

The success of the Pradhan Mantri Jan Dhan Yojana is questionable. While the government claims to have achieved a financial inclusion of 100 per cent, the urban poor remain excluded. Beggars, ragpickers, small vendors, slum dwellers and the homeless who live on the many streets of our large cities have been completely overlooked by the government in all its schemes, including the scheme for financial inclusion. More important, it's all very well to boast about 12.5 crore new bank accounts, but 24.13 per cent of the Jan Dhan bank accounts have reported zero balance. How does an empty bank account help change anyone's life? The money deposited in operational bank accounts isn't an encouraging figure either, the average deposit amount being ₹2,580 in April 2018.[549]

Coal auctions—imposed by the Supreme Court rather than a policy preference of the NDA—may have been a good idea, but their efficacy must be judged by whether the coal gets to the power stations that are currently starved of fuel sources, and by whether we can cut back on our imports of coal, which were always absurd in a country with the world's largest reserves of the black stuff.

And as for Swachh Bharat, as I've noted earlier, this is increasingly looking like a series of photo ops, with grandees picking up brooms for the camera and never touching them again until the next camera is scheduled to come by next year. Toilets are being constructed, but are they being used, and are they being cleaned? Is there water and electricity in them? Surveys suggested the real figures are dismal. From a Budget point of view, considering the importance of the campaign, it should be granted funds from core budgetary allocations to achieve reasonable targets. There

---

[548]'Full text of Arun Jaitley's Finance Budget 2015-16 speech', News18, 28 February 2015.
[549]'Banking for all: What lies beneath Jan Dhan Yojana's apparent success', Times of India, 24 April 2018.

aren't any, just vague talk of a possible Swachh Bharat Kosh or Clean India Treasury financed by levying a cess, much of whose expenditure seems to go to publicity campaigns. The government should focus on making hygiene and sanitation about human dignity and a community initiative rather than a tax liability. All credit to the PM for raising consciousness about this issue, but in the absence of credible central funding and community adoption of the scheme, it is bound to remain a laudable idea rather than a life-changer.

The finance minister regularly claps himself on the back over what he, echoing the Economic Survey, called the JAM Trinity—Jan Dhan, Aadhaar and Mobile—to implement benefits through direct transfer.[550] But this 'jam' was actually the UPA's 'bread and butter'—schemes devised by the UPA government and sneered at by the Opposition at the time. I'm sure it was too much to hope for Mr Jaitley to acknowledge this.

I don't see any reforms to improve the financial health of the banking sector, with an out-of-control Non-Performing Assets crisis which the government spends most of its energies blaming its predecessors for, even though the numbers have ballooned so much under Mr Modi that they are four times worse than at the end of the UPA government[551] and bank stocks across the country have been adversely affected. The government needs to resolve this issue of bad debts so as to free the worst affected borrowers, especially the power and infrastructure firms. But there has been no solution to this vital issue.

One major reform suggested in a Budget speech was the creation of a single market for agricultural goods, overruling individual states' agricultural produce marketing Acts. But given that the states have predictably resisted this encroachment on their

---

[550]'Jan Dhan, Aadhaar, mobile ushered in a social revolution: FM', *The Hindu*, 27 August 2017.
[551]'Govt banks' NPA write-offs double in three years', *Business Standard*, 22 December 2014; 'Banks' gross bad loans in December stood at ₹8.41 lakh cr', *Business Standard*, 9 March 2018.

prerogatives, how exactly does the Modi government hope to reconcile this reform with its much-vaunted spirit of 'cooperative federalism'?

The economy under Mr Modi has also witnessed a slackening labour market, with rural wages registering virtually no growth, after recording a high growth between 2008 and 2013, peaking at 38 per cent in 2014.[552] Agriculture and allied sectors have registered a decline in their growth rate. A fall in wages and employment opportunities will undoubtedly push rural youth into our limited urban spaces, where the NDA government can only offer them slogans about 'Make in India'. They need to 'make it' in India, but for that they need real jobs they can do. Where are these coming from? Slogans and sound bites don't make factories run.

Effective measures to help the poor, who constitute 29.5 per cent of the total population, have still not been introduced. Of India's total population, 30.9 per cent of the rural population and 26.4 per cent of the urban population is still living Below the Poverty Line (BPL).[553] The government has to still initiate schemes to fulfil its promise of creating slum free cities and little has been done to provide for pucca houses for the poor in rural areas, besides the UPA-created Indira Awas Yojana (IAY) which Mr Modi has renamed in order to convey the impression that his is a new scheme.[554] In fact overall allocations for housing and health have both been slashed since the UPA budgets.

Key areas have been neglected. Ambitious targets have been announced for new and renewable energy, especially vastly ambitious targets for solar power, but no concrete measures have been announced in the Budget to make them a reality: no tax-free bonds, specific allocations or tax incentives, for instance.

[552]G. Naga Sridhar, 'RBI paper points to sharp fall in rural wages since 2014', *Hindu BusinessLine*, 1 May 2018.
[553]C. Rangarajan Committee Report, 'Report of the expert group to review the methodology for measurement of poverty', Planning Commission, Government of India, June 2014, p. 10.
[554]Vipul Vivek, 'Modi has merely renamed 19 out of 23 Congress schemes', *The Quint*, 24 June 2017.

In Opposition, Mr Jaitley had long attacked the UPA's service taxes, joking that he couldn't use the 'sulabh shauchalaya' at Lodhi Garden on his morning walks because toilet use would be taxed since it's not on the negative list of service tax exemptions. Now, thanks to the hasty rollout of GST, the Modi government has in fact increased the number of items attracting Goods and Services Tax, and at much higher rates (see previous chapter), which will increase utility bills, food costs—and the cost of his urinal. He has flushed his own objections down the toilet. That's one thing he won't mind being accused of—taking Swachh Bharat too literally.

II

What does the aam aadmi look for in a Budget? At the personal level, he would obviously like more income, lower costs. At the broader level, he would like policies that will increase his job opportunities, reduce prices he has to pay for daily essentials and widen his life prospects.

What does the economist look for? At the macro level, he would look for policies that will create growth and jobs, improve exports, promote economic stability, tackle inflation and still help the government keep its fiscal deficit under control.

What does the politician look for? He looks for sops that he can sell to the voters. The government's five Budgets have had much to disappoint the aam aadmi, frustrate the economist and prove a mixed bag for the politician.

Any Budget must address five issues. One, fiscal consolidation, that is, the policy aimed at reducing the fiscal deficit. Two, job creation, usually through boosting manufacturing. Three, increasing savings in order to boost investments. Four, inflation control in our country; this is obvious. And five, improving investor sentiment, both domestic and foreign, so we can promote growth. Mr Modi's Budgets have fallen short on all these five criteria.

Yes, his are political Budgets. After a couple of years of gross pandering to corporate interests, the government at last discovered the virtues of attending to the needs of the agriculture sector and the rural poor. But this had much more to do with upcoming state elections than with a coherent economic vision. Real agricultural incomes have been stagnant since Mr Modi came to power in 2014. The 2016–17 Budget, for instance, fell between two stools, between sending reassuring signals to the rating agencies abroad and sending even more reassuring signals to the voters at home. In other words, it tried to satisfy both Modi's interests and Moody's interests. Nowhere was this contradiction more apparent than in the alarming unreality of some of the government's numbers, especially the fiscal deficit, when it was very clear from the Budget that there would be unplanned expenses and unrealized revenue. When Modi's government proclaimed a fiscal deficit target of 3.5 per cent, it actually clocked in at 4.1 per cent in fiscal year 2014–15 and 3.9 per cent in 2015–16; it was only in 2016–17 that 3.5 per cent was reached, by which time the target had come down to 3.3 per cent.[555]

The finance minister knew that he must fund expenditure for rural development, farmer welfare, housing for all, sanitation projects, grant of 'one rank one pension', recapitalization of stressed public sector banks. He also had to eventually accommodate expenditure of 0.7 per cent of GDP for the Seventh Pay Commission recommendations,[556] and a further investment of about 2 per cent of GDP to fund massive infrastructure projects. What about the additional expenses for implementing the National Food Security Act? I predicted in Parliament in 2015 that this exhaustive shopping list was certainly going to oblige the NDA government to breach Mr Jaitley's commitments of a fiscal deficit of 3.5 per cent. I take no great satisfaction in having been proved right within months. Then the government promised 3.3 per cent, with scant credibility; it finally reached that figure in 2017, though it had pledged to bring the fiscal deficit below 3 per cent by now.

---

[555]https://www.statista.com/statistics/802020/india-gross-fiscal-deficit-in-relation-to-gdp/
[556]'Here are the highlights of the 7th Pay Commission report', *Indian Express*, 22 July 2016.

More so, because the Modi government's tax collection targets have never been met. The revenue expenditure balance sheet is not encouraging. In addition, the disinvestment targets mentioned by the minister in his Budgets have been completely missed by the government every year, and what 'disinvestment' has happened has largely involved one public sector company buying up another—taxpayers' money essentially moving from one head to another. The government's desire to retain control even of its loss-making ventures was reflected most starkly in the attempted sale of Air India in 2018, which was so hedged about by conditions (including the government's wish to retain a 25 per cent stake) that not a single purchaser bid for the asset.[557] But the PM Modi Finance Ministry keeps financing itself by projecting ever-increasing tax revenue collections for successive years. These rely heavily on indirect taxation and on multiple hikes on excise duties (even as oil prices fell) which annually brings, of course, unpleasant news for every middle class and lower middle class tax-paying citizen.

Any economist will tell you that indirect taxes are essentially regressive. They hurt the poor more because the poor and the rich alike have to pay more for the same essential services. A rich man is buying petrol for his stretch limousine or a poor man is buying petrol for his scooter; they are paying the same price. So the government has been meeting its fiscal deficit targets on the backs of the aam aadmi instead of boosting the real incomes of the poor by cutting indirect taxes. So oil prices drop; excise duties go up. The aam aadmi in India gets no benefits while people in the rest of the world are saving at the petrol pump.

The Modi government is so tax-happy that its Finance Ministry undermines even the prime minister's policies. Thus the onus created by Mr Modi's Paris Commitments to encourage sustainable and eco-friendly consumption habits was defeated by Mr Jaitley levying 1 per cent infrastructure cess on small LPG and CNG cars.

---

[557]'Mihir Mishra, 'No taker for Air India stake sale as bids close without a single offer', *Economic Times*, 31 May 2018.

The Modi government rewards high ambition and aspiration with higher taxes. The tax exemption on profits for start-ups was a far cry from the much-needed rationalization of a tax on angel investors. In fact, let us face it, most start-ups do not, actually, book profits in the first few years of their operation. So, telling someone they do not have to pay tax on profits makes no difference because they do not have profits anywhere in the beginning. What you really need is to give angel investments, which are the bread and butter of these cash starved start-ups, a removal of the angel tax, which would, actually, strengthen the start-up ecosystem. (I suggested this in Parliament, but to no avail).

Corporates were hoping for tax cuts, but that never happened. Where is the proposed timetable for a roll out of the Direct Taxes Code? The UPA's last two finance ministers, Pranab Mukherjee and P. Chidambaram, had proposed a new direct tax code to replace the cumbersome Income Tax Act of 1961, but ran into obdurate resistance from the BJP and its chief ministers. Mr Modi loftily pledged to do better; he doesn't even seem to have tried.[558]

Meanwhile indirect taxes are gouging the common man. If a middle-class family of four in Delhi wants to go to a restaurant, they would have to expend some five litres of petrol on an average, given our distances and traffic, at over ₹80 per litre which would cost them ₹400 and which includes central and state taxes of over ₹200. Additional service charges and GST on their food bill, plus Swachh Bharat Cess of 0.5 per cent plus Krishi Kalyan Cess of 0.5 per cent, would ensure that this family's tax payments for their meal costs more than their dinner. The definition of success now in our country is when you spend more to support the government than you spend to support your family. For people living on fixed incomes and highly taxed salaries, that is an onerous burden, enough to discourage such outings. No wonder the economy isn't thriving, when the government has taxed middle-class people out

---

[558]'Road to reforms: Government sets up panel to rewrite direct tax law', *Times of India*, 23 November 2017.

of any incentive to spend.

Matters are worse if this family chooses to have an alcoholic beverage with their dinner, for then extortionate 'sin taxes' kick in. The government puts a high tax on liquor and then imposes such high taxes on everything else that they drive people to liquor. With due apologies, the middle class in India is reeling from a bad case of intaxication.

In a bid to achieve its ambitious GDP growth figures, the government has, therefore, burdened the aam admi. But, has the Modi government done enough to stimulate growth in the coming year and beyond? I am afraid not. On the contrary, it seems that the finance minister each year makes a conscious decision to tone down the previous years' growth aspirations. Given the sluggish environment of investment, there is an evident need for both enhancing public investment in social and physical infrastructure and also undertaking innovative measures to stimulate private investment. But private investment is largely not happening. In the last fiscal year, 2017–18, the announcement of new investments declined by 38.4 per cent and the completion of new projects declined by 26.8 per cent. Corporate sector profitability has been weak. The proportion of corporate debt that was owned by stressed companies has increased each year since Mr Modi's assumption of office. Talk to Indian businessmen, and it becomes clear that the Modi government's policies have discouraged any plans they may have had to invest in India. Many have done so abroad, and a startling number of well-heeled Indians have relocated to foreign countries and become NRIs—over 23,000 dollar millionaires have officially left India during Mr Modi's tenure alone.[559]

Growth, after all, depends on credit, and credit has been drying up in our country. The 'twin balance-sheet crisis' means that companies have unsustainable levels of debt, while banks, assailed by mounting non-performing assets (according to the RBI, banks'

---

[559]'23,000 dollar-millionaires have left India since 2014', *Economic Times*, 19 March 2018.

NPAs stand at a record 11.6 per cent of their total advances in
March 2018[560]), are reluctant to lend to them. The result is that
businesses can't borrow to grow themselves out of trouble. Growth
in bank credit to industry, which was steady under UPA, has never
crossed one digit in most months under the Modi government, and
by mid-2016 it was flat or negative. Demonetization exacerbated
the problem, with credit to industry declining by 5 per cent in
the first two months of 2017 and absolute annual declines every
month since then[561] Small and medium enterprises have been the
worst hit; small- and micro-enterprises were already battered by
demonetization, since many of them depend on cash flows that
dried up when rupee notes disappeared. And the finance minister
has failed to offer the nation a credible roadmap on how he intends
to recapitalize public sector banks when his allocations for the
purpose are a small fraction of the amounts needed.

The stark truth is that Gross Fixed Capital Formation (or
what is commonly known as the investment ratio) has steeply
declined from the 31.3 per cent it stood at in the last year of the
UPA government, 2013–14, to just 28.5 per cent today after four
years of stagnation.[562] Foreign Direct Investment (FDI), which the
Modi government loved to boast about, grew at 3 per cent in
2017–18, hitting a five year low.[563] Normally growth implies that
production, profits, wages, jobs and exports are all growing. That
is what we understand by growth. With the Modi government, we
have a peculiar situation where none of these elements is growing,
production is not growing, profits are not growing, wages are
not growing, jobs are not growing and exports are not growing.
And yet we are the fastest-growing major economy in the world!

So, how does the government still project a 7 per cent GDP
growth? The external debt of the country crossed the half a trillion

---

[560]'RBI sees gross NPAs at 12% by March', *Financial Express*, 27 June 2018.
[561]C. P. Chandrasekhar and Jayati Ghosh, 'Why we should worry about the fall
in bank credit', *Hindu BusinessLine*, 1 January 2018.
[562]P. Chidambaram, 'Across the Aisle: Debate, questions, but no answers', *Indian
Express*, 29 July 2018.
[563]'FDI growth hits 5-year low in 2017-18', *Economic Times*, 1 July 2018.

mark at $529 billion in March 2018, yet the finance minister carefully avoided mentioning external debt figures in his latest Budget presentation.[564] Growth slowed in all the key sectors— in manufacturing, in construction, in mining, in industries, in electricity and in agriculture. The index of industrial production was in the red, -1.3 per cent in December 2015. Though this picked up finally between November 2017 and February 2018, it faltered again in successive months, mainly thanks to a serious slowdown in manufacturing. The sale of consumer durables and capital goods was also in negative territory in fiscal year 2017.[565]

It has become increasingly clear that the official GDP data may well be accurate but it does not reflect the actual state of the Indian economy. What is worse is what lies ahead, which is that the battle is with the volatile global economy, declining exports, increased oil prices (up to almost $80 a barrel, more than double the anticipated $35 a barrel at which the Modi government's last Budget had been pitched), the risk of a poor monsoon and static domestic consumption.

On top of that it has been apparent that Modi's India is a laggard in relation to global figures: for instance, Indian exports went down for two successive years 2014–16, during a period when world trade actually went up by a modest 3 per cent. It is a long established principle in India that a one percentage point decrease in global economic growth normally translates into a 0.42 per cent decrease in our domestic growth; but in the Modi era we are seeing world trade and exports growing while India's slip into negative territory. The BJP government's 'Make in India' slogan sounds increasingly hollow since if we do not increase domestic consumption, we are not going to push up our growth rates because foreigners are not buying our goods.

The fact is that manufacturing is down. For manufacturing

---

[564]Gayatri Nayak, 'India's external debt rises by 12.4% on higher overseas borrowing and NRI deposits', *Economic Times*, 29 June 2018.
[565]Sahis Sharma, 'India's industrial output contracted by 0.1% in June', *LiveMint*, 12 August 2017.

to be internationally competitive, India requires policies that would reduce the cost of manufacturing, affordable interest rates, improved infrastructure, better trade facilitation, lower cost of power and, in other words, an entire ecosystem. Just having a slogan saying 'Make in India' will not do it. You need all of these—but in any case, the budget for 'Make in India' was cut by 35 per cent in 2017. (It was raised again the following year.)

In its last year, if anything, the Modi government appears to have abandoned much of its economic rhetoric and rediscovered the discredited virtues of a top-down command economy. More controls are being introduced, import substitution is being advocated, quantitative restrictions on imports being imposed, tariffs raised and non-tariff barriers erected. The government that once decried tax terrorism has dreamed up new retrospective taxes and unleashed an army of tax inspectors with greater punitive powers than ever upon the business community. Dirigisme has always been Mr Modi's preferred political style; it seems to have infected his economics as well. The days of the candidate who blithely declared 'the government has no business to be in business' are well and truly over.

The old joke is that only two things are inevitable—death and taxes. But death only comes once, whereas in our country, taxes keep coming and growing over and over again.

Having decried 'tax terrorism' under its predecessor, the Modi government has worsened the prospects of tax terror through its laws that permit administrative overreach. It has given customs and excise officials excessive authority to levy punitive actions against several people, individuals and even institutions like the Reserve Bank of India, the income tax and state GST bodies, state electricity boards and so on. Revenue officials will be exercising quasi-judicial functions as well, playing the role of the judge in disputes over their own decisions. An inspector raj will now be spread over other departments, causing the functioning of other departments to become coloured by the opinions and actions of revenue officials. A provision in the Finance Bill, 2017, allows excessive powers to IT officials for 'search and seizure'—this in a country where it is said that sharks wouldn't attack a tax inspector out of 'professional courtesy'.[566] Dealing with the Indian taxman these days is like dealing with a careless laundry—either way you lose your shirt.

At a time, when the government is trying to broaden the tax net, creating opportunities for the abuse of taxpayers is not wise policy. Allocating a disproportionate amount of punitive power with one branch of the government over the others is a recipe for strangling economic initiative.

Our taxes are already pretty onerous. Studying the ways in which they are implemented, and the powers given to tax inspectors to fulfil their demanding targets, really taxes the imagination— which was the one thing we thought the government could not tax. No doubt Mr Modi and his Finance Ministry will find a way to do that too.

Mr Modi's Budgets have confirmed the fears of many foreign observers that this government is not going to make any significant institutional reforms. What will be the effect of all this on the rupee? During the election campaign, Mr Modi was withering about the decline in the value of rupee, but it fell 18 per cent on his watch. It was 58.50 when he became the prime minister. He talked about it crossing the finance minister's age, but now it has overtaken his age. Having plummeted to the depths each successive month in 2018, the overall trend suggests that it will stay firmly on the wrong side of the 70 mark (as has been noted, it crossed 72 in September 2018) and join the BJP's margdarshak mandal.

III

A look at the Modi government's specific Budget priorities is also interesting and instructive. Initially, the allocations of Swachh Bharat were below the levels of the UPA sanitation budgets, but

---

[566]Shruthi Radhakrishnan, 'The taxman now has more powers thanks to the Finance Bill', *The Hindu*, 25 March 2017.

these have now gone up. About MGNREGA, the finance minister claimed the 2016–17 Budget was the highest ever allocation—it was not. It was still below the 2010–11 levels of the MGNREGA Budget of the UPA.[567] But, as a member of the previous government, I could not help feeling vindicated to see the government embracing UPA ideas that it had bitterly opposed, from strengthening the Aadhaar platform to MGNREGA itself, to welcoming 100 per cent FDI in food processing.

Many of Mr Jaitley's budgetary cuts over the years have been matters of grave concern. Food Security, Fertilizer Subsidies, Women and Child Development, Ministry of Minority Affairs have all been slashed, affecting the most vulnerable and marginalized sections of our society. Promised schemes like the one-stop crisis centres to deal with incidents of rape and sexual assault after the 'Nirbhaya' case have had to be scaled down to meaningless levels.[568] Where new ventures have been announced, funding has been grossly inadequate—for instance, the grand total of ₹500 crore allotted for five new IITs and IIMs, which seem doomed to being unworthy of their brand label unless considerable new resources are found.[569]

In the following paragraphs, I would like to repeat some facts and figures that have been placed on the record in Parliament in the government's own Budget documents.

The merger of the Ministry of External Affairs with the Ministry of Overseas Indian Affairs was seen as an opportunity to axe their combined budgets. As the Standing Committee on External Affairs repeatedly pointed out, the Ministry of External Affairs is already grossly underfunded. Budgetary cuts have further eroded its credibility: development assistance for the SAARC countries, for instance, had been cut in the 2016–17 budget. The

---

[567]Sangeeta Barooah Pisharoty, 'Activists reject Jaitley's claim of highest ever allocation for MNREGA', *The Wire*, 29 February 2016.
[568]R. K. Vij, 'One stop centres, which provide support services to survivors of gender violence, need to be revamped', *Hindustan Times*, 25 February 2018.
[569]'Union Budget 2014-15: Five more IIMs, IITs to come up', *Business Today*, 10 July 2014.

allocation for Nepal was reduced by 28.6 per cent, even though this is a country still recovering from a devastating earthquake, a terrible natural disaster, facing nation-wide shortages.[570] India makes commitments abroad at the highest levels and then finds the promised funds slashed by the finance ministry before they are disbursed.[571] After seeing the way in which every request of the MEA is hacked by North Block, I was moved to declare in Parliament that the biggest challenge for Indian foreign policy is not Pakistan—it is the finance ministry.

The same problem is at work when the Central Plan Outlay for the Ministry of Environment and Forests, including the National Afforestation Programme, saw savage budgetary cuts of 66 per cent in 2016–17, just after the minister had travelled to Paris and made extravagant commitments at the Climate Summit. Not only were no additional funds earmarked for the pledges made by India at COP-21; one cannot even find the faintest mention about the reserves needed to start fulfilling our requirements of $2.5 trillion announced by the Government of India for the Paris Commitments over the next fifteen years. Now, if we are going to spend $2.5 trillion over the next fifteen years, you had better start now, but the finance minister has not given even a one paisa for these commitments.

Let us face it. Making promises with no intention to fulfil them is not exactly unfamiliar territory for this government. In 2015, Mr Jaitley promised that six crore toilets would be built. The actual achievement, a year later, was barely 10 per cent, 62 lakh toilets and not all of those had water or electricity. The government should have completed the mammoth task of laying pipes or water supply for more than 60 per cent of rural households that do not have piped water. While ₹5,000 crore for 2016 was a bit of an increase from the previous year's allocation for water

[570]Suhasini Haidar, 'Sharp drop in aid to SAARC nations', *The Hindu*, 10 March 2016.
[571]'Promises that he can't deliver: Have Modi's 18 foreign trips brought in the desired results?', *FirstPost*, 22 March 2015.

supply, it was much less than the allocation of ₹10,500 crore by the UPA in 2013.[572]

Then, many of the government's promises are not new. Even though the government budgeted an increase in the central plan allocation for agriculture, including the newly named Pradhan Mantri Fasal Bima Yojana, it is still lower than the amount of ₹19,047 crore allotted by the UPA in its last fiscal year 2014 Budget. At that time, already the UPA had provided for weather-based crop insurance, agriculture insurance, the Rashtriya Krishi Vikas Yojana and National Horticulture Mission. Clearly, there is nothing for farmer welfare that was not already provided for earlier. In fact, the NDA reduced the UPA's allocations in 2015 and then increased them in 2016.

The finance minister also missed an opportunity to devote more resources, in a targeted way, to something that his colleagues have trumpeted repeatedly in the House—the need to instal broadband and increase Internet speed in both rural and urban areas. The National Optical Fibre Network is far behind its intended coverage of two and a half lakh gram panchayats. After four and a half years of rule, they have only reached 1 lakh gram panchayats.[573] The only progress has been in renaming the scheme as BharatNet. We have often said this is not a game changing government, it is a name changing government.

The Modi government's budget rhetoric also embraces the prime minister's vision for digitization. Digitization through public Wi-Fi, hot spots, e-books, online medical consultation, medicine supply, mobile banking, e-courts, e-police—Mr Modi mentioned all this in Parliament. But the reality is that rural India has just 13.7 Internet subscriptions per 100 people;[574] rural households often operate with barely any electricity, and using mobile phones that

[572]'Par panel expresses dismay over rural drinking water supply', *Times of India*, 2 May 2016.
[573]'One lakh gram panchayats become internet-service ready in Phase 1', *Economic Times*, 9 January 2018.
[574]Aarati Krishnan, 'How many Indians have Internet?', *The Hindu*, 26 March 2017.

do not have Internet connectivity. How can they access any of these services? The minister has been proudly talking about the so-called JAM trinity. I mean this may be JAM in the urban areas. But there is no butter or JAM in the rural areas because only 27 per cent of the villages in our country have a bank within a radius of five kilometres.[575] And, of course, all the online services the government wants to bring on stream require dramatic increases in bandwidth (rendered impossible by the miserly amounts of spectrum it is willing to relinquish to public use) and improved Internet speed, whereas India is struggling today with the connection speed of 8.80 mbps for mobile Internet speed, ranking 109 out of 122 countries, below Nepal and Pakistan.[576] How are we going to be able to deliver these services? Are Mr Modi's targets credible or is it an example of, with this very faith-based government, what one might call faith-based budgeting?

Some of the 2016–17 Budget's other omissions were also interesting. The government raised taxes on tobacco products—saying they cause cancer—but not beedis.[577] So, was it signalling that it is okay for the poor beedi smoker to die of cancer but the rich, middle-class and upper middle-class cigarette smoker must stay alive so that we can tax him?

According to World Development Indicators data, public spending on health and education is just 4.7 per cent of GDP in India compared with 7 per cent in Sub-Saharan Africa. People think Sub-Saharan Africa is the poorest part of the world, but they are spending 7 per cent on health and education whereas India is spending 4.7 per cent. East Asia is spending 7.2 per cent; Latin America is spending 8.5 per cent and the rich OECD countries are spending 13.3 per cent. So, it is not just a question of wealth or the amounts of money countries have. The figure

[575]Shaji Vikraman, 'Last mile banking', *Indian Express*, 20 September 2016.
[576]'India ranked 109 out of 122 countries in mobile internet speed; below Pakistan, Nepal', *Business Today*, 12 December 2017.
[577]'Centre's tobacco policy sclerotic? How else do you explain negligible taxes on bidis, chewing tobacco', *Financial Express*, 2 September 2017.

for all least developed countries is 6.4 per cent and India is only spending 4.7 per cent.

In regard to health, if you look at the fact that we need a colossal amount of money in order to achieve anything remotely like the declared objective of universal health coverage by 2030, the fact is that the public health system is in a pretty bad shape. The government has taken so long to deliberate on the National Health Policy, but the budget for the Transport Ministry is more than two and a half times the budget of the Health Ministry. Even customs duty exemptions on 76 life-saving drugs— cancer drugs, HIV drugs—were withdrawn by the 2016–17 Budget.[578]

When it comes to job creation—the grandest of Mr Modi's campaign promises, having pledged to create 2 crore jobs a year— some 31 million people have found themselves unemployed under the BJP, with the unemployment rate steadily growing, at 6.23 per cent in 2018.[579] The Centre for Monitoring of the Indian Economy has reported that the number of persons employed in the Indian economy went down to 406.2 million in 2017–18 from the 406.7 million employed in 2016–17; in other words, instead of creating jobs, Modi's India is shedding them. The labour force participation rate has been going down—42.7 per cent in 2018–19.[580] Another 50 million will enter the workforce in the term of Mr Modi. What work will his successive Budgets help them find? The female participation rate is even lower at 27 per cent.[581] But there are no targeted measures to help females work. The unorganized sector has been devastated by demonetization (Tamil Nadu alone reported 50,000 SMEs closed down as a result

---

[578]Vidya Krishnan, 'As customs duty exemption goes, 76 life-saving drugs to get costlier', *The Hindu*, 6 February 2016.

[579]Pragya Srivastava, 'Where are the jobs? Not in India; unemployment rate doubles, jobs decline', *Financial Express*, 24 April 2018.

[580]Mahesh Vyas, 'Employment stagnates in 2017-18', Centre for Monitoring of the Indian Economy, 17 July 2018.

[581]'India's female labour force is declining', *The Tribune*, 1 May 2018.

of demonetization, causing the loss of 500,000 jobs[582]), and the wage demands of the organized sector are not being met.

Mr Modi wrote an article in the *Economic Times* on the last Budget of the UPA in which he said: 'This Budget is a piecemeal exercise, and it appears that the UPA wants to play safe.'[583] He had repeatedly mocked the UPA for not thinking big. It is all the more disappointing that his Budgets have consistently failed to think big, tried to play it safe and approach the country's economic challenges piecemeal.

The joke going around about the 2016–17 Budget was that it was a good Budget only for the Aadhaar Card holding beedi smoker in need of dialysis who lost his degree certificate and planned to launch a loss-making start-up in a gram panchayat with MGNREGA funds. For everybody else, it was a huge disappointment. Something similar, alas, can be said about every one of Mr Modi's budgets.

---

[582]'Centre, Tamil Nadu blamed for 50,000 industries shutting down', *Indian Express*, 9 June 2018.
[583]'Budget 2013: UPA will always disappoint, says Narendra Modi, Chief Minister, Gujarat', *Economic Times*, 1 March 2013.

chapter thirty-eight

RAILROADING THE RAILWAYS

In 2017, the Modi government which, as I have pointed out repeatedly, is best known for empty gestures, came up with another one. For the first time since we attained Independence, the practice of the railway minister presenting the railway budget before the regular financial budget was stopped and the finance minister presented a combined fiscal budget, including the railway budget.

The curious practice of presenting the railway budget separately began in the days of the British raj, when the railway budget rivalled that of the rest of the Indian government. Of course, railway revenues today, at ₹48,642.68 crore in 2017–18, no longer dwarf the country's budget, which now stands at some $2.5 trillion.[584] But India's railways still produce other mind-boggling figures: 23 million passengers are transported daily (over eight billion per year, more than the world's entire population) on 12,617 trains connecting 7,172 stations across a 65,000-kilometre network. And, with 1.31 million employees, the railways are the country's biggest enterprise.[585]

In short, the railways are the lifeblood of India's economy, touching the lives of every segment of society and playing a key role in moving people, freight and dreams across a congested landscape. Yet much needs fixing.

India's trains carry four times the number of passengers as China's, despite covering only half as many kilometres, but still lose about 30,000 crore rupees annually.[586] The problem is that a

---

[584]Faizan Haidar, 'Railways posts highest revenue growth in three years', *Hindustan Times*, 28 April 2018 and Arun Jaitley, 'Budget 2018–2019', Government of India, 1 February 2018.
[585]In 2016–17, Indian Railways carried 8.1 billion passengers (source: Facts & Figures 2016–17, Ministry of Railways, Government of India).
[586]'Railways suffering losses in passenger sector every year', *Economic Times*, 29 March 2017.

succession of railway ministers, viewing the trains as poor people's only affordable means of transport, have refused to raise passenger fares, squeezing freight instead. This has proved popular with voters but disastrous for the country.

Though freight transport still accounts for 67 per cent of railway revenues, with 2.65 million tons carried every day, the higher fares needed to subsidize passengers have deterred shippers. As a result, the share of freight carried across India by rail has declined from 89 per cent in 1950–51 to 31 per cent today.[587]

Instead, an increasing volume of goods is shipped by road, choking India's narrow highways and spewing toxic pollutants into the country's increasingly unbreathable air. By contrast, China's railways carry five times as much freight as India's, even though China has a far better road network.[588]

Making matters worse, politicians have continued to add trains to please various constituencies—but without adding track. Indeed, owing to land constraints, India has laid only 11,004 kilometres of rail track since independence in 1947, adding to the 53,000 left behind by the British.[589] (China added nearly 80,000 kilometres to its rail network over the same period.) As a result, several lines are operating beyond their capacity, creating long delays. Exacerbating this inefficiency are slow train speeds, which rarely exceed 50 kilometres per hour (and 30 kilometres per hour for freight), partly owing to the need to stop at an ever-rising number of stations to appease political interests.

But perhaps the biggest problem is how dangerous the railways are. Aging rails, tired coaches, old-fashioned signals and level crossings dating back to the nineteenth century combine with human error to take dozens of lives every year.

Yet every railway minister had continued to insist on their

---

[587]'Railway Budget: why you need to know these 10 numbers', *NDTV*, 26 February 2016
[588]Vishnu Saraf, *India and China: Comparing the Incomparable*, New Delhi: Macmillan India, 2008, p. 112.
[589]'Indian rail network added 11,004 kilometres in 62 years, *NDTV*, 14 December 2012.

populist approach. With the government losing $4.5 billion every
year by subsidizing passenger fares, it has little money to spend on
upgrading infrastructure, improving safety standards, or speeding
up the trains.[590] According to the audit report by the CAG on the
performance of railways in 2015, the total planned expenditure of
the Indian Railways has increasingly exceeded its internal resources.
In the 2013–14 period, total plan expenditure was nearly ₹54,000
crore, while the internal resource generation was ₹9,700 crore
and budgetary support it received was around ₹29,000 crore.[591]
It is difficult to imagine how the railways will finance its ongoing
projects, much less invest in new ones.

It must be said to the Modi government's credit that it
recognized the problem and its second railway minister, Suresh
Prabhu, was candid about the need to eschew populism to focus
on renewal. (Ironically, he was himself the victim of his ministry's
failure to attend adequately to track safety, when one railway
accident too many forced his resignation in 2017.)[592] Mr Prabhu's
reformism seems to be in safe hands under his successor, Piyush
Goyal, though it is yet far from clear where the resources will
come from for all that needs to be done to place railways finances
on a sound footing.

And if all of this were not bad enough, India's leadership
seems not to recognize the challenges that the railways present.
In a country where rail passengers cannot even expect a clean
toilet, let alone an on-time arrival, Prime Minister Narendra
Modi has spoken of introducing bullet trains—the latest in a
string of irrationally grandiose aspirations. The bullet train
from Ahmedabad to Mumbai will cost an estimated ₹1.1 lakh
crore loaned by the Japanese government and will result in an

[590]Mahendra K. Singh, 'Now, government wants you to give up rail fare subsidy',
Times of India, 6 July 2017.
[591]Report of the Comptroller and Auditor General of India, 'Status of ongoing
projects in Indian railways', 2015.
[592]'Suresh Prabhu resigns; Piyush Goyal takes over as new Railways Minister',
Business Today, 3 September 2017.

economically unviable boondoggle,[593] whereas the 2018 budget for railways, focused on capacity creation, allocated just ₹1.48 lakh crore for the entire Indian Railways.[594] The contrast is glaring, made worse by the prime minister's rhetoric; his priorities are still bullet trains, installing CCTV cameras and Wi-Fi inside trains and announcing new world class trains, when the existing ones trundle along at an average of 35 kilometres an hour and have smelly or defective toilets.

Mr Prabhu had promised to raise $137 billion from market lenders, without clarifying how exactly they can be paid back, at rates of interest high enough to attract their investments in the first place.[595] The railways currently have an operating ratio of 98.5 per cent, barely 1 per cent of the amount needed to upgrade and modernize the network.[596] It is far from clear how the grand vision of a safer, cleaner and speedier Indian railway system will be achieved in practice. As one critic sardonically put it, this is a dream budget—because it's completely out of touch with reality.

But that has been the characteristic feature of the Modi government: high-pitched aspirations, soaring rhetoric, ambitious vision and quotable sound-bites, accompanied by few specifics, no implementation plan and no improvements in execution capacity. India's overburdened trains cannot run on hot air, but that seems to be what they are being offered for now.

---

[593]Arijit Barman, 'Sanjeev Sinha named adviser for ₹1.1 lakh crore bullet train project', *Economic Times*, 11 September 2017.
[594]'Rail budget 2018 highlights', *Financial Express*, 2 February 2018.
[595]Manoj Kumar, 'India aims to invest $137 billion in railways in next 5 years', *Reuters*, 26 February 2015.
[596]'Indian railways made its least ever profits in the last financial year, here's what it means', *News18*, 20 April 2018.

chapter thirty-nine

BOOSTING THE INDIAN ECONOMY

What should India do to improve its 'business quotient', and make itself a more desirable place for investors? For someone like myself, who believes the Modi government hasn't done enough to match the prime minister's promises, the answer is a complicated one.

Let's acknowledge the unusual features of the Indian economy. First, that policy choices are made in a democracy, and that too one with a majority of poor voters—every MP represents a constituency where a majority of his voters live on less than two dollars a day, and so the basic issues of survival and redistribution assume a high priority.

Most other democracies grew first and became democratic later. There was no real universal suffrage when most Western democracies were beginning to prosper during the Industrial Revolution. So Indian economic policy necessarily took the needs of the poor as a priority and sought to win their votes by offering them economic incentives. Redistributive policies have been high on the national economic agenda, because India has been a democracy since the start, and as an MP I know there is no escape from the political responsibility to pursue such policies.

Second, as a corollary of this, economic policy is driven largely by the interests of the poor, rather than taxpayers, since taxpayers are relatively few (less than 5 per cent of the voters) and non-taxpayers command more votes. The BJP's government's former Chief Economic Adviser, Arvind Subramanian, said taxpayers are only 4 per cent of voters.[597] In a democracy, the politician's accountability is inevitably more to the majority of the voters than to the minority of taxpayers. Of course, as the economy grows

---

[597]Puja Mehra, 'Only 5.5% who earn are tax payers: Economic Survey', *The Hindu*, 27 February 2016.

and the taxpayer base broadens, this will change, but that's for the long term.

Third, instead of developing through strong manufacturing, as most countries have done, and exporting goods, India's growth in recent decades has been led mainly by services exports. I don't think that's true of many other countries.

At the same time, India's economic development strategy has been affected by the fact that ours is a federal system.

Whereas the European Union is twenty-eight sovereign countries and one common market, we were—until the Goods and Services Tax was adopted in 2017—one sovereign country and twenty-nine markets, with differing state taxes and various limitations on inter-state commerce, including octroi and long lines of lorries lined up at check-posts at state frontiers. The UPA government tried to change this with a unifying GST, but ran into severe problems with the BJP governments in the states. When the Modi government finally did implement GST in July 2017, as I pointed out in Chapter 36, it made a thorough hash of it—among other things by multiple tax rates and exclusions it destroyed the single market vision that animated the GST idea.

Let us remember that since then-Finance Minister Manmohan Singh launched India on the path of liberalization in 1991, the country has visibly prospered, and despite population growth, per capita income grew 5.6 times.[598] In the last twenty-four years, India has pulled more people out of poverty than in the previous forty-four—averaging some 10 million people a year in the decade between 2006–16.

After the US and China, India is the world's third-largest economy, having overtaken Japan in PPP terms.[599] It is expected to perform the even more remarkable feat of becoming the world's third largest economy in real terms in slightly over a decade from

[598]Amit Mudgill, 'Since 1991, Budget size grew 19 times, economy 9 times; your income 5 times', *Economic Times*, 19 February 2018.
[599]Devika Banerji and Rishi Shah, 'India overtakes Japan to become third-largest economy in purchasing power parity', Economic Times, 19 April 2012.

now. India's meteoric rise has been fuelled by a remarkable shift in its economic fortunes. During a period when growth remained modest or sluggish across much of the industrialized world, India's gross domestic product (GDP) grew a remarkable 7.4 per cent in 2014.[600]

Even as the world has faced an unprecedented global economic crisis and recession, India continued to grow at a time when most countries in the world suffered negative growth rates in at least one quarter in the last four years. Many reasons have been attributed for this success. First, our banks and financial institutions were not tempted to buy the toxic mortgage-supported securities and engage in the fancy derivatives and credit-default swaps that ruined several Western financial institutions. Second, our merchandise exports increased by 20.2 per cent in May 2018 from 2017 and our services exports continued to do well.[601] Third, remittances from our overseas Indian community remained robust, reaching $55.75 billion in 2009–10 and nearly $69 billion in 2017, the bulk of which came from the hardworking blue-collar Indian expatriate community in the Gulf.[602] Fourth, most of our GDP does not come from the external sector but from Indians producing goods and services for other Indians in India.

Half of our growth has come from private consumption, less than 10 per cent from external demand; this compares with 65 per cent of China's real GDP growth coming from exports, and only 25 per cent from private consumption. India has the highest household savings rate in Asia, at 32 per cent of disposable income. In fact, 65 per cent of our national annual savings come from households (it's under 40 per cent in China). Indian banks have a fraction of the bad loans that China's banks suffer.

Around 4.75 million people are added to our workforce every

[600]'GDP growth (annual %)', World Bank <https://data.worldbank.org/indicator/NY.GDP.MKTP.KD.ZG?end=2017&name_desc=false&start=2014>.
[601]'India's merchandise exports jumps 20.2% in May 2018', *Business Standard*, 18 June 2018.
[602]'India highest recipient of remittances at $69 billion, says World Bank', *Economice Times*, 23 April 2018.

year, while China's has grown at a much lesser rate while growing older.[603] However, this demographic dividend will only work in our favour if we can educate and train our young people to seize the opportunities available to them in the twenty-first century—opportunities that entrepreneurs are creating. Our demographic dividend could become a demographic disaster if we continue to produce legions of uneducated (or undereducated) and unemployed (and largely unemployable), and therefore very frustrated young men and women.

Since we have a huge middle class, larger than every country bar the US and China, purchasing power is impressive. We have a big food grain surplus. Declining oil and commodity prices have favoured us. Inflation, which used to be very high a couple of years ago, had been contained, thanks largely to the collapse in fuel prices, but is now rising again as fuel prices rise. Our fiscal deficit has been going down. We have a manageable current account deficit. With China slowing and providing multiple barriers to entry, and Europe stagnating, there are very few places in the world that provide the opportunities that India does to investors. The country that looks best placed to provide the next engine for the world economy is India.

The Indian private sector is efficient and entrepreneurial and is compensating for the inadequacies of the state. India is good at the art of channeling domestic savings into productive investments, which is why it has relied so much less on foreign direct investment, and is even exporting FDI to OECD countries, as the sight of the British prime minister driving an Indian-owned car (the Jaguar) epitomizes. India's entrepreneurial capital and management skills are well able to control and manage assets in the sophisticated financial markets of the developed West.

It is possible for India to vastly step up its exports, be a hub of world-class education and take major strides in the manufacturing

---

[603]Sabina Dewan. 'Only 4.75 million join India's workforce annually, not 12 million as claimed', *IndiaSpend*, 21 May 2018.

sector. But for all this a combination of policies is needed, ranging from exchange rate management to micro-level stimuli.

The old joke runs that the Indian economy grows at night, when the government is asleep. But if we are to see the light of a new dawn, the government needs to wake up—and stay awake. The bad news is that it hasn't yet shown any signs of doing so.

Narendra Modi's election as prime minister in May 2014 was initially hailed worldwide as marking the advent of a more business-friendly government in the world's largest democracy. Encouraged by Mr Modi's pro-market sound bites, investors rushed to praise him as a new messiah of development.

Such talk continues, but it seems increasingly removed from the BJP's central preoccupations. In fact, as we have seen, Narendra Modi rose to power at the head of a family of right-wing organizations that largely do not share his economic priorities and that are obsessed with so-called 'cultural nationalism'—which is essentially just repackaged Hindu chauvinism.

The tension between Mr Modi's avowed economic reformism and the cultural nativism that animates his government's electoral base is a major impediment to progress. After all, the political majority that PM Modi needs to pursue his economic policies depends on the organizational capacity of the very people whose chauvinism is undermining him.

Investors are looking with mounting concern at Mr Modi's inability to manage this contradiction in his own support base. Foreigners are particularly concerned. As negative press increased abroad, potential investors have begun to feel skittish.

'What to think about the recent anti-Christian and Muslim tirades and conversion propositions?' said one foreign chief executive to me, on the verge of committing a major investment to India. 'Conversion and ethnic/religious cleansing doesn't ring well here in Germany particularly. The bizarre dream of a 100 per cent Hindu India would be an India with little or no foreign support. That is not what India deserves.' He added, in an email: 'I doubt the Middle Eastern investors would welcome an anti-

Muslim policy either. They could react by turning off the $-spigot. Europeans and Americans certainly would scale back considerably if Christians are exposed to an inquisition in reverse.'

Comments like these point to the dangerous economic implications of the Modi paradox. A domestic policy of Hindu–Muslim polarization might win the BJP votes and seats in Parliament but will grievously undermine the image he needs to project to attract foreign investment—without which the economic successes he needs to legitimize his rule will be impossible. What India ideally needs is communal harmony at home and enlightened economic policies that bring in goodwill and investment from abroad. With the Modi paradox, it increasingly seems you can have one or the other, but not both.

V

FLIGHTS OF FANCY

Narendra Modi has spent over a year of his four years as prime minister travelling around the world instead of attending to the problems the country faces. His tireless energy is admirable, measurable results few and far between. It would have been another matter if his extensive travels, the most by any Indian prime minister in history, had actually done the country much good. Not a chance. Our relationship with Pakistan is rocky, China is pushing us around, ties with the US are at a low ebb, Nepal mistrusts us and is moving towards China, the Maldives refuses new visas to Indians, and so on. The abandon with which Mr Modi hugs world leaders has clearly not borne much fruit. In this section I take a look at the various foreign policy failures of the prime minister and show how they could have been avoided.

chapter forty

MR MODI'S IMPROMPTU FOREIGN POLICY

As chairman of Parliament's External Affairs Committee, I have always proudly articulated our tradition that political differences stop at the water's edge—there isn't a Congress foreign policy or a BJP foreign policy, only Indian foreign policy. Yet I can't help feeling that there are aspects of the Modi government's foreign policy in the last four years that are not easy for many to swallow as India's, rather than his.

As the BJP celebrated its fourth anniversary of assuming office, it was safe to conclude that we have at its helm a prime minister whose foreign policy report card has largely been a tale of much activity and few results.

Like most Indians, I acknowledge the energy Narendra Modi has brought to his foreign travels—forty-one trips in four years to fifty-two countries, as of June 2018.[604] (Even if it means that his office still owes an outstanding amount of over ₹325 crore to the debt-ridden national carrier, Air India, as on 31 January 2018[605]). Mr Modi's desire to introduce himself to the world was entirely understandable after many years of international ostracism where the only country willing to grant him a visa seemed to be China. He can be forgiven for overcompensating somewhat: the website *Asia Times* calculated that Prime Minister Modi was out of his office every third day in his first four years in power, spending 477 out of 1,491 days—up till Tuesday, 26 June 2018—in his term as PM visiting other countries as well as various Indian states.[606] This

---

[604]'In 41 trips to 52 countries in 4 years, PM Narendra Modi spent ₹355 crore: RTI', *Indian Express*, 28 June 2018.
[605]'Govt owes Air India over ₹325 crore for VVIP chartered flights', *Times of India*, 11 March 2018.
[606]Vishakha Saxena and Aritry Das, 'Frequent flier Modi "goes missing on key issues at home"', *Asia Times*, 28 June 2018.

is equivalent to a year and three months out of his four years as prime minister. (PM Modi's favourite destination remains China, which he has visited six times, including twice in 2018, but the United States and Germany come close, with five trips each.)

While it is fair to depict the prime minister as an energetic salesman abroad for the Government of India, his travels came at the expense of domestic priorities, where—in an over-centralized government—key decisions and appointments were kept pending because of the prime minister's unavailability. And as India itself underperformed, the credibility of the star salesman himself increasingly came under question. After all, how long can a salesman impress by the sheer force of oratory and cleverly designed international spectacles if the package he is selling is empty?

Mr Modi has also proved unable to keep his domestic political interests out of his foreign policy. In countries with a substantial Indian population, including the US, UK and Australia but also the UAE, Philippines, Kenya, Singapore and Israel, he had special events arranged for him to address the resident Indian community, often in large stadiums like New York's Madison Square Garden. These events were designed to promote the greater glory of Narendra Modi and to denigrate India's achievements before he came to power; on more than one occasion he claimed Indians had been ashamed of their passports till his assumption of office.[607] This is scarcely a line calculated to enhance the country's image abroad, even if it served narrow political objectives back home (and reportedly enhanced the BJP's coffers through generous donations from attendees and other well-heeled expatriates).

Moreover, worryingly his visits inevitably sparked a justifiable fear among many observers that the headlines and speeches surrounding his visits were merely 'feel good' aspects that mask growing troubles elsewhere and the serious lack of a cohesive foreign policy blueprint for the country.

---

[607]'PM Modi says Indians were ashamed of their country before he assumed office; Twitter outrages', *News18*, 19 May 2015.

This is, of course, leaving aside the fact that the 'achhe din' that were promised to the people of India remain completely out of sight and the phrase has now silently been supplanted by the equally vapid 'New India', an anachronism if at all. Lofty foreign policy pronouncements have helped divert attention from domestic concerns and preserved the image of Mr Modi's India to a large extent, but even here a feeling of being let down has been mounting for some time. Even the most fervent sympathizers of the prime minister are now beginning to tire of the photo ops and the 'breaking news' stories of Mr Modi's tireless travels abroad, seemingly with little connection to the needs of the aam aadmi at home.

For a government driven by (and drawing political capital from) its lavishly funded publicity machine, this is becoming a problem. India, as I have said often, needs to strike a balance between its hard power and soft power: it is not the country with the bigger army that wins but that which tells the better story—at the moment, the story Mr Modi and his colleagues in government are pitching to the world looks less and less convincing with every passing month. If foreign policy were merely a question of making fine speeches, then the prime minister would score top marks. But substance must follow grandiloquent oratory and unfortunately for Mr Modi, he has very little substance to show for his efforts abroad, and only a shipload more of promises to add to the titanic stock already piled high at home.

Hindutva ideologues have tried to construct a distinctive "Modi doctrine" in foreign policy. A book of that name, published under the auspices of the RSS-affiliated Dr Syama Prasad Mookerjee Research Foundation, even lays out its five principal features: 'Samman—dignity and honour; Samvad—greater engagement and dialogue; Samriddhi—shared prosperity; Suraksha—regional and global security; and Sanskriti evam Sabhyata—cultural and civilizational linkages.'[608] But aside from the Sanskrit terms, it is

---

[608]Anirban Ganguly, in Anirban Ganguly, Vijay Chauthaiwale and U. K. Sinha, *The*

difficult to see how these five ideas differ from the policy principles of previous Indian governments. Mr Modi's foreign secretary for three years (2015–18), S. Jaishankar, the senior civil servant in the Ministry of External Affairs, famously suggested that India, earlier content with being a 'balancing power', was now seeking, under Narendra Modi, to be a 'leading power'.[609] But how precisely the Modi government has set about achieving this remains a mystery. A grandiloquent speech by RSS chief Mohan Bhagwat, head of the organization of which Mr Modi has been a lifetime pracharak, declaring that India was on its way to becoming a vishwa guru (teacher of the world), embarrassingly summed up both the pretensions and the embarrassment of India's global self-projection.[610] We have a government that believes its own press releases even when those they are directed at ignore them. The one concrete achievement of PM Modi's foreign policy appears to be that of getting the United Nations to adopt International Yoga Day, since it has meant people around the world following an Indian practice in a highly visible way that enhances our global image, with yoga events taking place at prominent locations around the world (though the manner in which the government subsequently pursued the Guinness Book of World Records over the issue was, to put it mildly, unseemly). That, alas, is the extent of the positive side of the ledger, where the PM's efforts have borne tangible results. For the rest, the report card is decidedly troubling.

India's foreign policy appears to many observers to be created impromptu, on the hoof, as it were, in the course of the prime minister's peripatetic travels. Key discussions which should have taken place in the preparation of these visits seem to follow the prime minister's pronouncements, rather than precede and justify them. The announcements, usually of investments to come, have

Modi Doctrine: New Paradigms in India's Foreign Policy, New Delhi: Wisdom Tree, 2016, p. 179.

[609]IIS Fullerton Lecture, Singapore, 20 July 2015, www.mea.gov.in.

[610]Manoj Anand, 'RSS strength not to domineer but to make India Vishwa Guru: Mohan Bhagwat', *Deccan Chronicle,* 21 January 2018.

largely failed to materialize. And stated goals, such as those accompanying the impressive India-African Summit in New Delhi or the bold promises of $100 billion in Chinese investments during Xi Jinping's visit in September 2014, do not seem to be accompanied by the investment of adequate resources to fulfil them or coordination with various government agencies to achieve their announced goals. The summit showcased this government's tendency to see such occasions as events to be well managed, rather than part of a strategy requiring meticulous implementation. And the $100 billion was eventually watered down to $20 billion, served with an embarrassing side of incursions by the PLA, audaciously while Xi was still on Indian soil.[611] Very little of that $20 billion has actually arrived.

Indeed, the External Affairs Ministry does not appear to be involved in much serious follow-up work to the PM's tours. Fundamental decisions are taken in the PMO, if not by the prime minister himself, along with his national security adviser. And while the external affairs minister is herself a respected and widely liked politician, her role in the formulation of foreign policy appears to be so tightly circumscribed that diplomats in Delhi have taken to referring to her, with a smile, as the minister for consular affairs. Her time seems to be spent largely on Twitter, replying to voters' complaints about her ministry's services, helping Indians who have lost their passports abroad and Pakistanis needing heart surgery in India—not to mention the totally pointless effort to splurge taxpayers' money to secure Hindi as an official language at the United Nations. Meanwhile, the ministry has had to swallow the embarrassment of seeing 'Yoga and Indian Culture Acharyas' (well-versed in Sanskrit, yoga and the Hindu scriptures) appointed with diplomatic status at Indian embassies to promote Hindu culture abroad, even as its core diplomatic staff languishes at levels comparable to New Zealand and Singapore, countries of

---

[611]Nayanima Basu, 'China dashes $100-bn hope, to invest $20 bn over 5 years', *Business Standard*, 19 September 2014.

considerably smaller population and modest global aspiration. The
gap between the aspirations Mr Modi loves to speak of and the
capacity of the Ministry of External Affairs to fulfil them has
never been more glaring.[612]

Where has Mr Modi's India been found wanting in the process?

The red ink on Prime Minister Modi's report card begins
with the neighbourhood, which is where any government must act
with the greatest caution and sensitivity to balance our national
interests with regional circumstances beyond our control.

Since Mr Modi's swearing in—a pageant of sorts that saw
the premiers of Pakistan, Nepal, Sri Lanka and Afghanistan in
attendance and which was lauded as the grand inauguration of
a new chapter in our international relations—India's ties with
Pakistan have witnessed more ups and downs than a child's yo-
yo. The prime minister—a man who systematically obstructed
the UPA government's peacemaking efforts with Pakistan and
whose campaign speeches thrived on demonizing that country—
had excoriated the Congress for 'serving chicken biryani' to a
Pakistani visitor.[613] Now he was exchanging shawls and saris with
his Islamabad counterpart, along with sentimental letters to each
other's mothers. (I mischievously tweeted my hope that chicken
biryani would be on PM Modi's dinner menu for his Pakistani
guest: it wasn't.)

By inviting Nawaz Sharif to Delhi when he took office in
2014, Mr Modi was believed to have turned a historic page and
opened a new era of bilateral relations. But less than two months
had passed before both countries were exchanging artillery fire
across the still-sensitive border. Talks between our respective
foreign secretaries were called off when the Pakistanis proposed
meeting Indian Kashmiri separatist leaders on their proposed visit—
something our visitors had always done and to which earlier

[612]Iain Marlow, 'India's Diplomat Shortage Leaves it far Behind China', *Economic Times*, 31 August 2018.
[613]Rajeev Sharma, 'Modi's swearing-in: Why Nawaz shouldn't expect chicken biryani', *FirstPost*, 26 May 2014.

governments had responded with confident official indifference.[614] In November of the same year, at the SAARC summit in Nepal, Mr Modi pointedly stared at a brochure to ignore his Pakistani counterpart as he walked past, though it was later revealed that the two leaders had met privately in a hotel suite belonging to an Indian businessman.[615] The pattern repeated itself in December 2015, when Mr Modi made an impromptu visit to Lahore to attend a celebration at Mr Sharif's home; a week later relations turned frosty again after seven Indians were killed by Pakistani militants at the Pathankot Air Force Base, later followed by an equally condemnable attack on the Indian army at Uri in September 2016 and at Nagrota the month after.[616] In retribution, the Indian army conducted a series of 'surgical strikes', lightning precision attacks, on terrorist camps operating out of Pakistani soil. While the nation rightfully applauded the swift response of our armed forces, the present government appeared to be more preoccupied with spinning the strike as the first of its kind—a testament to the supposed iron mind of their prime minister. This was blatantly untrue (it is now well known that similar strikes have been ordered in the past). Worse, the entire approach reflects the lack of a cohesive policy framework when it comes to negotiating the relationship with our most turbulent neighbour.

India–Pakistan relations have swung back and forth, as though they are determined more by the unpredictable moods of our leadership than on a coherent foreign policy and vision for peace, let alone a practical roadmap. One day the government declares its 'red lines' and twice calls off talks with Pakistan because its representatives met with the Kashmiri-separatist Hurriyat; the next day the red lines don't matter. One day the ruling party avers that talks and terror don't go together and that Pakistan cannot

---

[614]Suhasini Haidar, 'India-Pak. talks are off', *The Hindu*, 18 August 2014.
[615]'When Nawaz Sharif went for his speech, PM Modi read SAARC booklet', *NDTV*, 27 November 2014.
[616]Shivam Vij, 'Uri attack: Narendra Modi's aggressive stand on Pakistan might make India more vulnerable to terror', *Quartz*, 19 September 2016.

be rewarded with a visit till it makes progress on punishing the
perpetrators of 26/11; the next day the PM is winging impulsively
to Lahore, sending India's surprised high commissioner scurrying
to the airport to receive his boss.[617] This is foreign policy by
whim, not by design.

So too with Nepal—where New Delhi's de facto blockade
choked, which I explain in some detail in Chapter 46, the nation's
economy, cut off its oil supplies, created genuine hardship and
provoked a groundswell of hostility among ordinary Nepalis. This,
and the behaviour that accompanied the episode, was a blunder of
such Himalayan proportions that the only country on earth whose
relationship with us has been fraternal enough for us to maintain
open borders with it, now shows every sign of turning towards
China instead. Telling then, of the current strain in relations, is
the fact that once Prime Minister K. P. Sharma Oli was sworn
into office for the second time on February 15 this year, the first
leader to visit his country was his Pakistani counterpart Shahid
Khaqan Abbasi.[618]

One astute observer told me privately that 'PMO took its eyes
off the ball'. But when decision-making has been so centralized
in the Modi regime that every ministry has to send its important
files to the PMO for clearance, how many balls can Mr Modi
and his beleaguered minions keep their eyes on?

India's mess in Nepal adds to the growing sense of disquiet
amongst students of Indian foreign policy about the Modi
government's management of relations on the subcontinent. A
combination of arrogance and ineptitude is all too often visible
where subtlety and proactive diplomacy could have delivered the
desired results. A raid into Myanmar in hot pursuit of terrorist
sanctuaries had six precedents under the UPA, but each had
been shrouded in a discreet silence; the Modi government chose

[617]Suhasini Haidar and Kallol Bhattacharjee, 'PM goes to Lahore, makes a Christmas
date with history', *The Hindu*, 25 December 2015.
[618]Elizabeth Roche, 'Why India is keeping a close eye on Pakistan PM's visit to
Nepal', *Livemint*, 5 March 2018.

to announce their one raid with such bellicose rhetoric that it embarrassed Myanmar, the violation of whose sovereignty New Delhi was trumpeting.[619] Relations with our neighbours—Pakistan, Nepal and most recently, the Maldives—are worse than they have ever been. The Modi government's fecklessness has caused negative consequences for private Indian interests too. The Maldives has not only cancelled projects involving Indian companies, but started turning away Indian applications for employment visas, leading resorts to advertise posts open to any nationalities but 'Indians need not apply'.[620] Meanwhile China has been signing contracts previously offered to Indians, and Chinese and Pakistani warships have been calling on Maldivian ports.[621]

On the wider global stage, the list of failures is dizzyingly high. The US, for all of PM Modi's visits, has been playing fast and loose with the so-called '2+2' (where the foreign and defence ministers of both countries meet) dialogue with India being postponed twice and tensions over trade tariffs reaching an all-time high, with each country slapping tariffs on the other's products.[622] The US sent its Indian-origin ambassador to the UN, Nikki Haley, to instruct the Modi government to cut back its links with Iran, a principal supplier (and geographically the closest to India) of vitally-needed oil and gas.[623] At the same time the Modi government's unctuous currying of favour with the US has led to a precipitous decline in relations with Russia, with the much-touted joint fifth-generation aircraft project being abandoned.[624] European relations are adrift

---

[619]Sanjeev Miglani, 'India tries to assuage Myanmar after cross-border raid boasts', *Reuters*, 15 June 2015.

[620]Suhasini Haidar, 'Downturn in ties with Maldives hits Indians' job opportunities', *The Hindu*, 13 June 2018.

[621]'Maldives signs trade pact with China', *The Hindu*, 8 December 2017 and 'Pakistan Navy ships visit Maldives', *Daily Times*, 21 April 2017.

[622]Yashwant Raj, 'Why friction between India, US is rising when the two nations are trying to improve ties', *Hindustan Times*, 29 June 2018.

[623]'US Ambassador to UN Nikki Haley meets PM Modi, calls for cutting dependence on Iranian oil', *Indian Express*, 27 June 2018.

[624]Amrita Nair-Ghaswalla, 'Russia drops "decade-old" stealth fighter project with India', *Hindu BusinessLine*, 17 July 2018.

and Britain remains bemused by its dealing with our prime minister. Despite a few announcements of aid and trade made during Mr Modi's visit to Africa for the BRICS summit in July 2018, our engagement with the continent has proved to be a sorry tale of high-level neglect.

China's is a particularly disappointing story. Indeed the most glaring embarrassment in our recent foreign policy has been the way Modi's government has handled India's relationship with China, starting with the fiasco of President Xi's over-hyped visit in 2014 and culminating in the complete mismanagement of the military stand-off between the two countries in Doklam, which the government claimed had been resolved in a triumph for Indian diplomacy in August 2017. The PR exercise that Modi Inc. managed to spin from that event was undone a few months later when consistent reports and publicly available satellite imagery all pointed to the likelihood that the Chinese were consolidating their presence on the Himalayan plateau that directly overlooks India's strategic Siliguri corridor, and had been doing so for some time.[625]

But the inconsistency in this government's foreign policy style and narrative is not new. In the lead-up to and during his election campaign in 2014, Narendra Modi and the BJP had constantly berated the Government of India for being unable to do anything about frequent Chinese incursions across the disputed frontier. Two years later, the same Mr Modi not only embarked on a stream of effusive meetings with both the Chinese president (with whom he shared much publicized bonhomie on several occasions) and foreign minister, but also invited China to help modernize the Indian railways and has removed government restrictions on Chinese investment in sensitive sectors like ports and telecoms.[626] As to the border incursions, the BJP government echoed the very line it had denounced when the Congress government uttered it—

[625]Jonathan Marcus, 'China–India border tension: satellite imagery shows Doklam plateau build-up', *BBC*, 26 January 2018.
[626]Dipanjan Roy Chaudhury, 'Chinese companies plan big investment across sectors in India', *Economic Times*, 26 May 2016.

that since the two countries have differing perceptions of where the border lies, each patrols in areas the other considers to be theirs. What was excoriated by Mr Modi as pusillanimity and appeasement in the Congress have now, overnight, become wisdom and statesmanship in the BJP.

Meanwhile China has shown no inclination to make progress on the intractable border dispute between the two countries; it has extended overt protection to Pakistan after the Modi government's belligerent PR offensive on the 'strategic strikes'[627]; it has displaced India in the Maldives; thwarted an Indian deal to set up a naval base in the Seychelles[628]; and through the China–Pakistan Economic Corridor, a $62 billion project, it has outflanked India by creating a strategic transportation link between the Pakistani port of Gwadar (which China, to all intents and purposes, controls and runs) to its own western provinces, partly through territory that India claims.[629]

There have of course been some foreign policy successes, but these have almost entirely been in areas where Mr Modi and his party chose to follow the path already laid by successive previous governments without upsetting the delicate balance upon which these relationships rested. One of the prime minister's greatest achievements is that he has reversed the BJP's formal opposition in Parliament to the Indo–US Nuclear Deal and to the seminal land boundary agreement with Bangladesh—both of which were UPA initiatives and both of which were wise policy reversals by the NDA government of the positions the BJP had taken in opposition. In a continuation of UPA policy and as a reflection of the country's image as a responsible nuclear power, India was subsequently

---

[627]'After Modi's warning, China says international community should support Pakistan on counter-terrorism efforts', *Outlook*, 20 April 2018.

[628]Vinay Kaura, 'India's Seychelles naval base plan hits wall: New Delhi must commit greater economic, military resources to preserve its interests', *FirstPost*, 30 March 2018.

[629]'China-Pakistan sign new deals for Gwadar port's development: CPEC may turn out to be India's security and strategic problem', *FirstPost*, 31 January 2018.

admitted to three global missile-nuclear technology groupings.[630]

In the election campaign, Narendra Modi had breathed fire and brimstone about Bangladesh, accusing it of sending millions of illegal immigrants into India and promising that the moment he won the election, they would all have to 'pack their bags' and leave India for home.[631] Bangladeshi officials had publicly and privately expressed their disquiet that any attempt to do this could be deeply destabilizing for their politically fragile state. Within weeks of his victory, however, Mr Modi's foreign minister was all smiles on her first official visit abroad—to Bangladesh. Illegal immigration wasn't even mentioned in Dhaka.[632] However, the BJP government in Assam has unwisely reopened the issue of deportations, and disquiet is mounting in our friendly neighbour as the National Register of Citizens identifies individuals to be 'foreigners' who are potentially deportees. There is, however, no deportation agreement in place between India and Bangladesh.[633]

The Land Boundary Agreement with Bangladesh concluded by Prime Minister Manmohan Singh, which Indian diplomats had considered vital to removing bilateral irritants, had never been implemented because UPA couldn't win the BJP's support in Parliament to ratify the territorial swaps required. But now the Modi government is the biggest votary of the Land Boundary Agreement, which the Opposition cooperated fully in ratifying.[634]

The BJP had been virulently critical of the Indo–US nuclear deal, Manmohan Singh's signature foreign policy triumph. They had even supported a no-confidence motion against the UPA

[630]'India and the clubs that control war tech exports', *Indian Express*, 30 January 2018.
[631]'Mamata dares Modi on Bangladeshi migrants issue', *Indian Express*, 3 May 2014.
[632]'Sushma bid to build Dhaka bridge - No breakthrough on two pacts opposed by Mamata, say officials', *Telegraph India*, 27 June 2014.
[633]Annie Gowen, 'India's crackdown on illegal immigration could leave 4 million people stateless', *Washington Post*, 30 July 2018.
[634]Smriti Kak Ramachandran, 'RS passes Bill on land pact with Bangladesh', *The Hindu*, 6 May 2015.

government on the issue of the deal.[635] Yet, in a quiet and under-reported move, the Modi government wisely ratified the India-specific additional protocol, a UPA undertaking to grant greater access to India's civilian nuclear sites to the UN's International Atomic Energy Agency.[636]

I would also say this government's Africa policy has been a qualified success, although a lot more could have been done and the level of inattention is disappointing. Here again, though, what PM Modi is doing, more often than not, is building on the foundations laid by the UPA government.

I will explore some of India's specific foreign relationships under Narendra Modi in the chapters that follow. However, what is clear about Mr Modi's foreign policy is that his stance today, now that he is sitting in South Block, is different from what it was when he was in Gandhinagar.

The cerebral American politician, New York Governor Mario Cuomo, once memorably observed that you campaign in poetry, but govern in prose. Hard reality, he suggested, replaces the flights of policy fantasy that afflict those without power.

Welcome to the foreign policy world of Narendra Modi.

---

[635]'A look back at the 2008 floor test when UPA faced no-confidence', *Hindustan Times*, 22 July 2018.
[636]'Nuclear deal: India to ratify additional protocol to Indian specific safeguard agreement', *Indian Express*, 23 June 2014.

chapter forty-one

THE INDIA-PAKISTAN YO-YO

I

When Pakistan was created in 1947, its founder, Muhammad Ali Jinnah, publicly expressed the hope (and the expectation) that its relations with India would come to resemble those between Canada and the United States.[637] His idea was of two countries with more in common than not—separate politically but united culturally and linked by strong economic ties and close human relationships. As we all know, that was not to be. Today, over seventy years later, with a cricket hero the newly anointed prime minister of Pakistan, how should we look back at this relationship, and look forward to the uncertain future?

Pakistan was carved out of the stooped shoulders of India by the departing British in 1947 as a homeland for India's Muslims, but (at least until very recently, if one can extrapolate from the two countries' population growth trends) more Muslims have remained in India than live in Pakistan. Pakistan's relations with India have ever since been bedevilled by a festering dispute over the divided territory of Kashmir, India's only Muslim-majority state. Decades of open conflict and simmering hostility, punctuated by spasms of bonhomie that always seem to sputter out into recrimination, have characterized a relationship that has circumscribed India's options and affected its strategic choices. The knowledge that our nearest neighbour, populated as it is by a people of a broadly similar ethnic mix and cultural heritage, defines itself in opposition to India and exercises its diplomatic and military energies principally to thwart and undermine us, has inevitably coloured India's actions

---

[637]Somak Ghosal, 'Jinnah did not want India and Pakistan to be permanent enemies: Husain Haqqani', *Huffington Post*, 28 July 2016.

and calculations on the regional and global stage. The resort by Pakistan to the sponsorship of militancy and terrorism within India as an instrument of state policy since the 1980s has made relations nearly as bad as in the immediate aftermath of independence.

There is, in Indian eyes, a deep-seated pathology at work here. Former Pakistani ambassador Husain Haqqani has written of 'Pakistan's near pathological obsession with India' and the 'paranoia' of its elite, fuelled by the resentment of emigrés from India who developed 'a national narrative of grievance'.[638] These migrants, who did not hail from the territory of the country they were ruling, had to develop and sustain an ideological narrative about Pakistan, giving birth to a nationalism that was reductive: Pakistan's principal raison d'être became that it was not India and that it defined its interests in opposition to India's.

The 'two-nation theory' that Hindus and Muslims could not live together and the notion of a thousand years of conflict between the two peoples had to be created, justified and propagated, including through the 'prescribed myths' of tendentious history textbooks. As the Pakistani commentator Khaled Ahmed observed: 'Pakistani nationalism comprises 95 per cent India hatred. They call it Islam because that is how we learn to differentiate between ourselves and India.'[639] Islam became central to Pakistan's sense of itself: as the academic Waheed-uz-Zaman put it in 1973, 'If the Arabs, the Turks, the Iranians, God forbid, give up Islam, the Arabs yet remain Arabs, the Turks remain Turks, the Iranians remain Iranians, but what do we remain if we give up Islam?'[640] One Pakistani official answered the question to the New York Times in 1980: 'second-rate Indians'.[641]

If this visceral hatred of India is, to Pakistanis, the main casus

[638]Hussain Haqqani, India vs. Pakistan: Why Can't We Just Be Friends?, New Delhi: Juggernaut Books, 2016, pp. 7, 9 and 21.
[639]Ibid., p. 159.
[640]Quoted in Haqqani. Waheed-us-Zaman, The Quest for Identity, Islamabad: University of Islamabad Press, 1974, p. i.
[641]Quoted in Haqqani. Michael T. Kaufman, 'Pakistan's Islamic revival affects all aspects of life', New York Times, 13 October 1980.

belli, embellished by the 'just cause' of Kashmir, the horrors that
were inflicted on Mumbai by terrorists from Pakistan at the end
of November 2008 remain the starting point for any Indian's
discussion of Pakistan. They have left an abiding impact on all
Indians. India picked itself up after the assault, but it counted
the cost in lives lost, property destroyed and, most of all, in the
scarred psyche of a ravaged nation. Deep and sustained anger
across the country—at its demonstrated vulnerability to terror
and at the multiple institutional failures that allowed such loss of
life—prompted the immediate resignations of the home minister in
Delhi and the chief minister and his deputy in Maharashtra. But
'26/11' in Mumbai represented a qualitative change in Pakistan's
long-running attempts to pursue 'war by other means'. The assault,
and the possibility of its recurrence, implied that there could be
other consequences, yet to be measured, that the world will have
to come to terms with in the future—consequences whose impact
could extend well beyond India's borders, with implications for
the peace and security of the region, and the world.

After the killings, the platitudes flowed like blood. Terrorism
is unacceptable; the terrorists are cowards; the world stands united
in unreserved condemnation of this latest atrocity, and so mind-
numbingly on. Commentators in America tripped over themselves
to pronounce the night and day of carnage India's 9/11. But India
has endured many attempted 9/11s, notably a ferocious assault
on its Parliament in December 2001 that nearly led to all-out
war against the assailants' sponsors, Pakistan, and continuing
into a series of assaults on Indian installations in 2017. In 2008
alone, terrorist bombs had taken lives in Jaipur, in Ahmedabad,
in Delhi and (in an eerie dress rehearsal for the effectiveness
of synchronicity) several different places on one searing day in
Assam. Mumbai, however, combined all the four elements of its
precursors: by attacking it, the terrorists hit India's economy, its
tourism and its internationalism, and they took advantage of the
city's openness to the world. So the terrorists hit multiple targets
in Mumbai, both literally and figuratively. They caused death

and destruction to our country, searing India's psyche, showing up the limitations of its security apparatus and humiliating its government. They dented the worldwide image of India as an emerging economic giant, a success story of the era of globalization and an increasing magnet for investors and tourists. Instead, the world was made to see an insecure and vulnerable India, a 'soft state' besieged by enemies who could strike it at will.

This has been the fate of successive governments in India. Prime Minister Vajpayee's extraordinary overland visit to Lahore in 1999, his historic speech at the Minar-e-Pakistan repudiating his earlier hawkish views, and the signing of the Lahore Declaration were followed within months by the Pakistani incursion into Kargil. While to his credit Prime Minister Modi made attempts to reach out to his Pakistani counterpart Nawaz Sharif—particularly with the invitation to his inauguration in May 2014 and the subsequent impromptu trip to Pakistan on the occasion of Mr Sharif's birthday on Christmas Day 2016—this did not stop the Pakistani 'deep state' later sponsoring multiple attacks in Pathankot, Uri and Nagrota.

India responded in kind with what it called 'surgical strikes', lightning precision attacks on terrorist camps operating within Pakistani soil (something which, as I've said earlier in this book, India has resorted to in the past without boasting about it).[642] With the publicly-announced strikes, India has made clear that inaction is not the only possible response to terrorist provocations.

It is a brave and slightly risky strategy, because it obliges India to pursue a similar course of action when the next significant terrorist strike occurs. Still, a country that refuses to suffer repeated body blows earns more respect than one whose restraint can be interpreted as weakness. If this determination, and Pakistan's ensuing diplomatic isolation, prompts Pakistani generals to rethink their policy of sponsoring terrorism as an instrument of state policy, peace between the neighbours could once again become a

---

[642]Prateek Joshi, 'India-Pakistan relations: New Delhi signals strategic shift across LoC, but escalating costs won't deter Rawalpindi', *FirstPost*, 22 January 2018.

possibility. But, for India, as subsequent attacks have demonstrated, such hopes have been betrayed too often in the recent past for it to continue to turn the other cheek.

II

For India, the central problem blighting the relationship between the two subcontinental neighbours is not, as Pakistani propagandists like to suggest, Kashmir, but rather the nature of the Pakistani state itself—specifically, the stranglehold over Pakistan of one of the world's most lavishly funded militaries (in terms of percentage of national resources and GDP consumed).[643] To paraphrase Voltaire on Prussia, in India, the state has an army; in Pakistan, the army has a state. Unlike in India, one does not join the army in Pakistan merely to defend the country; one joins the army to run the country. The military has ruled Pakistan directly for a majority of the years of its existence, and indirectly for most of the rest. Until 2013, no previous elected civilian government had been allowed to complete its full term[644]; Zulfikar Ali Bhutto was an exception but he was arrested (and later hanged) immediately after he completed his initial tenure. The army lays down the 'red lines' no civilian leader—and not even the 'free' media—dare cross.

This situation goes back to the very founding of the country. At Partition, Pakistan received, thanks to the lopsided application of the 'martial races' theory by the British, a larger share of undivided India's military than of either its population or territory. With 21 per cent of India's population and 17 per cent of its revenue, Pakistan got 30 per cent of the Indian Army, 40 per cent of the Indian Navy and 20 per cent of the Indian Air Force, obliging its government to devote 75 per cent of the country's first budget to cover the costs of maintaining this outsize force. The disproportionately large military establishment had a vested

---

[643]Imtiaz Ahmed, 'Pakistan defence allocation at $9.6 billion, up by whopping 18%', *Hindustan Times*, 28 April 2018.
[644]Najibullah Azad and Aditya Manubarwala, 'The Murder Of Democracy in Pakistan', *Indian Express*, 25 July 2018.

interest in its own perpetuation; as Haqqani points out, it 'needed a threat if it was to be maintained'.[645] Sadly, instead of cutting back on its commitments to the military, Pakistan kept feeding the monster till it devoured the country itself. Even when Pakistan lost half its territory in the disastrous Bangladesh war of 1971, the army continued to expand.

In return, the military establishment enjoys privileges unthinkable in India. In addition, serving and retired military officials run army-controlled shopping malls, petrol stations, real estate ventures, import-export enterprises and even universities and think tanks.

For half the country's existence, the military has ruled Pakistan directly after a series of coups; the rest of the time it has stayed in the shadows, controlling the elected civilian governments and calling the shots on foreign and security policy (especially vis-à-vis India) that no government dares challenge. Even civilian leaders with a popular base, like Zulfikar Ali Bhutto, bribed the military with generous allocations in the vain hope that this would forestall a coup against them. No Pakistani leader has had the courage, or the foolhardiness, to confront the military's stranglehold on power. There is no reason to believe Imran Khan, heading a minority government, will be any different.

III

In the interests of full disclosure, I should mention that, like hundreds of Indians, I do know Imran Khan, the new prime minister of Pakistan. I first met him nearly three decades ago in New York, at the home of his sister Rubina, a UN colleague. I have since encountered him a few more times in India, and duelled with him on television. When I led an Indian parliamentary delegation to Islamabad in 2017, he sought a meeting with me. When told that security restrictions would not permit me to leave the hotel, Imran came over and spent an hour with me and my colleagues.

---

[645]Haqqani, p.15.

He wanted to talk mainly about my book *An Era of Darkness*, which he had read and could cite extensively.

The problem is that he has two faces—a liberal, cosmopolitan and urbane one, which is seen in London and Mumbai—and an uncompromisingly hawkish Islamist one, an image he reserves for his Pakistani audiences. This is the man who, after all, has had Hafiz Sayeed address his early rallies, consorted with extremist parties and movements like the Tehreek e-Labbaik Pakistan and the virulently anti-Shia Sipah-e-Sahaba Pakistan, opposed repealing the blasphemy law, supports the de-recognition of Ahmaddiyas as Muslims[646]—and called Nawaz Sharif a coward for not responding militarily to India's 2016 'surgical strikes'.[647] Imran Khan's loudly-expressed sympathy for the Taliban even earned him the nickname 'Taliban Khan'.

But after his victory, he reached out to India, decrying each country's habit of blaming the other for its misfortunes. 'If India takes one step, we will take two steps,' Imran Khan said to New Delhi.[648]

It is clear that the military, having encouraged and perhaps sponsored Imran Khan's rise, sees him as the most plausible and useful instrument for whichever policy they decide to adopt towards us—and the 'India policy' has always been the prerogative of the military, as every PM who was inclined to cross the military's red lines found out. This means that—if, as some recent statements of General Bajwa suggest, Pakistan feels the policy of hostility has stopped paying dividends and must be changed—Imran Khan will turn on the charm and lean towards India.[649] But if the army's general headquarters in Rawalpindi decides it prefers to turn the screws on India again, encouraging the Lashkar-e-Taiba to conduct

[646]'5 of Imran Khan's most controversial positions', *NDTV*, 30 July 2018.
[647]'Imran Khan targets Modi, says Pakistanis not cowardly like Sharif', *Hindustan Times*, 1 October 2016.
[648]'If India takes one step, we'll take two to resolve Kashmir issue: Imran Khan', *Deccan Chronicle*, 26 July 2018.
[649]'Pakistan Army chief backs India talks to resolve tangles, including Kashmir', *The Hindu*, 15 April 2018.

another 26/11, Imran will be the mediagenic face of a belligerent approach.

Indeed, there is no shortage of evidence for the proposition that Imran's views on foreign policy largely mirror the army's. Both oppose the US presence in Afghanistan, and have condemned US–Pakistan military operations and drone strikes in the area. Imran dismissed US President Donald Trump as 'ignorant and ungrateful' for his criticisms of Pakistan's double-dealing (accepting American aid against terror while financing terrorists itself).[650] And Imran has rarely parted from the military's position on India.

But this Pakistan election wasn't really about foreign policy. India was barely mentioned by the candidates, other than the ritual references to Kashmir. It was about the Pakistani public's widespread disillusionment with a corrupt and ineffective establishment in power for too long (all civilian governments since 1971 have featured either the Bhuttos or the Sharifs). Imran Khan built his victory on a promise of 'clean, transparent and accountable government', fealty to 'true' Islamic principles, overt religious devotion (epitomized in his marrying a spiritualist 'pirni'), and a fierce social conservatism that many find hypocritical, given his colourful personal life and the sensational personal revelations of his former wife, Reham Khan.

Millions of hopes are riding on Imran Khan today. The dust is yet to settle as these words are written, but the most significant aspect of Imran's win must lie in the excuse it provides for those who really control Pakistan to promote a change. When Nawaz Sharif sought to reach out to India, the army stopped him. If now the army wants peace with India, it knows that a change of prime minister will justify turning the page—New Delhi would always want to give a new government a chance. We will need to wait a while to see if the page can be turned, and whether Mr Modi will show the wisdom and statesmanship necessary to turn it.

---

[650]"Ignorant and ungrateful" Trump has humiliated Pakistan: Imran Khan, *Times of India*, 3 January 2018.

Whether this will or will not happen is hard to guess because, since Mr Modi took office in May 2014, India–Pakistan relations have experienced more ups and downs than a child's yo-yo. The victory of a Hindu chauvinist hardliner—a man who had systematically blocked his predecessor's peace-making efforts while in Opposition and demonized Pakistan in his campaign speeches— was naturally assumed to portend a bilateral chill. Instead, Mr Modi invited the then Pakistani Prime Minister Nawaz Sharif to his inauguration. Since then the relationship has veered wildly from one extreme to the other—moments of extreme cordiality succeeded by incidents of virulent acrimony.

Now that there is a chance of a new beginning, a well-considered and pragmatic approach should inform our way forward with Pakistan, not brinkmanship and posturing as have been seen from the Modi government.

The challenge is, of course, that the nature of the Pakistani state makes peace difficult. Since the only way to justify the military's disproportionate dominance of Pakistani state and society is to preserve the myth of an 'Indian threat', the Pakistani military will, many in India believe, continue to want to keep the pot boiling, even if Kashmir were to be handed over to them on a silver salver with a white ribbon tied around it. In the analysis of the Pakistani commentator Cyril Almeida, the army is not strategically interested in peace; it may not want war (which general relishes dying?) but it does not want peace either.

From an international perspective, support for Pakistan from other countries has also dealt the country a great deck of cards. American backing for Pakistan as a Cold War ally absolved the country of the obligation to deal constructively with India—a practice continued till recent times (and the jury is still out on whether things will comprehensively change under Trump). More worryingly, China's backing of Pakistan in multiple international forums, notably the Security Council and its Sanctions Committee, as well as its deep strategic economic commitment to Pakistan, has only strengthened as American commitment appears to be weakening. The China–Pakistan Economic Corridor (CPEC), which India justifiably argues undermines its sovereignty since it runs through territory in Pakistan-controlled Kashmir that China itself recognizes as disputed, has been a significant cause of worry for New Delhi.

Similarly, Pakistan's strategic choice of drawing closer to Arab West Asia accentuated the sense of inveterate Islamism within Pakistan and brought petrodollars and fundamentalist interpretations of Islam into its prevailing ethos. Pakistani clerics and worse, official (and officially directed) mass media, evolved and assiduously reiterated the theory of the Ghazwa-e-Hadith, under which the Prophet himself had predicted a 'final battle' in Hind before the End of Times. Jihadi groups were spawned, nurtured and indoctrinated with the belief that every one of their assaults on Indians were part of the Battle for India promised by Islam's Prophet. But as Dr Frankenstein discovered when his monster escaped his control, such doctrines can bite their own creators; some jihadi groups, notably the Pakistani Tehreek-e-Taliban, realized that 'Hind' in the Prophet's time included what is today Pakistan, and used the same Ghazwa-e-Hadith to justify terrorist attacks on 'godless' installations of Pakistan's military establishment in the name of Islam.

On the other side, Indians have learned to endure the unspeakable horrors of terrorist violence ever since malign men in Pakistan concluded that it was cheaper and more effective to bleed India to death than to attempt to defeat it in conventional war. There had, after all, been four unsuccessful wars—the failed attempts by Pakistan in 1947–48 and 1965 to wrest control over Kashmir, the 1971 war that resulted in the birth of Bangladesh from the ruins of the former East Pakistan and the undeclared Kargil war of 1999, in which Pakistani soldiers were dressed in mufti to conceal their identities when they surreptitiously seized the heights above Kargil in Kashmir until being repelled in a heroic but costly action by the Indian army. Attack after attack on Indian soil since then has been proven to have been financed, equipped and guided from across the border, including two suicide bombings of the Indian embassy in Kabul, the first of which was publicly traced by American intelligence to Islamabad's dreaded military special-ops agency, the Inter-Services Intelligence (ISI) and its 'Directorate S' that collaborates with and directs terrorists and militants.

India's response has been defensive, not belligerent. India is a status quo power that seeks nothing more than to be allowed to grow and develop in peace, free from the destructive attentions of the Pakistani military and the militants and terrorists it sponsors. Pakistan has sought to obscure this reality by seeking to convince the West and China that its militarism is in response to an 'Indian threat', a notion assiduously peddled in Washington and London by highly paid lobbyists for Islamabad. The rationale for this argument goes back to 1971, when India, in their version of the narrative, attacked and dismembered Pakistan. This action, it suggested, reveals India's intentions: it is simply waiting for the opportunity to do to what remains of Pakistan what it did to the country's old political geography.

Yet it is clear that we want peace more than Pakistan does, because we have more at stake when peace is violated. To those who suggest that we should simply ignore our dysfunctional neighbours, accept the occasional terrorist blast (and prevent the ones we can), tell ourselves there is nothing we need from Pakistan and try to get on with our development free of the incubus of that benighted land, there is only one answer: we cannot grow and prosper without peace, and that is the one thing Pakistan can give us that we cannot do without. We cannot choose to be uninterested in Pakistan, because Pakistan is dangerously interested in us. By denying us the peace we crave, Pakistan can undermine our vital national interests, above all that of our own development. Investors shun warzones; traders are wary of markets that might explode at any time; tourists do not travel to hotels that might be terrorist targets. We should be aware of this too, and we should ensure they are aware that we are aware. And yet we must engage

Pakistan because we cannot afford not to.

The differences that bedevil our relations with Pakistan can be surmounted if we can arrive at mutually acceptable parameters that can define our relationship in the future. Terrorism is certainly not one of those parameters. When Narendra Modi's surprise visit to Lahore seemed to augur a thaw, Pathankot, Uri, Nagrota were all great setbacks on the path of normalization. It will take concerted and credible action by Pakistan on two fronts to set things right: action to bring the conspirators and perpetrators of the 26/11 attack to justice and action to begin dismantling the infrastructure of terrorism, the platform from which so many attacks have been launched against our country in the last two decades. If these are done, India will respond. But only credible action by Islamabad will instil a modicum of confidence in the people of India that dialogue is worthwhile and that our neighbours are as determined as us to give peace a chance. If such action is taken—for instance, against individuals and organizations known to be fomenting violence against India—the basis for building trust again can be laid.

And yet, at the same time, it is important to recognize that the problem will not be solved overnight. Even if, by some miracle, the Pakistani civilian and military establishment suddenly saw the light, concluded that terrorism was bad for them and decided to make common cause with India in its eradication, the task will not be accomplished with a snap of the fingers. Extremism is not a tap that can be turned off once it is open; the evil genie cannot be forced back into the bottle. The proliferation of militant organizations, training camps and extremist ideologies has acquired a momentum of its own. A population as young, as uneducated, as unemployed and as radicalized as Pakistan's will remain a menace to their own society as well as to ours. As a former Indian high commissioner in Pakistan, Satyabrata Pal, noted: 'These jihadi groups recruit from the millions of young Pakistanis who emerge from vernacular schools and madrassas, imbued with a hatred for the modern world, in which they do

not have the skills to work. So while young Indians go to Silicon
Valley and make a bomb for themselves, young Pakistanis go to
the Swat Valley and make a bomb of themselves, the meanness
of their lives justifying the end. Pakistan has betrayed its youth,
which is its tragedy.'

This is not a counsel of despair. It is, instead, an argument
to offer a helping hand. A neighbour full of desperate young men
without hope or prospects, led by a malicious and self-aggrandizing
military, is a permanent threat to twenty-first century India. If India
can help Pakistan transcend these circumstances and help it develop
a stake in mutually beneficial progress, it will be helping itself
as well. In such an approach lies the slender hope of persuading
Pakistan that India's success can benefit it too, that, rather than
trying to undercut India and thwart its growth, Pakistan should
look to the advantages that might accrue to it as a neighbour and
partner of an upwardly mobile and increasingly prosperous India.

IV

A former Indian high commissioner to Pakistan, G. Parthasarathy,
once famously remarked that promoting peace between India and
Pakistan is like trying to treat two patients whose only disease is
an allergy to each other.[651] This allergy has to be overcome. India
does not covet any Pakistani territory. Because we wish to focus
on our own people's development and prosperity in conditions of
security, we remain committed to long-term peace with Pakistan.
If the civilian government in Islamabad sees that the need is for
concerted action against terrorists wherever they operate, whether
in Pakistan, in India or in Afghanistan, we can find common
ground. Our willingness to talk will best be vindicated by their
willingness to act.

Trust can be earned, which is why peace must be pursued.
But we must pursue peace with our eyes wide open.

---

[651]Quoted in Stephen B. Cohen. *India: Emerging Power*, Washington DC: The
Brookings Institution, 2001.

To do so is, in the words of the veteran Indian diplomat K. Shankar Bajpai, the 'right, rational choice for a mature power'.[652] One of the problems in the India–Pakistan relationship is that it is the last one left with sharply opposed binaries. The two sets of ideas in India for dealing with Pakistan involve a choice between those advocating a military attack on the sources of terrorism, and 'peace at any price'. Our leaders are either exchanging sentimental letters about their mothers or ignoring each other in a stagnant silence. Too much of Indian public opinion is divided into sharply polarized camps of hawks and doves—the former insisting on nothing less than implacable hostility towards Islamabad, the latter advocating talks with whoever is in office in Islamabad, through a process 'uninterruptable' even if new terrorist strikes emanating from Pakistan were to occur.

Neither position, in my view, is tenable. Hostility is not a policy, and hostility in perpetuity is neither viable nor desirable between neighbours. And while the doves may be right that New Delhi's visceral reaction to the terror attacks is tantamount to giving the terrorists a veto over our foreign policy choices, no democratic government can allow its citizens to be killed and maimed by forces from across the border, without reacting in some tangible way that conveys to Pakistan that there is a price to be paid for allowing such things to happen. We have no choice but to punish each incident of violence by freezing official talks: let the Pakistanis understand that if they want to talk to us officially, they have to take credible steps to rein in Lashkar-e-Taiba and Hafiz Sayeed, and they have to punish the 26/11 killers whose trial has so far been a travesty.

At the same time, insisting that Pakistan must change fundamentally before India can make peace with it is not particularly realistic. A creative Indian government must seize on whatever straws in the wind float its way from Pakistan to explore

---

[652]Quoted in David M. Malone, *Does the Elephant Dance?: Contemporary Indian Foreign Policy*, New York: Oxford University Press, 2011, p. 112.

the prospects of peace. Foreign policy cannot be built on a sense of betrayal any more than it can be on illusions of love. Pragmatism dictates that we work for peace with Pakistan precisely so that we can serve our own people's needs better. So New Delhi must do its best to ensure that the Islamabad establishment abandons the conviction that terrorism is the only effective instrument that obliges India to sit up and pay attention to Pakistan and engage with its interests.

But we must do this without illusions, without deceiving ourselves about the existence of genuine partners for peace across the border and without being taken in by the insincere press releases of the civilian rulers who are occasionally allowed to don the masks of power in Pakistan. Imran Khan has friends and admirers in India, but his charm and charisma cannot change this reality. We must not be deluded into making concessions, whether on Kashmir or any other issue, in the naive expectation that these would end the hostility of the ISI and its extremist cohorts. As Haqqani says, Kashmir is not a cause of the conflict between the two states, but rather a symptom of it.[653] We have to look beyond Kashmir.

V

What, then, is the way forward for our two countries? Jawaharlal Nehru, India's first prime minister, had predicted of the two countries that 'we can either become more than friends or more than enemies'[654]. The latter seems to have happened. From the Indian perspective, the elephant in the room remains the Pakistani army. Until the military men are convinced that peace with India is in their self-interest, they will remain the biggest obstacles to it. One hope may lie in the extensive reach of the Pakistani military apparatus and its multiple business and commercial interests. Perhaps India could encourage its firms to trade with enterprises

[653] Haqqani, *India vs. Pakistan*, p. 46.
[654] Jawaharlal Nehru, *Jawaharlal Nehru's Speeches*, Vol. 2, New Delhi: Publications Division, Ministry of Information and Broadcasting, Govt. of India, 1983, p. 447.

owned by the Pakistani army, in the hope of giving the military establishment a direct stake in peace. More military-to-military exchanges, even starting with such basic ideas as sporting contests between the two armies, might also help. Of course, advancing such ideas in India would inevitably be seen as naiveté bordering on blasphemy, since the military complex in Pakistan has shown no sign of changing its policy of attempting to 'bleed India to death by a thousand cuts', to quote a phrase from a Pakistani strategic document that has now passed into folklore. Indeed, Indians accept that the very nature of the Pakistani state condemns us to facing an implacable enemy in the self-perpetuating military elite next door, for lasting peace would leave them without a raison d'etre for their power and their privileges.

But in keeping with the hypothetical, though the idea of joint exercises between the two militaries seems preposterous today, it may entirely be feasible in a UN peacekeeping context: to take one example, several years ago Indian aircraft strafed Congolese rebel positions in support of besieged Pakistani ground troops as part of a UN peacekeeping operation, MONUC. In my UN days I personally witnessed the extraordinary degree of comradeship between Indian and Pakistani officers serving in the UN Peacekeeping Department headquarters in New York; perhaps being among foreigners served as a constant reminder of how much more they had in common with each other, so that they were frequently lunching together, visiting each other's homes and seeing the local sights together. Such contacts can and should be built upon to develop the right atmospherics for peaceful relations, which unavoidably require engagement with the Pakistani military. Indians are, understandably, among the strongest supporters of Pakistani democracy, at least in theory, but we have to live with the realities next door, and that requires us to see the Pakistani military not just as the problem, but as a vital element of the solution.

An India striving for peace can build on the generosity it has often shown—as witness the unilateral Most Favoured Nation

(MFN) status it gave Pakistan—by extending itself to its neighbour, offering a market for Pakistani traders and industrialists, a creative umbrella to its artists and singers and a home away from home for those seeking a refuge from the realities of Pakistani life.[655] Many Pakistanis now realize that perpetual conflict with India is hampering Pakistan's own aspirations for economic growth and development. Multiplying our channels of contact—with 'backchannel diplomacy' conducted by 'special envoys' of the two leaderships (a formula used effectively by Pervez Musharraf and Manmohan Singh), direct contact between the two militaries (of which there is very little) and extensive people-to-people contact— is indispensable to the peace effort.

Non-governmental organizations and civil society—particularly those that channel the energy of young people, who are impatient with decades of hostility— can also play a useful role in developing relations that go beyond the prescriptions and the proscriptions of governments. Trade is another obvious area. Tell Pakistani businessmen that if they can get their government to reciprocate India's two-decade–old practice of MFN status in trade relations, it will result in India taking concrete steps to reduce the non-tariff barriers relating to security inspections and clearances that have limited the extent of Pakistani exports to our country. India's financial services industry and its software professionals could also offer themselves to Pakistani clients, giving themselves a next-door market and providing services that Pakistan could use to develop its own economy. These are all 'easy wins' waiting to be pursued at the first opportunity.

Sadly India has reacted to 26/11 and other Pakistani provocations by punishing the wrong people—tightening visa restrictions and restraining other possibilities of cultural and social contact. The terrorists of 26/11 did not apply for Indian visas before coming onshore with their deadly baggage. Those

[655]Kanishka Gupta, 'Most Favoured Nation status to Pakistan: What is it all about?', *Indian Express*, 27 September 2016.

who apply are genuinely people of goodwill towards, and interest in, India. The advantages of openly issuing visas and enhancing opportunities for Pakistanis in India outweigh the dangers; after all, almost every Pakistani visitor here is entranced by the land that Partition has denied to them. This may be an area in which risks are worth taking, since the advantages of openly issuing visas and enhancing opportunities for Pakistanis in India outweigh the dangers; after all, anyone who is willing to give his fingerprints and biometrics to the visa section of the Indian high commission in Islamabad is hardly likely to be a security risk.

VI

I am strongly in favour of a liberal visa regime, which would require India to remove its current restrictions on which points of entry and exit the Pakistani visa-holder can use, the number of places that may be visited and the onerous police reporting requirements. To begin with, a list can be drawn up of prominent Pakistanis in such fields as business, entertainment and media, who would be eligible for more rapid processing and for multiple-entry visas. It will be argued that Pakistan will not reciprocate such one-sided generosity, but India should not care. Insisting on parity with Pakistan is to bring ourselves down to their level. Let us show a magnanimity and generosity of spirit that in itself stands an outside chance of persuading Pakistanis to rethink their attitude to us.

After all, though it seems scarcely believable today, passports and visas only became required for travel between the two countries as late as 1965. Initially, despite Partition, national identities remained fluid: Pakistan's first nominee as high commissioner to India, Mohammad Ismail, wished to remain an Indian citizen (to protect his properties in UP) while being accredited to New Delhi as an envoy![656] Though those days are long gone, reaching out to Pakistanis is the right thing to do. We've tried everything else.

---

[656]Omair Ahmad, 'The Gorakhpuri', *Hindu BusinessLine*, 28 November 2014.

The big questions—the Kashmir dispute and Pakistan's use of terrorism as an instrument of policy—will require a great deal more groundwork and constructive, step-by-step action for progress to be made. Afghanistan is an area of contention that, given a new climate of peace, could become an area for cooperation rather than a site of proxy conflict. By showing accommodativeness, sensitivity, foresight and pragmatic generosity in all the ways suggested above, India might be able to turn the bilateral narrative away from the logic of intractable hostility in which both countries have been mired for too long.

From such a diagnosis, the only possible prescription is that of cooperation, to build peace and security together. We hope that those who rule Pakistan will also make that diagnosis and share the same prescription. To reiterate the point made earlier in this chapter, accepting Pakistan the way it is but pushing for peace nonetheless is, in my view, the only way forward. It will mean isolating those elements and those issues that both sides consider intractable and placing them on the back burner for now, in order to proceed with those that can be solved. Trust and understanding can be built on the basis of small agreements on seemingly marginal issues, thereby improving the atmosphere within which the more difficult problems can be tackled.

Ultimately, the fundamental principle of relations between two foreign and sovereign nations, even one sharing a history as tumultuous as ours, is reciprocity. Dealing with homegrown terrorism, reforming the nature of the military complex, providing actual negotiating power to the civilian government of the day, accepting in letter and spirit the 1972 Simla Agreement and the 1999 Lahore Declaration, the provision of MFN status in return to India, are all important steps that must be taken by Pakistan before one can contemplate getting the two countries back to the drawing board in the hope of chalking out a lasting peace in our lifetime. It is widely known that, during the latter stages of the Musharraf regime, the two countries came extremely close to a definitive conclusion on a number of pending issues, including

Kashmir, until Musharraf's mounting domestic political difficulties made it impossible for him to clinch a deal. (Musharraf himself has implied that an agreement was also close with the previous Indian prime minister, Vajpayee, until the BJP called an election that it lost; the process had then to start all over again.)[657]

It is surely not impossible to pick up the threads, but it is very difficult to pick up the threads in an atmosphere of violence, intimidation and mayhem. This is where Pakistan, too, bears the major share of the responsibility for making progress towards peace. No democratic government worth its salt, and certainly no Indian government, will negotiate with a gun pointed at its head. A New Delhi that is prepared to make concessions will not want to make them if there is the slightest suggestion that it is doing so because it is intimidated by terrorist action. If Pakistan can make serious efforts to curb its extremists sufficiently to create a more propitious climate for a peace process, India would more readily seize the opportunity. But the primary onus for confining, if not destroying, the deadly virus that it has long incubated must rest on the Pakistani state. If it seizes that responsibility, it will not find India lacking.

Given the Modi government's track record this far in its relationship with our western neighbour, I am not holding my breath that the path I'm advocating will be chosen. However, in the hope that some counsel will be heeded, let me try and outline in this chapter some of the things that will need to be kept in mind while dealing with Pakistan. First, it is important to recognize that Pakistan has failed to fulfil any of the minimum requirements for dialogue that Mr Modi himself has cited. It has not prosecuted the perpetrators of the 2008 Mumbai massacre or constrained the terrorist forces that operate with the complicity of the military establishment on its territory. It has not even handed over Dawood Ibrahim, the fugitive don of the Mumbai underworld.

---

[657]Uday Singh Rana, 'When Vajpayee and Musharraf "Almost Resolved" the Kashmir Dispute', News18, 13 February 2018.

There continue to be acts of aggression on the border. So am
I being unrealistic in thinking there is a way forward that will
enable us to end decades of hostility?

In a famous 1947 article in *Foreign Affairs*, George F. Kennan
argued that the Soviet Union's hostility toward the United States
was chronic and incurable, since it was rooted not in a classic
conflict of interest between two great powers, but in deep-seated
nationalism and insecurity on the part of Russia which the US
could do nothing about. Something similar could be said about
India and Pakistan. Straightforward disagreements between two
states can be resolved through dialogue and compromise. But how
can that work when Pakistan's abiding hostility towards India is
rooted in fundamental insecurity about its national identity as the
'not-India' for the subcontinent's Muslims, and even worse, driven
by the self-interest of a rapacious military which commands a
greater share of the national GDP than the military of any other
country in the world, and needs this hostility to justify its power
and privileges?

For two and a half decades, as has been noted, Pakistan
has pursued a policy of inflicting on India 'death by a thousand
cuts'—bleeding the country through repeated terrorist attacks,
rather than attempting an open military confrontation which it
cannot win against India's superior conventional forces. The logic
is that India's response to this tactic would always be tempered
by its desire not to derail its ambitious economic development
plans, as well as the Indian government's unwillingness to face
the risk of a nuclear war.

But this predictable and repetitive pattern of India–Pakistan
relations was suddenly disrupted on 29 September 2016, when
India's Director-General of Military Operations (DGMO),
Lieutenant-General Ranbir Singh, announced that Indian
commandos had conducted 'surgical strikes' across the Line of
Control (LoC) in Kashmir, the de facto international border
between the two countries. The DGMO stated that the strikes,
in the early hours of that morning, had destroyed terrorist 'launch

pads' and eliminated significant numbers of militants poised to cross over for attacks on the Indian side, as well as some who were protecting them (presumably a reference to Pakistani soldiers).[658]

The Indian public and the country's notoriously fractious political class reacted with great pride to the news, unanimously hailing the decisive action as long overdue. For the preceding quarter-century, Indians had watched helplessly as their attempts at peacemaking with their belligerent, military-dominated neighbour had collapsed repeatedly, thanks to terrorist attacks from Pakistan that the government in Islamabad seemed unable or unwilling to prevent.

Pakistani reactions were a curious mixture, ranging from dismissive declarations (backed by orchestrated bus tours of journalists to selected parts of the LoC) that no surgical strikes had even occurred, to angry statements declaring that irresponsible Indian firing across the LoC had killed two Pakistani soldiers. For once, the Pakistani military appeared to have been caught off guard by Indian action.

Indians braced themselves for the international community's disapproval—the fear of nuclear war between the subcontinental neighbours usually dominates world opinion whenever bilateral tensions flare. But this time, thanks in part to the DGMO's measured and precise statement and an absence of military triumphalism in India's official tone (the braggadocio of the ruling party's publicists came later), the world seemed to consider India's response justifiable.

Pakistani attempts to seek support against India were widely rebuffed, with Pakistan's usual supporters, China and the US, mildly calling for both sides to defuse the tensions.

India also tightened the diplomatic screws on its recalcitrant neighbour, persuading other members of the South Asian Association for Regional Cooperation (SAARC) to call off a planned summit

---

[658]'India destroys 7 terror launchpads in Pakistan in surgical strikes along LoC', *Deccan Chronicle*, 29 September 2016.

in Islamabad as punishment for Pakistan's bad behaviour.[659] India's government also announced that it was undertaking a review of the Indus Waters Treaty, under which India has conceded to Pakistan, on generous terms, the waters of the Indus River, which originates in India, not even using the share to which it is entitled.[660]

It has since emerged that the operation announced by Singh was not India's first military strike across the LoC; several had occurred under the previous government as well, in response to military raids on Indian territory. But the strikes were the first to be announced publicly, providing a clear signal of intent and a bold statement that business as usual—Pakistani pinpricks followed by Indian inaction—is no longer to be expected.

With its calibrated and targeted strikes, India made it clear that inaction is not the only possible response to terrorist provocations. Although brave, the strategy was not without risk, because it obliges India to pursue a similar course of action when the next significant terrorist strike occurs. Still, as I have said before, a country that refuses to suffer repeated body blows earns more respect than one whose restraint can be interpreted as weakness.

VII

However, even as it is important to show our belligerent neighbour that we cannot be attacked with impunity, the path of negotiation cannot be abandoned. Too much of Indian public opinion is divided into sharply polarized camps of hawks and doves—the former insisting on nothing less than implacable hostility towards Islamabad, the latter advocating talks with whoever is in office in Islamabad, through a process 'uninterruptable' even if new terrorist strikes emanating from Pakistan were to occur.

As I've said earlier, it is time for a different approach: one that separates the issue of political dialogue and a targeted military

---

[659]'Islamabad SAARC Summit cancelled, announces Pakistan', *FirstPost*, 30 September 2016.
[660]'Modi chairs meeting to review Indus Water Treaty', *The Hindu*, 26 September 2016.

response to acts of violence from that of trade and people-to-people contact. Yes, punish each incident of violence by freezing official talks or by surgical strikes. At the same time, whenever appropriate or when the drums of war have grown muted, we should open our doors and hearts to Pakistanis who have nothing to do with the military establishment. Multiplying our channels of contact away from Track-I and Track-II to embrace the ordinary people of Pakistan would put both countries back on the right track—towards genuine peace.

The late prime minister Atal Bihari Vajpayee had once declared that you can change history but not geography.[661] He was wrong: history, once it has occurred, cannot be changed. The time has come, instead, for the victims of geography to make history.

---

[661]Quoted in *World Development Report 2009: Reshaping Economic Geography*, Washington DC: World Bank, 2009, p. 120.

chapter forty-two

ALL HAT AND NO CATTLE

The unpredictable and unruly actions of President Donald Trump have shaken the world. And India has been buffeted too. Given the way he has treated some of his closest allies, such as Canada, Britain and the EU, it would be foolish to imagine that India is going to be exempt from Mr Trump's eccentric and combative politics. With the volatility that both our countries have faced since early November 2016, the future of India–US relations is certainly an important question to ponder, one which has left many seasoned analysts and observers of relations between our two countries perplexed. Indeed, it appears that for now the only thing that we can all be certain of is how uncertain things seem to be in the Trump era.

The Indo–US relationship has evolved significantly over time. In the first decades of India's independence, its relations with the US were far from close. This should have been surprising, since the two countries had a lot in common then too, as they do today. Both are vibrant democracies that believe in human rights, the free press, fundamental freedoms and more, besides having both experienced colonialism and, thereafter, broken new ideological and political ground in world history. As Henry Kissinger noted, the two countries have 'no conflict of interest in the traditional and fundamental sense.'[662] Mutual trade and investment are growing steadily. And people-to-people relations, strengthened by a common language, by around 150,000 Indian students a year spending more than $6 billion ($6.4 billion in 2016–17) on American educational and related services, and by nearly 2 million people of Indian origin who have made their lives

---

[662]'Kissinger hails India as world power', *The Hindu*, 7 November 2004.

in the US, have been characterized by friendship and warmth.[663]

But in 1947, Indian Americans were just a handful, and there were two major factors that didn't help the cause of Indo–US amity: US ignorance and Indian unwillingness to take sides in the Cold War.

America's initial indifference was best reflected in President Harry Truman's reaction when Chester Bowles asked to be named ambassador to India: 'I thought India was pretty jammed with poor people and cows round streets, witch doctors, and people sitting on hot coals and bathing in the Ganges...but I did not realize anybody thought it was important.'[664]

If that was bad, India's political orientation was worse. The American preference for making anti-communist allies, however unsavoury, tied Washington to Pakistan's increasingly Islamist dictatorship, while India's non-aligned democracy drifted towards the secular Soviet embrace. The US government regarded non-alignment with distaste; Eisenhower's secretary of state, John Foster Dulles, notoriously declared that 'neutrality between good and evil is itself evil'. In a world divided between two uncompromising superpowers, India's refusal to ally with its fellow democracies seemed like appeasement at best, and aid and comfort for the enemy at worst.

India's arch-enemy and perpetual irritant, Pakistan, on the other hand, became an essential component in America's strategy of containment of the Soviet Union and in its later opening to China. From India's point of view, US indulgence of Pakistan became overt hostility when the US sent the Seventh Fleet into the Bay of Bengal in support of the Pakistani military genocide in Bangladesh in 1971. Tempers cooled soon enough, but India was always regarded as tilting towards the Kremlin, hardly a recommendation for warm

---

[663]'Indian students in US dwarf America's FDI in India, spend whopping $6.54 bn', *Financial Express*, 14 November 2017 and Corinne Abrams, 'This map shows where India's huge diaspora lives', *Wall Street Journal*, 19 January 2016.
[664]Quoted in Andrew J. Rotter, *Comrades at Odds: The United States and India, 1947–1964*, Ithaca: Cornell University Press, 2000, p. 15.

relations in American eyes. Matters plumbed their depths during two historic lows: 1971, when the US and India found themselves on opposite sides during the Bangladesh war and India signed a treaty with the Soviet Union; and 1998, when India tested its nuclear capabilities at Pokhran, the US imposed sanctions on it.[665]

But since then we have seen a sea change, with China's rise, India growing economically more vibrant and an increasing convergence of Indian and US views of strategic priorities in the Indo-Pacific region. The Indo–US nuclear deal signed by Prime Minister Manmohan Singh and President George Bush in 2005 marked an astonishing breakthrough. The 123 agreement for nuclear cooperation essentially recognized India as a de facto nuclear state and enshrined an 'Indian exemption' that opened up an entire new vista of security and defence possibilities.[666] The narrative today can be seen as a remarkable success story: the record shows both how far the strategic partnership has come, but also how much more can be done.

The nuclear accord simultaneously accomplished two things. It admitted India into the global nuclear club despite its principled refusal to sign the Nuclear Nonproliferation Treaty (which Indians overwhelmingly reject as the last vestige of apartheid in the international system). More important, it acknowledged that US exceptionalism had found a sibling. Thanks to the US, which strong-armed the forty-five countries of the Nuclear Suppliers' Group into swallowing their concerns that special treatment for India could constitute a precedent for rogue nuclear aspirants such as Pakistan, North Korea and Iran, there is now an 'Indian exception.' Few things could have been more gratifying to a deeply proud nation that was tired of being constantly hyphenated by Washington with its smaller, dysfunctional neighbour, Pakistan.

Under Mr Obama, nothing quite so dramatic occurred. First of all, the US's grand strategic orientation inevitably focused on

---

[665]'U.S. imposes sanctions on India', *CNN*, 13 May 1998.
[666]'Chronology of the Indo-US nuclear deal', *Times of India*, 9 October 2008.

the rise of China, which as Secretary of State Hillary Clinton had indicated, was Washington's most important bilateral relationship on the planet. And on the subcontinent, the Obama administration's understandable concerns in Afghanistan inevitably made Pakistan loom much larger in its consciousness than India. To Mr Obama, it was clear that there could be no successful outcome in Afghanistan possible without Pakistan, and was therefore attentive to Islamabad's priorities in ways that New Delhi occasionally found irritating. It is fair to say that during Mr Obama's Nobel Prize-winning first year in office, sceptical India was largely immune to the wave of what one might irreverently call 'globama-ization' that swept the rest of the planet.

Making things seem more difficult is what Narendra Modi stands for. He shared an excellent personal relationship with Mr Obama, but his background as someone who subscribed to illiberal, majoritarian ideas came in the way of the India–US relationship making any real progress. As I have pointed out earlier, it was telling that Barack Obama said pointedly in a Town Hall speech in New Delhi in January 2015: 'India will succeed so long as it is not split along the lines of religious faith.'[667] Mr Obama's message was clear: if India did not resolve the problems that were dividing the country, Mr Modi's proclaimed ambitious development plans would be thwarted. It is the central element of the Modi paradox I have explored throughout this book. But coming from a US President, whose visit was being hailed by the government as a diplomatic triumph and whose 'bromance' with the Indian PM saw first names and much friendly banter, it was a pointed reminder of the fundamental contradiction at the heart of Mr Modi's regime.

The tensions between the two tendencies—the economic reformism preached at the top and the cultural nativism that animates the majority beneath—have affected the government's

---

[667]'India will succeed so long as it's not splintered on religious lines: Barack Obama', *Financial Express*, 27 January 2015.

agenda. What makes it worse is that the political majority needed
by the prime minister to pursue his economic policies relies entirely
on the political campaigns and organizational capacity of the
very people whose chauvinism is undermining him. The Modi
paradox we have mentioned throughout this book affects Indo–
US relations too: Mr Modi wasn't elected PM in order for the
minorities to be vilified and assaulted, but to fulfil an aspirational
development vision he effectively articulated. Mr Obama's speech
was a way of telling him he can't do that without abandoning his
old religious intolerance that earned him those American strictures.
If Narendra Modi acolytes hoped that President Trump would be
less ideological, the president cannot be indifferent to the concerns
of evangelical Christians, a key part of the president's ideological
base, about mounting bigotry in Modi-run India.

Nonetheless, a certain affinity between Mr Modi and
Mr Trump is hard to escape. The journalist and commentator
Varghese K. George summarized it best, citing both men's election
campaign speeches: 'Modi said India's election commission was
acting against him; "illegal" immigrants from Bangladesh were
voting against his party. So he promised to deport them. But he
was of the view that Hindus coming from other countries must
be protected. Trump said "illegal" Mexicans were voting for the
Democratic Party and they would be deported, while Christian
refugees [from Europe and the Middle East] would be given
preference. Modi said Manmohan Singh—the first non-Hindu
prime minister of India—was weak and indecisive and foreign
leaders did not respect him.... Trump said Barack Obama—
America's first non-white President—was indecisive and weak and
foreign leaders did not respect him... Modi called journalists "news
traders"; Trump called them "the lowest form of life". The more
I heard Trump, the more the territory felt familiar to me.'[668]

The similarities between both men and the nature of their

[668]Varghese K. George, *Open Embrace: India-US Ties in the Age of Modi and Trump*, New Delhi: Penguin Books, 2018, p. viii.

appeal as leaders harnessing a public disenchantment with their countries' political establishments can, however, only go so far. As heads of government, each espouses the same assertive nationalism: Mr Modi speaks of 'India First', Mr Trump of 'America First'. The two slogans, though similar, cannot always be compatible, as quarrels over trade policy quickly bore out.

The same contradictions affect not just government, but relations with US civil society as well. In 2015, in what was widely hailed as a triumph, Mr Modi not only made the first prime ministerial visit to Silicon Valley but met with the CEOs of top cutting-edge tech firms like Adobe, Facebook, Google and Tesla, pitching 'Digital India' to a receptive audience where 'StartUp India' and 'StandUp India' went down well with the familiar 'Make in India'. His carefully pre-scripted Town Hall with Mark Zuckerberg, the announcement that Google would bring broadband to 500 Indian railway stations and the prime minister's manifest interest in innovation and tech entrepreneurship undoubtedly made a positive impact.

But to acknowledge this is not to tell the whole story. You didn't have to listen to the liberal protestors of the #ModiFail campaign or read the petition signed by Indian Studies academics to know that Mr Modi's sales pitch battled a strong counter-narrative of his government's own making. While Mr Modi was smooth-talking in California, his government had shut down the Internet in Kashmir for three days, repeating a similar action in Gujarat the previous week. A Twitter report revealed that government agencies reporting accounts for objectionable content rose from 15 in the last six months of 2014 to 341 in the first six months of 2017. There was also an increase in requests from government agencies for information—a 55 per cent increase since July–December 2016.[669] This instinctive illiberalism does not go well with 'Digital India'. Sure, China has banned Facebook and

---

[669]'Twitter report shows rise in govt requests to remove info', *Indian Express*, 21 September 2017.

Twitter altogether, but India is a democracy, and will be held to different standards.

Mr Modi is a highly effective salesman for India, and there is no denying the energy and dynamism he has brought to taking India's message abroad. But, as I have noted in this book and elsewhere, every good salesman is only as effective as his product allows him to be, and this is where Mr Modi's sales pitch falls short of reality. It's not just the openness of 'Digital India' versus the trigger-fingers of the BJP government's censors. It's also the lack of substance behind his other claims. Bill Gates waxes eloquent on how important it is for Mr Modi to expand healthcare spending in India,[670] but Mr Modi doesn't admit he has slashed the health budget.[671] Mr Modi releases a carefully calibrated tear at the mention of his mother, but doesn't acknowledge his government has gutted the budget of the Women and Child Development Ministry.[672] Mr Modi talks about the importance of the Swachh Bharat Abhiyan, but fails to concede that while its publicity budget has gone up five-fold, his government allocates less money to sanitation than UPA's had done (with considerably less fanfare).[673]

Mr Modi's fundamental problem in America remains his growing credibility deficit in India—the perception that he talks a good game but delivers little (or, in the marvellous Texan phrase about cowboy braggadocio, that he is 'all hat and no cattle'.) He is an excellent salesman for his version of India, but Americans are increasingly beginning to feel that behind the packaging there is no product.

But there has been progress on other fronts—the small but

---

[670]'Bill Gates to Narendra Modi: You need to generate new healthcare models for India', *FirstPost*, 14 August 2015.

[671]'Big Modi govt push for health? Key schemes face cut in funds', *Times of India*, 12 February 2018.

[672]Abantika Ghosh, 'Activists cry foul as WCD Ministry funds slashed by half', *Indian Express*, 1 March 2015.

[673]'Swachh Bharat: Who Built More Toilets? UPA Did Better Than NDA', *The Quint*, 5 August 2015; Aroon Deep, 'Swachh Bharat spent ₹530 crore on publicity in three years—but little on grassroots awareness', *Scroll.in*, 22 November 2017.

significant steps that add up to strengthening the sinews of any relationship. Agreements on seemingly mundane subjects like agriculture, education, health and even space exploration and energy security testified to enhanced cooperation, and the two governments also proclaimed 'initiatives' on clean energy and climate change as well as educational linkages between American and Indian universities.[674]

The problem is that the pattern down the decades has been one where every few years, with much optimism, declarations are made, or at least hopes loudly expressed, that India–US relations have entered a new, positive era, only to be undone by one setback or another. In recent times, much has been said and written in this regard about the meetings between President Trump and Prime Minister Modi, both when Narendra Modi visited the US in July this year and on the sidelines of the G20 Summit in Hamburg.

For the first interaction, the bar of expectations was certainly set quite low primarily because there was considerable uncertainty regarding President Trump's personal convictions on foreign policy. For example, though he had developed a fairly hardline rhetoric on the issue of US–China relations and appointed a number of known China-bashers to key positions, we were all well aware of the much publicized bonhomie that was on display when President Xi visited Mr Trump at his Mar-A-Lago resort, something that took everyone watching by surprise. This reaffirmed the growing belief that with Mr Trump no assumptions can be taken for granted. Many Indian-Americans had enthusiastically supported the Trump candidacy, believing his victory would be good for India; now Indians were not so sure. There was the episode of Mr Trump's singling out of India in his statement withdrawing from the Paris Accord, unfairly accusing India of not contributing adequately to the fight against climate change and being essentially a freeloader on global energy policies.[675] This was understandably seen in Delhi

[674]'U.S.-India Joint Statement and Fact Sheets', U.S. Embassy & Consulates in India.
[675]'What Donald Trump said about India in his announcement on Paris climate accord', *Indian Express*, 2 June 2017.

as a setback for Indo–US relations.

The Indians approached the summit with a mixture of anxiety and low expectations. New Delhi was anxious to ensure that a personal rapport could be established between Narendra Modi and Donald Trump, who till then had only interacted briefly over a congratulatory phone call; but they had no reason to expect any significant breakthrough. Though the visit didn't end up generating a 'bromance' between the two, unlike Mr Modi's first-name-terms relationship with 'Barack', it went well enough, featuring Narendra Modi's famous public hug of the former president, which seemed to take Donald Trump by surprise but did not seem to displease him.

Still, the summit was low on actual substance, once you examine the nuts and bolts of the joint statement that was published. PM Modi did say a lot of things that President Trump wanted to hear, including promising to spend more taxpayer money buying American goods, including purchasing twenty Guardian drones. Indian investment in the US, based on data from the Department of Commerce, also creates nearly 197,000 jobs in that country—and that, given the transactional nature of Donald Trump's calculations, should be something the US appreciates.[676] On the Indian side however there was a feeling that India accomplished very little in return. The issue of H1B visas, an area of significant concerns for India with its ever expanding IT sector but a campaign target for Donald Trump, wasn't brought up. And overall, while the joint statement highlighted several aspects of what India could offer to the US, particularly defence acquisitions and market access, there was little discussion on what the US could offer India.[677]

The up-and-down pattern has continued: a strong speech by the Trump administration and its then secretary of state on Pakistan's habit of running with the terrorist hares while hunting with the American hounds have given Indians much cheer,[678] but a strong

---

[676]'Briefing document, 11 January 2018', US India Strategic Partnership Forum, p. 2.
[677]'Full text of the joint statement between PM Narendra Modi and US President Donald Trump at the White House', The Hindu, 27 June 2017.
[678]Ashok Kumar Mehta,'The enigma that is US-Pak ties: Pakistan must stop

attack from the president himself on Indian tariffs, singling out Harley Davidson motorcycles,[679] has inaugurated a trade skirmish of mutual retaliatory tariffs that could yet plunge the countries into a trade war. Amid all these mixed signals, reports indicate that Prime Minister Modi has invited President Trump to be the chief guest at India's Republic Day commemorations on 26 January 2019, though the President has not apparently accepted the invitation yet. If he does accept, though, a word of caution might be in order. As the respected military historian, Srinath Raghavan, wrote in *The Print*, 'If the government expects Trump to turn solicitous of India's interests after presiding over the pomp of a Republic Day parade, it is clearly out to lunch. As America's closest allies have realized, pandering to Trump is useless and counterproductive.'[680]

But it is undeniably true that whether it is Republicans or Democrats in America or the Congress or, more recently, the BJP in India, the fundamentals of the relationship between our two countries are sound and will survive political change in either country.

The transformation of the India–US relationship from estrangement to strategic partnership is well advanced, and the relationship has clearly acquired a depth that goes beyond the utilitarian measurement of successful transactions even if it faces the occasional setback. The strong foundations I just mentioned have been developed both by various governments over the past two decades but very often also in spite of governments.

Ideologically, India identifies and has a close relationship with American democracy, liberal internationalism, and so far anyway, the cosmopolitanism emerging from widespread immigration. As I have observed frequently before, for both countries, soft power is

---

providing sanctuaries to terrorists', *DNA*, 18 October 2017.
[679]Datunorro Clark, 'Trump attacks Harley-Davidson for moving production overseas to offset tariffs', *NBC*, 26 June 2018.
[680]Srinath Raghavan, 'Narendra Modi's charm and grand Republic Day invite won't fix ties with Donald Trump', *The Print*, 17 July 2018.

an integral component of what drives their role in the world—the
power of attraction. For Harvard's Joseph S. Nye, who invented the
concept, the United States is the archetypal exponent of soft power.
The fact is that the US is the home of Boeing and Intel, Google
and the iPod, Microsoft and MTV, Hollywood and Disneyland,
Coke, jeans, McDonald's and Starbucks—in short of most of the
major products that dominate daily life around our globe. The
attractiveness of these assets, and of the American lifestyle of
which they are emblematic, is that they permit the US to persuade
others to adopt the US's agenda, rather than relying purely on the
dissuasive or coercive 'hard power' of military force. For India
too, Bollywood, bhangra and bhelpuri have done more to enhance
its presence in the world than the Ministry of External Affairs or
the Indian army. When you can find an Indian restaurant or a
yoga class in any small town in America, you know Indian soft
power is working in the US.

The prominence of Indians in American life and on US
television screens, their vital role as fundraisers for US politicians,
their presence on Congressional staffs and governmental office,
all point to Indians playing an influential role in American public
life. Congressman Raja Krishnamoorthi has jokingly talked about
the 'samosa caucus': there have been two Indian-American
governors, and currently six Congresspersons, a senator and the
US ambassador to the UN are of Indian descent. For the most
part, they have shown a willingness to stand up and be heard
on issues that matter to India. I believe that in the long term,
Indian Americans will come to play the same role in relation to
US policy on India as Jewish Americans play in relation to US
policy on Israel, and for similar reasons.

But soft power is at risk from hardline Hindutva. Reports of
assaults on minorities in India reflect poorly on India's soft power
in America. And when protestors at a World Hindu Congress
organized in Chicago are beaten up by delegates, as occurred in
September 2018, it casts doubt both on the homeland's values and

on those of the people espousing them in America.[681]

But there are also harder factors at work than soft power. In economic and transactional terms, cooperation has been growing steadily stronger, despite occasional irritants. Take arms sales: in 2001–04 India purchased arms and defence supplies worth $400 million from the US. From 2005 to 2008 this multiplied into $3.2 billion (with the purchases including the USS Trenton, twenty General Electric F-404 engines for the Tejas fighter, six C-130J Super Hercules mission aircraft, and eight Boeing P-8I maritime control aircraft). Thereafter, between 2009 and 2013, India's defence purchases went even higher to $5.7 billion (including 500 CBU-97 sensor-fused weapons for Jaguar aircraft, 40 Harpoon anti-ship missiles, six C-130J Hercules, and 10 Boeing C-17 Globemaster-III transport aircraft).[682] In other words, the total value of defence purchases made by India between 2008 and 2013 was ten times the value of deals signed in 2001–04. However, so far India has largely bought non-combat support equipment from the US, and little lethal equipment. Still, the US has now overtaken Russia, India's traditional defence supplier, in terms of the value of trade.[683]

Where do we go from here? India has, admittedly, a low defence technology base, which does not allow it to take advantage of all the options the US could offer and while this is a good beginning, the challenge is to raise the bar and take our technological cooperation to the next level.

So the fundamentals undergirding our relationship include our democratic systems, mutual understanding, no significant areas of difference with the end of the Cold War, growing defence cooperation, comparable soft power assets and a thriving Indian-American community. There is also an increasing convergence of

[681]Varghese K. George, 'Jostling and arrests at World Hindu Congress', *The Hindu*, 9 September 2018.
[682]Ajai Shukla, 'India-US defence ties grow with assertive Modi govt', *Business Standard*, 21 January 2015.
[683]Rajat Pandit, 'US pips Russia as top arms supplier to India', *Times of India*, 13 August 2014.

geopolitical views, particularly on China's rise and the threat it poses in East Asia, including to India.

Yet for all these areas of convergence, there have been equally strong areas of divergence in the relationship and how our two countries manage and navigate these differences will prove crucial to developing an enhanced strategic partnership.

It's in the nature of democracies to disagree—including with each other. In examining defence cooperation, for instance, it is apparent that constraints exist on both sides of the fence: Indian defence procurement procedures, which are being revised, do not go down well with US suppliers, while US licensing constraints do not agree with India. For instance, the Government of India's latest Make in India campaign is reinforcing our traditional preference for, if not entirely developing weaponry at home, at least co-manufacturing it with foreign investors, instead of making full purchases from abroad. There are structural difficulties on the American side for such a Make in India strategy, since the US has longstanding export control requirements that make any transfer of technology in such fields conditional on direct and close scrutiny of End Use Monitoring, to which India cannot fully agree, besides requiring an assortment of bureaucratic sanctions. Both countries, ultimately, need to make an effort to find a compromise that is mutually agreeable. In fact, it was to facilitate this that in 2012 the Government of India set up the Defence Technology and Trade Initiative (DTII), under which so far India and the US have agreed to start cooperation on various pathfinder projects—but given that by the beginning of last year progress has only been made on two of those projects it is clear that big, momentous developments are yet to occur.[684]

It has helped that the Government of India has now decided to increase Foreign Direct Investment (FDI) in defence to 49 per

[684]Benjamin Schwartz, 'The Trajectory of US-India Defense Trade', U.S. Chamber of Commerce and 'Defence Trade and Technology Initiative: India, US agree on 2 new "pathfinder" projects', *Economic Times*, 14 July 2018.

cent,[685] making its traditional formula somewhat more palatable to the US, but in general, the Indian preference to domesticate high technology, including in defence, goes against the American tendency to embed India into the global defence supply chain. While increased FDI will soften this impasse somewhat, legislation on this alone will not satisfy the US, which also wants clarity on labour laws, control of management and on intellectual property rights. So it is too early to get hopes too high.

Beyond defence procurement, trade between the two countries has also seen progress over time albeit still nowhere close to optimal levels. Data from the Department of Commerce suggests that the bilateral trade relationship between the United States and South Korea, a country whose GDP is just around 40 per cent of India's, enjoys a volume of trade nearly twice the size of India's current trade with the US. The US–China trade for that matter is six times the Indian figure. India is currently the ninth largest goods trading partner of the US at $67.7 billion in goods trade as of last year.[686] The deficit in trade stands at more than $30 billion, in favour of India, with trade between the two countries estimated at $140 billion in 2017.[687] This modest deficit is really not such a big deal for an economy the size of the US, but when President Trump keeps mentioning it as an issue, it really doesn't help.[688]

Similarly, FDI between the two countries has also witnessed a marginal increase between 2015–16, US FDI in India stood at $28.3 billion in 2015, an increase by 4.4 per cent from the previous year, while India invested a more modest $9.3 billion in FDI in 2015, an improvement by 3.7 per cent from the previous year. The numbers from trade and defence relationships do point to a

---

[685] Amrita Nair Ghaswalla, 'Govt may soon allow 100% FDI in defence', *Hindu Business Line*, 20 August 2017.
[686] 'U.S.-India Bilateral Trade and Investment', *Office of the United States Trade Representative*, 22 March 2017.
[687] 'India-US trade estimated to touch $140 billion in 2017', *Hindu BusinessLine*, 3 February 2018.
[688] Amiti Sen, 'India to tell US not to judge ties on the basis of trade deficit', *Hindu BusinessLine*, 8 July 2018.

healthy relationship, though a lot more can be done in this regard.

But areas of convergence are only one side of the coin and naturally as two leading powers of the twenty-first century, the two countries do not necessarily see eye to eye on all issues.

There is a perception among critics, not just in India, that these areas of convergence are 'soft' and 'feel-good' aspects of the relationship that mask a lack of substantive progress on the hard strategic, economic, political and security issues that analysts here consider more important. Take the issue of H1B visas, an area of critical importance in US–India relations. Since 2007, Indian citizens have been the largest group of H1B applications to the United States, with over 21 lakh applicants between 2007–17.[689] But with Mr Trump's pursuance of his campaign goals to ensure less H1B approvals and therefore more security for US jobs, Indians who want to work in the US have been significantly affected. This is particularly true for India's IT sector professionals who have been recognized globally for their capability and skill.

Similarly, at a national security level, how understanding is the United States of India's security concerns, especially vis-à-vis Pakistan? Here President Obama and, to an extent, President Trump, after some recent tough talk about Pakistan's sponsorship of terrorism, have inspired confidence that the United States does indeed pay serious attention to India's core national security interests. But the past hyphenation of India and Pakistan is an area of significant irritation for the leadership on the Indian side, and needs to be abandoned again as it was under President George W. Bush.

It almost appears that there is a strategic attempt of mollifying India in this regard without developing a narrative of concrete substance. To take a simple example, just prior to PM Modi and President Trump's interaction in July 2017, the US had assigned the tag of 'global terrorist' to Syed Salahuddin, the leader of the

---

[689]'Over 21 lakh Indians applied for H-1B visa in 11 years', *Hindu BusinessLine*, 1 August 2017.

Hizbul Mujahedeen.[690] But it has no practical effect: as they say in New York, that and 65 cents will get you a cup of coffee. While it was a token of recognition of India's security concerns, it was unfortunately not accompanied by, or followed up with, any action against Pakistan, the state that provides Salahuddin and his terrorist colleagues safe haven and succour in the first place.

Similarly, while there has been some appreciation from President Trump for India's role in Afghanistan, there continues to be greater receptivity to Pakistani objections than New Delhi considers reasonable. New Delhi remains seriously concerned about the possibility of a US withdrawal from Afghanistan that implicitly leaves the country to the mercies of the Pakistani ISI, which has been known to foment and guide terrorist actions against India. Cooperation between India and the United States on counterterrorism has improved after 26/11, but the two countries have not gone much beyond information sharing (though the access somewhat belatedly granted to the Pakistani-American terrorist enabler David Coleman Headley helped overcome Indian misgivings about the depth of this cooperation). This is one area where real teeth could be added, not least to reassure Indians that the United States' understandable desire to cut its losses in 'Af-Pak' would not leave our country more vulnerable to the depredations of those who stand to gain from an American departure.

India is also wary of the possibilities of a greater US–China relationship under President Trump. As some analysts have observed, China's greatest bargaining chip with the United States has been its capability of keeping a leash on North Korea, something that the Trump administration will greatly value. Should Mr Xi present himself as a suitable middleman between the two countries and assuage the heightening tensions, President Trump may take America closer to China. At a time when ambitious Chinese expansion projects such as the Belt and Road Initiative

---

[690]'Why US tag of "global terrorist" for Salahuddin matters to Indian govt', *Indian Express*, 28 June 2017.

(BRI), China–Pakistan Economic Corridor (CPEC) and Silk Route are being viewed with increasing concern by New Delhi, which views these developments as national security and sovereignty concerns, such a warming up of US–China relations could to some degree come at the expense of the US–India relationship.

The US could also show more interest in resisting China's irredentist claims to Indian territory, particularly its habit of dubbing Arunachal Pradesh as 'South Tibet', an issue on which the United States has stayed conspicuously neutral. The question of the strategic content of the relationship goes beyond the subcontinent. Barack Obama's support in the Indian Parliament for New Delhi's claims to a seat on a reformed security council has not been followed by any instructions to American diplomats around the world to execute this commitment or even to pursue this objective.[691] The suspicion remains that what Indians saw as a substantive triumph during President Obama's visit in fact amounted to little more than a rhetorical flourish.

Of course Indians must beware of seeing the US relationship in terms of a checklist of Indian expectations alone.

Former US ambassador Robert Blackwill was once reported to have said: 'India wants the US to invest, India wants the US to keep its markets more open, India wants more visas for its professionals, India wants us to be helpful on Kashmir and in dealing with Pakistan, India wants US support for membership of the UN Security Council, India wants this and India wants that. Tell me what will India give in return?'[692] This is not elementary transactionalism alone, since Mr Blackwill was very much an exponent of the support-India-for-its-own-sake school of American foreign policy-making. Rather, it reflected a genuine level of exasperation. The fact is that Washington has reason to feel that New Delhi has not done enough to define its own sense

---

[691]Ed Henry and Sara Sider,'Obama backs permanent seat for India on Security Council', CNN, 8 November 2010.
[692]Ashley Tellis, 'New Delhi, Washington: Who gets what?', Times of India, 30 January 2010.

of its role as an emerging great power, and consequently has no settled vision of what it wants from a strategic partnership with the United States.

India is gradually moving from its traditional obsession with preserving its own strategic autonomy in the face of external pressure to a broader acceptance of its own responsibilities in shaping the world in which it wants to thrive. But it has been curiously diffident, even reluctant, to do so. The vision I depicted in my 2012 book *Pax Indica: India and the World of the 21st Century* is no closer to realization five years later. India has the capacity, the human and technological resources to play a major role alongside the US in the stewardship of the global commons, from cyberspace to outer space. But there is not yet a fully-fledged consensus on what that entails and how far it permits the two countries to flesh out the meaning of the expression 'natural allies' first used by both governments at the beginning of the century. And India needs to find the political will to play such a role with confidence.

Unfortunately, the turbulence of the Trump era and the backlash against globalization may make the management of our areas of divergence difficult, but given the alignment of our strategic interests, this will not be impossible.

Part of the success of the India–US relationship will lie in how effectively the two countries manage the differences that inevitably will arise between them. Diplomats like to pretend that there are no difficulties or misunderstandings, when in fact several have arisen in the recent past. An illustrative list in recent years would include different priorities on terrorism and mismatched threat perceptions, incompatible views on Pakistan as a credible partner for peace and continued disagreements on aspects of trade relations, none more evident than in their duelling positions on the Doha Round. There are also issues of style—American insensitivity and Indian preachiness have tended to rub each other the wrong way. But on geopolitical fundamentals, there is no real clash of interests. On no issue of vital national interest to either country (with the possible exception of Iran) is the other arrayed on the 'wrong' side.

The twenty-first century world is one in which an emphasis on the shared values of both countries—democracy and pluralism, tolerance and transparency, and respect for personal liberty and human rights—has greater salience than ever. For the first time in human history, a majority of the world's population lives in democracies. The idea that the two principal ones have special interests and responsibilities is not a fashionable one, but it could become one of the defining features of the new era.

As democracies, India and the United States have the additional responsibility of establishing and running international structures to cope with the myriad challenges of the twenty-first century that go beyond the capacity of any one state or alliance to resolve. These include terrorism and nuclear proliferation, but also less conventional threats: state failure, transnational organized crime, the spread of pandemics, piracy in international waters, the management of cyberspace and the military misuse of outer space, to name a few. The threat of Islamist fanaticism and the rise of an authoritarian China also pose specific national security challenges to the United States and India that, if handled well and in cooperation, could assure a safer world.

The United States has to come to terms with a world whose centre of gravity has clearly moved away from the Atlantic to Asia, and to determine where it sees itself in relation to the incontestable rise of China and the growing prowess of India. If the relationship with India is going to become as important to American security as Europe's once was, wouldn't America need to revise its own positions on the threats and challenges faced by India? And yet the fundamental driver for long-term relations between the United States and India remains the importance of America—the nation, not just the government—as a partner in India's own remaking. As I have argued before the basic task for India in international affairs is to wield a foreign policy that enables and facilitates the domestic transformation of India. The relationship with the United

States is part of an effort to make possible the transformation of India's economy and society through our engagement with the world, while promoting our own national values (of pluralism, democracy, social justice and secularism) within our own society.

The India–US partnership contributes towards a global environment that is supportive of these internal priorities, and that facilitates our energy security, our food security and our environmental future. When we succeed in our national transformation, we will be including more and more of our people in the great narrative of hope that has been the narrative of social and economic development in America over the last two hundred years. If all goes well, India will be bringing 500 million villagers into the global village. That will mean 500 million more in the market for American products, 500 million more consumers, service providers and partners. India hopes the US will welcome them to the global village; and America hopes that India will pursue policies that will make it easier for America to do so.

But when one looks at Mr Modi's substantive contribution to this important relationship, once we get past the theatrics, it is surprisingly thin. After Mauritius, the US is the largest investor in India, but there's been no significant uptick.[693]

And now with President Trump having mentioned India as one of the countries with which the balance of trade has to be 'rectified' the road ahead will only get rockier, not smoother. Will Prime Minister Modi have the sagacity to make our relationship with the US what it should be, as his prime ministerial term lurches towards its inglorious conclusion? On the basis of what he has been able to accomplish thus far, I doubt it very much.

---

[693]'Mauritius largest source of FDI in India, says RBI', *Economic Times*, 19 January 2018.

chapter forty-three

KOWTOWING TO CHINA?

The kowtow (or koutou in the pinyin form of Mandarin Chinese) was to be performed before the emperor of China from ancient times. Although it possibly originated in an even earlier era, it was well established by the time the Qin dynasty came to power around 221 BCE. Although there are various forms of the kowtow, it is essentially a gesture of deep respect towards one's elders and superiors and can involve bowing, prostrating, kneeling or a combination of all three. In the past, the requirement of the kowtow in the presence of Chinese rulers caused resentment among foreign ambassadors and non-Chinese dignitaries because it was a gesture of submission. Today, the kowtow is no longer in vogue. But as President Xi Jinping grows ever more powerful it is clear that he expects most of the foreign heads of states he deals with to kowtow to him in all but form. This is a problem that India has to deal with head-on, as more than most we have to figure out how to deal with China and its all-powerful ruler in a way that best suits our own interests.

As I have pointed out earlier, Narendra Modi has visited China and the US more than he has visited any other country in the world.[694] He and President Xi Jinping have met on numerous occasions, most recently in Wuhan and then in Johannesburg. But for all this, there doesn't seem to have been much headway made on the most serious issues confronting the two nations—border conflicts, the trade imbalance, China's growing aggressions as it seeks to fulfil its regional and global aspirations, to name just a few. As with the chapter on Indo–US relations that precedes this, a detailed analysis of the India–China relationship is beyond the

---

[694]Varun B. Krishnan, 'Modi's foreign visits: A look at the PM's travel patterns and expenses', *The Hindu*, 21 July 2018.

scope of this chapter, so let me just focus on a few aspects.

Possibly the most pressing issue is the conflicts on the border, the Doklam standoff continued for many months in 2018 before the two sides stood down; but the problems this year have their genesis in a long-standing dispute over the border that does not seem to be likely to ease up any time soon, notwithstanding the conciliatory noises that are made from time to time. To sort out the long-unresolved border issue alone would require an extraordinary act of statesmanship and there are no signs that Mr Modi, as prime minister, has either the inclination or capability to achieve it.

Before Doklam, relations between the two countries took on an icy chill when Chinese leaders turned furious over the Dalai Lama's April 2017 visit to the northeastern Indian state of Arunachal Pradesh, which China claims as its own. On 8 April, over loud protests from China's government, the Dalai Lama addressed devotees from far and wide at the historic monastery in the border town of Tawang, where the sixth Dalai Lama was born more than three centuries ago.[695]

India and China view both the Dalai Lama and Arunachal Pradesh very differently. From India's perspective, the Dalai Lama is the spiritual leader of the Tibetan Buddhist community, and so has the right to minister to his followers at the great Tibetan Buddhist monastery in Tawang. And, because Arunachal Pradesh is a state of the Indian union, what happens there is India's decision alone.

In China's view, however, Arunachal Pradesh is not really India's. Yes, it officially belongs to India, they say, but only because of the McMahon Line, a boundary drawn by British imperialists in 1911, which China no longer accepts (though China did settle its boundary with Myanmar along the same line). The Chinese government refers to Arunachal Pradesh as South Tibet.

In any case, says China, the Dalai Lama is not a spiritual leader, but a political one. And, given his support for Tibetan

---

[695]'Live: China Wrong to Slam Delhi Over Dalai Lama, Says Arunachal CM', *The Quint*, 5 April 2017.

self-rule (Chinese officials angrily call him a 'splittist'[696]), his visit
to a sensitive border area was viewed as a deliberate provocation.

According to China's spokesman, allowing the Dalai Lama
to visit Arunachal Pradesh could harm bilateral relations, with
India facing the 'consequences.' China also summoned Indian
Ambassador Vijay Gokhale to register a formal protest.[697]

India, for its part, took a conciliatory approach. The Ministry
of External Affairs first attempted to assuage China, stating that
'no additional colour should be ascribed to the Dalai Lama's
religious and spiritual activities.' And, in the face of China's
increasingly intemperate fulminations, Prime Minister Narendra
Modi's government reiterated its respect for the 'One-China' policy,
urging China's government not to generate 'artificial controversy.'[698]

But China was not mollified. Instead, when the Dalai
Lama arrived in Arunachal Pradesh, the Chinese official media
declared that China might be 'forced to take tough measures.'
The *Global Times*, an English language tabloid published by the
Chinese Communist Party mouthpiece the *People's Daily*, took a
particularly belligerent tone. Citing China's GDP, which is 'several
times higher than that of India,' and its military capabilities, which
'can reach the Indian Ocean'—not to mention its proximity to
troubled Kashmir—it asked, 'if China engages in a geopolitical
game with India,' who will win?[699]

The same *Global Times* editorial stressed that this visit by the
Dalai Lama to Arunachal Pradesh was different from his previous
six—the last of which was in 2009—because he was 'received
and accompanied' by India's junior home minister, Kiren Rijiju.
India saw nothing unusual in Rijiju, an Arunachali politician,
being present for a major spiritual occasion. In democracies, such

---

[696]Jaime FlorCruz, 'Analysis: Why the Dalai Lama angers China', *CNN*, 18 February
2010.
[697]Apurva, 'Don't use Dalai Lama to harm our interests: China to India', *Indian
Express*, 7 April 2017.
[698]'Elizabeth Roche, 'India stands firm on Dalai Lama's Arunachal visit in face of
China opposition', *Livemint*, 5 April 2017.
[699]'India's use of Dalai Lama card tactless', *Global Times*, 6 April 2017.

public events involving popular religious figures are common, and politicians often enjoy the attention they attract by attending them.

But China preferred to use Rijiju's attendance as evidence that the event was, in fact, political, suggesting that India was using the visit as 'a diplomatic tool to put pressure on China.' The fundamental point, the *Global Times* stressed, was that the Dalai Lama 'is a highly politicized symbol in China's diplomacy,' so much so that a country's attitude toward him affects almost 'the entire relationship' with China.[700]

Despite the Modi government's refusal to back down in 2017, it climbed down in 2018, when it asked 'senior leaders' and 'government functionaries' to stay away from events planned in March and April by the Tibetan government in exile to mark the 60th anniversary of the Dalai Lama's arrival in India; this move was, ostensibly, to avoid exacerbating the Doklam crisis.[701]

The Modi government has been engaged in an awkward diplomatic trapeze act to avoid provoking China while simultaneously avoiding the impression of bending too far to accommodate its powerful neighbour. To give credit where credit is due, Mr Modi has tried to work with China, but with little to show for his efforts. His government hailed his July 2018 meeting with President Xi Jinping as an example of getting diplomacy back on track, only to be confronted with the embarrassment of confirming that it had been a 'no-agenda meeting'—in other words, one in which India has been unable to raise any of the issues relating to its neighbour's troublesome conduct, from Kashmir and CPEC to Masood Azhar, stapled visas, Arunachal Pradesh and Doklam. It does not appear to have occurred to Mr Modi that to have no agenda is in fact to adopt your adversary's agenda, since he prefers to talk on his own terms rather than about your issues.

Such setbacks in dealing with China have been common throughout Mr Modi's tenure. For example, in 2014, PM Modi

---

[700]Ibid.

[701]Shubajit Roy, 'Dalai Lama events in Delhi cancelled, Tibetans shift "Thank You India" function to Dharamsala', *Indian Express*, 6 March 2018.

not only welcomed Chinese President Xi Jinping to his hometown, Ahmedabad, on his own birthday; on that same trip, he also lifted the previous government's restrictions on Chinese investments in sensitive sectors of the Indian economy, such as ports and telecoms.[702] Chinese soldiers promptly crossed the disputed frontier with India in the Ladakh region of Jammu and Kashmir, going so far as to pitch tents on land that India considers its sovereign territory.[703]

That mini-crisis was followed by a series of policy setbacks that reflected China's scant regard for India's sensitivities on various issues. China opposed India's bid (strongly supported by the United States) for membership in the Nuclear Suppliers Group.[704] It blocked India's request to name Masood Azhar, the head of Jaish-e-Mohammed (a Pakistani terrorist group), to a United Nations Security Council blacklist, despite support for the move from the council's fourteen other members.[705]

China has also built its CPEC through Pakistan-controlled parts of Kashmir.[706] China itself recognizes that the territory is disputed, yet its government completely ignored India's objections to the violation of its sovereignty.

Against this background, China's expectation that India would respect its sensitivities was a bit rich. Yet China's arrogant approach is not new. In fact, its reaction to the Dalai Lama's visit to Arunachal Pradesh as well as Doklam, is of a piece with its behaviour in the South China Sea, where China insists that sovereignty should be determined according to its 'nine-dash line.'[707]

China expects other countries to fall into line when it makes

[702]'PM Modi welcomes Xi Jinping in Ahmedabad; India, China sign 3 pacts', *Times of India*, 18 September 2014.
[703]Victor Mallet, 'China-India border stand-off overshadows Xi Jinping's deals', *Financial Times*, 18 September 2014.
[704]'US reaffirms support to India's NSG bid', *Indian Express*, 11 January 2018.
[705]Elizabeth Roche, 'China again blocks bid in UN to list Masood Azhar as a global terrorist', *Livemint*, 2 November 2017.
[706]'China-Pakistan Economic Corridor: Pakistan's road of high hopes', *Indian Express*, 18 April 2016.
[707]David Lague, 'Analysis: China's nine-dashed line in South China Sea', *Reuters*, 25 May 2012.

such a demand, as the Philippines has done under President Rodrigo Duterte.[708] And China has proved willing to turn up the heat on those that don't, such as Japan and Vietnam.[709]

But India is somewhat bigger than China's other regional neighbours, and is made of sterner stuff. Rather than adopting a confrontational stand, China's leaders should work with us. If they don't, and instead move to follow through on their threats, they may well discover that India, too, has cards to play.

In *Pax Indica: India and the World of the Twenty-first Century*, I laid out a number of areas for possible co-operation with China, particularly in the multilateral arena. It is entirely possible that the relationship with China can veer away from confrontation towards at least coexistence if not extensive cooperation. That was also the conclusion reached by the Parliamentary Standing Committee for External Affairs in its review of India-China co-operation in 2017–18. But to pull this off successfully requires an adroit combination of political firmness, military preparedness to discourage any PLA adventurism (strong defences would serve to prevent military means actually having to be used), hard-headed economic negotiations and skilful diplomacy. It cannot be achieved through bursts of enthusiasm followed by sullen negativity, which have characterized the Modi government's attitude so far. Polite namaskars must be India's alternative to the kowtow.

---

[708]Panos Mourdoukoutas, 'Duterte's South China Sea Flip-Flops Will Put The Philippines In A Place It Doesn't Want To Be', *Forbes*, 30 May 2018.
[709]'Japan Will Soon Help Vietnam Extract Gas from the South China Sea. How Will China Respond?', *National Interest*, 11 August 2018.

chapter forty-four

BARGAINING WITH BANGLADESH

Of the many foreign policy decisions made by the Modi government, the only one I would deem an unqualified success was its ratification of the Land Boundary Agreement with our eastern neighbour. The boundary dispute dates back to the partition of the subcontinent in 1947.

The Partition of India by the British was a slapdash affair, concocted by a collapsing Empire in headlong retreat from its responsibilities. The border between the new states of India and Pakistan was hastily drawn by a lawyer, Sir Cyril Radcliffe, who had never visited India, and left numerous practical problems in its wake. In the eastern part of Pakistan, now (since 1971) the independent country of Bangladesh, Radcliffe's lines left two sets of anomalies behind: territories 'awarded' to one country that the other country (and its citizens) refused to relinquish (known to the lawyers as 'adverse possessions'), and tiny enclaves formally belonging to one country but located within, and totally surrounded by, the territory of the other. There are 111 Indian enclaves in Bangladesh spread over 17,000 acres and 51 Bangladesh enclaves in India spread over 7,110 acres,[710] so that a settlement would involve a net transfer of some 40 square kilometres of territory from India to its eastern neighbour.

Initial attempts to resolve these anomalies soon foundered on the hostility that had sprung up between the two nations soon after Partition. Bangladesh's independence from Pakistan as a result of Indian intervention in 1971 opened up the possibility of a resolution, and a Land Boundary Agreement was actually concluded in 1974, but a military coup in Bangladesh and

---

[710]Shubhajit Roy, 'Everything you need to know: Land swap in offing with Bangladesh to end disputes', *Indian Express*, 2 December 2014.

subsequent strains in the relationship with India put that agreement on indefinite hold. Though there were periodic bouts of bonhomie in the two countries' relationship through the 1990s, a succession of Indian governments proved unable, or unwilling, to squander the political capital necessary to legitimize the transfer of territory required to settle the dispute.

In 2011, then Prime Minister Manmohan Singh pushed anew for a permanent settlement, but his efforts stumbled in the face of domestic resistance, both from a coalition ally and from the Opposition, especially the BJP, whose votes would have been indispensable for the constitutional amendment required to implement the deal. The BJP had blocked the Bill in Parliament, with the then Leader of the Opposition in the Upper House, Arun Jaitley, a lawyer himself, arguing that the territory of India was an integral part of the Constitution and 'cannot be reduced or altered by an amendment.'[711]

The BJP's victory, however, was followed by a U-turn on most of the policy positions it had adopted in Opposition. The boundary with Bangladesh proved no exception. Visiting Dhaka as her first foreign stop after becoming foreign minister, the BJP's Sushma Swaraj pledged to go through with the Land Boundary Agreement, and referred it to the Parliamentary Standing Committee on External Affairs for review.[712] The committee, which I head, deliberated over three weeks of hearings, summoning senior representatives of the Foreign Ministry, the Home Ministry and the government of the most affected state, West Bengal. On Monday, 7 December 2014, it unanimously recommended that Parliament proceed to ratify the Constitutional Amendment. Mr Jaitley, now the country's finance minister and a prominent member of the cabinet, refrained from reiterating his previous views, and with Prime Minister Modi himself announcing his support for the

---

[711]Manan Kumar, 'Why Narendra Modi made a U turn on Land Boundary Agreement?', *DNA*, 2 December 2014.
[712]'Sushma bid to build Dhaka bridge - No breakthrough on two pacts opposed by Mamata, say officials', *Telegraph India*, 27 June 2014.

deal, passage through Parliament seemed assured. But it took the government four more months—and a last-minute hurdle in the form of a demand by the Assam unit of the BJP that the state be left out of the deal, something stoutly resisted by the Congress—before they finally brought it to Parliament, unchanged, for passage.[713]

The agreement faced no hurdles in Bangladesh, which gains the most from a settlement, both territorially and in stature in relation to its giant neighbour. In India, the most problematic issue remains the perception of a surrender of territory. It has never been sufficiently explained to the public that neither country will, in fact, actually be giving up any territory it currently controls. The enclaves are lawless tracts within sovereign countries, where the writ of their nominal overlord does not run. India, for instance, has no access to the Indian enclaves within Bangladesh—there are no customs posts, border markings, post offices or police thanas to reflect their notional Indian sovereignty. The people inhabiting these enclaves are theoretically Indian citizens, without any of the rights and privileges Indian citizens in the rest of India are able to exercise. Ending the anomaly will merely regularize the reality, and any loss of territory is purely on paper.

Still, any residents of the Indian enclaves who wish to migrate to India after the settlement would have a legal right to do so. If they fail to exercise this option, their status is converted to Bangladeshi, along with the territory they inhabit. Most people are expected to opt to remain where they are, though, since any connection to the rest of India must have faded since 1947.

The agreement will be a major boost to the already warm relations between New Delhi and Dhaka. The Awami League government in Bangladesh under Sheikh Hasina Wajed has extended India an unprecedented level of cooperation in the area of security and counterterrorism. Under less friendly regimes, Bangladesh had

---

[713]P Vaidyanathan Iyer, 'Congress braces for a fight if Assam kept out of land boundary deal', *Indian Express*, 1 May 2015.

been a haven for assorted terrorist and militant groups who used to wreak havoc in India and find refuge in Bangladesh. Hasina's government has not just denied these groups shelter but actively intercepted them, arrested some of their leaders and even handed wanted terrorists over to the Indian government. As she pointed out to me when we met in Dhaka in October 2014, if bombs are not going off in Assam these days, it is because of her government's actions against the terrorists who used to set them off.

If Indians and in particular Assamese are sleeping safer these days, it is thanks to the government in Dhaka. Giving Bangladesh legal rights to territory within its own borders is the least India can do to say thank you. With the 100th Constitutional Amendment, we have finally done so.

chapter forty-five

HAVE WE LOST NEPAL?

In the United States of the early 1950s, as Mao's Communist party regime consolidated its hold on China and marched into Tibet, exiling Washington's favourite Generalissimo, Chiang Kai-Shek, to the island of Taiwan, the American strategic community was convulsed in a debate over 'Who Lost China?' I only hope that nearly seven decades later their Indian equivalents will not be letting out the anguished cry, 'Who Lost Nepal?'

As a result of a slew of unpopular decisions, India seems bent on driving Nepal into the arms of China and others. As I have pointed out, it is significant that the first state visitor, Prime Minister of Nepal K. P. Sharma Oli received, after being sworn in on 15 February 2018, was the Pakistani prime minister, S. K. Abbasi.[714]

There is, of course, only one place for fingers to be pointed, and that is at our own government in New Delhi. Despite its increasingly feeble denials, India's de facto blockade of Nepal for the past few years has choked the country's economy, cut off its oil supplies, caused genuine hardship and provoked a groundswell of hostility against our country—from the one place on the planet whose relationship with us is so fraternal that we maintain open borders with it.

How did this come to pass, and why? India's displeasure at Nepal's new constitution and its refusal to accommodate the desires of its Madhesi and Tharu population was understandable. The people of the Terai (or the Madhes, as Indians prefer to call the region south of the hills abutting our border) are in many ways kin to—and essentially indistinguishable from—their brethren on

---

[714]Elizabeth Roche, 'Why India is keeping a close eye on Pakistan PM's visit to Nepal', *Livemint*, 5 March 2018.

our side of the frontier.

Some Nepalis consider Madhesis to be essentially transplanted Biharis, but they have been there for centuries and more, and no one contests their legitimate claim to an honoured role in shaping Nepal's political destiny. But rather than choosing an inclusive path by giving them their own autonomous regions or provinces, the new constitution of the country that came into effect in September 2015 essentially rendered them a minority in almost every province bar one.

The unhappiness of most of the Madhesi people with this decision, and the rioting that followed the announcement of the new provinces, added to India's disquiet, since problems in Nepal inevitably spill over into India. It is unofficially estimated that at the height of the Nepalese civil war less than a decade ago, 7 million of Nepal's 27 million people had sought refuge in India (undocumented, since Nepalis need no passports to come here).

If the anger in the Terai leads to a separatist movement, for instance, India will likely bear the brunt of a new refugee crisis. New Delhi felt, understandably, that Kathmandu's leadership, overwhelmingly composed of the dominant hill elites, should have taken India's concerns into account before announcing a constitution so fraught with potential problems.

But it's a far cry from feeling fraternal concern about a vital neighbour making a major political error and manifesting that irritation through virtually cutting off that country's lifeline from our country, thereby giving rise to profound resentment of what is justifiably portrayed as Big Brother's bullying. The suspicion that in doing so the BJP government was pandering to voters in Bihar's assembly polls that were being held at the time was not entirely unfounded.

The fact is there's enough blame to be cast on our side too. The foreign secretary was sent as a special envoy to warn Kathmandu not to embark on a negative course, but that was just days before the constitution was promulgated and after it had already been agreed among all the major national political parties. The time for discreet but strong-arm diplomacy was months earlier, when the signs were apparent that the constitution was likely not to be the inclusive one India had hoped for.

The then foreign secretary was an outstandingly able diplomat, but he was no Nepal expert and had never served there. A political envoy, or an all-party team of Indian political leaders with well-established contacts in that country, should have been dispatched before the summer with a clear and unambiguous message of the importance India attached to a formula acceptable to all shades of Nepali opinion.

I have reason to believe our embassy, which was led by Ambassador Ranjit Rae (who was succeeded by Manjeev Singh Puri in 2017), read the warning signs in time and sent urgent messages to New Delhi calling for early diplomatic intervention. These were ignored. As I have mentioned earlier, one astute observer told me privately that the 'PMO took its eyes off the ball'.

That was the Modi government's first mistake. By the time it woke up to the impending crisis and dispatched the foreign secretary to Kathmandu, it was already too late. The time for quiet, discreet but effective diplomacy had long since passed; the constitution was already a 'done deal' before we even showed our cards.

When the constitution-makers in Kathmandu went ahead and issued the constitution they had already agreed upon, India reacted with a pique unbecoming of a major regional power. We showed our displeasure publicly by, in effect, cutting off essential supplies on which all Nepalis are dependent.

The problem was not just that this came across as overbearing, but that it had all the subtlety of a blunderbuss: instead of sending a message to the elite in the hills, we hurt people we didn't want to hurt—the aam aadmi of Nepalis. An ordinary worker in Kathmandu who can't get an auto-rickshaw to take his pregnant wife to a hospital because there's no petrol in the pumps isn't going to worry about the niceties of constitutional inclusiveness. He is just going to curse India for doing this to him. We made enemies of the very people we have always claimed are our brothers.

And what has the Modi government achieved by doing this? A basic rule of international politics is that you apply pressure calibrated to a desired outcome—in this case, changes acceptable to the people of the Terai. But instead we imposed a blockade after the constitution had already been adopted; it would be impossible for any government in Kathmandu to change it at this stage under Indian pressure without being perceived as surrendering its sovereignty. So we incurred deep unpopularity in the hills without gaining anything concrete for the Madhesis—a lose-lose proposition.

On top of that New Delhi allowed itself to be identified with the losing side in the prime ministerial race, unsubtly backing Sushil Koirala and turning the once-Indophile Oli into a raging anti-Indian chauvinist. Well, Oli is now the prime minister, Delhi: deal with it.

That was how an over-centralized Modi regime succeeded in alienating Nepal. Today, China is busy making inroads into the north, building roads, opening railway lines into Nepal, and grandly offering landlocked Nepal access to its ports as an alternative (though hardly a credible alternative, given their distance from the country) to Nepal's traditional sea outlet in Kolkata. For all the professions of fraternal bonhomie that have accompanied later interactions between the Indian and Nepali prime ministers, it is clear that a significant change has occurred in the relationship, to which India has no choice but to adjust. The decision by Prime Minister Oli to pull his country out of the BIMSTEC (Bay of Bengal Initiative for Multi-Sectoral Technical and Economic Cooperation) military exercise at the last minute in September 2018 pointed to continued mistrust between the two governments, to which Mr Modi's policies and conduct appear to have contributed.[715]

---

[715]Shastri Ramachandran, 'Nepal PM KP Oli sees "mischief" in India visit of ruling party chairman', DNA, 13 September 2018.

The Modi mess in Nepal adds to the growing sense of disquiet amongst students of Indian foreign policy about the Modi government's management of relations on the subcontinent. A combination of arrogance and ineptitude is all too often visible where subtlety and pro-active diplomacy could have delivered the desired results.

chapter forty-six

LET US BE HUMANE TO THE ROHINGYAS

I

The Rohingya crisis has led to a great deal of incoherent commentary in our media and around the world of late. Globally, the story has centred around the demonization of Daw Aung San Suu Kyi, the Nobel Peace Prize laureate who is the de facto leader of her country. She is being assailed as complicit in her military's ethnic cleansing of the Rohingya minority. There have even been calls to strip her of her Nobel; headline writers have dubbed her 'ig-nobel'. This is misguided and ill-informed, since it is the Burmese military that controls the Rohingya policy and not her, but that is another story and need not detain us here.

There are roughly 40,000 Rohingyas in India at the moment and our attitude towards them has ranged from the appalling to the less than humanitarian. When the crisis first spilled over our border our response was disgraceful. The minister of state (Home), Kiren Rijiju, declared his government's intention to deport all Rohingya refugees—even those with documents from the United Nations High Commissioner for Refugees (UNHCR) recognizing them as such—as illegal migrants.[716]

This would have been an extraordinary step to take, because India has had a proud humanitarian record of granting asylum to persecuted groups for over 2,000 years. Swami Vivekananda, in his famous address to the World Parliament of Religions in Chicago in 1893, spoke of his country as a haven for the persecuted, taking pride in Hindus' acceptance of Jewish and Zoroastrian refugees.[717]

---

[716]Krishna N. Das and Sanjeev Miglani, 'India says to deport all Rohingya regardless of U.N. registration', *Reuters*, 14 August 2017.
[717]'Full text of Swami Vivekananda's Chicago speech of 1893', *Business Standard*, 11 September 2017.

In recent years, Tibetans, Bengalis persecuted by the Pakistani army in 1971, ethnic Tamils from Sri Lanka, Nepalis fleeing their civil war, the Chakmas of Bangladesh, Afghans and an assortment of individual Iranians, Iraqis and Syrians, and Africans have been among those given refuge in India, with various degrees of formal legality. This is our traditional practice and there has been little serious dissent about it anywhere in the country.

There is one major difference, though: unlike the majority of those cases (the individual Middle Easterners and Afghans excepted), the Rohingyas are all Muslim. The arguments advanced by Mr Rijiju all revolve around this inconvenient fact. The Rohingyas, he says, are susceptible to recruitment by terrorist groups; they 'pose grave security challenges'; their presence leads to social, political and cultural problems; and the government is anxious to 'ensure the demographic pattern of India is not disturbed'.[718] In other words, we didn't want to play host to large numbers of Muslim refugees. This is, in a word, appalling (and the government has not offered a shred of evidence for the suggestion that Rohingyas are in any way complicit in terrorism in our country).

There was no immediate threat to the Rohingyas, however, because our government had overlooked an inconvenient fact before Mr Rijiju made his statement: we had no place to deport the Rohingyas to. They all hail from Rakhine province in Myanmar, where their ancestors settled under British rule some 150 years ago, but Myanmar refuses to recognize them among the 135 ethnic groups listed under its 1982 Citizenship Act, considering them foreigners.[719]

Yangon therefore has no obligation to take back people it considers foreigners, whose presence in their country they, however outrageously, deem illegal. (Indeed, in Myanmar, the very word Rohingya is taboo: they can only be called 'Bengali', in other words

---

[718]Deepak K. Singh, 'Embrace the Rohingya', *Indian Express*, 13 September 2017.
[719]Angela Dewan, 'Who are the Rohingya and why are they fleeing?', *CNN*, 13 September 2017.

illegal migrants from Bangladesh.[720]) But Bangladesh acknowledges no responsibility for people who have, for the most part, resided in the Arakan area for a couple of centuries.

After a massive outcry, the government walked back its inhumane idea of involuntary deportation and has now begun talking of providing assistance to Bangladesh to resettle Rohingya refugees there as well as providing assistance to Rakhine state so that the refugees can return there safely.[721] All this is much better than our government's initial reaction to the Rohingyas, but it is still far from implementability. In the meantime, the legal status of these unfortunates remains indeterminate, depriving them of the possibility of finding legal employment, or of improving their makeshift (and often wretched) living conditions.

Legalities aside, there is also a simple moral case here. Our so-called Hindu nationalists are, as usual, forgetting the values on which the Hindu faith is based, one cardinal principle of which is 'atithi devo bhava', the guest is like God. The timeless values invoked by Swami Vivekananda—and more recently by Pandit Nehru in welcoming the Tibetan refugees—cannot be cast aside to suit the prejudices of the ruling party, without doing violence to the principles they embody. To make matters worse, the BJP government has been actively promoting the passage of a new law, the Citizenship Amendment Bill, that would grant the right of Indian citizenship to refugees from Myanmar and every other of India's subcontinental neighbours, provided they are not Muslim.[722] The Bill proposes citizenship to six persecuted minorities who come to India from neighbouring countries, but it names Hindus, Jains, Sikhs, Parsis, Christians and Buddhists alone—not Muslims. Humanitarian policy that discriminates on the basis of religion is not humanitarianism at all, but bigotry.

---

[720]'The Most Unwanted: A gripping account of Rohingya refugees living in India', *Indian Express*, 26 June 2018.
[721]'India extends support to Bangladesh for resolving Rohingya crisis', *The Hindu*, 9 April 2018.
[722]Nafees Ahmed, 'Rohingyas flee Myanmar: India must drop religious criteria in refugee law', *Business Standard*, 6 September 2017.

Refugees bring a great deal to their host countries. Albert Einstein was a refugee. Tom Stoppard was a refugee. In our own country, Milkha Singh was a refugee. They fled their homelands for their lives and found a welcome in a new home, to which they brought lustre through their own achievements.

A country of over 1.3 billion people can easily welcome 40,000 Rohingyas. Let us stop allowing the ruling party's bigotry to undermine more than two millennia of Indian tradition. Let us be humane to the Rohingyas—and in that way, let us be true to ourselves.

II

The Rohingya situation finds an echo in a second potential humanitarian disaster that also involves Bengali Muslims, this time in Assam. Seventy-one years after the partition of India, and forty-seven years after the subsequent rebirth of the former East Pakistan as Bangladesh, one of the legacies of the messy division of the subcontinent has come back to haunt the country. The crisis in mid-2018 over the publication of a National Register of Citizens (NRC) in the Indian state of Assam has thrown into doubt the citizenship, and the future, of some four million human beings, with incalculable consequences for the peace of the region.

The departing British partitioned India in 1947 on the basis of religion, in order to create a Muslim state, Pakistan, out of Muslim-majority provinces in the West and East of India. East Pakistan seceded in 1971 to form Bangladesh after a brutal and genocidal campaign by the Pakistani army had driven some 10 million refugees to India. Once India had vanquished Pakistan in war and the Pakistani army in the east surrendered, the refugees streamed back home to newly-independent Bangladesh. But some, perhaps, stayed on in India, merging seamlessly into the population.

Over the course of the next few years, they were joined by millions of other migrants from Bangladesh, fleeing economic hardship and land scarcity in an overcrowded country. While those who slipped into the Indian state of West Bengal were easily assimilated by their fellow Bengalis, those who made new homes in the north-eastern state of Assam were culturally, linguistically, ethnically and religiously different from the majority of their Assamese neighbours. Fearing they were being squeezed out of land and job opportunities in their own country, Assamese students began mass protests in the 1980s, which occasionally erupted into violence and made Assam all but ungovernable. A pair of savage massacres of Bengali Muslim migrant groups, including of some 3,000 in the Assamese village of Nellie in 1983, revealed the extent of the crisis. The agitation was only defused when then Indian Prime Minister Rajiv Gandhi concluded an 'Assam Accord' in 1985, pledging to identify all those who had migrated illegally from Bangladesh into Assam since 1971.

This was easier said than done, and despite estimates of 20 million illegal immigrants from Bangladesh, an assortment of tribunals set up to identify foreigners failed to spot more than a few thousand over the years. No concrete action was taken, and the problem was left to simmer for decades by successive governments. But the election of a hardline Hindutva government in 2014 revived the process, under Supreme Court supervision. When it concluded the main phase of its work at the end of July, it published the NRC, a list of persons who could provide proof of antecedents in Assam preceding the accord's cut-off date of 1971. Just over 4 million people, who could not, found themselves rendered, in effect, stateless.

There is still time to appeal the findings of the register, and it is anticipated that some of the more obvious errors of omission— some members of a family listed and others not, for instance—will be swiftly rectified. But the question that bedevils Assam today is: what happens to the rest?

The ruling Bharatiya Janata Party of Prime Minister Narendra Modi is simultaneously taking credit for having identified 'foreigners', and sheltering behind the protection of the Supreme Court's supervision of the process. The implication is that this is a neutral exercise that has nothing to do with politics. But at bottom the exercise is indeed intensely political—since it is about who can own land, claim jobs and vote in BJP-ruled Assam.

Whatever the size of the final list of foreigners deemed ineligible for Indian citizenship, it is assumed that the excluded will be overwhelmingly, if not entirely, Bengali Muslims. What will happen to them? Some speak glibly of deporting them to Bangladesh. But there is no deportation agreement in place between New Delhi and Dhaka, and Bangladesh has made it clear that it assumes no responsibility for people who are not on its soil. Will they be turfed out of their homes in Assam and find themselves with no place to go?

Some suggest the setting up of camps to house these people temporarily till Bangladesh can take them back, a prospect that has human rights groups horrified—not least since that day may never come. Indeed, Bangladesh is one of the few neighbouring countries with which the present government of India has been able to maintain good relations. Creating a migration crisis, or worse still, attempting forced deportations, will destabilize a relationship that is vital to India.

The human implications of the NRC list are also troubling. Many who may indeed have come to India after 1971 (and are therefore deemed ineligible under the terms of the accord) have lived in Assam for over four decades and know no other home. Can they now be stripped of the rights they have exercised in democratic India most of their lives?

It has been cynically suggested that a principal purpose of the exercise has been to strip Bengali Muslims of the right to vote, as general elections loom in early 2019. In a state of 26 million inhabitants, disenfranchising 4 million could have a significant impact on the electoral fortunes of the ruling party, which is not known to enjoy much support among India's Muslim electorate. But the legal implications of such an action have yet to be parsed, and will be open to challenge in the courts.

So far, the crisis created by the NRC has been non-violent, but as tensions mount on both sides of the issue, the risk of an eruption is ever-present. Is an accord arrived at in 1985, setting a cut-off date in 1971, necessarily the best framework to resolve the issue in 2018? Can democratic India afford to ignore the human rights of a few million people who have been living on its soil for decades? While protecting India's sovereignty and the integrity of its citizenship are laudable principles, can they be applied in practice to create stateless people whose lives would suddenly be plunged into limbo?

There are no clear answers to any of these questions, though passionate voices on both sides of the argument have no doubt what those answers should be. At a time when the BJP's majoritarian assertiveness has already raised concerns around the world, the answers India finds will mark a hugely important step in the evolution of its turbulent democracy.

chapter forty-seven

LOOTING AND SCOOTING

One of the questions that maddens right-thinking Indians is this one: why do so many Indians accused of fraud and cheating flee abroad, particularly to London, and why can't we just bring them back to face justice?

The string of high-profile fugitives from the law who have managed to escape India in recent years—in order of disappearance, Lalit Modi, Vijay Mallya, and Nirav Modi, but also many lesser-known figures before and between them—has brought the spotlight on to the issue of extradition. One of the basic principles of criminal law is that it is applicable to only the territory of the state of origin; it does not extend to foreign jurisdictions. However, because of the increasingly transnational nature of crime, and the habit of criminals taking refuge in foreign countries to escape the reach of the law, extradition laws were framed to bridge the limitations of criminal law.

Extradition is the transfer of a person by a state in which he or she resides, to another state where such person is required to face a criminal trial or to serve a sentence for an offence for which that person has already been convicted. Therefore, a request for extradition can take place when a person is under investigation, under trial or when convicted.

The Extradition Act, 1962, governs the law of extradition in India. Section 3 of the Act states that the Act is applicable to foreign states notified by the central government. That notification takes place when India enters into an extradition treaty with another country. This has to be negotiated; when both countries agree, an extradition treaty sets out the conditions and procedure for extradition, which, by and large, incorporate the basic internationally accepted principles of extradition law.

The extradition request must be in relation to an 'extraditable offence': not all criminal offences come under this definition, as it usually encompasses serious offences. This is determined by each individual treaty. For instance, Article 2 of the 1997 Extradition Treaty signed by India and the USA states that if an offence attracts more than one year of imprisonment, then it shall be considered an 'extraditable offence'. Extradition treaties also incorporate the principle of 'dual criminality', whereby the offence for which a person is being extradited, must be a criminal offence in the requesting country as well as in the requested country.

But that's not all. When you request extradition, you have to furnish compelling justification—that is, the requesting country must provide material to establish a prima facie case against the concerned person, to the satisfaction of the requested country, in order to commence an extradition process. Legal principles specify that the extradited person must be only prosecuted for the offence mentioned in the extradition request, and not for any other offence. If the requesting country wishes to prosecute the person for additional offences, the person must be returned to the requested country and a fresh process of extradition has to be considered.

Finally, the person must be assured a fair trial in the requesting country, in line with internationally accepted human rights standards. The requested state is not supposed to enquire into the nature of the criminal justice system in the requesting state; however, if the criminal justice system in the requesting state is seen, on the face of it, to be contrary to fundamental tenets of justice, then the requested state may question the procedure of the requesting state. These principles are incorporated to protect individuals from political persecution and fishing expeditions by vindictive foreign governments. Many European states refuse to extradite wanted criminals to India on the grounds that India retains the death penalty, which most European democracies consider a barbaric practice. India has, in some cases, promised a European court that the extradited offender will not be executed, and has obtained extradition only on the basis of such an assurance.

That was how Portugal agreed to extradite the notorious gangster Abu Salem; had he been arrested in India, he would almost certainly have faced the noose for the crimes for which he was convicted.

Extradition treaties are also governed by the 'principle of reciprocity', under which, if a foreign country has a stated position that it won't extradite its nationals to other countries, then India also bars the extradition of its nationals to such a country. This practice is followed by India in relation to certain countries in the Middle East, such as Kuwait, Bahrain, Saudi Arabia and the UAE, whose nationals are not extraditable to India from their home countries.

India has extradition treaties with forty-two countries and more limited 'arrangements' with nine others.[723] While India's treaty partners have treaty obligations to consider India's requests, in the absence of a treaty, it is a matter for the foreign country to consider, in accordance with its domestic laws and procedures, whether it wants to agree to India's extradition request or not. Nevertheless, India can extradite individuals from countries with which it does not have extradition treaties if it is backed by the principle of reciprocity. In other words, if India assures the requested state that in future it will similarly extradite a person from the country if a proper extradition request is made, then the requested state may extradite a person wanted by the Indian authorities. But just because we have an extradition treaty does not mean we will immediately get a fugitive extradited; there is a process to be followed, and we have not been doing too well with it.

An extradition request is sent by the requesting country through appropriate diplomatic channels. If a case is pending before a court in India and the accused evades the summons of the court, then it may issue a warrant of arrest. This can be sent to foreign authorities for execution, if the accused is in a

---

[723]Poulomi Banerjee, 'Chinks in India's armour: Why Mallya may escape extradition', *Hindustan Times*, 22 May 2016.

foreign jurisdiction, as per Section 105 of our country's Criminal Procedure Code, and the procedure for this process is governed by the Mutual Legal Assistance Treaties (referred to as 'MLATs') between the concerned countries.

However, despite the existence of an extensive legal framework to extradite fugitives, India has a dismal record in successfully convincing other jurisdictions, particularly the UK, about the need to extradite such people.[724] Why has London become such a haven of choice for fleeing Indian crooks? The dismal conditions in Indian jails, the slow pace of our criminal prosecution mechanism as well as the presence of the death penalty, have been cited by British courts as reasons for their denial of extradition requests by India. In a case seeking the extradition of Sanjeev Kumar Chawla, a man accused of cricket match-fixing in 2000, even though the court in London was convinced that there existed a prima facie case against him, it held that the poor conditions in Tihar Jail amount to a violation of his basic human rights and therefore declined the request.[725] Similarly, India's request for the extradition of Jatinder Angurala, a person accused of financial fraud, was declined by a court in the UK, as the request was made in 2015, even though the acts were supposedly committed in the early 1990s. The British court concluded that it would be unfair to extradite an aged person after such a long passage of time.

The largest number of successful extraditions since 2002 (nineteen persons out of a grand total of just sixty-five fugitives extradited to India altogether[726]) has been from the UAE. It is depressing to note that despite numerous extradition requests against various individuals in the UK, only one person has been extradited to India in the past twenty-five years. The failure of the Indian authorities to undertake prison reforms and improve our system of criminal prosecution has therefore acted as a major

---

[724]'From Mallya to Nirav Modi, the UK remains the preferred hideout of Indian fugitives', *Times of India*, 15 June 2018.
[725]'UK rejects two Indian extradition requests', *Times of India*, 5 November 2017.
[726]'List of fugitives extradited by foreign governments to India', www.mea.gov.in

hurdle in India's efforts to nab fugitives abroad.

The case now proceeding against Vijay Mallya, and the failure to proceed against Lalit Modi, are litmus tests for the Indian extradition process. If India fails to successfully rebut Mallya's reported claims of political victimization, then the courts in the UK may look at the Indian request in a negative manner. As his lawyers have once again harped on the poor conditions of jails in India, the lawyers for the Government of India have stressed that Mallya will be kept in Arthur Road Jail in Mumbai, with facilities better than the average Indian jail. At the time of writing, it remains to be seen how the UK courts will react to this in Mallya's case. However, in relation to Lalit Modi, even though India was reported to have forwarded the warrant for arrest against Modi for money laundering, his sympathizers in the present government, who have been revealed to include the foreign minister herself, have shown no interest in proceeding with a formal extradition request. Indeed, in response to a question in the Lok Sabha on 9 August 2017, the MoS for External Affairs claimed that 'the Ministry of External Affairs has not received any formal request for extradition of Mr Lalit Modi from the concerned law enforcement agencies in India.'[727]

India's dismal record in extraditing fugitives, particularly those in the UK, must be immediately corrected through a comprehensive review of the manner in which we present our extradition requests, as well as undertaking extensive reforms in our criminal justice system in order to end the perception of our jails as being guaranteed horror houses of grime, deprivation and torture. The abolition of the death penalty, which has no deterrence value nor any penological justification, would also improve our image as a country committed to the ethos of justice. At the same time, we must undertake a review of our bilateral extradition treaties, in order to strengthen our ability to seek the extradition of individual

---

[727]'No formal extradition request submitted against Lalit Modi to MEA', *Hindustan Times*, 14 May 2017.

fugitives. However, above all, we require firm political will, which has been singularly lacking in the Modi government, to ensure that the cases are brought to their logical conclusion—otherwise we will soon become known as the country of choice for those who wish to loot and scoot, since so few are successfully brought back.

chapter forty-eight

PROTECTING OUR MIGRANTS

Among the unsung factors in India's near-miraculous survival of the global economic recession some years ago were the remittances that kept coming in from our mainly blue-collar workers in the Gulf. India receives the highest amount of remittances in the world at roughly $69 billion, almost three times the amount of FDI that comes into the country.[728]

By far the largest share comes from the Gulf countries—Bahrain, Kuwait, Oman, Qatar, Saudi Arabia, and the UAE—which contributed 32 per cent to the total amount in 2017. And most of those represent the sweat and toil of labourers, masons, clerks, shop assistants and other working class Indians who never lost their faith in our country, or diluted their commitment to India, at a time when well-heeled Indian capitalists preferred to invest their money abroad.

And yet, despite their invaluable contributions to our country, many Indian migrant workers continue to face exploitative working conditions, forced labour, non-payment of wages and other forms of human rights abuse that sometimes plunge them into slavery-like conditions. These workers, the majority of whom are low-paid and semi-skilled or unskilled, are employed as cooks, cleaners, domestic workers, plumbers and construction labourers. And India could do far more to help them in their distress.

Let us look at the kinds of challenges that migrant workers face:

- *Deception by visa brokers and recruiting agents*: They are victims of various forms of deception and trickery at the recruitment stage. These include excess charges for visas and other travel documents, processing of fake travel documents

---

[728]'India highest recipient of remittances at $69 bn', *The Hindu*, 23 April 2018.

without informing the workers of their illegitimate status, recruitment for non-existent jobs, misrepresenting the job and working conditions, providing falsely inflated loans that lead to situations of bonded labour. As an MP, I have heard countless stories of migrant workers landing in the wrong country and being stranded there, being jailed for having the wrong documents, finding their salary or work conditions are not what they were promised. This is compounded by:

- *Lack of awareness of pre-departure training*: Lack of authentic and timely information relating to overseas employment, recruitment agencies and emigration procedures makes workers dependent on intermediaries and vulnerable to exploitation. And:

- *Lack of access to remedies*: The power differential between workers and recruiting agents makes it difficult for workers who face abuse to secure justice. Enforcement mechanisms are not strong enough and complaints registered rarely lead to convictions.

International Migrants Day, 18 December, celebrates the spirit of millions of migrants across the world. It recognizes that a large section of these men and women put their freedom and sometimes even their lives at risk to follow their dreams and aspirations. It's a good occasion for us in India to think of how we can protect our migrants better.

The Emigration Act, 1983, which has been used to regulate the recruitment and employment of migrant workers, has been criticized by government commissions and NGOs such as Amnesty International India. The government-commissioned report by the Ministry of Overseas Affairs in 2009 stated in its recommendations: 'The institutional failure in effectively addressing corruption and fraudulence in the overseas recruitment system cannot be rectified by cosmetic changes but calls for a comprehensive institutional reform. The new institution should be liberal but capable of tackling the complex layers of corruption and multiplicity of players with greater coordination and efficiency to ensure free but orderly emigration of Indian workers to the overseas labour market. It should also be preventive and remedial in its focus when it seeks to streamline the overseas recruitment system.'

Amnesty International India's 2014 report titled 'Exploited dreams: Dispatches from Indian migrant workers in Saudi Arabia'[729] highlighted how India has failed to meet its international obligations to protect the rights of migrant workers and prevent trafficking and forced labour. The Philippines law on migrant workers in its statute places the dignity of its migrant workers above their contribution to the national economy through their foreign exchange remittances—and to that end seeks to provide adequate and timely social, economic and legal services to its migrant population. 'The existence of the overseas employment program rests solely on the assurance that the dignity and fundamental human rights and freedoms of the Filipino citizens shall not, at any time, be compromised or violated' says the Migrant Workers and Overseas Filipinos Act, 1995.

Our Emigration Act expresses no such sentiment.

Their law also recognizes NGOs as key partners in the protection of migrant workers and seeks to cooperate with them for the promotion of migrant welfare. Ours doesn't.

Recognizing the severe deficiencies of the existing law, the UPA government had started the process of trying to improve emigration legislation on the lines of the Philippines Migrant Workers Act, but this new legislation has not yet come about. Previous reports by the Ministry of Overseas Indian Affairs have specified the shortcomings of the recruitment process and expressed the need to modernize the legislative framework into a more effective instrument in facilitating legal migration and empowering emigrants.

Now it's time for the Modi government to treat this issue with the seriousness it deserves. Based on research and field experiences, organizations like Amnesty International India and MPs like myself

[729]www.amnesty.org, 4 July 2014, Index number: ASA 20/025/2014.

have come forward to call for a new law that provides adequate protection services to migrant workers before they depart. When it comes to migrant workers, it should be the state's number one priority to protect their lives and dignity in a foreign country. A new law that empowers workers with adequate information and support from their home country will help reduce the likelihood of exploitation abroad.

In a country like ours, with unemployment and underemployment problems and excess human resources, a robust emigration law will help fulfil the aspirations of millions of India's citizens going abroad in search of better economic opportunities.

chapter forty-nine

A MAN OF DESTINY? NOT QUITE

The phrase 'man of destiny' is most commonly associated with Napoleon Bonaparte. It is used to describe Napoleon's unshakeable belief in his own destiny as someone who would rule the world despite his origins as a member of an impecunious Corsican family and the numerous setbacks he encountered in his drive to greatness.

Narendra Modi can certainly be described as Napoleonic in his single-minded pursuit of power and his belief in his own destiny from a very young age. Many of his admirers point to his visionary speeches, his soaring ambition, and his unshakeable faith in his own and India's destiny, as evidence that he has the special qualities that the iconic French leader possessed. However, while Napoleon is remembered, despite all his shortcomings, for his brilliant foresight and his belief in, and implementation of, many of the ideas that are fundamental to the world today—among them religious tolerance, property rights, and equality before the law—the same cannot be said of Narendra Modi. His speeches have been compelling, but he has been unable to implement his ideas. At the same time, he has failed to prevent or stop forces that have undermined India's prospects. On his watch, forces of bigotry, communalism and division have been unleashed that have set India back decades, and make it difficult to rate him positively on practically any quality that defines a great statesman and ruler.

In this chapter I will try and sum up much of what I have examined in this book about the record thus far of India's paradoxical prime minister. (Any repetition of ideas previously expressed in the book is deliberate as I am seeking here to reiterate what I believe are the main failings and contradictions inherent in Narendra Modi.)

Let's start with Mr Modi's impact on the lives of Indians and Indian society that I look at in Section II, 'The Modi-fication of

India'. Just one incident will serve to sum up the deleterious effect he has had on so much that is good and intrinsic to our country. His failing was hammered home to him by Atal Bihari Vajpayee, the greater BJP prime minister in most Indians' reckoning, in 2002, when Mr Vajpayee rapped Mr Modi on the knuckles for failing to observe raj dharma, the dharmic code of conduct that rulers are expected to follow. One of the texts in which raj dharma is explicated is the Shanti Parva of the Mahabharata. In the last essay he ever wrote, 'Living with the Mahabharata', published in *Seminar* in April 2010, the great philosopher, writer and Mahabharata scholar Chaturvedi Badrinath (1923–2010) defined the dharma of the ruler in the following way: 'The protecting of the people, this is the highest dharma of the king. Indeed, the protecting of all living beings with kindness towards them, is the highest dharma. Therefore, that king who has the character of protecting with kindness, those who know what dharma truly is regard as the highest dharma.'[730]

Mr Badrinath then goes on to say that good governance, according to the Mahabharata, is to protect people from fear. He quotes the epic as laying down the following injunctions: 'Let the king protect his subjects from their fear of him; from their fear of others; from their fear of each other; and from their fear of things that are not human.' Yet today the Modi regime has generated what I have already quoted a columnist as dubbing 'an ecosystem of fear'. On every one of these counts, Narendra Modi and the government he leads have failed dismally. The India we live in now is a society that is polarized and fearful. Minorities, liberals, women and Dalits are harassed and brutalized with impunity and lumpen thugs terrorize all and sundry in the name of Hindutva.

This is the India Prime Minister Narendra Modi presides over, not the secular, plural, free and equal society that our founding fathers had envisioned and was built in its first six and half decades as a free nation. This is the first test Prime Minister Modi fails

---

[730]Shanti Parva, 71.26, 27.

when it comes to being regarded as a 'man of destiny'. No leader whose destiny is built on corroding the destinies of millions can be said to be worthy of the name.

Let's move on to his sorry record of misgovernance. In Section III, 'Moditva and Misgovernance', I take a close look at the multiple areas in which Mr Modi and his government have made a hash of governing India, often taking the country backwards rather than letting it surge forward. The rise of widespread communal violence, mob lynchings and the bizarre phenomenon known as 'cow vigilantism'; the shrinking space for dissent, with those who dare to think differently experiencing the daily fear of vulnerability to intimidation and coercion; the etiolation of freedom of expression and freedom of the press, the bulwarks of any democracy; the sidelining and often demonization of India's minorities, to a point where many feel unwelcome in Modi's new India; the unleashing of a crude form of mob bigotry, both on the streets and on social media, that are perceived as enjoying the patronage of the authorities; the hollowing out of institutions built up over decades, whose independence and impartiality are being systematically stifled; the eradication of checks and balances and the exaltation of government-sponsored definitions of nationalism that reduce alternative viewpoints to the category of 'anti-national' and 'anti-Hindu', themselves seen as largely synonymous; and the creation of a 'new normal' in society which makes acceptable the diffusion of a malevolent communal poison in the name of a triumphant majoritarianism that has eroded the fundamental values of India's secular and nominally egalitarian republic—all of these have cast a blight on the meaning of our citizenship in Modi's new India.

Moving on, we come to an area in which PM Modi's performance has been inglorious—the economy, as described in Section IV, 'The Failure of Modinomics'. The book details a checklist of spectacular failures, headed by a GDP growth rate that, as has been noted, has fallen by nearly 2 per cent because of the twin self-inflicted blows of demonetization and the botched rollout of GST. Demonetization, in particular, has badly dented investor confidence, drastically reducing much-needed investment in the economy. The recently released 'back-series' figures show that GDP growth under UPA-1 (8.87 per cent) and UPA-2 (7.65 per cent) was higher than the first four years of NDA-2 (7.35 per cent). Worse, the GDP fell for five consecutive quarters under Mr Modi, hitting a low of 5.7 per cent in the first quarter of 2017–18. The IMF projects GDP growth of 7.3 per cent in the current financial year, lower than it was under UPA and than it might have been had the economy not been dealt the 'double tap' of demonetization and GST. The growth that has occurred has largely been because of an unsustainable government spending spree (at two and a half times private consumption). Manufacturing has contracted, exports have declined (well below the UPA-era peak of $312 billion in 2013–14)[731], growth in industrial production has slowed and agriculture is stagnating (or worse, given the annual rise in the number of farmer suicides). The current account deficit is projected to grow from 1.9 per cent to 2.6 per cent of GDP this year. Unemployment is on the rise, despite far-fetched claims of new jobs being generated, which are not apparent to those who should supposedly be working in them. Petrol and diesel prices, whose worldwide fall was not reflected in India thanks to the Modi government's disgraceful decision to dip its hands into the pockets of the public with record levels of fuel taxes, are again on the rise, hurting the common man and having a knock-on effect on the prices of all essential commodities. [732] And after declaring 'No more tax terrorism', the Modi government inflicted tax demands on entire new categories of victims, shaking investor confidence.

Amid this sorry catalogue of economic ruin, the BJP has built

---

[731](In a few places in the text figures denominated in foreign currencies have not been converted into Indian rupees for reasons of context, source material or comparison.)

[732]As of 3 September 2018, a litre of petrol was selling at ₹79.15 in Delhi, ₹86.56 in Mumbai, ₹82.24 in Chennai and ₹82.06 in Kolkata; 'Petrol, diesel prices hit all-time high', *NDTV*, 3 September 2018.

itself up into the wealthiest political party in India by far.[733] It is flush with funding from business and has passed a law allowing political parties to receive foreign financial contributions that permit it to tap into its network of supporters abroad who no longer carry an Indian passport.[734] It has also introduced 'electoral bonds' that can be purchased anonymously and donated to political parties, in order to ensure that it can collect additional contributions while assuring contributors that the sources of its funding need not be revealed.[735]

Finally, we come to another great example of the image-building PM Modi excels at, this time on the global stage. Here we have a decidedly mixed record of pretension—the prime minister claims that India's standing has gone up in the world thanks to him, that an Indian passport finally has value it did not enjoy before his ascent, and that prior to his ascendancy, Indians abroad were ashamed to call themselves Indian—that contrasts embarrassingly with what has actually been achieved on the ground and the reality of global perception as I have discussed in Section V, 'Flights of Fancy'.

Yes, Mr Modi is capable of evolution. His reaction to my Dubai Ports World proposal was in my mind when I publicly raised the question of why Mr Modi, in the extensive international travels of his first year, had not visited a single Islamic country. It must be said that he amply made up for it in subsequent years, in particular focusing on improving bilateral relations with the UAE and Saudi Arabia, to both of which he made successful visits. (He nonetheless also managed a visit to Israel in a way that did not elicit any protest from the neighbouring Arab states, and welcomed an Israeli prime minister to India for the first time.) If as prime minister he has been able to overcome his prejudices

[733]Sunetra Choudhury, 'BJP richest national party, with ₹1,034 crore declared income: report', *NDTV*, 11 April 2018.
[734]Pragya Srivastava, 'Modi govt legitimises foreign poll funding; Subramanian Swamy calls it "terrible": What you must know', *Financial Express*, 22 March 2018.
[735]Anshuman Tiwari, 'Electoral bonds: How Modi government is incentivising India's biggest political scam', *DailyO*, 18 January 2018.

and those of his followers in the greater interests of the nation, that is certainly to be welcomed. But in this he was following the well-worn footsteps of his predecessors, who had laid the groundwork for him to tread upon.

Where he acted in accordance with the time-honoured traditions of continuity in foreign policy, Mr Modi kept India on an even keel. But where he attempted his own initiatives, he has left behind a sorry legacy—with Narendra Modi's India snubbed in the Seychelles, marginalized in the Maldives, negated in Nepal, sidelined in Sri Lanka, undermined in the US, compromised by China and provoked by Pakistan (and found wanting). Meanwhile, India's inestimable asset, its global soft power, was battered by the unsavoury reporting worldwide of the mounting intolerance, bigotry and lumpen violence unleashed by his supporters.[736] To compound matters came the Rafale fighter deal. The UPA government had chosen to purchase 126 Rafales from France that would be assembled by the public-sector Hindustan Aeronautics Limited in Bangalore. Prime Minister Modi abruptly reduced these to 36 aircraft off the shelf at three times the price per aircraft. In addition, there were several other questions that were raised, especially by Congress president Rahul Gandhi who demanded a JPC probe into the Rafale deal; the prime minister has simply refused to answer them.[737]

. As I hope I have managed to show in this book, much of what the Modi government is all about has turned out to be little more than a series of empty gestures and marketing gimmicks, while only smidgens of substance have been achieved on the ground. I have demonstrated how all his highly touted initiatives in Gujarat, over three terms as chief minister, have actually left the state worse off on several fronts. In similar fashion, as he nears the end of his

---

[736]Ellen Barry, 'Toll From Vigilante Mobs Rises, and India Begins to Recoil', *New York Times*, June 2017;
[737]Aviral Virk, 'Why the Cost of the Rafale Deal is Modi Govt's Worst Kept Secret', *The Quint*, 26 July 2018; Sagar, 'On a Wing and a Prayer', *Caravan*, 1 September 2018.

term as prime minister, the country is reeling on several fronts—a fearful populace, an economy that has been hobbled by foolhardy initiatives, a painful lack of jobs, a devastating number of farmer suicides, insecure borders, instability in Kashmir and the palpable failure in implementation of even laudable initiatives like Swachh Bharat, skill development and Beti Padhao Beti Bachao. In short, Mr Modi's rule has been bad for India, and it all rises from the Modi paradox that I have described in chapter after chapter—his inability to rise above his narrow-minded, mean-spirited, sectarian political origins to the levels of statesmanship and good governance that a country like India needs and that many hoped he could deliver. Winning elections thanks to the ruthless management of constituencies, as well as the exploitation of the worst traits of his core constituency, does not a great leader make.

As the writer Arundhati Roy observed in late August 2018, when a half-dozen left-leaning civil rights activists were suddenly arrested on what were widely seen as a flimsy grounds, 'the BJP and Prime Minister Narendra Modi are losing popularity at an alarming pace (for them). This means that we are entering dangerous times. There will be ruthless and continuous attempts to divert attention from the reasons for this loss of popularity, and to fracture the growing solidarity of the opposition. It will be a continuous circus from now to the elections—arrests, assassinations, lynchings, bomb attacks, false flag attacks, riots, pogroms. We have learned to connect the season of elections with the onset of all kinds of violence. Divide and Rule, yes. But add to that—Divert and Rule.'[738] The arrests and prosecutions would be one form of diversion; worse might yet follow, though perhaps warning about it in advance might discourage it.

There is no doubt that the one area Narendra Modi has succeeded in is his own self-projection. Many who have not examined his record in detail still ascribe to him qualities of

---

[738] Arundhati Roy, 'My Name is Arundhati Roy and #MeTooUrbanNaxal', *The Wire*, 30 August 2018.

decisiveness, devotion to duty, incorruptibility and determination that in their eyes mark him out as a great leader. He continues to lead in most public opinion polls as the most deserving prime minister of the country. This may be a tribute to his marketing savvy, his stirring speeches, his repeated projections of his own personality, his assiduous and mellifluous use of every communications tool from monthly radio broadcasts to daily tweets, his relentless burnishing of his own outsize image, or simply a reflection that mass public opinion can be easily swayed by rhetorical flourishes and skilled PR. But this is really the ultimate paradox of our paradoxical prime minister—that his perceived stature rests on appearances that are themselves belied by the multiple failures of the administration he leads.

Compounding all this is the man's extraordinary ego. Narendra Modi had been seen, even as chief minister, as being above his party affiliation; he reported to no one, felt accountable to no one (especially after the BJP lost power in the national general elections in 2004) and took his own decisions, without regard even for the views of his old organization, the RSS. In the end, therefore, he must be judged for himself; since he claims all successes as his own, his transcendent failures must inevitably also be laid at his own door.

It is all very well to say, as PM Modi did during his Independence Day address on 15 August 2018, that he was 'impatient because many countries have moved ahead and India has to go forward... I am restless because I have to improve the quality of life of our citizens... I am concerned because India has to be at the forefront of the Fourth Industrial Revolution... I am eager because I want the country to use its resources and abilities...'[739], but what the citizens of India need to ask their prime minister is this: when will you go beyond making fine speeches and actually do something good and lasting for this country, where

[739]'PM's address to the nation from the ramparts of the Red Fort on the 72nd Independence Day', www.pmindia.gov.in, 15 August 2018.

in addition to being 'impatient', 'restless', 'concerned' and 'eager', you show through your actions that you are concerned about the welfare of every last Indian rather than just winning elections and imposing your fraudulent agenda on a hapless nation?

In recent months, it has become increasingly apparent that people are no longer taking PM Modi at his word. The Modi paradox is beginning to take effect. His government's failures are being highlighted and it is to be hoped that voters in 2019 will no longer give him the mandate to play fast and loose with the lives and fortunes of millions of his countrymen.

Perhaps one indication that the tide may be turning against him is the fact that some of his closest supporters are breaking ranks with him and his party. A BJP MP, Nana Patole, resigned from his party and from the Lok Sabha in 2017, declaring that the prime minister was a one-way communicator who did not care to listen to voices on the ground, even of his own party. His two largest allies in the NDA coalition (in terms of Lok Sabha seats), the Telugu Desam and the Shiv Sena, have repeatedly and publicly expressed their disenchantment with him, with the Telugu Desam going so far as to quit the coalition and move a motion of no-confidence in his government in 2018.

On 12 March 2017, writing in *The Pioneer*, erstwhile BJP Rajya Sabha MP and newspaper editor Chandan Mitra had this to say: 'Indians cutting across caste and class, religion and belief have reposed faith in a man they believe is India's Man of Destiny, one who will lead the country to a Golden Age of Peace and Prosperity.' In July 2018, Mitra quit the BJP and shortly thereafter joined the Trinamool Congress party of Modi's bitter critic Mamata Banerjee, in whom he now publicly reposes his faith. If so many of Modi's most prominent erstwhile followers no longer see him as India's 'Man of Destiny', then neither should anyone else.

chapter fifty

THE NEW INDIA WE SEEK

'New India' is the latest phrase our current prime minister has been trying to create a buzz around. During his address to the nation from the ramparts of the Red Fort on the occasion of the anniversary of India's 71st Independence Day in 2017, he is reported to have used the phrase ten times in one hour. Or in other words, as the old saying goes 'Every speaker has his moment. The problem is that most of them stretch that moment to an hour.'

What is this 'New India' he is urging us to create? The prime minister speaks of an India free from the shackles of casteism and communal tension, an India that successfully solves its endemic problems of corruption, nepotism and terrorism, an India where every woman, man and child would be given an empowered and dignified standard of living, thanks to a society that harnesses India's entrepreneurial spirit to become an economic powerhouse. But, as usual, between the rhetoric and the reality there falls a great shadow. For all these statements and ideals (which one can find very little to disagree with), one is struck by the complete lack of any idea of how our country is going to achieve any of this. On the contrary, the road to New India appears littered with the wreckage of all that was good and noble about the old India.

Whether it is the 'Achhe Din' of 2014 or the 'New India' of the present, under the BJP government, these phrases appear to be mere subterfuge, a smokescreen for the real agenda of New India that this government has pursued since coming to power four years back.

As a progressive Indian, I too want a New India. But not this kind of New India.

The New India I want is a country where you won't get lynched for the food you eat, marginalized for the faith you hold dear, criminalized for the person you love and imprisoned for making use of fundamental rights guaranteed by your own Constitution.

Instead, we must look forward to a New India that celebrates and welcomes pluralism, an idea vindicated by history itself.

To me, this New India must be fundamentally rooted in the idea of India that our founding fathers believed in. After all, as I've asked in a different context, if you don't know where you are coming from, then how can you know where you are going?

This nebulous 'Idea of India'—though the phrase is Rabindranath Tagore's—is, in some form or another, arguably as old as antiquity itself.[740] Pandit Jawaharlal Nehru saw our country as an 'ancient palimpsest' on which successive rulers and subjects had inscribed their visions without erasing what had been asserted previously.[741] We not only coexist, but thrive in our diversity which is our strength. Swami Vivekananda spoke of a Hinduism that not merely tolerates other faiths but accepts them as they are. This acceptance of difference has been key to our country's survival, making 'unity in diversity' the most hallowed of independent India's self-defining slogans.

India, as I have long argued, has always been more than the sum of its contradictions. I write in the introduction about the Indian idea, which is that a nation may endure differences of caste, creed, colour, conviction, culture, cuisine, costume and custom, and still rally around a consensus. And that consensus is around the simple idea that in a democracy you don't really need to agree—except on the ground rules of how you will disagree. It is the idea of an ever-ever land—emerging from an ancient civilization, united by a shared history, sustained by pluralist democracy.

India's democracy imposes no narrow conformities on its citizens. As I have stressed here and elsewhere, the Indian pluralism is you can be many things and one thing. The Indian idea is the opposite of what Freudians call 'the narcissism of minor

---

[740]Sisir Kumar Das, ed., 'Chapter VII', *The English Writings of Rabindranath Tagore, Volume Three: A Miscellany,* New Delhi: Sahitya Akademi, 1996, p. 288.
[741]Jawaharlal Nehru, *The Discovery of India*, New Delhi: Oxford University Press, 1994, p. 59.

differences'; in India, we celebrate the commonality of major differences. So the idea of India is of one land embracing many. For New India to succeed and indeed thrive, it will have to embrace this inclusive vision and draw its inspiration from the key tenets of the core 'Idea of India'. Only by maintaining a commitment towards a democratic and pluralistic ethos can New India be able to fulfil the aspirations of all Indians. Interestingly, the need for our government to preside over a harmonious plural society springs not just from the core values of our country and need for insaniyat (or humanity), to use Mr Vajpayee's phrase, to guide our leaders' actions, but also from good old-fashioned economics. An eye-opening report,[742] first published on *Indiaspend.org*, a public interest NGO, pointed out that 'if India discards religious beliefs that perpetrate caste and gender inequalities it could more than double its per capita GDP growth of the last sixty years in half the time.' Did someone say, '*sabka saath sabka vikas*'?

At the same time, we must also be conscious that preserving our ideological commitment to pluralism, acceptance and the freedom provided by our democratic systems is only one-half of the battle. Providing a decent standard of living to the people of India, particularly those from economically vulnerable groups, is the second commitment that we must undertake in our blueprint for a New India.

Our inclusive vision of New India must be complemented by inclusive development as we move forward. We can talk of a New India, and yet, many of the battles India has been fighting—and must continue to fight—continue to centre around our principal

---

[742]'Secularisation the path to growth', *Business Standard*, 19 August 2018; The study, entitled 'Religious Change Preceded Economic Change in the 20th Century', was published in the journal *Science Advances* and was conducted jointly by researchers at the University of Bristol in the UK and the University of Tennessee in the US. Its key finding was that 'secularization precedes economic development and not the other way around, as is commonly believed'. One of the co-authors of the report, Damian Ruck, a post-doctoral researcher at the University of Bristol said that India's per capita GDP growth per annum 'could have been higher if Indians were less rigid in their religious views'.

basic problems of roti, kapda, makaan and now, sadak, bijli and paani, plus no doubt broadband (to most people in our mobile phone age, 4G is more important than Modi-ji). The prestigious *Forbes* magazine list of the world's top billionaires had to make room for 119 Indian dollar billionaires in 2018, with a combined net worth of $440 billion, greater than the GDP of a majority of member states of the United Nations.[743] But at the same time we have 363 million people living below the poverty line. And it's not the UN/ World Bank's poverty line of $1 a day, now revised to $1.25, but the Indian poverty line, which in the rural areas is ₹32 a day—in other words, a line that's been drawn just this side of the funeral pyre.[744] This is our reality and this is what our blueprint for a New India must address—creatively, quickly, and securely.

New India must be built on the liberalization we embarked upon in 1991. Economic growth remains vital to pulling people out of poverty. But the fruits of that growth—the revenues that come from it—must be shared with those who are excluded from its benefits. The magic of the market will not appeal to those who cannot afford to enter the marketplace. As India navigates its development, we must focus on ensuring that the benefits of growth are shared across the nation—by our youth, who are struggling to find jobs, and by our poorest, for whom true development would be life changing.

Any discussion about New India, about India's future, centres on India's youth. After all, who else are we building this New India for if not the young? We have trained world-class scientists and engineers, but nearly 40 per cent of our compatriots are illiterate, and we have more children who have not seen the inside of a school than any other country in the world does.[745] We have a potentially young, dynamic labour force that could deliver to us

---

[743]'Forbes billionaires 2018 ranking: With $40 bn, Mukesh Ambani richest Indian; Jeff Bezos tops global rich list', *FirstPost*, 7 March 2018.
[744]'New poverty line: ₹32 in villages, ₹47 in cities', *Times of India*, 7 July 2014.
[745]'India has a third of world's illiterates', *Times of India*, 8 March 2017.

that demographic 'dividend' so often proclaimed across global platforms. China, Japan, and even South Korea (our major East Asian competitors) are facing a serious demographic squeeze, and the rest of the world is ageing. India's youth should not only be part of India's development, but drive it.

This requires us to provide them with both education and employment opportunities on an unprecedented scale. The last Budget, however, had no specific schemes for youth unemployment, except the unsuccessful old skill development scheme. Ignoring the problem has only made matters worse. Young people may be celebrated as 'bhagyavidhatas' by our prime minister, but their current reality is one of shrinking opportunities. As I have pointed out, the prime minister's boasts about creating crores of jobs have no grounding in the harsh reality. His own government's figures show he is nowhere close to meeting his own target. It is no wonder, then, that as a recent survey reported 70 per cent of young people are anxious about their job situation and prospects.[746] Development cannot be the preserve of older generations. New India cannot be the plaything only of Old Indians.

Achieving inclusive development also rests on the government working for its poorest citizens. It is painful to see their struggles exploited for political gain. Promises are made in abundance during desperate election campaigns with little thought for their realization. When the dust settles, they are left as observers to economic growth.

However, the exploitation of the poor that we see today seems to continue beyond elections. They are abused as a part of government projects for the purpose of ostensibly meeting targets. A UN Special Rapporteur recently reported after a trip to India, that public authorities coerce individuals into building and using toilets by threatening to revoke their ration cards.[747]

[746]'Youth unemployment bucks India's rapid growth', *Financial Express*, 21 April 2017.
[747]Leo Heller, 'End of Mission Statement by the Special Rapporteur on the human rights to safe drinking water and sanitation Mr. Léo Heller', United Nations

We cannot claim to be helping the poor if we are treating their human rights as dispensable, free to be traded for the purpose of fulfilling individual policy aims. No matter how much it needs to be done, for those affected, sanitation is certainly not a substitute for food. Until their needs and rights are considered in a holistic way, for every policy made, we cannot hope to include them in India's development.

Ad hoc policies to improve the opportunities available for India's poorest and India's youth are clearly insufficient for the size of the problem that we are facing in the present, let alone its growth in the future. To include these groups in India's development, they must be protected from adverse effects from other policies. We need grown-up economic management, not slogans and sound bites. Policies must be conceived in consultation with all stakeholders and implemented carefully in coordination with everyone affected to ensure that ill-thought plans do not cause inadvertent harm to our economy, especially to the most economically vulnerable.

We may yet be able to address our staggering economic challenges if our leaders develop the capacity to look at the bigger picture. Even during the best phases of our growth in recent years, growth was never only about per capita income figures or enabling businesses. It was always a means to an end. And the ends we cared about were the uplift of the weakest sections of our society, the expansion of possibilities for them, the provision of decent healthcare and clean drinking water.

So what should be the animating idea of our New India? It is the idea of one nation made of many different kinds of people. An India where it does not matter what religion you practise, what language you speak, what caste you were born into, what colour your skin is. In our New India it should only matter that you are Indian.

Our New India must be an India that respects all religions, all faiths, all beliefs, all cultures, all languages, all regions, all

---

Human Rights Commission, 10 November 2017.

castes and all classes. That Idea of India is under threat today from those who seek not just to rule India, but to change India's very heart and soul.

What we want in India is unity. They want uniformity.

We believe in an India that unites our people. They seek to divide us.

Our ideology binds our people together. Theirs separates one Indian from another.

What we need in New India is the strengthening of democratic institutions at all levels, with transparency and accountability enforced through the Right to Information Act and an active Parliament. They seek to weaken these institutions, hollow out RTI, disregard Parliament and promote one-man rule.

What we require in our New India is a leadership that empowers people and harnesses their collective strength in the pursuit of national objectives, not someone who sees people as instruments of his own power.

Our New India must derive its support and strength from all sections of our diverse society. Their 'New India' speaks of one faith and reduces others to second-class status.

Their idea of 'New India' is one of exhortation: Make in India, Digital India, StartUp India, StandUp India, Sit Down India. Our New India must be one of consultation. We must never speak of 'India Shining' without asking who India is shining for. Our New India must follow policies that both promote higher economic growth and also ensures that the benefits of our growth are enjoyed by the poor and disadvantaged sections of our society.

The choice is clear. We can have a New India that belongs to all of us, led by a government that works for all of us. Or we can have a 'New India' that belongs to some, and serves the interests of a few.

You can choose a New India that embodies hope, or one that promotes fear. You can support a New India united in striving, or an India divided by hatred.

I believe we can look forward to a New India with confidence, if not with optimism. But we must build this New India on solutions to our major challenges. We have to overcome our poverty. We have to deal with the hardware of development, the ports, the roads, the airports, all the infrastructural progress we need to make, and the software of development, the human capital, the need for the ordinary person in India to be able to have a couple of square meals a day, to be able to send his or her children to a decent school and to aspire to work a job that will give them opportunities in their lives to transform themselves. We have to tackle and end corruption. We need to conquer these challenges, real challenges which none of us in India can pretend don't exist. But it must take place in an open society, in a rich and diverse and plural civilization, one that is open to the contention of ideas and interests within it, unafraid of the prowess or the products of the outside world, wedded to the democratic pluralism that is India's greatest strength, and determined to liberate and fulfil the creative energies of its people.

We must remain faithful to our founding values of the twentieth century if we are to conquer the challenges of the twenty-first and build the New India that we seek.

Our New India will shine. But it must shine for all.

ACKNOWLEDGEMENTS

This book, more than any of my other works, has been in many ways a collective effort, with the author being inspired, guided, assisted and pushed by the extraordinary team at Aleph Book Company. My friend and editor, David Davidar, whose original idea this volume was, has been closely associated with the book at every stage of its conception and execution. His colleague, Simar Puneet, and the tireless researcher Rosemary Sebastian have also played a vital, indeed indispensable, role in bringing *The Paradoxical Prime Minister* to readers. Bena Sareen came up with a great cover. No words of gratitude can do justice to their role—so I will have to content myself with a heartfelt 'thank you, team'.

There was little time, in this process, to consult and seek inputs from others, but I have benefited from the counsel of those close to me who have read parts of the manuscript at various stages, especially Manu Pillai, Raghav Sharma, my niece, Ragini Tharoor Srinivasan, and my son, Kanishk Tharoor. Some of the material in the book also benefited from the inputs of my dedicated colleagues John Koshy and Arvind Abraham. To all of them, my grateful thanks. Though their insights have greatly improved the book, the responsibility for its contents and conclusions remain mine alone.

I aired some of the ideas in the book, in different forms, in my columns and writings for a variety of publications, notably *Project Syndicate*, *NDTV.com*, *The Quint*, *The Print*, *The Week*, *The Hindu*, *Urbane*, *National Herald* and *Indian Express*. Their offering a home to my words and ideas is gratefully acknowledged.

Shashi Tharoor
September 2018

INDEX